INTERNAL WAGE STRUCTURE

STUDIES IN INDUSTRIAL ECONOMICS

EDITED BY

J. L. Meij, *Professor of Industrial Economics, State University of Groningen, The Netherlands*

E. M. Hugh-Jones, *Professor of Economics, University College of N. Staffordshire, England*

John Perry Miller, *Professor of Economics, Yale University, New Haven (Conn.), U.S A.*

V

1963

NORTH-HOLLAND PUBLISHING COMPANY
AMSTERDAM

INTERNAL WAGE STRUCTURE

EDITED BY

J. L. MEIJ

Professor of Industrial Economics,
State University of Groningen

Mey, Jacob Louis

1963

NORTH-HOLLAND PUBLISHING COMPANY
AMSTERDAM

PRINTED IN THE NETHERLANDS

INTRODUCTION TO THE SERIES

As business life becomes more complex, so the field of industrial economics grows increasingly important. Though the problems in the micro-world of the firm and the influence of its behaviour on society as a whole are studied extensively there still exists a lack of that collaboration between students of different nationalities which has proved to be so fruitful in other sciences and even in other parts of economics.

Another obstacle to the development of this field of our science is the relatively few contacts in many countries between economists and business men.

The principal aim of this present series is to stimulate study and research in this part of economics and to further an interchange of ideas and results on an international basis. In general it is expected that contributors will not only give the present state of informed opinion in their respective countries on the subjects treated but also include the results of their own study and research. Although this may sometimes lead to some overlapping the editors feel that this may not be undesirable, in so far as it serves to link together the parts of the subject.

As the reader will see, the level of treatment is that appropriate to an audience of graduate academic standard. Nevertheless, the volumes are not addressed to academic scholars only but also to those engaged in management. A knowledge of basic economic principles is assumed.

If the publishing of this series gives an impulse to the fostering of international collaboration in this important section of economics and focuses attention on the necessity for further development of industrial economics and on the mutual benefit economics as well as practical business life may derive from it, the goal of the editors will be achieved.

THE EDITORS

BIOGRAPHICAL NOTES

H. M. DOUTY: Chief, Division of Wages and Industrial Relations of the Bureau of Labor Statistics, U.S. Department of Labor, Washington D.C., U.S.A.
Author of: Union impact on wage structures, in *Monthly Labor Review*, Febr. 1954; Labor status and collective bargaining, in *Monthly Labor Review*, June 1956; Some effects of the $ 1,00 minimum wage in the United States, in *Economica*, May 1960.

M. P. FOGARTY: Professor of Industrial Relations, University of Wales, Cardiff, U.K.
Author of: *Human relations in industry*, Oxford; *Economic control*, London 1955; *The just wage*, London 1961.

W. GALENSON: Professor of Industrial Relations, University of California, Berkeley (Calif.) U.S.A.
Author of: *Comparative labor movements*; *The Danish system of labor Relations – a study in industrial peace*; *Labor productivity in Soviet and American industry*.

G. H. HILDEBRAND: Professor of Industrial and Labor Relations, Cornell University, Ithaca (N.Y.) U.S.A.
Author of: Economics by negotiation, in *American Economic Review*, May 1959; Growth and Stability in the postwar Italian economy, in *American Economic Review*, May 1961; *The pacific coast maritime shipping industry*, 1930–1948 (with W. Gorter); *The economic effects of unionism*, University of California 1958.

E. KOSIOL: Professor of Industrial Economics at the Free University of Western Berlin, Western Germany.
Author of: *Theorie der Lohnstruktur* (*Theory of wage structure*); *Grundlagen und Methoden der Organisationsforschung* (*Principles and methods of organization theory*).

J. L. MEIJ: Professor of Industrial Economics, University of Groningen, The Netherlands.
Author of: *Weerstandsvermogen en Financiële Reorganisatie van Ondernemingen* (*Flexibility and Financial Reorganisations of Corporations*); *Leerboek der Bedrijfshuishoudkunde I en II* (*Principles of Industrial Economics, Vol. I and II*).

CONTENTS

PREFACE

From its earliest stage the problem of the distribution of the national dividend has been considered the principal problem of political economy. In particular economists were interested in the share of labor and its determining factors, "the wealth of nations" depending for the largest part from what was the source of income of the great mass of the population.

Apart from changes in the percentage of unemployment, the share of labor is determined by the general level of wages. The more the latter increases the larger the part of labor in the national income. For that reason economists have turned their interest particularly towards the wage-level. Unfortunately, there does not exist one wage-level but a multitude of levels for different jobs and occupations. Theories on the general level of wages therefore could not be developed without a high degree of abstraction. Studying the factors determining the wages paid for different categories of labor seems very helpful to bring economic theory closer to reality. Recently, this problem therefore has drawn more and more the attention of economists. Not only of economists, however, but also of sociologists, statisticians and students of other social sciences. Differences in wages perhaps are more important for the social welfare than the general wage-level. Thus the problem of wage structure, that is, the factors determining the relationships between wages paid for labor in different industries, companies, geographic regions, occupations and jobs, to mention only some of the principal structure-dimensions, ought to be considered of utmost importance for the understanding of social life, its tensions and its tendencies.

Scholars of the so-called managerial sciences are also showing a remarkable interest in the forces determining the different wages paid within the enterprise. As I stated elsewhere, management offers a problemarea shared by different sciences*. The reason why is quite simple. Management problems have different aspects, such as sociological, psychological, technological and economic ones. Therefore these problems are also studied by scholars in various fields, who are principally

* Management, a Common Province of Different Sciences, *Management International*, 1962/5.

more concerned with the micro-world of the independent units of our society than with the phenomena related with its macro-aggregates such as population, national income, social stratification and others. Unmistakably the wage structure within the enterprise is a substantial problem for management. Moreover the wage structure within the company cannot be considered apart either from the wages within the industry or from those within the nation.

According to the aim of our Series a book was planned which deals in particular with the economic aspects of the wage structure, but nevertheless in such a way that its other aspects are not neglected, a book bringing together the knowledge acquired by specialists of different countries.

This volume on Internal Wage Structure treats a series of questions regarding the wage structure within the firm. It will be followed by a volume on External Wage Structure, edited by Professor E. Maurice Hugh-Jones, University of Keele, N. Staffordshire, England.

The volume on Internal Wage Structure opens with a "Portrait of a Pay-Structure" by Professor M. P. Fogarty. Stress is laid principally on the factors "that differentiate between employees within their firm".

In the second chapter, written by the editor, some thoughts are to be found on the relationships between wage-structure and organization-structure. Therefrom some conclusions are drawn for the wage-policy both of employers and unions. The author is convinced that a lot of research has still to be done in this area. He is equally convinced that future developments will pave the way for new policies in wage-administration and wage-control for employers and their organizations as well as for unions.

Professor Erich Kosiol from the Free University of Western-Berlin gives a detailed description of the principal systems of wage determination and their effects on income, production and cost.

Just as in the preceding volume the European contribution to the Series is enlarged. We hope to continue this policy. In this volume the contribution of Americans and Europeans is equally divided, the last three chapters being written by American authors. They are, however, by no ways the least important ones.

Wage-structure in our days is in a substantial degree determined by collective bargaining. Through this procedure the unions have a far reaching influence on wage-differentials even within the factory. An expert like Dr. H. M. Douty from the U.S. Department of Labor, gives in chapter 4 his views on the impact of trade-unionism on the wage-structure and on how this influence differs with the way unions are organized, whether on a craft-basis or on an industry-basis.

Professor George H. Hildebrand from Cornell University, Ithaca (N.Y.) has contributed a chapter in which he emphasizes the links between the wage structure and some internal and external influences viz. the internal job-structure, the labor-market and the product-market, whereby especial attention is paid to the product-market.

The volume is completed by a study concerning the wage structure in the Soviet-industry. The author, Professor Walter Galenson from the University of California, Berkeley, who is an expert on Soviet wage-administration, gives a very interesting view on the problem of wage determination in a collective system.

It seems very important to state how in a system which is formally still based on the philosophy of economic equality, a wage-structure could be developed, showing a remarkable similarity with that in capitalism, even to a certain extent with the wage structure in the earlier days of capitalistic development.

I hope that this volume will give a picture of the problems of wage structure within the company, problems arising for a great deal from the amphibious nature of this wage structure because it is partly a consequence of the social wage structure, and partly it originates from the particular needs for labor of different kinds and qualities within the company.

Finally I wish to thank my assistants of the department of industrial economics at the University of Groningen for their help in my editorial work and last but not least professor Ernest H. Weinwurm of Chicago (Ill.) for his fruitful remarks on behalf of my own contribution.

J. L. MEIJ

CHAPTER 1

PORTRAIT OF A PAY STRUCTURE

M. P. FOGARTY

University of Wales, Cardiff, U. K.

1. Differentials in Direct Wages and Salaries

a. *Differentials by Skill, Responsibility, and Occupation*

In a study of unrelated British firms – two engineering works, a food plant, a chemical plant, and a bank – Elliott Jaques finds that there is a general recognised "equitable work payment scale" relating pay to a wide range of factors which he sums up as "responsibility". In more usual job evaluation terms, the factors underlying this are responsibility, skill, and the working pace (physical and mental) normal to each person (Fig. 1).* People paid according to this scale are likely to feel that justice has been done to them by their firms, though they may still think that the economy as a whole could be organised to provide a higher standard of living all round. Even a small deviation from the scale – as little as 2% – may cause dissatisfaction. Deviations of around 10% from the equitable level "lead to an active sense of grievance, complaints or the desire to complain, and if no redress is given, an active desire to change jobs, or to take collective action if an organised group is involved." These reactions become very strong once the deviation reaches 15–20%. Deviations above the equitable level tend to be rare in an inflationary economy, where rates often tend to lag behind rising prices. Jaques finds that many types of manual and some types of office work tend to be underpaid by amounts of the order of 5–12% as compared with technical work of similar responsibility. But when upward deviations do occur they:

> "are accompanied by feelings of being relatively well off as compared with others; at the 10 to 15 per cent level of deviation there is a strong sense of receiving preferential treatment, which may harden into bravado, with underlying feelings of unease about how long the relatively advantageous position can be maintained."[1]

* Use of Jaques' factual observations should not be taken to imply commitment — at any rate the commitment in Jaques' own terms — to the particular technique of job evaluation, that of the "timespan of responsibility", with which they are associated.

TABLE 1. Typical Rates of Pay, Men, Various Grades, Great Bri

Coefficient	Operative grades Manual (1950–9)	Operative grades Clerical (commerce and industry, 1958)	Trade unions (c. 1952)	Works Managers (1953–4)
70–75		least skilled (Grade A, adults)		
75–80				
85–90	unskilled	semi-skilled (Grade D)		
100	average, all manual workers	skilled (Grade E)		
110	craftsmen			
to 125(c.100–125)				starting r
125–150	supervisory or super-skilled grades: e.g. Grade F Clerk, office supervisor: foreman (industry, 1948–50) controlling 25–50 employees and 1 or 2 chargehands: army sergeant.			
to 200 (junior management or professional)			organiser: assistant secretary	superintende department or works manag controlling 1– employees.
to 400 (middle management or professional)			general secretary	department deputy work manager co trolling over 2 employees: wo or general ma ager (not Dire tor) controlli up to 100 Director co trolling up to 2

's. Average Earnings of Manual Workers = 100

Personnel Managers (1956)	Professional and Managerial: Doctors (1959)	Teachers (1959)	Civil Service (1959)	Army (1958)
	Starting rate (House Officer first post)			
		starting rate (Asst. Teacher, minimum qualification)		
verage for trainees.				
versity graduates				
rsonnel manger, firms emloying under 0: assistant or puty PM, firms ploying under 00, personnel istant, trainee.	senior house officer: registrar	Assistant teacher (school): assistant lecturer or junior lecturer, university	Executive officer	lieutenant, captain
rsonnel manrs and heads of ecialist depts, ms employing 00 or more		headmaster: senior or Senior Lecturer, Reader, university	Principal	major, lieutenant-colonel

TABL

Coefficient	Operative grades Manual (1950–9)	Clerical (commerce and industry, 1958)	Trade unions (c. 1952)	Works Managers (1953–4)
marginal to middle and higher grades			ceiling, most trade union salaries, 400–500	
to 1,000 (senior management and professional)				Directors co trolling over 2 employees: ot general or wo managers co trolling ove 1000
1000+ (super-grades)				ceilings in: nationalised in dustry 1,05 (Board membe 1,500 (Chairme private firm 2000–3000 a upwards

The base for calculating all coefficients is the average weekly *earnings* of adult male manual workers, as published at 6-monthly intervals in the Ministry of Labour Gazette.

Manual workers. It is assumed that differentials in the *earnings* of more and less skilled manual workers are approximately the same as the differentials in basic *rates* of pay, as given in the Ministry of Labour's *Time Rates of Wages and Hours of Labour.* This assumption holds unequally in different industries. Evidence bearing on it will be found in the series of wage studies by K. G. J. C. KNOWLES and others appearing since 1951 in the Bulletin of the Oxford Institute of Statistics.

Clerks. Data from the biennial *Clerical Salaries Analysis* by the Institute of Office Management, 1958 ed.

Supervisors. Clerical Salaries Analysis: Report of the Royal Commission on the Civil Service, Cmd. 9613 (1955) par. 676 and Minutes of Evidence, 8th Day, pp. 248–51: National Institute of Industrial Psychology, *The Foreman*, Staples (1951), pp. 130–132: White Paper on Service Pay and Allowances, Cmd. 365, 1958 (see below on Army).

Trade unions. B. C. ROBERTS, *Trade Union Government and Administration in Great Britain*, Bell (1956) pp. 305–7: H. A. CLEGG and others, *Trade Union Officers* (Blackwell 1961) pp. 55–60, 66–67, 209–216.

Works managers. Institution of Works Managers, *The Works Manager and his Responsibilities* (1954).

ntinued)

	Professional and Managerial			
Personnel Managers (1956)	Doctors (1959)	Teachers (1959)	Civil Service (1959)	Army (1958)
	general practitioner	professor	Assistant Secretary	Colonel
rsonnel Direc- r: top 25–30% f Personnel nanagers in ms employing over 3000	consultant (ceiling 840)		Under-Secretary: Deputy Secretary	Brigadier; General
			Permanent Secretary 1,050: two posts at up to 1,200	

Personnel managers. Institute of Personnel Management, *Personnel Management Salaries* (1957): see also *Personal Management Salaries* (1961)

For business salaries generally see also Federation of British Industries, *A Career for the Graduate in Industry* (1954): Royal Commission on the Civil Service, Minutes of Evidence, 7th Day, p. 182, and 8th Day, pp. 248–51: G. Copeman, "Promotion and Pay for Executives", Business Publications Ltd., (1957): and Table 2 (E. Jaques). Average total remuneration of directors can be worked out from company reports: see also R. Stewart and R. Lewis, *The Boss* (Phoenix, 1958) Ch. 10. Rates for top jobs in nationalised industry are given in the White Paper on Public Boards, Cmd. 332, 1957.

Graduates – starting rates. Political and Economic Planning, "Salaries of Graduates in Industry" *Planning* (March 1957) and Federation of British Industries, loc. cit.

Doctors. Basic data in Minutes of Evidence of the Royal Commissions on Doctors' and Dentists' Remuneration, 1957–60, introductory memorandum. The rates used in the table took effect from 1st January 1959: *The Times*, 24.12.58.

Civil Servants. The rates quoted for higher Civil Servants took effect from 1st February 1959: *The Times*, 24.4.59. The basic structure of Civil Service Pay is as recommended by the Royal Commission on the Civil Service, Cmd. 9613, 1955.

Army. All rates are for married officers. From the White Paper on Service Pay and Allowances, Cmd. 365, 1958.

Equitable rates of pay change, of course, with changing prices. But the slope of the equitable payment curve in Britain does not seem to have changed substantially during the 1950's. Some of the relativities it establishes are shown in more detail in Table 1. These are actual relativities: but, as Jaques shows, they are usually not far from the ideal of the equitable payment curve. The base of the table is the average earnings of

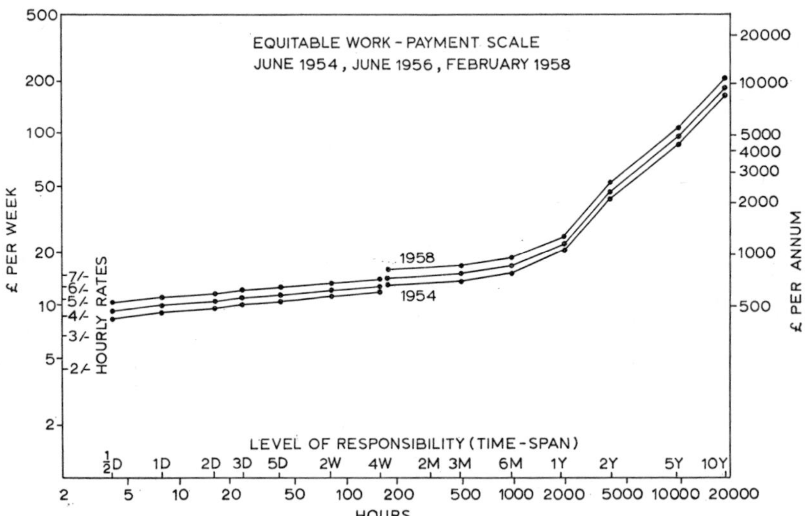

Fig. 1. Pay related to "timespan of responsibility" in a selection of British firms – rates commonly accepted as equitable.

The graphs are based on the rates found to be regarded as "fair" in studies of two engineering firms (including Glacier Metal Ltd., where this approach was originally worked out), a food firm, a chemical firm, and a bank. The studies included analysis of some thousands of jobs at all levels. The break in the curves "represents the point at which people stop thinking in terms of overtime, and therefore expect rather higher basic pay". Level of responsibility "is measured by finding the maximum period during which the worker's discretion must be exercised without review by a higher authority".

E. Jaques, "An Objective Approach to Pay Differentials", *The New Scientist* (July 3rd 1958).

adult male manual workers in the trades covered by the Ministry of Labour's twice-yearly census. Taking these as 100, unskilled workers have coefficients around 85–90 and craftsmen about 110. The table may understate the skilled man's differential over the labourer, for it treats differentials in earnings as if they were the same as differentials in basic rates of pay. On that basis, it puts the labourer's rate at about 80% of the craftsman's. But in a nation-wide sample of incomes in 1952–3 the Oxford

Institute of Statistics found that unskilled manual workers were earning on the average about 80% as much as semi-skilled and skilled workers together, so that their earnings must have been less than 80% of those of skilled workers alone. There is evidence from several trades – engineering,[3] railways,[4] shipbuilding * – that the gap between skilled and unskilled tends to be wider on earnings than on rates: though it is often semi-skilled pieceworkers who have the best chance of all of earning over their basic rates.

Clerks' earnings run below those of manual workers. The direct pay of a skilled clerk in commerce or industry (his fringe benefits often compare better) compares only with that of an average or semi-skilled manual worker, and the least skilled grades of clerk often compare badly with labourers.

Supervisors, the next grade up, may have very different levels of responsibility. One may be little more than an operative, another in effect a manager. For a standard of comparison we may take what the National Institute of Industrial Psychology calls the "level B" supervisor, who in mass-production industry might have 25–50 men and one or two assistants and charge-hands under him. This man, or his opposite number in an office or the Forces, might have a coefficient of 130–150. Since clerks' earnings are lower than manual workers', this means that the office supervisor often has a wider margin over the employees he controls than the industrial foreman. The spread for different grades of industrial supervisor can be illustrated as follows:

National Institute of Industrial Psychology survey, 1948–50, (as in Table 1). Actual average excess of earnings of male supervisors over male operatives supervised		Courtaulds Ltd., 1959. Normal excess of supervisors' earnings over average of operatives supervised	
	%		%
chargehands, assistant foremen	10–15	chargehands	20
foremen (Level B)	30–35	junior foremen	35
superintendents etc. (Level A)	60–65	senior foremen	55

There are still occupations, such as general practice in the solicitors' branch of the legal profession, where trainees are paid little or nothing even after they have completed their formal education and are working on the job. But the general rule is for beginners in professional and manage-

* As between shipbuilding timeworkers, labourers compare better with craftsmen on earnings than on rates. But the proportion of craftsmen on piecerates in 1950 was 83 %, against 33 % for labourers. Overall, therefore, craftsmen do better on earnings [5].

rial work to be paid at rates corresponding to those of operatives or clerks. Junior managers and equivalent technical and professional grades have coefficients in the range up to 200. Middle management grades, such as department or colliery manager, or the works or personnel manager of a medium works, are usually in the range from 200 to 400; so is the headmaster of a school, the commander of a battalion, or a Principal in the Administrative Grade of the Civil Service. What Rosemary Stewart and Roy Lewis collectively call "the boss", the staff who take major decisions in medium or large businesses, the civil service, or the armed forces are likely to have coefficients from 400 to 1,000. The ceiling for public service jobs is usually about 1,050, with a few at up to 1,200 or 1,500. That for private industry may run up for the chief executives of the largest firms to 4,000 or 5,000.

In industrial management salaries at all levels tend to be higher (though with wide variations) in the largest firms. But this is naturally most marked in the highest ranks. A firm which expands employs more foremen, but not necessarily better foremen; but it will still only have one managing director, who must be capable of a higher level of responsibility. The most relevant criterion of size appears to be turnover rather than capital or number of employees.

It is interesting to watch a new or developing branch of management or the professions creep up the salary scale as the responsibility of its members widens. There has in particular been a tendency for the rates paid to some functional specialists in industry and the public services to rise relative to those paid to line specialists. This happened around the turn of the century with engineers (Inspectors and upwards) in the Post Office.[6] It has happened more recently and generally with personnel managers and also scientists.* For scientists in the public services the turning-point came in 1945. A White Paper on the Scientific Civil Service pointed out that though enough and good enough scientists were being recruited for routine posts, the Government had not shown enough appreciation of the need for scientists of high quality. The chances of promotion in the Scientific Civil Service were therefore improved, the number of senior posts increased, and salaries at the senior level related to those of the Administrative class.

Trade union salaries are rather awkwardly balanced, as might be expected, between the operative and the managerial brackets. General secretaries' salaries usually reach at least the edge of the middle manage-

* The salaries quoted for personnel managers seem to have at least double from 1947 to 1956, more than keeping pace with the rise in operatives' earnings.[7]

ment grade; the most common coefficients in 1952 were about 175–260.[8] But they do not always go over it, even in major unions. In 1959 the President and General Secretary of the Electrical Trades Union (who are paid the same rate) had their salaries raised: but even the new and improved coefficient was only 180.[9] Very few union salaries go much beyond the top of the middle management bracket.

This outline of differentials for skill and responsibility is of course a framework round which there may be considerable variations, though these usually keep within the limits of what, on Jaques' showing, can be tolerated without provoking severe reactions. Some of these variations are systematic. The steel industry offers manual workers a few very highly paid jobs in departments such as melting and rolling, so that the spread of differentials among manual workers is much higher than usual. In 1950–1 junior melters are estimated to have earned on the average 35–50% as much as first-hand melters, and labourers 30–40% as much.[10] In a North Wales steelworks in 1955 fourth-hand melters were earning 55% as much as first-hand.[11] It puts figures like these in perspective, however, to note that if all the production departments of that works are taken together labourers were averaging 67% as much as "leading hands", the class which includes categories such as first-hand melter, and 78% as much as the less skilled members of production crews. These are much more like normal differentials.

In dock work, on the other hand, there is no formal recognition of skill differences at all, though this does not prevent their recognition in less formal ways, such as a better chance of membership in favoured gangs.[12] Supervisors in most industries are offered a margin such as was described above, but there is a long-standing tradition in coal-mining that deputies, firemen, and similar grades ("this curious post of Government safety-inspector-cum-foreman") should average less than skilled men on the coal face.[13] The National Coal Board laid down immediately after nationalisation that deputies' earnings were "not to exceed the average shift earnings of pieceworkers" – which means largely faceworkers – "in the Division or wages district." [14]

There are also less systematic variations. There are important elements of accident and looseness in the British wage and salary structure, and differentials for skill and responsibility are often cross-cut by others, such as the different chances open to workers even within one firm to earn incentive or other supplementary payments. So for instance in a comparison of the average earnings of timeworking fitters and labourers in engineering firms within one region in 1952 Hill and Knowles found that in the great majority of cases labourers' earnings were above 70% and below 90% of fitters' – close, that is, to the ratio generally recognised in the industry – but that they ranged in a few cases as low as 60% and as high as 110% or even, in one startling case, 140%.[15] The evaluation of rates for white-collar staff was till twenty years ago often rough and ready. Management salaries show the widest variations of all, and the British Employers' Confederation has shown itself distinctly sceptical of attempts to standardise them.[16]

But as time goes on these unsystematic variations are being progressively ironed out. Trade union policy has generally favoured standardisation: so for instance building craftsmen's rates today are all on the same level, whereas in 1913 the recognised rate for the lowest-paid craftsman in a given area was commonly 10–20% below the highest, and could be as much as 33½% below it.[17] The sort of standardised wage scale that has emerged from recent tidying-up operations in large British concerns is illustrated in Tables 2(a) and 2(b). Vauxhall Motors, the British subsidiary of General Motors, in 1956 revised and consolidated their wage scale, eliminating incentive though leaving merit rates. The resulting scale (Table 2(a)) provides a rather wider spread than usual between top-skilled and labouring jobs, and also a more marked differentiation between skilled jobs. The National Coal Board (Table 2(b)) was saddled after nationalisation with a vast and complicated inheritance of rates, related to the history of each pit and coal-field, in which even the names of jobs were unstandardised and pay for similar jobs might vary in the ratio of 2½ to 1. In 1955 the task of standardising the pay of day (that is, time) workers was completed with the results shown in the Table. 6,500 jobs, each with its own rate, were re-classified in this operation under 400 titles divided between 13 pay grades: five for general workers below ground, five for general workers above ground (with a deduction of 4/11, or 8% of the minimum rate, for women), and three for craftsmen, with a supplement of 3/4 (10% of the lowest craftsman's rate) for craftsmen working underground. Payments for special conditions, other than for wet work, were consolidated into the main rate, though special payments for overtime and weekend work remained.

Clerical workers, at least in large concerns, are normally on standardised scales, and Table 2(c) shows the outline national grading scheme worked out by the Institute of Office Management and used in its biennial surveys of clerical salaries. The assessment of management and professional salaries also becomes steadily more precise both in the public services and (in spite of the British Employers' Confederation's scepticism) in private

TABLE 2

Three Examples of Reorganised Wage and Salary Structures

(a) *Hourly-paid wage scales, Vauxhall Motors.* Reorganised 1956
Rates quoted effective as from September 1958. Men aged 21 and over

Coefficient	Typical jobs: Indirect	Typical jobs: Production
100	sweeper, general labourer	
107	mates (millwright's, plumber's, electrician's): bricklayer's labourer: stoker: swarf handler	
111	internal trucker: storekeeper	
114	driver (crane, loco, transport)	
117	stockchaser, slinger	
124	bricklayer, painter, plumber, inspector (semi-skilled)	
126		metal cleaner and washer, swarf sorter, wood machinist helper
129		enamel plant worker
130	carpenter, pipe fitter, welder, repetition machinist	
134	fitter or electrician (rectification: vehicle service section): body repairer	
135		assembler, paint sprayer, welder, machinist
138		wood machinist
140		sawmill spindle hand
142	skilled machinist, jig and tool maker, pattern maker, millwright, fitter, (vehicle bench: engine and testing), inspector (skilled), electrician (general maintenance and various skilled jobs)	
144		setter

(i) employees with two years' service receive an increase of 1d. an hour (1.7% on the general labourer's rate).

(ii) setters, group leaders on production work, and most indirect grades can earn "merit money", equivalent to 5 % on the general labourer's rate.

(iii) production grades (other than setters and wood machinist helpers) and most indirect grades with coefficients of 130 or more can be graded as "grou pleaders", with a supplement equivalent to 5% on the general labourer's rate.

(iv) the rates quoted are for Grade 1 of each job. On each job there is a hierarchy from:
Trainee, improver
grade 2
grade 1
special grade (setters and most indirect jobs only).

(v) overtime and shift rates but not incentive bonus, remain payable in addition.

From Vauxhall Motors Ltd., *Grading Scheme–Hourly Paid Wage Scales,* 21st edition, effective Sept. 19th, 1958.

(b) *Consolidating of day (i.e. time) wage rates, National Coal Board,* 1955

6,500 local job titles → reclassified under 400 national titles → and 13 job grades: ↑ general workers (underground; surface); ↓ craftsmen

		age 21 or over		
		grade	rate per shift February, 1955	
general workers	underground	I	34/1	
		II	33/1	
		III	32/1	
		IV	31/1	
		V	30/1	
	surface	I(a)	33/9	
		I	29/9	less 4/11 for women
		II	28/9	
		III	27/9	
		IV	26/9	
craftsmen		I+	34/9	plus 3/4 for work underground
		I	32/3	
		II	29/9	

All additional allowances abolished except allowances for wet work and rest and bonus for working a full 5 shifts in a week.

From National Coal Board, Report for 1955, and Ministry of Labour, *Time Rates of Wages and Hours of Labour*

business. The public services commonly have fixed scales, whereas in private business it is more usual to have a range of salaries for a post at a given level, with the possibility of placing the holder of the post at different points within the range according to his ability.[18] But the range is not chosen at random. Large firms, in particular, have more and more elaborate machinery for comparing management and professional jobs both inside and outside each firm so as to ensure that pay and responsibility correspond.

Skill and responsibility differentials have narrowed markedly since 1913 and especially since 1938, but the process has been stepwise and not continuous. There was little sign of any narrowing of differentials before 1913. A. L. Bowley estimated that if a hundred typical adult male British wage-earners were ranked in order of their earnings, the ninetieth man's earnings for a full normal week would have been $44\frac{1}{2}\%$ of the tenth man's in 1860, 44% in 1880, and $44\frac{1}{2}\%$ in 1914.[19] In the case of builders the craftsman's margin over the labourer seems to have been much the same in 1914 as in the Middle Ages.[20] There may have been some narrowing of management differentials over the rank and file. A Permanent Secretary in the Civil Service earned 29 times as much as an average

(c) *Grading scheme for clerical workers, Institute of Office Management*

Grade		Median salary of adults, 1958, as % of salary for Grade E. Men	Women
A	Simple tasks allotted under close supervision.	71	71
B	Simple copying and making of entries from original documents. Tasks requiring the knowledge of a limited number of well-defined rules. Simple operations requiring manual dexterity. Measure of responsibility small, work mostly checked or closely supervised.		
C	Work of a routine character but where the responsibility is somewhat greater than B Grade. Checking of B Grade work.	84	82
D	Work calling for the exercise of some initiative. Daily routine varying. Little supervision given.	88	84
E	More important clerical work with a measure of control over the sequence of jobs or over the work of small groups of staff. Non-routine queries. Work requiring special knowledge or involving individual responsibility without supervision.	100	100
F	Supervision of sections and responsibility for the efficient execution of a complete division of the work. Regular contact with the management and administration. Work demanding knowledge of a special character, e.g. legal, accounting, statistical, engineering, or industrial, and requiring experience, discretion, and judgment.	121	123

Institute of Office Management, *Clerical Salaries Analysis.*

adult male manual worker in 1876–9 and only 26 times in 1914; the coefficient for an average member of the then equivalent of the Administrative Grade fell from 8 to 6.7.[21] But most of this shift occurred in the years of mild inflation after 1895. At such times higher Civil Service salaries then and now, change more slowly than wages, and a temporary lag need have no permanent significance. There is no evidence to judge what happened to the less sticky salaries in business.

Differentials between skilled and unskilled manual workers narrowed sharply in the first World War, widened a little in the years of deflation after it, and stabilised again from 1924 to 1939. There was then another sharp squeeze during the second World War and the years of acute inflation and shortages till 1949. Differentials then once again levelled off, and there has been no further general change till the present.

TABLE 3

Unskilled workers' rate as per cent of skilled, Great Britain, 1880–1957

	1885/6	1914	1920	1924	1938	1945	1950	1957
building	64	66½	81	76	76	81	84	88
shipbuilding	54	55	77	69	72	81	82 }	
							84 }	84
engineering	60	59	79	71	75	82	85	84
railways	50½	54	81	68	61	76	77	74
police	82	—	70	70	62	70	76 }	
							74 }	70
printing							79	83
flourmilling							84	75
baking							86	89
leather currying and tanning							90	92
drugs, fine chemicals							91	91

from K. G. J. C. KNOWLES and D. J. ROBERTSON, "Differences Between the Wages of Skilled and Unskilled Workers," *Bulletin of the Institute of Statistics* (April 1951) and Ministry of Labour, *Time Rates of Wages and Hours of Labour.*

Clerks' salaries (Table 4) seem to have slipped relative to manual workers chiefly during and just after the second World War. Table 4 understates clerks' advantage over manual workers in 1909–10, since clerks' salaries for 1909–10 are medians for clerks of all ages and are compared, in a period of rising incomes, with manual wages for 1914. It is possible, for example, that the index for commercial and industrial clerks should be 85–90 rather than 79. Allowing for this, the salaries of average clerks in 1909–10 in all main industry groups were clearly ahead of the average for manual workers, and usually approached or exceeded those of skilled workers. Clerks also of course had greater security and other fringe benefits. Some clerks, such as the higher paid clerks in the Civil Service, had their rates squeezed relative to manual workers between 1913 and 1924.[22] But in London and Liverpool at least the general picture in 1929–30 seems still to have been rather like that of 1909–10, though Table 4 makes the picture seem more favourable than it is by excluding the relatively low-paid clerks aged under 25. Clerks in industry, commerce, and transport seem to have made a marked relative gain. Clerks seem to have slipped a little, but probably not significantly, by 1939: in June 1939 the index for manual workers' wages was 105½ (1924 = 100), but for salaries only 99.[23] But early in the 'forties this slip became a landslide. There was an apparent recovery at the end of the second World War, when manual workers' earnings were damped during the transition from war to peace. But except in that year or two, the salary of a median clerk in commerce or industry – somewhere towards the top of Grade D – was now well below the earnings of even average, let alone skilled, manual workers, and the salary of a skilled clerk was barely on a level with them. Also, though banking still pays above the general average, public service clerks have lost their former privileged position and come down to the level of clerks in commerce and industry.* Since the end of the 'forties these relationships have levelled off. In 1960 the ratio of adult male clerks' salaries in commerce and industry to adult male workers' earnings was much the same as in 1952.

Management and professional differentials were also sharply squeezed during and just after the second World War (Table 5). But after 1950 differentials for managers and professional employees (though not for the free professions) levelled off or even expanded somewhat, though rarely back to their pre-war level. From 1949–50 to 1954–5 "salaries increased fairly uniformly and by an amount larger than the 16% increase in earned income as a whole." [24] The earnings of Fellows and Associates of the Royal Institute of Chemistry increased in 1953–6 at exactly the same rate as those of industrial workers, and, if anything, the increase was greater for the more senior members aged 30 to 60 than for their juniors. There is some uncertainty about the course of salaries at this level from 1956 to 1960, but the evidence is on the whole that percentage differentials did not change.[25]

There has been a marked tendency for white-collar salaries within a given industry or profession to slide down so to speak *en bloc*, keeping their relativity to one another though falling in relation to manual earnings. So for instance a Permanent Secretary's coefficient compared to a manual worker was 17 in 1939 and less than 10 in 1956, and a general's coefficient fell from 16 to 8 (1958): but there was scarcely any change in the relation of the general to the captain or colonel or of the Permanent Secretary to the Clerical Officer (Table 6). University professors earned 3–3½ times as much as assistant lecturers and demonstrators in both 1923–4 and 1938, and were still doing so in 1957–9, though colleagues in the intermediate range from lecturer to reader had caught up on them

* In the Civil Service this is explicit and deliberate: Civil Service rates are now based on "fair comparison" with rates in outside work. There are confirmatory data for local government and the nationalised industries in the Office Management Association's analyses.

TABLE 4

The Clerks' Downfall. Salaries of Adult Male Clerks and Manual Workers, 1909–58

(a) clerks' salaries, average or typical earnings of skilled manual workers = 100.

	insurance	banking	civil service	local government	commerce and industry	transport
U. K. 1909–10 (manual workers' earnings for 1914: salaries, median for clerks of all ages)	126	125	109	102 (including senior officers)	79	72 (railways)
1929–30, clerks aged 25 or more:						
London	131 (insurance and banking)		125 (civil service and local government)		106	109
Liverpool	all industries or trades, clerks aged:					
	25–34		101			
	35 or more		108			
1942–58, Great Britain (assuming skilled manual workers' earnings to average 110% of average for all adult male operatives):						
				semi-skilled		skilled
1942				(Grade D)		(Grade E)
1946				74		91
1952				94		109
1958				81		91
1960				80		92
				77		89

(b) clerks' salaries; median or average earnings of all manual workers = 100.

U. K. 1909–10 (Manual workers' earnings for 1914: salaries, median for clerks of all ages)	184	183	159	148	115	105
1929–30, clerks aged 25 or over:						
London	168		160		136	140
Liverpool	all industries or trades, clerks aged:					
	25–34		121			
	35 or more		129			
1942–58, Great Britain			semi-skilled (Grade D)			skilled (Grade E)
1942			82			100
1946			103			120
1952			89			100
1958			88			101
1960			85			98

Sources 1909–10: clerical data estimated from F. D. KLINGENDER, *Conditions of Clerical Labour in Britain*, Martin Lawrence, (1935) p. 20: Klingender's calculations are based on CANNAN and BOWLEY, *Amount and Distribution of Income* (*Other than wages*) *Below the Income-Tax Exemption Limit in the U. K., Since* 1860 (Cambridge 1937) pp. 46 and 51. 1929–30: *New Survey of London Life and Labour*, King 1934, VI 79, VIII, 305–6, and *Social Survey of Merseyside* (Liverpool, 1934), II 27, 331. 1942–58: Institute of Office Management, *Clerical Salaries Analysis*.

TABLE 5

Increase in Wages and Salaries at Various Levels, 1936–55 Great Britain

grade (1954–5)	equivalent wage or salary 1936–7 £	1954–5 £	Increase per cent
adult male operative (average earnings)[a]	179 (1938)	580	224
middle management:			
middle of bracket	655	1,500	129
near top of bracket	925	2,000	116
higher management	1,220	2,500	105

[a] based on earnings in October.

"Equivalent" salaries are salaries at the same point (e.g. five-thousandth or five hundred thousandth from the top) in the distribution of salaries in the two years compared.

From R. D. G. ALLEN, "Changes in the Distribution of Higher Incomes." *Economica* (May 1957) p. 148.

somewhat.* There is evidence (Table 7(a)) that differentials between clerks and department managers in some branches of private business after falling in 1939–47, had recovered by 1954 to almost their prewar level. But it is not possible to compare differentials among top salary earners in British private firms before and after the war. In America the ratio between the pay of the top executive and the third in command of a typical corporation does not seem to have varied significantly since 1929 (Table 7(b)).

As a result of nationalisation, the problem has arisen of adjusting the high pay of senior managers and professional staff to the lower ceilings usual in the public service. This has been done in several ways.

(1) The nationalised section of the road haulage industry contained many small firms, whose owners' high incomes rested on the fact of their being owners. They were bought out and compensated as owners, and re-employed (if qualified) at normal salaries.[26]

(2) The National Coal Board inherited a number of executives at salaries (including bonus) up to £10,000, whereas the maximum even for Board members was fixed at £5,000 for ordinary members and £8,500

* Memoranda of the Association of University Teachers. The A.U.T. data for 1923–24 and 1938 do not include Oxford, Cambridge, or the Scottish universities.

for the chairman. Some were dismissed, if necessary with compensation. Others were re-employed at personal rates up to £7,500: but these rates were kept frozen while inflation pushed the rest of the salary scale up.[27]

TABLE 6

Differentials Within Certain Public Service Occupations and Between Them and Average Adult Male Operatives

(a) *Civil Service.* Maximum salaries for various grades: maximum for clerical officers = 100.

	1939	1956
Permanent Secretary	857	870
Under Secretary	486	471
Assistant Secretary	429	377
Principal	314	283
Higher Executive Officer	186	178
Executive Officer	150	145
Clerical Officer	100	100
Manual work: average earnings of adult men, October	51	90

(b) *Army.* Pay (on promotion): Lieutenant-Colonel's pay = 100.

	Married		Unmarried	
	1938	1958	1938	1958
General	294	253	302	293
Major-general	194	181	198	198
Brigadier	145	141	146	150
Lt.-Colonel	100	100	100	100
Major	75	78	69	75
Captain	55	58	46	50
Lieutenant	38	47	32	36
Manual work: average earnings of adult men, October	18	32		

Sources for Army figures: *Army Estimates* (1938) pp. 330 and following (ration, servant, lodging, fuel and light, and furniture allowances are included, but corps and command pay excluded): and White Paper on Service Pay and Allowances, Cmd. 365 (1958). Operative's earnings from Ministry of Labour Gazette.

TABLE 7

Relative Salaries Before and After the Second World War

(a) *Great Britain*

	1939	1947	1952	1954
(i) five manufacturing companies (accounts departments were chiefly studied) and one insurance company				
average salaries of clerks = 100:				
average salary of:				
section leaders	142	139	139	140
assistant department managers	195	178	184	186
department managers	257	228	242	246
average salaries of section leaders = 100:				
average for assistant department managers	137	128	132	133
average for assistant department managers = 100:				
average for department managers	132	128	132	132
(ii) banks and insurance companies. Maximum salaries for comparable grades of manager as per cent of maximum salaries for clerks.				
Big Five banks	189	—	197 [a]	
insurance companies	180	—	—	158

a) managers' salaries 1953–4 compared with clerks' for 1952.

All data from a study by *The Economist* Intelligence Unit, submitted in evidence to the Royal Commission on the Civil Service, Minutes of Evidence, 8th day, pp. 248–51, May 1954. The manufacturing firms studied were in oil, chemicals (2), rubber and textiles.

(b) *United States*

Ratio between the pay of senior executives in American corporations, 1929–57

	1929	1936	1954–7 (average)
top executive	100	100	100
second	75	69	70
third	58	54	57½

Data from J. C. BAKER, *Executive Salaries and Bonus Plans* (McGraw-Hill 1938) and "Annual Report on Executive Compensation" *Harvard Business Review* (Sept.–Oct. 1958).

(3) Consultants under the National Health Service were at the start (1948) paid salaries and distinction awards which equated all of them to senior management and some to Permanent Secretaries and members of nationalised boards. But distinction awards were then held for twelve years at the same cash value in spite of rising prices; for consultants at the top of the basic scale they were actually reduced. The rise in the basic scale itself was damped, so that whereas in 1949 a consultant on the basic rate could expect to earn 4 to 8 times as much as an average manual worker, in 1960 even the improved scale recommended by the Royal Commission on Doctors' and Dentists' remuneration offered him only 3.6 to 5.5 times as much.[28]

In some branches the drop in managerial and professional relative to manual salaries during and just after the second World War was offset by faster promotion. This is true of banking [29] and of the Administrative Grade of the Civil Service: entrants to the Administrative Grade in 1925–35 were likely to reach any given rank in roughly two-thirds of the time needed by their predecessors of 1909–14.[30] In industry it has certainly been possible to get rapid promotion. One survey of successful executives' careers shows average annual salary increases, during the time of most rapid movement, of around 20%.[31] But there is no way of saying how much the possibilities of promotion have been improved in trade and industry generally.

In some cases the speeding up of promotion has been a once-for-all operation, arising out of changes, such as the expansion of the general machinery of the State during the formative period of the Welfare State, which are not likely to be repeated. There are general tendencies at work to keep the demand for higher-qualified staff rising even in the long run, but it does not follow that demand will go on rising in relation to supply.

This calls for a rather careful consideration of demand and supply, for appearances can be deceptive. The ratio of administrative and technical to operative staff in British industry has nearly trebled since 1907 (Table 8(b)), and the proportion of non-wage-earners in the whole work force has doubled. (Table 8(a)). But the increase has consisted largely of a wave of clerks, and especially women clerks. Women's work has been revolutionised. Whereas seventy years ago only one in eight of the women in the work force was a white-collar worker, today nearly half are. But the number of male white-collar workers, and above all of better-paid ones, has not increased nearly in proportion, if indeed at all. The increase in the number of salaried jobs has been offset by a fall in the number of independent employers, and on balance the proportion of adult men who hold

TABLE 8

The Changing Structure of the Work Force. Great Britain

(a) Per cent of the occupied population in certain categories

	England & Wales	Great Britain		England & Wales		Great Britain
	1851	1870	1881	1921	1931	1951
farmers:						
employers	1.9			0.9		0.5
working on own account	1.1			0.9		1.0
non-farmers:						
employers	6.2[a]			2.6		1.5
working on own account	3.4			4.4		4.0
Total, business middle class	12.6			8.8		7.0
Managers, officials	1.0			2.5		3.3
professions	2.6			4.2		9.4[b]
clerks, shop assistants, etc.	3.5			12.1		13.6[c]
Total, new middle class	7.1			18.8		26.7
Total, all middle class as per cent of all occupied:				Great Britain		
males			22.4	24.4	26.0	26.9 } England & Wales
females			12.6	31.3	32.0	45.1 } England & Wales
males and females	19.7	15.9	19.5	26.4	27.8	33.7
wage-earners as % of all occupied	80.3	84.1	81.5	73.6	72.2	66.3

From F. D. KLINGENDER, *Conditions of Clerical Labour in Britain*, Martin Lawrence (1935) Introduction: A. L. BOWLEY, *Wages and Income in the U.K. since* 1860 (Cambridge 1937) Appendix E: E. H. PHELPS BROWN and P. E. HART, "The Share of Wages in National Income," *Economic Journal* (June 1952): D. V. GLASS (ed.), *Social Mobility in Britain* (Routledge and Kegan Paul, 1954) pp. 192–4: Censuses of Population 1931 and 1951.

a) Employing 1–10 employees.
b) "Operatives in Social Class I and II".
c) Socio-economic classes 6 and 7.

TABLE 8 (*Continued*)

(b) Manufacturing industry: administrative, technical, and clerical staff as per cent of number of operatives

	%	%
1907	8.6	
1924	13.0	
1935	15.0	
1948	20.0	19.0
1958		26.9

1907–48: based on Census of Production:
1948–58: Ministry of Labour Gazette, July 1959.

(c) Proportion of males in each occupational grade, England and Wales

Grade at end of career or in 1949	Mean date of entering work		
	1875–80	1905–10	1935–40
professional, managerial, executive	6.7	6.2	5.7
inspectional, supervisory, other non-manual:			
higher	8.7	9.1	8.2
lower	14.5	14.3	9.0
skilled manual, routine non-manual	46.5	37.8	47.8
semi-skilled manual	13.5	16.5	19.9
unskilled manual	10.0	16.0	9.4
	100.0	100.0	100.0

GLASS, *op. cit.*, p. 268.

(d) Ratio of non-operative to operative staff, sample of firms in S. E. Essex, 1953–7

(i) Number of non-supervisors per manager or supervisor in firms with each type of production system.

Employment in firm	Unique article	Mass production	Mass production & process	Process
450–550	21	15	10	9
850–1,100	38	16	10	9
3,000–4,500	26	22	15	8

(ii) number of operatives per member of the monthly or weekly paid staff: median for firms of all sizes with each type of production system.

5	5	6	3

JOAN WOODWARD, "Control and Communication," *Journal of the Institution of Production Engineers* (September 1957).

jobs above the ordinary manual or clerical level changed very little from the nineteenth century to 1949 (Table 8(c)). However, it is probably increasing now for the reason brought out in Table 8(d); namely that the advanced methods of production now more and more used in offices as well as factories require a higher proportion of managers and technicians. These managers and technicians have to be not only more numerous but also more highly trained. Among managers in a recent sample of large British private firms, 10% of those who reached the age of 21 in 1916–20 were graduates, but 34% of those who were 21 in 1940–5.[32] Another recent estimate suggests that, whereas in a progressive economy the total manpower employed of course increases less rapidly than output, the ratio between increase in output and increase in the employment of scientists and engineers may be about 1 : 1.[33]

Whether this rising demand for higher-qualified staff will lead to continued changes and rapid promotion – or, failing that, to pressure to keep up or raise the pay of higher grades – depends on what happens on the supply side. Supply seems at the moment to be rising more or less in step with demand, though with a lag (which however does not seem to be increasing) in some scientific fields. The output of university graduates has trebled since 1938, and the proportion of boys and girls with six or more years of secondary education seems likely to rise between 1959 and 1970 from 14% to 34%; by 1980 it may reach 52%.[34] The rising tide of higher education is limited by the quantity of ability available in the country. But there seem still to be substantial unused reserves of ability: though much less so in the case of first-class ability than of ability of lower grades.[35] The chances therefore seem to be that though rising demand will let rising supply be absorbed, it will not for the time being lead to any general acceleration of promotion or raising of the value of higher-grade staff: though it may well do so here and there.

During and just after the second World War differentials were narrowed by changes in the cost of living to the disadvantage of higher earners. It is estimated (Table 9(a)) that in 1947 the cost of living had risen 18% more for families with incomes of a 1938 value of £700 a year (say £2,000 at the prices of the late 'fifties) than for those with 1938 incomes of £200. The cost of directly-charged public services, which do not enter into ordinary cost of living indices, also changed to the disadvantage of the well-to-do. The fairest way of stating this is as in Table 10(a), which compares direct taxes on incomes not of equal purchasing power but at corresponding points on the income scale. A married man (no children) on the margin between middle and senior management would have paid about 26% of

TABLE 9

Changes in the Cost of Living for Different Income Groups, 1938–57: Great Britain

(a) 1938–47

Income, 1938 £	cost of living, 1947) June) as % of 1938	Corresponding real gross income, 1947 £
200	156	312
700	185	1295

(b) 1945–57. Man, wife, and one child. June 1947 = 100

	Household income, £					
	under 6	6—	8—	10—	14—	20—
1945	93	93	93	93	93	93
1946	94	94	94	94	94	94
1947	99	99	99	99	99	99
1948	108	108	108	107	107	107
1949	111	111	111	111	110	110
1950	116	115	115	115	114	114
1951	127	127	127	127	126	125
1952	141	140	139	139	137	136
1953	143	145	144	143	141	140
1954	148	147	146	145	144	142
1955	156	155	153	152	150	148
1956	162	161	159	159	156	155
1957	167	166	165	164	162	161

Table (a) from D. SEERS, *The Levelling of Incomes since 1938* (Blackwell 1951).

Table (b) from K. R. HUTCHINGS, *Prices, Taxation, and the Family*, cyclostyled (1959).

his income in direct tax in 1953, but only 14% in 1938, an increase of 12%: the increase for an operative was only 6%.

But these shifts against the well-to-do stopped after the war years. Such changes in the relative cost of living of different income groups as there has been since 1945 (Table 9(b)) has been in favour of the higher income groups: in all, the general cost of living for a married couple with one child rose from 1945 to 1957 about 4% less for families with incomes of over £1,040 a year in 1957 than for those at the bottom of the scale. The cost of directly-charged public services also moved somewhat in favour of better-off families (Table 10(b)).

TABLE 10

Effects of Direct Taxation on Incomes at Certain Levels and Periods

(a) Per cent of income retained by a married couple after income tax and surtax at corresponding income levels, 1938 and 1953. A 1953 income is at the level corresponding to one in 1938 if it is at the same point in the hierarchy of incomes: e.g. if it is the five-thousandth or five-millionth from the top when incomes are ranked in order.

Income £		Per cent of income retained after tax	
1938	1953	1938	1953
180	500	100	94
400	900	93	84
1000	2000	86	74
	2500		68
1500		83	
	3000		64
2000		80	
	4000		57

"Corresponding" incomes as estimated by R. G. D. ALLEN, Report of the Royal Commission on the Civil Service, Cmd. 9613 (1955) p. 216.

(b) Per cent of income aid by a married couple in income and surtax on incomes of approximately equivalent purchasing power

Income £			Per cent of income paid in tax		
1938	1948	1959	1938–9	1948–9	1959–60
234	407	600	0	9	7
264	476	700	1	11	10
445	850	1,250	5	21	18
859	1,700	2,500	13	29	26
1717	3,400	5,000	17	41	38
3434	6,800	10,000	26	56	53

£ 600–700 in 1959 represents average adult male operatives' earnings: £ 1,250 the margin between lower and middle management: £ 2,500 that between middle and senior management. Prices are adjusted with Dudley Seers' index for 1938–48 (see Table 9(a)), with the consumer price index as given in *National Income and Expenditure* 1958 for 1948–57, and with the cost of living index from the Ministry of Labour Gazette for 1957–9. Deflation with an index such as that in Table 9(b) would make the 1938 and 1949 incomes corresponding to £ 1,250 and over in 1959 somewhat lower and the tax percentage rather less.

TABLE 10 (*Continued*)

(c) Effect on higher incomes of the tax on university education: married couple with one child at the university and no other children. Great Britain, 1958–9

	£	£	£
income	600	1,250	2,500
jobs typical of each income level	operative	department manager	works manager
income and surtax payable	11	187	606
additional charge payable, compared to operative, for university fees and maintenance	—	70	245
net income	589	993	1,649

In estimating the additional charge payable it is assumed that all three men are living in rented houses, or, if owner-occupiers, have charges for mortgage interest and-ground rent equal to the Schedule A valuation.

The cost of living index in Table 9(b) lumps together all incomes above £1,040, a year, which in 1953–4, the base date for weighting the index, was the margin between lower and middle management. It would be interesting to explore further with the help of an index that discriminated between middle and higher management. One factor, for example, that markedly affects the relative cost of living of families at the lower, middle, and higher management levels is the tax on higher education. Since the second World War responsibility for the fees and maintenance of students has been partly nationalised. University students receive grants from public funds, either State or local authority, on a national scale intended to cover their fees and term-time maintenance. But these grants are made under a means test, which affects chiefly families above the lower management level (Table 10(c)). In effect, earners at the middle and higher management level have to pay an educational tax from which the general run of the population is exempt. In the 1950's, as the table shows, this could represent a very substantial addition to their tax liability. New regulations in 1961 reduced this tax at the £2,500 level by about 40%, but still left it significant. There is at present no means of saying whether, when liabilities of this kind and any offsetting advantages are taken into account, the overall trend in the price of public and private services has been less or more favourable to households at the higher management level than to the average of households with incomes of more than £1,040 a year.

b. *Supplementary and Substitute Payments*

Supplementary and substitute payments, in addition to or replacement of basic wages or salaries, take three forms: what is sometimes called "effort bargaining": [36] payments for inconvenience and awkward conditions: and market bargaining rates, that is payments to bring a lagging standard rate up to a true equitable or equilibrium level, or bidding up rates beyond that level to attract labour.

1. *Effort bargaining.* Effort bargaining aims at adjusting pay not only to the standard requirements of each job but to the individual's performance in it. It is common at all levels. Payment by item of service or capitation fee is the rule in many professions, as for instance among barristers and solicitors, doctors in general or private practice, dentists, accountants in independent practice, or auctioneers. It is also of course the rule for the farmer and the independent shopkeeper or craftsman. The pure milk of payment by results is seen in the enterprising citizen convicted in 1957 of purveying some hundreds of purloined cats to the National Health Service at twelve-and-six apiece. After a time, he told the court, he did not see cats any more: only twelve and six on four legs. Occasionally an independent profession has a fall-back rate, a minimum below which earnings will not be allowed to fall. Doctors starting practice in under-doctored areas may in this way have their income made up to a fixed minimum for not exceeding three years.[37] The payment of doctors in general practice also has another – for the professions – unusual feature in that it is geared to encourage output at but not exceeding a certain level: capitation fees are increased by two-thirds for the 501st to 1,500th person on each doctor's list.[38] But for most independent occupations there is neither gearing nor a lower limit to incomes. After allowing for operating expenses it is perfectly possible for a doctor, barrister, or farmer to make a net loss.

Salaried managers and professional men in private industry are commonly paid, not on fixed scales, but within a range which gives scope for adjustment for individual merit. One large firm, for example, fixes a maximum rate for each job done with standard competence, but may fix the personal maximum for individuals holding any job at up to around ten per cent above or below the job maximum; in practice it is found that about 10% of staff have personal rates above or below (say 7% above, 3% below) the ordinary job rate. This firm also pays a "service" bonus of up to 15% of salary, related to profits, to staff above supervisory level, with a minimum of three years' service, who sign a six month or three-yearly (according to their level in the firm) contract of service. Sales staff such as commercial travellers, canvassers, insurance agents or shop managers are commonly paid commission, though, a recent survey suggests, decreasingly so; in recent years the percentage of salesmen paid by salary and the percentage of salary in the total remuneration of sales forces have both increased.[39] Scientists may have a bonus on inventions.[40] Managing directors, the Federation of British Industries note, are often paid a bonus, though they do not say how much.* In a sample of five manufacturing industries in 1955 gifts and bonuses (including profit-sharing, which is referred to again below) added from 1.1% to 6.3% to the salaries of all administrative, technical, and clerical staff.[41].

TABLE 11

Teachers' Merit Awards in Local Authority Maintained Schools, England and Wales, February 1959

(a) Number of teachers paid at various rates

	Men	Women
Head teachers	15,000	15,000
Deputy Heads	6,000	9,000
Department Heads	11,000	6,000
Assistants holding graded posts:		
with maximum allowance	500	500
middle rate	3,000	3,000
lowest rate	16,500	13,500
Assistants	50,000	106,000
	102,000	153,000

(b) Awards for graded posts as per cent of maximum basic salary of Assistants with various qualifications:

	% of maximum salary		
	Lowest allowance	middle rate	maximum
qualified, 2-year trained	8.3	13.9	19.4
graduate, 3-year trained	7.5	12.5	17.5
good honours graduate, four-year trained	7.0	11.6	16.3

W. P. ALEXANDER, *What Teachers are Paid*, Association of Education Committees (1959). The rates are calculated on men's salaries. The sex differential was wiped out in teaching in 1961.

* See note to Table 1.

In public enterprise it is usual to have fixed salary scales rather than a range of rates. But here too bonuses and merit awards appear in various shapes. Up to 34% of medical consultants may receive distinction awards: and consultants are often paid by hospitals on a part-time basis, the rest of their time being free for private practice.* Merit awards under various labels have long been common in school teaching (Table 11), and are occasionally found in the universities. University staff also expect examining, tutorial, and other miscellaneous fees, in amounts differing from college to college. Personal merit is often recognised in the public services by placing a member of a staff, especially on promotion or first appointment, higher on a scale than he could normally expect. So far as the statistics of salaries are concerned this of course appears as a change in the distribution of basic salaries, not as a supplementary payment.

TABLE 12

Wage-Earners on Payment by Results, Great Britain

(a) Percentage of wage earners in selected industries who were on payment by results, 1900–1953

	Shoes		Engineering %			Shipbuilding		Docks
	Men	Women	Skilled	Semi-skilled	Un-skilled	Skilled	Un-skilled	(London)
1900	—	—	—	—	—	—	—	c. 20
1906	31	21				35	4	
1926			51		14			
1931			56		16			
1938			62	81	15			
1939	67	61						
1942			70	82	23			
1943	58	49						
1948			61	84½	23			
1949	53	46						
1950						83	33	c. 75
1953	57	50						

From K. G. KNOWLES and D. J. ROBERTSON, "Earnings in Engineering", 1926–1948, *Bulletin of the Institute of Statistics* (June 1951), p. 187, and "Earnings in Shipbuilding", *ibid.* (November and December) p. 359. K. G. KNOWLES and MONICA VERRY, "Earnings in the Boot and Shoe Industry", *ibid.* (Feb.–March 1954) p. 49. R. LYNTON and S. KING, "The London Docks" (1950) p. 18.

* See Reference 37.

TABLE 12 *(Continued)*

(b) 1938–61: percentage of wage-earners on payment by results

(i) all industries

	% of all wage-earners of each category				
	Men	Women	Boys	Girls	All
1938	18	46	21	21	25
1947	24	39	20	35	28
1951	28	44	22	38	32
1955	29	42	23	39	32
1957	28	41	22	39	31
1961	30	44	22	44	33
(ii) manufacturing					
1938	29	48	26	27	33
1951	38	48	28	39	40
1955	38	45	28	40	40
1957	38	45	27	40	39
1961	41	47	30	45	42

(iii) manufacturing, by size of establishment

Number of wage-earners per establishment:	per cent of wage-earners on pbr in establishments this size					per cent of establishments this size having pbr schemes			
	1951	1953	1955	1957	1961	1953	1955	1957	1961
1–10	8	7	7	7	13	12	11	11	24
11–24	12	12	12	12	13	23	22	23	24
25–99	24	24	23	23	24	44	42	42	45
100–499	39	38	38	38	39	68	67	66	68
500–999	47	47	47	47	49	84	81	80	81
1,000+	57	57	57	56	56	89	89	88	86

From Ministry of Labour Gazette and Ministry of Labour, *Industrial Relations Handbook.*

Among the industries excluded from the tables are:

- farming
- coal-mining (39½% of male workers in 1951 were on piece-rates)
- dock work (80% of work is on piece-rates: Knowles & Romanis, 1952, p. 334)
- shipping
- railways
- distribution
- catering
- entertainment
- domestic service

The tables cover, in addition to manufacturing:

- building and contracting
- gas, water, electricity
- government industrial employees
- local government services
- mining and quarrying (not coal)
- road transport; waterways; other transport and storage; laundries and cleaners.

At the operative level gifts and bonuses are rarely important. In the five manufacturing industries just referred to they added an average of 0.4% to wages in 1955. Commission is paid in some distributive or service occupations, such as hairdressers or bread or milk roundsmen, and catering staffs still expect tips. The allowance for this has been a bone of contention in fixing catering wages. The rule in licensed hotels is that minimum rates for waiters, boots, and other service staffs may be reduced – in 1959 by 23/– a week, 17% of the rate for waiters in large towns – if the employer undertakes to make up the amount received in gratuities to at least this sum.[42] In industry generally the importance of payment by results, including both individual and group incentives but excluding merit rating and profit-sharing, increased progressively from before the first World War till just after the second (Table 12(a)). By 1951 some 40% of all wage-earners in manufacturing industry were on payment by results, including 57% of those in plants employing 1,000 or more: more than four-fifths of the plants employing 500 or more had incentive schemes (Table 12(b)) and (c). But since then the trend has levelled off, and among the larger firms there have been some signs of a decline. Payment by results is relatively uncommon in the public utilities, including road transport: in distribution, catering, repair, and small-scale craft services, in building and contracting: in a few manufacturing industries, notably cement, chemicals, printing, and some food industries: and in national and local government service.[43] It is significant that this list includes some of the most advanced process or automated industries, such as electricity, chemicals, or cement. It is among the more advanced automated firms that the first hint of a retreat from payment by results has appeared. These firms may however and since the second World War increasingly do use merit rating. An example is Vauxhall Motors; one of the purposes of the new wage-scale summarised in Table 2(a) was to replace a former bonus scheme with time rates plus merit rating. In some industries – it is not known precisely how many – a negative form of payment by results is found in the form of fines or deductions for bad work, carefully regulated by the Truck Acts.

Employees of any grade, whether paid by wage or salary, may also have their income increased by profit-sharing (Table 13). In 1954 some 551 profit-sharing schemes were known to the Ministry of Labour, including 2% to 3% of all employees in the work force and adding on the average 5% to 10% to their earnings. There had not at that time been much increase in profit-sharing since 1938. The tendency has been for schemes to arise and die, being succeeded by others; of those noted by the Ministry in 1954, only 31 dated from 1918 or earlier.

TABLE 13

Profit-sharing Schemes in the United Kingdom, 1938 and 1954

(a) Schemes whose existence is known to the Ministry of Labour

Year	Type of Scheme	No. of schemes	No. of firms	Employees in these firms: Total	Employees in these firms: Participating in scheme	% added to employees' other annual earnings
1938	All	404	399		261,000	
		48	45		not known	
		452	444			
1954	Share-out on predetermined base. Open to:					
	all employees	400	408	571,000	381,000	5.8
	staff or other special group	21		43,000	8,600	10.1
	No predetermined base for share-out	130		163,000	133,000	7.4
		551		777,000	522,600	

(b) Participants by main industry groups. (Schemes with share-out on a pre-determined basis)

Firms other than cooperative societies

Chemicals	106,000
Engineering, shipbuilding vehicles	75,000
Other	164,000
Cooperative societies	45,000
Total	389,000

(c) Percentage added to employees' other annual earnings under schemes in cooperative societies.

	%
Retail cooperatives	2.3
Productive societies	5.0
Agricultural	9.1

(d) Type of payment made to employees, non-cooperative society schemes.

Type of payment	No. of schemes	No. of participants	% added to employees' other annual earnings
(1) Cash or savings deposits	223	212,650	6.9
(2) Provident, superannuation, etc. fund	7	4,800	3.8
(3) 1+2	12	7,000	9.0
(4) Bonus retained and invested in firm	3	92,200	4.8
(5) 1+2+4	9	1,800	8.2
(6) Share issues on free or favourable terms	37	17,400	
(7) Capital deposit certificates	14	6,300	
(8) Other or mixed	5	2,600	7.1
		344,750	

From Ministry of Labour Gazette (May 1956).

The amount added to managers' or professional men's incomes by effort bargaining can be large. The lowest rate of distinction award to a medical consultant adds, in round numbers, 20–30% to his salary, and a maximum award may add 100% to 160%. In the industrial example quoted, the highest personal rate for a given job may be 25% above the lowest. Special responsibility allowances – quite apart, that is, from promotion to Deputy or Department Head – could in 1959 add 7% to 19½% to the maximum basic salaries of an assistant teacher. Higher proportions than these occur in the case of sales staffs on commission or of bonuses to top managers.

TABLE 14

Recognised Differentials for Workers on Payment by Results: United Kingdom, 1955

(a) Schemes providing that pieceworkers shall earn a specified margin over minimum time rates or ordinary time rates.

Margin	Examples of industries paying this
46½–52½%	Roller leather
37½%	shoes (most skilled and experience workers)
33–⅓%	Heavy chemicals: seed crushing, etc: soap: coopering
25%	Sand and ballast; brick (Midlands): Glass container (misc. workers): cement: Fine chemicals: scrap: metal finishing: gold, silver, jewellery (Birmingham and London): surgical dressings: asbestos: leather: shoes (except most skilled): biscuits: cocoa, chocolate, etc.: food manufacturing: home-grown timber: wooden box etc.: paper making
20%	Pottery: stoneware: opthalmic optical: gloves: building: wholesale grocery and provision
18–19%	Rubber
17½%	Yorkshire woollen
16–2/3%	Envelope and stationery
15 %	Electrical cables: silk: tobacco: civilian transport (maintenance)
13 %	Hosiery (women workers, Scotland)
10%	Toys
1–6%	Men's and some women's occupations in dressmaking, hat, cap etc., shirts, wholesale mantle
0	Dressmaking (women, England and Wales): Some other women's clothing occupations: docks: milk distribution (England and Wales)
Various	Carpets: printing: needle, fishhook, etc.

TABLE 14 (*Continued*)

(b) Schemes providing as in (a), but with a difference between individual and collective payment by results.

Margin	Examples
30% on individual schemes, 20% on group schemes	Glass processing: piano manufacture (London): Furniture (Great Britain)
25% and 15%	Furniture (Northern Ireland)

(c) Schemes in which the margin for payment by results is related to a notional figure less than actual time rates.

Notional margin	Are pieceworkers entitled to a fixed supplement, based on time, over and above their piece earnings?	True margin over time rates	Examples (industry and occupation on which calculation based)
45%	Yes	7½%	Brass and copper rolling etc., Birmingham district, (rollers, all grades)
		7%	Brass working and foundry, Great Britain (Grade E)
		3½%	Heavy coil spring, Sheffield (most skilled)
		7%	Engineering (fitters, Birmingham)
27½%	Yes	14%	Railway workshops (fitters etc.)
		20%	Building brick and clay goods (fillers)
25%	Yes	9½%	Textile bleaching, dyeing, finishing, (men 21 years and over)
20%	Yes	14%	Surgical instrument manufacture (skilled men)

From Ministry of Labour, *Time Rates of Wages and Hours of Labour* (1955).

For manual workers, Table 14 shows for 1955 the standard margins over time rates which an operative of ordinary efficiency would be expected to earn on payment by results. A few trades set the minimum expected addition at 33⅓% or 50% over time rates. Several others mention figures of this size, but relate them to a fictitious base rate in such a way that a nominal 45% may in fact come out at 3% or 7% (Table (14c)). But the commonest rates are 15–25%. In the clothing trades and the docks it is common to set no fixed margin at all, the minimum expected yield being no more on piece rates than on time. Premium bonus systems, under which the rate per unit diminish as output goes up, were increasingly common until after the first World War. But they have been found to cause a sense of injustice among workers, and one of their main virtues, that they save employers from heavy wage costs where rates are loosely fixed, has become less important as rate-fixing has become more accurate. They have therefore tended to go out of fashion. Under the piece-rate and bonus plans now most commonly used in Britain – British practice here is not necessarily typical of other countries – payments increase either exactly in proportion to output or, less often, more than in proportion.[44]

TABLE 15

Pieceworkers' and Timeworkers' Earnings in Certain Industries, 1906–1953, Great Britain

(a) Shoe manufacturing

	Pieceworkers' weekly earnings as % of dayworkers'		Approximately half[a] of all earnings lie within following percentage of median			
			Pieceworkers		Dayworkers	
	Men	Women	Men	Women	Men	Women
				%		%
1906	88	111	over 18	25	11	15
1938	112	113				
1943	134	133				
1949	127	130	11	15	8	4
1953	127	127	12	16	over 7	5

(b) Engineering

	Pieceworkers' weekly earnings as % of timeworkers'			"Implied"[b] and actual difference in earnings between piece and timeworkers (pieceworkers' wages as % of timeworkers')			
				Fitters		Labourers	
	Skilled	Semi-skilled	Unskilled	Implied	Actual	Implied	Actual
1926	116		119	127	124½	125	128
1931	114		112	116	116	113	115½
1938	115	119	110	114	118	111	116
1942	126	124	112	112	131	108	114
1948	107	120	110	110	113	107	113
1953	107	116	109	108	113	106	111

[a] Quartile deviation: half the inter-quartile spread expressed as a percentage of the median.

[b] Implied by the difference between minimum time rates and the minimum rates which pieceworkers are entitled to earn.

TABLE 15 (*Continued*)

In approximately half[a] of all firms in 1952 average hourly earnings lay within the following percentages of the median:

	Pieceworkers %	Timeworkers %
Fitters	8	8
Labourers		6

(c) Shipbuilding

	Pieceworkers' weekly earnings as % of timeworkers'	
	Skilled	Unskilled
1906	145	133
1940	132	
1942	129	
1946	126	
1948	123	
1950	120	132

(d) Coal-mining

	1955	1956
(1) Weekly rate for a Grade I underground worker, including 5-day week bonus, one week-end shift, and average value of allowances in kind	234/– (from April 1955)	252/4 (from February 1956)
(2) Average earnings of all coal face workers	296/5	320/11
(3) (2) as % of (1)	127	127

From K. C. KNOWLES and MONICA VERRY. "Earnings in the Boot and Shoe Industry", *Bulletin of the Statistics* (Feb.–March 1954): K. G. KNOWLES and T. P. HILL, "The Structure of Engineering Earnings", *ibid.* (Sept.–Oct. 1954): and "The Variability of Engineering Earnings", *ibid.* (May 1956): K. G. KNOWLES and L. J. ROBERTSON, "Earnings in Engineering, 1926–1948", *ibid.* (June 1951) and "Earnings in Shipbuilding", *ibid.* (Nov.–Dec. 1951): Ministry of Labour Gazette, and Ministry of Labour, *Time Rates of Wages and Hours of Labour*, 1956–6.

TABLE 15 (*Continued*)

(e) Various departments in individual firms (study by University of Birmingham)

Firm	industry		earnings of employees transferred from time to piecework: timework earnings = 100
A	engineering	(1)	113
		(2)	143
C	food processing		145
D	engineering	(1)	113
		(2)	135
		(3)	149
		(4)	125
		(5)	141
		(6)	137
		(9)	119
E	industrial accessories		113

From J. P. DAVISON, P. S. FLORENCE, BARABARA GRAY, and N. S. ROSS, *Productivity and Economic Incentives*, (Allen and Unwin, 1958) p. 57.

What actually happens under payment by results for manual workers, as apart from what appears in the lists of minimum rates, is shown in Table 15. A series of very careful studies by the University of Birmingham (Table 15(e)) in a selection of industries showed increases of earnings on going over from time to piece work of from 13% to 49%. The shoe industry (Table 15(c)) aims to give most pieceworkers 25% more than day-workers, and a few up to 37½% more. In recent years pieceworkers have in fact averaged 25–30% more. In shipbuilding the actual margin has been 20–30%, in mining probably around 25–30%. In engineering, where pieceworking labourers' and craftsmen's national minimum margin is 45% and their implied margin about 7%, their actual margin has been 5% to 10%; the actual margin for semi-skilled workers has been 15–20%. Steel maintenance workers' tonnage bonus – a collective bonus, so normally likely to add less than an individual bonus – increased a day worker's earnings by 10½% in 1949 and 18½% in 1956. In the Manchester docks (Table 18(b)) piecework bonuses in 1950–1 added 15–20% to dockers' basic pay.

Payment by results margins are not in general a compensation for unusual or excessive effort; the Birmingham studies showed that most pieceworkers feel that they are working up to their comfortable capacity but not beyond it. They are probably to some extent a recognition that timeworkers tend to be both under-employed and underpaid. But they do not very precisely reflect the extra intensity of piecework as against timework. The Birmingham studies covered cases of transfer from time to piecework with a minimum of accompanying change in production methods. The increase in output, mainly on semi- or unskilled work, ranged up to 291%, the commonest being 50% to 103%, but increases in pay ranged only from 13% to 49%. Payment by result margins also certainly reflect a desire to compensate workers for the gambling element in piecerates. There is a ceiling to the margins that considerations like these are felt to justify. Skilled men, who are more likely than unskilled to work near to their capacity on timework, and men normally on piecework and working at piecework speed, may have to be paid lieu rates (or whatever the term appropriate to a particular industry may be) to keep their earnings in line with those of pieceworkers.[46] But within these rather vague limits there seems to be no very clear-cut reason, except tradition and convention, why payment by result margins should stand at the precise level that they do.

Payment by results does not necessarily increase the dispersal of earnings among pieceworkers themselves, or not by much. A work group which does not accept a payment by results plan may impose a ceiling on earnings or group its earnings closely round one or two modes.[47] But ordinarily the spread of earnings does increase. A commonly quoted rule of thumb is that in a large department the best workers may be expected to produce around twice as much work as the least efficient. It is not clear, though, whether the distribution of outputs is likely to be normal or log-normal. The evidence on the whole is that, if workers are not specially selected and restriction of output is not practised, the log-normal distribution is most likely; the curve has a long tail reaching out towards the right, with a few workers making high earnings and a tendency for most to concentrate round a mode lower than the average.[48]

2. *Inconvenience and awkward condition payments.* Inconvenience and awkward conditions payments are in part an expense allowance, as when builders are paid for travelling or slaughterers a clothing allowance. As such, they should properly be excluded from a reckoning of wages and salaries: but it is often hard to draw the line. In part they are a response to differences in the readiness of workers to enter what in effect are different labour markets; the market for labour willing to move from place to place, for example, or willing to work under conditions worse than are usually associated with a given level of responsibility. They take two main forms: inconvenient time payments and payment for awkward conditions.

Overtime pay is prerogative of operative grades, both manual and clerical. One of the traditional joys of being an industrial supervisor is to do without overtime pay; 56% of the National Institute of Industrial Psychology's sample in 1948–50 got none.[49] In mining the under-official, like the colliery manager, is paid an "upstanding wage", with nothing extra for overtime or weekends.[50] In the Civil Service ordinary clerical staffs are paid from time and a quarter to double time if they work extra hours. But Executive Officers and similar lower management grades, so the Royal Commission on the Civil Service noted in 1955, had to work four extra "free" hours before getting overtime, and then had only plain time rates. "Extra duty allowance", roughly equivalent to plain time rates, was at that time paid to all grades up to and including Principal – that is up to and including middle management level – who were on systematic overtime. But this was abolished in 1956, though senior grades of Executive Officer can still claim long hours gratuity if they are on systematic overtime for six months or more. This is equivalent to rather less than plain time rates: 8% for staff who have averaged 5 extra hours a week and 10% for those who have averaged 6 or more. Both before and since 1956 higher management grades – Assistant Secretaries and upwards – have been free to work unlimited hours for no extra pay.

For manual workers overtime ordinarily begins at time and a quarter, rising to time and a half after two hours – or for workers on a 5½ day week, after normal stopping time on Saturday – and to 1¾ or double time on Sundays. Some trades, among others heavy chemicals, shipbuilding, baking, paper-making, electricity supply, electrical contracting, and the docks start at time and a half, and a few, of which the most important are engineering and vehicles, at time and a third. In recent years the proportion of manual workers on overtime has been consistently around a quarter, and the average number of hours worked overtime each week by those working overtime has been equally consistently around eight.* The standard working week fell after the second World War from 48 to 44 or 45 hours, and more recently has fallen again to around 42 or 42½. But the actual average hours worked by adult men, after dropping to 46 hours in 1947, came back by 1950 to 47½ and has remained at 47½–48½ ever since. Overtime is worked chiefly by men, and rather more, on the whole, by the less skilled: women's hours have averaged consistently 41–42.[51] The contribution of overtime rates to workers' budgets is illustrated in Table 18(a). For engineers in 1953 overtime represented 10–15%

* Figures of operatives on over and short time are given quarterly in the Ministry of Labour Gazette.

of total earnings. For industrial wage-earners as a whole overtime probably accounted for not more than 2% or 3% of earnings in October 1936, but for over 10% in October 1954.[52]

TABLE 16

Shift Premiums, Great Britain, 1956

(a) Trades where premiums are expressed in cash.

	Commonest rates		
	pence per hour	per cent of average hourly earnings of operatives, Oct. 1956	
	d.	Men	Women
two-shift workers	1–3	2–5	3–8½
three-shift	2–4 (some up to 6)	3½–7 (up to 10)	5½–11

(b) Percentage or other proportionate premiums. Per cent addition to normal rates.

Two-shift systems			Three-shift systems		
First shift	% Second shift	Industry	First shift	% Second shift	% Third shift
5	5 or 15	Asbestos cement	10	10	10
0	16–2/3	Leather tanning, etc.	0	16–2/3	16–2/3
0	15(night)	Baking (England and Wales)	0	15	15
12½	12½	Biscuits	12½	12½	12½
20	20 or 25	Printing (general England and Wales)			
½ hour's pay	½ hour or ½ hour + 20	Rubber	½ hr.	½ hr.	½ hr. + 20
20	20	Gas	20	20	20
		Civil Air transport:			
16–2/3	16–2/3 or 25	engineering etc. staffs	16–2/3	16–2/3	25
6–2/3	10 or 20	goods handling etc.	6–2/3	10	20
15	15	Engineering[a]	15	15	15
		Steel maintenance craftsmen	9	9	23

[a] This rate is expressed, not as a percentage, but in terms that men are expected to work only 37½ hours for a normal 44-hour week's pay.

From Ministry of Labour, *Time Rates of Wages and Hours of Labour*, 1956, and Report of Court of Inquiry into the iron and steel craftsmen's dispute, Cmd. 9843, 1956.

A survey of shift and night duty payments for manual workers in 1956 [53] showed that night duty payments were usually 12½% to 25% on day rates, though a group of engineering and electrical trades paid 33⅓% and the general printing trade in London 50%. But a number of trades paid fixed money premiums per hour of night work, and as a result of inflation these might yield less than the normal percentage margin: 5–10% instead of 12½–25%. Nightwork premiums might or might not be taken into account in calculating overtime and piece rates.

Shift premiums are illustrated in Table 16. Where they are paid, they commonly replace night duty payments: these are then payable only to workers ordinarily on daywork who transfer to nights. Like nightwork premiums, shift payments fall into two main groups, fixed cash margins and proportional rates: but in their case cash margins were in 1956 the commoner of the two. Proportional rates generally offered 10–25% for a night shift and 5–20% for at least one of two day shifts. Fixed cash payments on the other hand rarely reached as much as 10% of average hourly earnings even for the lowest paid workers. "It appears to be the rule", an Institute of Personnel Management Survey notes:

> "that the salary structure for staff employed on shift work at least reflects the inconvenience payments made to operatives employed on the same shift system". (F. P. Cooke, *Shift Work*, Institute of Personnel Management, 1954, p. 26).

Awkward condition payments are as varied as the awkward conditions themselves. Civil Servants may claim removal expenses, and transfer grants up to £100, on transfer to a new area. Forestry workers collect an extra penny an hour for work in water or with creosote or tar, and water board workers for work in dirty conditions or requiring rubber boots. Coalminers also are paid extra for wet work. Constructional engineers are paid extra for hot or dirty work or work at exceptional heights, and a "radius allowance" for travelling to work sites. Slaughterers have a clothing allowance of 2/6 a week. Builders may collect a penny an hour for loading or stacking dry cement, 2d. for dirty or wet work or work in slings or boatswain's chairs, 3d. for hot work on furnaces and the like, and up to 4d. for high work. Bus, canteen, and hotel workers are paid spreadover allowances if the gaps between spells of duty within a given day are unusually long. Hospitals pay a penny an hour to staff who are looking after mental patients, 2d. while disinfecting bedding, books, or clothing, 3d. for boiler cleaning and 6d. a day while washing foul linen. Hospital staffs may also get spreadover allowances, and standby allowances of 5/– a night for the case where they have to be accessible in off-duty hours. Ship-repairing workers can claim special allowances for work on oil ships, submarines, or ships with dangerous cargoes, or in boilers or double bottoms. Dock workers can claim for dirty or awkward cargoes or wet work. Cumberland shepherds claim "lonely money" for work on the high fells.

3. *Market bargaining rates*: Examination of the wage structure of many British enterprises reveals a number of supplementary payments which, whatever their nominal form, cannot strictly be brought under either of the two previous headings. They may be formally labelled as overtime rates or payment by results, or may appear more simply and straight forwardly, under various names, as workshop supplements to standard rates established in national negotiations.[54] Their purpose is to adjust standard rates to the actual requirements of the market in two ways, either or both of which may contribute to any particular payment.

The difference between the two ways may be defined by reference to the "equitable work payment scale", to use Jaques' term again, which is found in any labour market at any given time. It is the same as the long-term equilibrium rate towards which pay would tend in a purely competitive market. Subject to any further adjustment that may be made by way of effort bargaining, inconvenience or awkward condition payments, or to factors to be considered in the next section, it represents equal pay for equal trained ability in all jobs at the same level of work; the steepness of the gradient between jobs being determined by the scarcity of trained ability at each level; that is by the *general* scarcity, not by the scarcity for particular classes of work in relation to the use which employers of representative efficiency can make of it.[55] Short-term market bargaining consists of paying above the rates determined in this way in the hope of attracting labour in general, or particular grades of it, to a particular firm or industry. Fair comparison payments, on the other hand, are made when the "equitable work payment scale" has risen, but the standard wage for some group of workers has not yet caught up with it.

Fair comparison supplements can be very substantial. The standard rate for engineering fitters on timework rose from 1948 to 1959 by only 75%, whereas the earnings of industrial workers generally rose about 105% and those of pieceworking fitters by 108%. Supplementary payments, (other than overtime), which added only 9% to timeworking fitters' standard rates in 1948, accordingly rose to 35% in 1959. Overtime payments, as a proportion of total earnings, remained nearly constant. Overall, thanks to the massive increase in other supplementary payments, timeworking fitters' earnings rose 111%, keeping actually a little ahead of the rise in other industries. Fitters on piecework, by contrast, had in this period an increase of 99% in their standard rates, and consequently needed only a small increase - 7½ % - in the addition to their earnings through supplementary payments.[56] There has been a general tendency for payments above nationally negotiated wage rates — wage drift — to be highest in industries where standard rates have lagged.[57]

Short-term market bargaining supplements are much less substantial and significant than fair comparison supplements. H. A. Turner records strong resistance in many sectors of the British economy to plus-payments of any kind, and *a fortiori* to short-term bargaining payments. The typical situation in British labour markets is one of oligopoly.[58] Employers will increase the rate for a grade if this is necessary to catch up with what is being paid by others, but are unwilling to make the first move in upsetting the long-term relation between rates, and disapprove of any of their number who do it. This attitude is reinforced by the pressure of employers' associations and even of trade unions. Cotton union officials have been heard to refer to payments over standard rates as "malpractices". The efforts in several industries to standardise wage structures and eliminate unauthorised margins have had strong union support.[59]

Speaking generally and without distinguishing betweenfair comparison and short-term bargaining payments, Turner says flatly that "plus-payments appear negligible in most non-private employments." They happen, at the salaried as well as the wage-earning level, but not on a significant scale. When they do occur, they often take the form of upgrading an employee on a salary scale rather than of changing the scale itself. In private business Turner finds that plus-rates for wage-earners are significant chiefly in two areas. One is competitive, unstable trades with little habit of mutual discipline and, often, poorly developed collective bargaining, such as some sections of the clothing trade. The other is giant firms with strongly established positions, which may have and be known to have (which deters other firms from bidding against them) a margin to spare for bidding up rates. There is a general tendency for the biggest firms of an industry to pay up to 10% more than the smallest.[60] In a few cases the margin is much larger. Motor firms, for example, may go 50% over the general rates for the occupations in which they are interested.[61] In between comes the general run of private employers, even in small-unit trades such as building, printing, or agriculture. Plus-rates exist among these but not on a large scale.

Among salary earners there is a great difference between the disciplined policies of public and big private concerns and the more casual methods of small private businesses. Big firms take a great deal of care over the grading of their senior staff, both collectively and on an individual basis, and are reluctant to let rates get out of line with one another or, usually, with those of other firms: though some big firms do systematically pay above standard rates for salaried staff as for wage-earners. Small employers on the other hand pay at this level more haphazardly, as the accidents of the market may provide. It is likely that plus-rates occur quite often among them on an unsystematic basis. In the case of salaried as of wage-earning staff public employers usually avoid plus-rates, at least in any open form.

It does sometimes happen that a whole profession or occupation not only comes to be paid above the general level for the work it does but is able to maintain this position for some time. A case in point is the medical profession. At the start of the National Health Service in 1948 doctors in the service, whether in hospitals or in general practice, where paid at well above the rates for other professions with similar qualifications and responsibilities. This created anomalies not only in the service itself but in other industries where doctors were in a minority. In local government service authorities insisted on paying doctors on scales similar to other professional officers, so creating a grievance among the doctors. In the universities, on the other hand, doctors were paid as doctors, and therefore above the rates for their colleagues in other specialisms. A similar situation arose among dentists, whose initial rates under the National Health Service put them in the top management bracket. In their case the situation was dealt with by a ruthless and immediate cut in piece-rates, by which general dental practitioners' net incomes were halved. The doctors held out longer. Their position was gradually whittled away, but it was only in 1960 that they were brought back decisively into line with other professions.[62]

4. *Overall effects*: Taken together, effort bargaining, market bargaining, and inconvenience or awkward condition rates account for a very respectable part of many wages and salaries. To some extent they are a substitute for basic rates, but commonly they add a supplement to them. In the first years of the second World War (Table 17) operatives' earnings increased about 25% faster than basic wage rates. They have kept this lead but not increased it, for since then additions to base rates have been as near as makes no difference in the same proportion as additions to total earnings. The formula is:

let earnings in October 1938 (which were then close to wage rates) = 100 for a standard working week (i.e. excluding overtime).

let a = the per cent increase in basic ("industry") wage rates for a standard working week thereafter, corrected for changes in the age, sex, and industrial distribution of the work force and for the length of the standard working week.

b = the index of earnings at any date thereafter on the base 1938 = 100

then for any later data:

$$b = 100+5a/4.$$

The effect of this formula is that standardised earnings are gradually coming closer to a ceiling of 25% above baserates. In 1949, when base rates were at 200 (1938–9 = 100), earnings were at 225–30. In 1955, when base rates reached 300, earnings were at 350. But the tendency for earnings to creep ahead of rates is slow and confined to a limited number of industries. In the ten years 1948–58, in the whole range of industries covered by the Ministry of Labour's earnings enquiries, earnings (excluding overtime payments and the effect of changes in the distribution of the work force) increased only 6 % more than rates. This figure was increasing steadily at about ½% a year. Greater overtime at various times during the ten years made the increase in earnings run a further 2½% to 6% ahead of the increase in rates: but this addition showed no permanent trend. Had there been no rise in standard rates, market pressures might have brought the increase of earnings due to supplementary payments up to 2% to 4% a year. But most of this potential rise was forestalled by annual wage rounds or consolidated by them into base rates, leaving for 1952-1959 a balance of 0.7% a year. In industries which did well in the annual rounds the unconsolidated balance was very small or even negligible; for example 0.1% a year in engineering (all grades of workers together) and the woodworking industries. The largest balances tended to appear in industries such as textiles, which lagged in the general rounds.[63]

Table 18 shows in more detail the effect of supplementary and substitute payments on certain operatives' earnings. For engineering labourers and craftsmen supplementaries accounted for 27½% to 35% of total earnings in 1953, and for from 20% to 70% of the total increase in earnings since 1926. In particular cases (Table 18(c)) the proportion contributed by supplementaries might be higher still. For dockers in 1950–1 "overtime", including what in other industries might appear as shift or night duty premiums or spreadover allowances, accounted in 1950–1 for 20–35% of

TABLE 17

"Workplace" and "Industry" Weekly Wage Rates, 1938–55

	increase per cent since October 1938 workplace	industry	increase in industry rates / increase in work-place rates
1940 July	30	24	.80
1941 July	42	33	.80
1942 Jan.	46	37	.80
July	60	48	.80
1943 Jan.	65	52	.80
July	76	62	.81
1944 Jan.	79	58	.74
July	82	62	.75
1945 Jan.	76	56	.74
July	80	59	.74
1946 Jan.	74	57	.77
Oct.	90	70	.78
1947 April	94	77	.82
Oct.	103	83	.81
1948 April	114	90	.80
Oct.	120	96	.81
1949 April	124	97	.79
Oct.	129	101	.79
1950 April	133	103	.78
Oct.	140	108	.77
1951 April	156	124	.80
Oct.	165	131	.80
1952 April	177	142	.81
Oct.	185	148	.81
1953 April	196	157	.81
Oct.	201	162	.81
1954 April	213	173	.82
Oct.	223	180	.81
1955 April	242	195	.81
Oct.	250	199	.80

From H. A. TURNER, Wages: *Industry and Workplace Rates* (Manchester School, May 1956), p. 116. "Workplace" rates are earnings, from the Ministry of Labour's surveys. "Industry" rates are based on the Ministry's index of wage rates for a standard working week (i.e. excluding overtime). Both series are standardised for changes in the age, sex, and industrial distribution of the work force and the length of the nominal working week.

TABLE 18

Total Effect of Supplementary Payments in Certain Industries, Great Britain

(1) Supplementary payments and engineers' earnings, 1926–53.

	% of total earnings							
	Timeworkers				Pieceworkers			
		Earned in standard week				Earned in standard week		
Fitters	Total	Standard rate	Supplementaries	Overtime earnings	Total	Standard rate	Supplementaries	Overtime earnings
1926 (Oct.)	100	93.0	6.8	0.3	100	97.2	4.7	−1.9
1931 (Oct.)	100	94.1	8.1	−2.2	100	96.0	7.9	−3.9
1938 (Oct.)	100	81.0	9.5	9.3	100	80.9	12.5	6.6
1942 (July)	100	64.5	16.3	19.2	100	57.4	27.1	15.5
1948 (July)	100	72.5	19.8	7.7	100	74.7	23.2	2.2
1953 (July)	100	65.4	21.5	13.3	100	65.2	25.1	9.8
Labourers								
1926	100	89.9	6.6	3.6	100	94.4	9.0	−3.3
1931	100	95.2	6.4	−1.5	100	96.3	8.6	−4.9
1938	100	83.0	6.6	10.4	100	83.9	10.8	5.3
1942	100	67.1	11.6	21.3	100	64.7	15.1	20.2
1948	100	76.8	12.9	10.3	100	74.7	17.3	8.0
1953	100	72.5	12.0	15.5	100	70.2	15.7	14.1

(−) = short time

(b) Increase or decrease (−) in supplementary payments as % of the increase in standard or minimum piecework rates in each period.

		Timeworkers %	Pieceworkers
Fitters	1926–31	46	−56
	1931–8	34	76
	1938–42	83	202
	1942–8	36	−38
	1948–53	48	63
	1926–53	50	70
Labourers	1926–31	−4	20
	1931–8	15	36
	1938–42	47	61
	1942–8	15	23
	1948–53	16	20
	1926–53	21	31

From K. G. J. C. KNOWLES and T. P. HILL, "The Structure of Engineering Earnings", *Bulletin of the Institute of Statistics* (Sept.–Oct. 1954), pp. 291–2.

TABLE 18 (*Continued*)

(c) Earnings in a Glasgow engineering firm, March 1953.

	Average hours worked	Total	Earnings				
			Earned in Standard wk.		Earned in overtime		
			Hourly rates (1)	Bonus	Hourly rates (1)	Bonus	Overtime provision (2)
skilled	50.2	100	54	25	8	4	9
semi-skilled	53.1	100	54	20	11	4	11
unskilled	58.0	100	55	11	17	3½	13½

(1) including national bonus. (2) including some payments for night shift.

From D. J. ROBERTSON, *Factory Wage Structures and National Agreements,* (Cambridge 1960) p. 34.

(2) Dock workers' earnings on "overtime" and piece-rates. 1950–1.

(a) Percentage of all earnings accounted for by "overtime"[a] in certain ports, 1951:

London	over 35%
5 large port groups (Liverpool, Manchester, Hull and Goole, Bristol and Severn Glasgow)	20–35

(b) Dockworkers' average earnings, Manchester, April–June 1950.

	About
Basic pay, including attendance money and holiday pay	£5
Piecework bonuses	1
"Overtime"[a]	2
	8

a) "Overtime" includes what in other industries would be known as shift premiums, nightwork premiums, or, sometimes, spreadover or split duty allowances. A dock worker may therefore be working a substantial amount of overtime even though his actual hours add to the standard week or less.

From K. G. J. C. KNOWLES and ANN ROMANIS, "Dock-workers' Earnings", *Bulletin of the Institute of Statistics* (Sept.–Oct. 1952) p. 349, and University of Liverpool, *The Dock Worker* (1954) Diagram IX.

TABLE 18 (*Continued*)

(3) Supplementary payments in London Transport, 1936 and 1951.

	Earnings (men) as % of maximum rates	
	1936	1951
Railways		
Motormen	113	120
Guards	115	120
Stationmen	124	120
Roads		
Central bus drivers	105	113
Conductors	104	111

The supplementary payments in question are notably for overtime, weekend work, and spreadover duties.

From K. G. J. C. KNOWLES and H. J. COLE, "Rates and Earnings in London Transport", *Bulletin of the Institute of Statistics*, (August, 1953).

earnings, and "overtime" plus piece-rates added up to 35–40% of the earnings of dockers at Manchester. London Transport employees (men) earned in 1951 10–20% above their maximum basic rates.

Supplementaries widen the scatter of pay between persons, though not necessarily between grades: that has to be judged from case to case. They also make pay less stable. When the economy is working at high pressure and rates are in any case tending to rise, supplementaries accelerate the rise and increase the threat of an inflationary spiral. Some kinds of supplementary pay, such as piecework earnings or overtime, are in any case linked to the level of economic activity and increase with it. Others, such as piecework rates, are often negotiated at work-place level, and are changed more quickly than rates which depend on national negotiation. For both these reasons supplementaries provide the leading edge in the movements for advance of pay that tend to go with a high level of activity. They move first. Basic rates in trades where supplementary earnings are small are pulled up after them in an effort to keep pace. But this in turn creates a demand for higher basic rates in the trades where supplementaries are large.*

When on the other hand the pressure of work falls off, this is very likely to be reflected in a fall in supplementary earnings. Base rates can fall, but only under very severe pressure – much more severe than has been experienced in Britain since 1939. History shows that the general

* See Reference 62.

tendency of rates of pay is upwards, even at times of general stability of prices: rates may stand for very long periods at a given level, but a ratchet effect operates to ensure that a rate once raised does not fall.[64] But supplementaries such as overtime or piece-rate earnings can certainly fall. It is estimated that in the stagnation of 1955–9, from 1955 to the end of 1958, the number of hours worked by operatives in British industry fell 7%. The proportion of the work force unemployed, whether or not recorded in the official statistics, rose 4–4½%. The difference of 2½–3% reflected itself in reduced piece, overtime, or other supplementary earnings.[65] This figure does not sound large. But it must be remembered firstly that marginal hours or output are likely to be paid at exceptionally high rates, and secondly that the recession fell unevenly on different firms and industries, so that the cut for some was much more severe.

Supplementaries tend to be unstable in detail as well as in this rather general way. Studies in steel, dock work, engineering, and clothing show differences in individual workers' earnings in good and bad weeks over periods up to a year of as much as two or three to one.[66] It would be interesting to have a similar record of fluctuations in the income of those middle-class professions which are paid mainly or largely by item of service.

A final and obvious effect of supplementary and substitute payments is of course to complicate the pay structure, adding to the cost of administering it and making it harder to understand. In an extreme case like that of engineering they may reduce the structure to little better than chaos. One aspect of this is that it often becomes difficult to see how best to use supplementary and substitute payments themselves. Overtime premiums are conventional, and there is reason to think that they no longer correctly reflect the actual disadvantage to workers or gain to employers from longer hours. Overtime is often used as a substitute for a straightforward wage increase; where the market demands an increase it may be given by lengthening hours of work or allowing week-end work, without this necessarily leading to any increase in output. Overtime is also commonly used by family men to make up for the deficiency of provision under the social security system for family needs. Shift and piece-work premiums are also commonly conventional. There is reason to think that piece-rates, like overtime, are sometimes used not as a genuine incentive but in substitution for a basic wage increase, and that in some industries the use of piece-rates has been extended into areas to which they are inappropriate.[67]

Considerations of this kind were among those which brought about the reorganisation of the wage structures at Vauxhall Motors (desire to get rid of payment by results, though merit rating was retained) and in the National Coal Board (proliferation of awkward conditions and perhaps short-run market bargaining rates) recorded in Table 2. They have also led in the last few years to discussions with a view to reforming the wage structure in the engineering industry as a whole. There has been a growing general interest in recent years in the idea of high time rates associated with performance standards set by work study.

c. *Age, Sex, and Family or Race Differentials*

Boys starting work in British industry at the legal school leaving age can expect (Table 19(a)) to get 25–30% of a skilled man's wage, rising to 57–58% at age 18. The young labourer's rate, as a percentage of the adult

TABLE 19

Juvenile and Adult Pay, Clerks and Manual Workers, Great Britain

(a) manual work	Age						
	14	15	16	17	18	19	20
juvenile wage rates, 1937, as % of average adult wages:							
boys and youths	21	25	31	38	48	57	68
girls	31	38	47	59	72	79	86
boys' and youths' wage rates, 1956:							
craft apprentices, % of journeyman' rate		(26) [a]	34	44	57	70	92
labourers:							
% of labourer's rate		34	44	56	72	83	91
% of journeyman's rate (taken as 125% of labourer's).		27	37	45	57½	66½	73
(b) clerks							
medians of young clerks' minimum salaries as % of salaries of fully skilled clerks (Grade E). Industry and commerce, 1956:							
boys and youths		25	28	34	40	45	53
girls		32	36	42	50	55	61

[a] in many trades apprenticeship starts at age 16.

Juvenile wage rates 1937: A. L. BOWLEY, *Studies in the National Income* (Cambridge 1942) pp. 67–8.
boys' and youths' rates, 1956: Ministry of Labour, *Time Rates of Wages and Hours of Labour*: unweighted average of rates for seven trades (pottery, engineering, blacksmiths, sawmilling, paper manufacture, printing, building, electricity supply).
clerks, 1956: Office Management Association, *Clerical Salaries Analysis.*

labourer's, is usually higher than the young craftsman's as a percentage of the skilled man's, and for the first two or three years the labourer may earn a little more than the craftsman. But by age 18 the craft apprentice tends to draw level and then ahead. Girls are expected to complete their training more quickly, and are often on adult rates by 18 or 19. Young clerks (Table 19(b)) start at much the same percentage of skilled adult rates as manual workers, but have a much longer and slower climb before they reach their peak. At age 20 an apprentice craftsman may be earning 90–95% of the full adult rate, but a young clerk aiming at a post of corresponding skill only 50–60%. This must be read in the light of the fact that the skilled clerk's full rate is likely, on the average, to be less than the craftsman's. The clerk's climb is not only longer: it also leads to a lower peak. Young graduates, coming in at age 21 or over, usually start by being paid about the same as an average manual worker (Table 1).

TABLE 20

Earnings of Boys and Girls as Per Cent of Average Earnings of Adult Men and Women in Manual Work, Other than Agriculture: United Kingdom, 1886–1959

	boys and youths as % of men	girls as % of women
1886	39	57 [a]
1938	38	57
1943	39	55
1946	38	59
1950	40	65
1956	41	66
1959	43	64
1960	44	65

[a] Textiles only.

A. L. BOWLEY, *Wages and Incomes in the United Kingdom since 1860* (Cambridge 1937) p. 50, and Ministry of Labour Gazette.

At all levels the gap between young workers' and adult rates has narrowed since 1938. Before the second World War craft apprentices were commonly paid less in cash – not merely less in proportion to adult rates – than unskilled learners.[68] Young manual workers in general (Table 19(a)) were paid less in proportion to adult rates than today; though (Table 20) since adults' earnings have risen much more than juveniles' since 1938 relative to base rates, the closing of the gap has till recently been much more marked in terms of rates than of earnings.

Young clerks' rates rose much faster than those of adults in the second World War and immediately after it. In professional work the habit of charging premiums or paying beginners nothing, or only nominal rates, has tended to die out.

Some typical relations between age and ability to take responsibility, at different levels of capacity, are illustrated in Fig. 2. At the operative level – "timespan" of up to one week – ability rises to a peak and then falls towards retiring age. But at the middle and still more the higher management level, with a timespan of two years and upwards, it shows no fall and may go on rising or at least appearing to rise to the end. Tables 21 and 22 and Fig. 3 on the whole confirm the impression of Fig. 2.

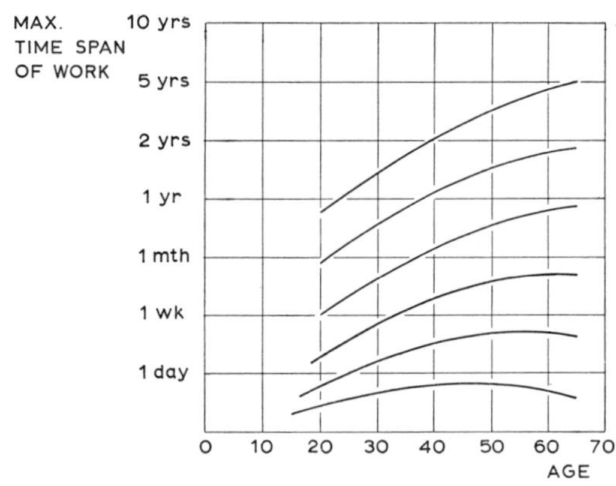

Fig. 2. Capacity for responsibility, related to age. West London firms, about 1955.

From E. Jaques, *Measuring Responsibility* (Tavistock Publications, 1956) p. 95.

Unskilled manual workers' earnings reach their peak about age 30, and drop more sharply than any other class up to age 65. Whereas at age 25–34 unskilled manual workers in 1953 averaged 86% of the earnings of semi-skilled or skilled, from 45 onwards they averaged only 76–78%. Semi-skilled and skilled manual workers had peak earnings around age 40, and a rather smaller drop to retirement. White-collar workers, on the average – if an average of junior clerks and managing directors means anything – were more likely to have a peak about age 50, and rather little drop from then on. The higher the qualifications the later the peak. The less highly qualified members of the Royal Institute of Chemistry (Fig. 3(a)) may reach their peak by 45–50, but the most highly qualified not till 55 or 60. The graphs in Fig. 3(c) show that the same holds for

TABLE 21

Income of Income Units (Normally Husband and Wife) whose Head has a Given Occupation and is of a Given Age, Great Britain, 1953

(a) Age of head	Head's occupation				
	Salaried, self-employed	Manual	Retired, unoccupied	All	All-average number of earners per "unit"
	Gross income of unit (£'s)				
18–24	219	309	183	269	1.05
25–34	541	463	243	482	1.19
35–44	772	494	278	574	1.29
45–54	788	464	439	560	1.30
55–64	752	377	222	409	1.15
65+	970	382	163	240	1.06
All	642	437	195	434	1.18

Average numbers of earners per "unit"	self-employed	Managerial, Technical	Clerical, Sales	Skilled	unskilled		
	1.35	1.12	1.14	1.23	1.21	1.07	1.18

(b)	Average annual earnings of heads of units where head was a male manual worker [a]		
	Skilled £	Unskilled £	All £
18–24	335	335	335
25–34	444	383	432
35–44	470	381	447
	454	345	421
55–64	409	317	370
65+	478	323	388
All	441	352	414

[a] Excluding any who were absent from work through sickness or unemployment for more than 4 weeks in the year.

From H. F. LYDALL, "The Life Cycle in Income, Savings, and Asset Ownership", *Econometrica* (April 1955), and *British Incomes and Savings* (Blackwell, 1955), p. 34.

TABLE 22

Incomes of Income Unit Whose Head had a Given Occupation, Great Britain, 1953

(a) Age of head

	Head's occupation	
	Average for unskilled manual as % of skilled manual	Average for salaried and self-employed as % of all manual
18–24	100	71
25–34	86	117
35–44	81	156
45–54	76	170
55–64	77½	199
65+	67½	254
All	80	147

(b) Fall in income from peak to age 55–64 as % of peak income

	%	peak age
Unskilled manual	17	25–34
Skilled manual	13	35–44
Salaried and self-employed	5	45–54

Derived from Table 21. "Salaried etc." and "all manual" from (a), "unskilled" and "skilled manual" from (b).

many other professions. A number of big firms now use age- and-salary graphs on the lines of those in Fig. 3 for deciding the career patterns to offer to staff at different levels of ability. The bottom 10% of even managerial or professional staff may follow a pattern like that of the lowest curve in Fig. 2. The top 1%, on the other hand, may follow a line that stands straight up without a break. One possible way of using career curves, once they are established, in judging the suitability of staff for promotion, transfer, or relegation is illustrated in Fig. 3(e).

But the data in Fig. 3, and particularly in 3(c), suggest a reservation. Is the smooth, unbroken rise of the age-and-capacity curve for higher grades of ability in Fig. 2 an illusion? In fee-paid professions such as medicine or dentistry Fig. 3 shows a marked peak and drop. Dentists reach their peak in their thirties and early forties; but they may not be typical of the professions, for they practice what is essentially a manual craft of a type demanding physical endurance. But doctors too have their

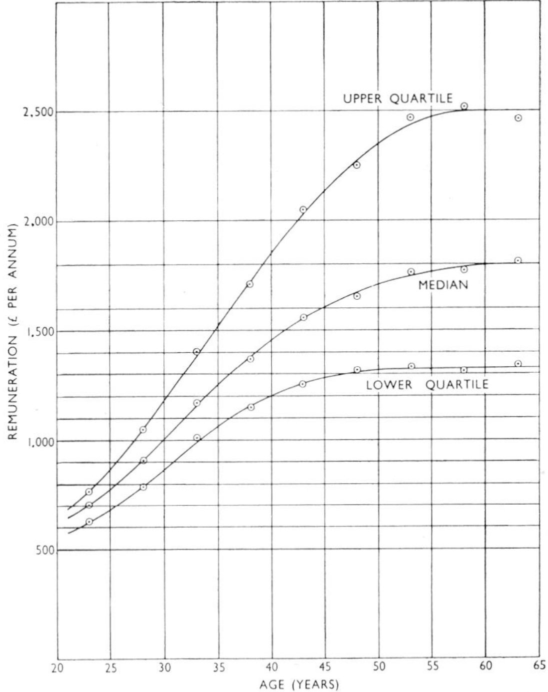

Fig. 3(a). Age and pay in certain professions.

(a) Corporate members of the Royal Institute of Chemistry, 1956.
Median and quartile remuneration of corporate members. Variation with age (21–65).
Note: Median points at £ 1390 and £ 1790 are displaced downwards by about £ 20 in the diagram. Their true positions fit as well or better on the curve as drawn.

Royal Institute of Chemistry, *Remuneration Survey* (1956). *Journal of the Royal Institute of Chemistry* (September 1956) p. 529.

Fig. 3(b) Medical practitioners (general practice)

		Age					
(i) 1936–8, male		under 35	35–9	40–4	45–54	55–64	over 65
Net income (average):							
	urban areas	£ 959	1158	1175	1220	1006	754
	mixed	£ 1012	1192	1256	1255	1260	728
	rural	£ 839	1038	975	1063	928	797
(ii) 1955–6, all (median)		£ 1710 (30–34)	2120	2260	2460	2180	2160

Report of the Committee on the Remuneration of General Practitioners (Cmd. 6810) (1946): and Royal Commission on Doctors' and Dentists' Remuneration, Cmd. 939 (1960).

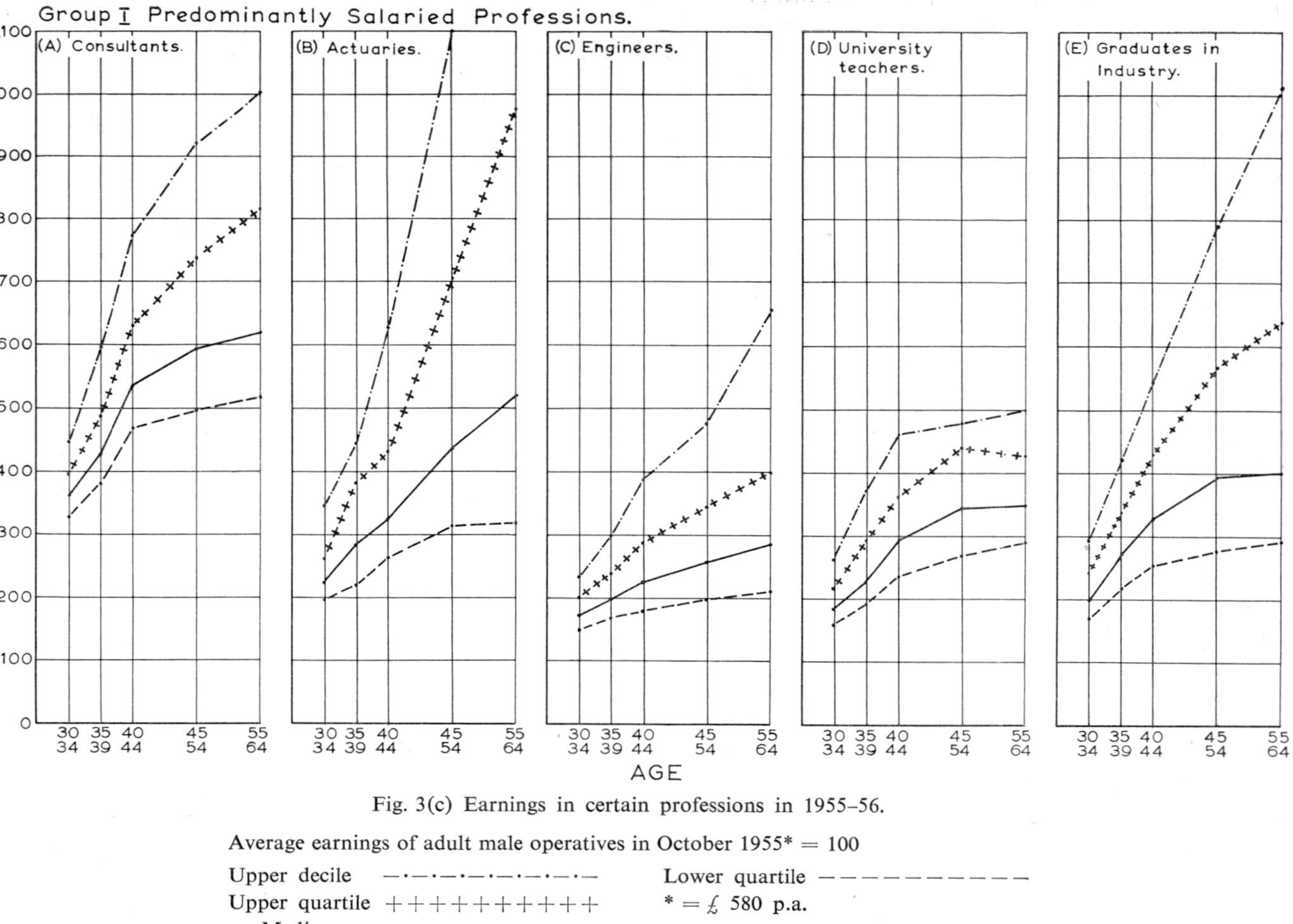

Fig. 3(c) Earnings in certain professions in 1955–56.

Average earnings of adult male operatives in October 1955* = 100

Upper decile —·—·—·—·—·—·—
Upper quartile + + + + + + + + + + +
Median ————————
Lower quartile — — — — — — — — —
* = £ 580 p.a.

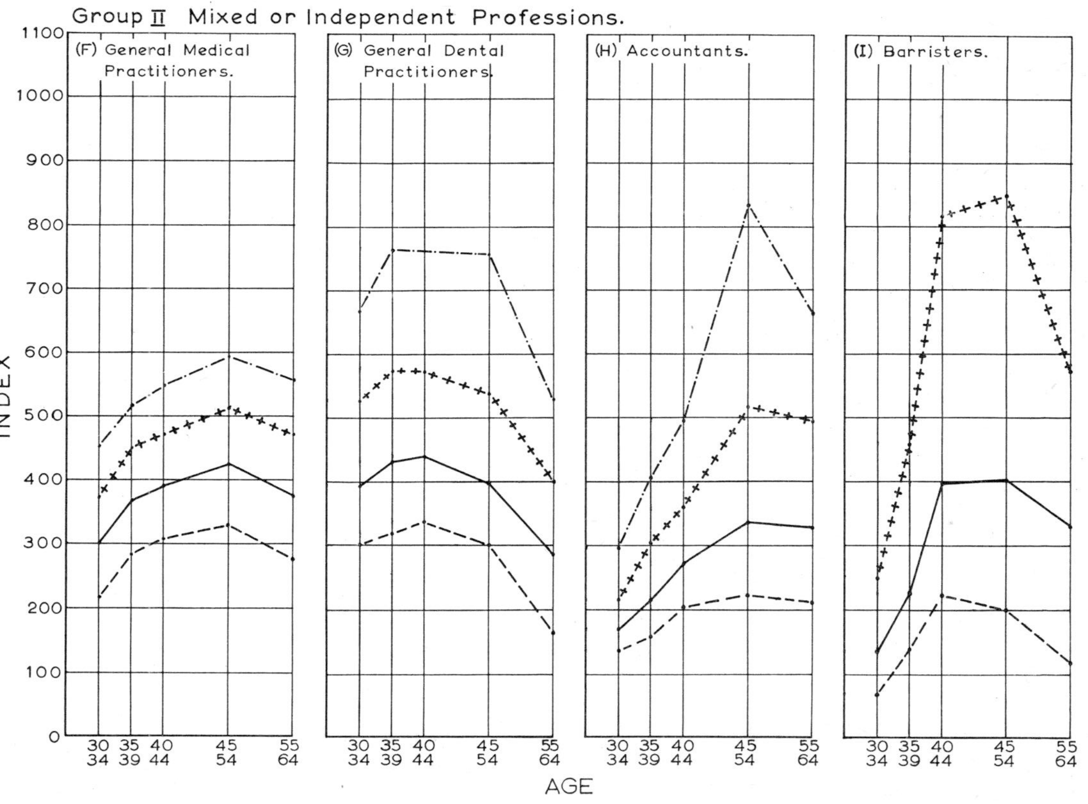
Group II Mixed or Independent Professions.
(F) General Medical Practitioners.
(G) General Dental Practitioners.
(H) Accountants.
(I) Barristers.
INDEX
1100
1000
900
800
700
600
500
400
300
200
100
0
30 34
35 39
40 44
45 54
55 64
AGE

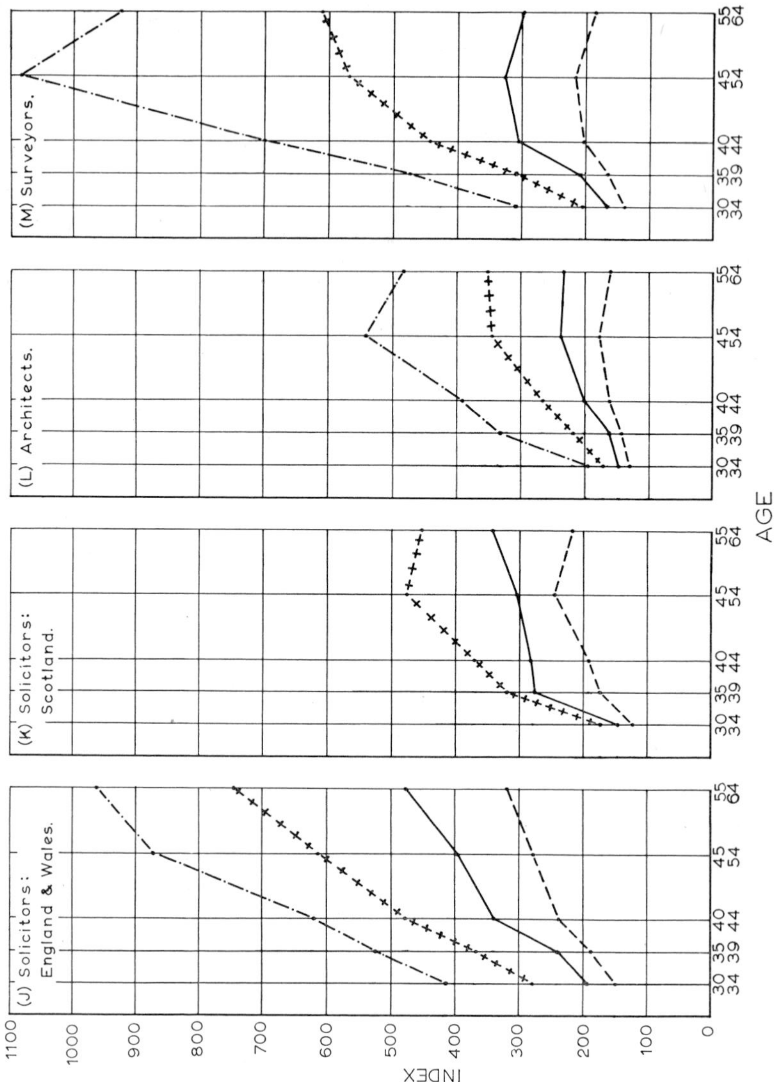

Fig. 3(d). Earnings and age in industrial management, 1960

(Average salaries in 5-year age group)

	25–29	30–34	35–39	40–44	45–49	50–54	55–59	60 & over
Chairmen & Managing Directors	–	2138	3587	3420	2761	3942	4958	4762
General Managers	1861	1925	2270	2350	2630	4180	3296	2159
Sales & Marketing	1464	1810	2345	2510	1953	2619	3050	–
Works & Production	1112	1505	2077	2080	2492	2002	2930	–
Technical Managers	1085	1785	1514	2110	1999	2462	3037	–
Personnel Managers	1080	1507	1954	2212	2189	1650	1900	2050
Company Secretaries	1240	1560	2000	2100	2825	1870	1784	2573
Accountancy	1233	1395	1665	1762	2189	2202	1983	1910

From G. Copeman's annual survey in *Business*, (December, 1960).

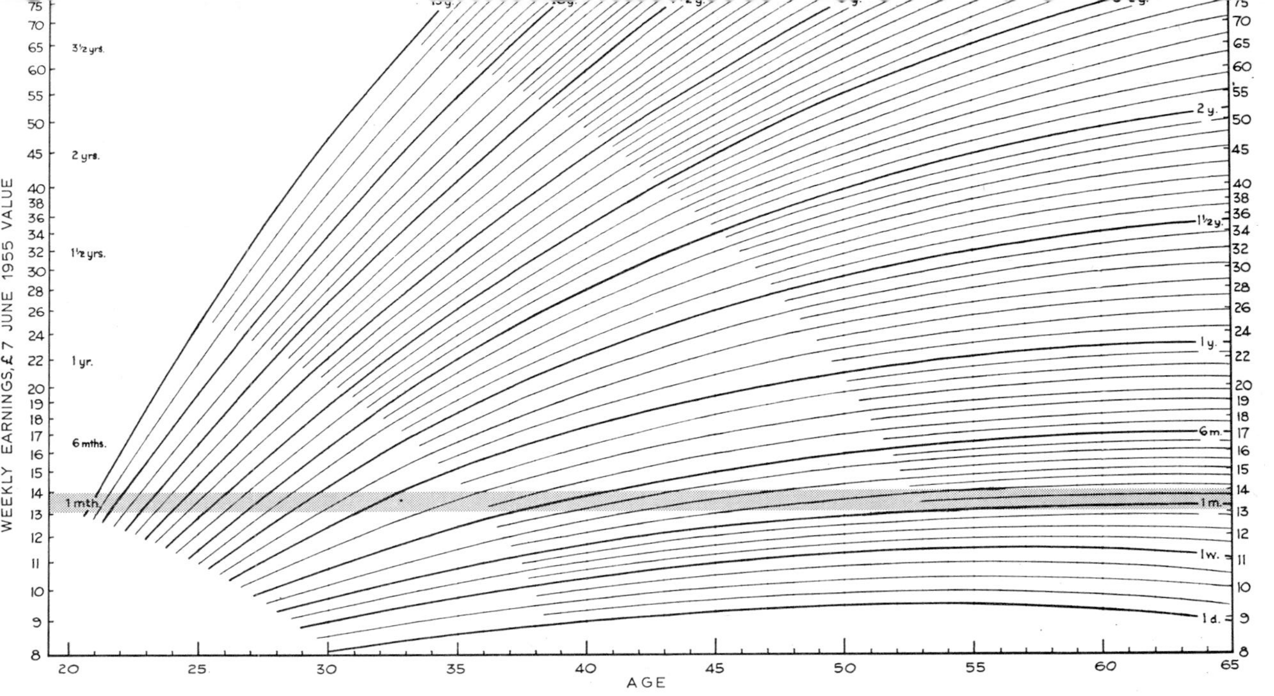

Standard Wage and Salary Curves

Fig. 3(e). Typical salary curves for industrial executives, 1959.

This chart, devised and copyrighted by Dr. Elliott Jaques, is a means of comparing actual earnings with those which might be expected in a normal career pattern. In the absence of illness or other exceptional interruption, the growth of a man's capacity might be expected to follow one of the age-capacity lines curving across the graph. Capacity is measured in "time-span", the unit devised by Dr. Jaques. The curves are drawn so as to indicate the pattern likely to be followed by the capacity of a man whose "time-span" at age 55 is, for example, one year, six months, or two years. Ideally, Jaques suggests, earnings, converted into pounds of 1955 value, and measured up the left-hand side of the graph, should follow the same curve of capacity. The use of these graphs is explained fully in E. Jaques, *Equitable Payment*, Heinemann 1961.

From G. Copeman, "Executive Salaries – A New Approach," *Business Publications* (1960) p. 6, and E. Jaques, *Equitable Payment*, (Heinemann 1961) Part IV.

peak around age 50, and a definite drop from it. This also happens in the case of accountants, barristers, architects, surveyors, and self-employed chemists, who in Fig. 3(a) are lost among the far greater numbers of employees. There is a similar peak and a drop in some though not all branches of business management. Older men may be dismissed, demoted, or, in a period of inflation, refused the pay increases granted to their younger colleagues (Fig. 3(d)).[69] If in other branches of higher salaried work salaries go on rising till retirement, or at least reach a plateau and stay there, does this reflect genuine maintenance of capacity? Or is it rather the case that by custom these employees are allowed to go on receiving their maximum rate of pay even after the point where, in a fully competitive profession, younger and more active men would have replaced them or have begun to cut into their earnings? It may be that, because the old men sit on in the salaried seats of power, younger men are prevented from developing their full capacity, and this is reflected in the apparently steady increase of capacity with age in Fig. 2.

The custom of not openly cutting pay when capacity declines with age is certainly strong at all occupational levels. When older employees' earnings drop, this is rarely because rates are cut. It is usually because men have to transfer to less strenuous jobs and avoid overtime and piece-work: or because they are no longer welcome in regular work teams and may have to accept awkward marginal work: or perhaps because they retire formally from work and are re-engaged in a lower grade. So for instance in 1952 the least skilled grade of the Office Management Association's classification, Grade A, included only 2–4% of the male clerks aged 30–54, but 8% of those from 55 to 64 and 16% of those over 65.[70]

Sex differentials are often hard to track down, for they may take the form of not only of paying different rates for the same job but also, while preserving the principle of the rate for the job, of denying women access to favoured job categories. Very broadly, employment in Britain falls from this point of view into three sectors.[71]

The first is the professions. Here the rule has long been the same pay for the same job. But this rule is not and never has been universal, as the difference in grade-for-grade rates in personnel management in Table 23(a) shows. It is also consistent with a tendency to keep women out of the best-paid work, or rather to discourage them, often in subtle ways, from striving officiously to enter it. The gap between women and men chemists widens (Table 23(a)) as both get older, and no one is surprised if women in general medical practice earn less than men.

TABLE 23

Women's Earnings as Per Cent of Men's in Certain Areas of Discrimination, Great Britain

(a) professional work	%
social work, 1951 (expected earnings)	70–75 (starting rates) to 42½ (maxima)
personnel management, 1956 (grade for grade)	60–80
Fellows and Associates of the Royal Institute of Chemistry, 1956 (average earnings in each age group):	
age 26–40	75–80
over 40	60–70
doctors in general practice:	
1936–8 (urban areas)	40–60
1955	73

E. YOUNGHUSBAND, *Social Work in Britain* (Carnegie Trust, 1951) p. 11: Institute of Personnel Management, *Personnel Management Salaries*, (1957): Royal Institute of Chemistry, *Remuneration Survey* 1956. For doctors see reference to Fig. 3.

(b) clerks (industry and commerce)

	GRADE					
	A	B	C	D	E	F
	(Older clerks only)			(all clerks)		
1942				64	66	62
1946				64	68	63
1952	75	75	68	70	74	72
1956	70	75	71	68	74	72
1960	74	73	68	69	71	74

Office Management Association, *Clerical Salaries Analysis.*

(c) Industrial supervisors (Level B – foremen) 1948–50.

	Average weekly earnings, shillings								
Percent of supervisors with pay in each range:	60–99	100–139	140–159	160–179	180–199	200–219	220–259	260 or over	Total
men	–	4	12	23	19	21	17	4	100
women	23	40	10	–	7	7	13	–	100

National Institute of Industrial Psychology, *The Foreman*, Staples (1951), pp. 130–132.

TABLE 23 (*Continued*)

(d) Manual work: women's earnings as per cent of men's.

	Women and girls as per cent of men and boys
1906	44
1924	48
1931	49
1935	48
	Women as per cent of men
1938	47
1943	51
1946	54
1950	55
1956	52
1960	51

A. L. BOWLEY, *Wages and Incomes in the United Kingdom since 1860.* (Cambridge 1937) and Ministry of Labour Gazette.

The second area is administrative, professional, and technical work in the public services: that is the public services excluding operatives and a few clerical grades such as typists. Here the usual practice till 1946 was to pay women at lower rates, usually two-thirds to 85% or 90% of the men's rate, for similar jobs. Equal job rates were by then beginning to be introduced. They were applied generally to administrative, professional, and technical staffs in local government in that year. This movement continued, and in 1955 the Chancellor of the Exchequer announced that equal pay would be introduced in the Civil Service and in teaching by seven instalments, to be completed by 1961. Several nationalised industries, including gas, electricity, and British Railways, followed this lead in the next two years and agree to apply equal pay to their administrative, technical, and general clerical staff, though leaving typists and telephone operators on special rates of their own.

But though equal job rates are established or on the way, women still find it hard to reach the best paid grades of the public services. Some formerly existing barriers have been dropped, particularly the marriage bar, which at one time cut short many promising careers in teaching and the Civil Service. In teaching and among Administrative Grade Civil Servants half or more of the women excluded by the marriage bar in the 1920's and 1930's would have wished to stay on [73] and, perhaps, qualify for promotion. This bar has now gone. But there is still no woman judge (through there is a Recorder). The first woman Permanent Secretary was appointed only in 1955, and the second in 1959. Women teachers outnumber men by half (Table 11), and by no less than 2 : 1 in the ages from 50 to retirement. But men hold 50% of the posts as Head. Among local authority social workers, staff in the field work grades, of whom 99% have salary maxima below £1,000, are divided equally between men and women. But the administrative grades, where 60% of the staff have maxima over £1,000 and 7½% over £2,000, are 98% male.

The third sector is manual work together with clerical work in industry and commerce, and with the exceptions mentioned in the public services. Here there is equality neither of job rates nor of job prospects.

Women clerks in industry and commerce (Table 23(b)) earn 70–75% of men's rates, grade for grade, or say 75–80% (allowing for the fact that women tend to get the worse paid jobs in each grade) on a comparison of actual jobs.[75] These are much better rates than prevailed in the past. To the 70–75% of 1958 corresponds 60–65% in 1942, and less in 1938.[76] A median woman clerk in 1956 earned about 65% as much as a median man; in 1909–10 she would probably have earned only 45%.[77] Women clerks' rates seem to have been rising relative to men's even before 1909, judging by Civil Service data going back to 1876.[78] It seems that women clerks, typists, telephonists, telegraphists, and related grades in the Civil Service gained markedly relative to men from 1876–9 to 1913 as well as from 1913 to 1924; some ground was lost from 1924 to 1938, but was made up again from 1938 to 1950. But in industry and commerce this long upward progress of women relative to men halted during the fifties. There is no sign of forces within the industrial and commercial sector itself which would cause it to resume. The Institute of Office Management did however note that between 1958 and 1960, as equal pay progressed in the public sector, competition from that sector began once again to level up women clerk's rates relative to men in London, the area where public service demand is strongest.

In manual work women's earnings rose relative to men's in the first World War, hold their position till 1938, and then rose again till 1950. They have since fallen, and stood in 1960 at 51%. This impressively low figure in the product chiefly of two factors. First, though women's rates for a given job are not always below men's – London Transport, for instance, pay women station staff and conductresses at the same rates as men [79] – they very often are. Though women's rates improved relative to men's during the second World War, in 1946 minimum rates for adult women in the industries under statutory regulations averaged only 65%

of the nearest corresponding rates for men. In 1950–52 women's rates reached 70–71% and there they have remained. For women workers in general wage rates bore almost exactly the same relation to men's in 1959 as in 1948.[80] Secondly, women may find it harder to enter skilled or at least better paid jobs. The Royal Commission on Equal Pay illustrated the combined working of these factors in piece-rate industries by distinguishing four common methods of fixing women's piece-rates:[81]

(1) piece rates are fixed, as in engineering, on the basis of time rates which are lower for women than for men.
(2) piece rates are lower for women than for men, on the ground that in spite of identical job titles women do work inferior to men's in respects such as range of work, weight handled, skill, degree of supervision, or responsibility for setting work up.
(3) piece rates are identical, but the work is demarcated, as in the shoe industry or some branches of the clothing trade, to give the best paying work to men.
(4) piece rates are identical, but men are required, formally or by custom, to run more machines.

It is also true that women get and indeed seek less overtime than men, and in that respect earn smaller supplements over their basic rate. Also, they are more likely than men to quit their jobs and so get less benefit from increments for length of service. It is for these two reasons that women in London Transport earn less than men, job for job, in spite of equal rates. But in other industries these factors are offset by the high proportion of women on piece-rates: though women earn less of some sorts of supplementary pay they earn more of others.

Women industrial supervisors (Table 23(c)) meet the same discrimination as the women under them. A median woman Level B supervisor in 1948–50 earned about two-thirds of the rate for a median Level B man.

Differentials based on family, race, nationality, or religion rarely take the form of paying lower or higher rates for a given job. If the boss's son is paid a high salary, it is likely to be because he has become a director sooner than he could otherwise have expected, not directly because he is the boss's son. After the first World War shipowners could and did pay lower rates to coloured crews signed on overseas, and this led to race riots in several ports.[82] More recently, it is possible that refugees or coloured immigrants or domestic servants from the Continent have been paid for a time, here and there, at less than market rates. But there is no reason to think that there has been more underpayment in their case than in that of native workers under statutory wage regulation.[83] The much more usual effect of family, race, or nationality is to facilitate or block access to well-paid types of work.

In some ways this sort of discrimination has become less common than it used to be.

> "The custom of patrimony, that is to say a privilege enjoyed from time immemorial, by the journeyman in certain occupations, of bringing their own sons into the trade" [84]

no longer flourishes as it did when the Webbs described it. Few trade unionists would today defend the brutal frankness of the nineteenth century Sheffield Razor Hafters, "that no boys be admitted to the trade except members' sons." [85] It has become less necessary than it used to be (Table 24) to be "spoken for" by relatives or friends in the plant.[86]

TABLE 24

Kinship Ties in a North Wales Steel Plant, to 1954

Average number of relatives working in plant, now or formerly. Employees recruited:	Wage-earners	Staff and Managers	All
before 1925	4.5	3.6	4.4
1925–38	4.9	4.7	4.9
1939–46	4.2	3.7	4.0
1947–54	2.4	2.4	2.4
Percentage of new entrants in each period who were "spoken for" by relatives or friends:			
before 1925	41	54	42
1925–38	22	37	25
1939–46	28	44	30
1947–54	10	30	12

From W. H. SCOTT *and others*, *Technical Change and Industrial Relations* (University of Liverpool, 1956) p. 53 and 56.

In the 1930's a prospective bank clerk's chances of getting the job depended a good deal on whose name appeared opposite "by whom introduced?" on his application form; but it is no longer so today.[87] The number and importance of private business owners has diminished, an important sector of the economy has been nationalised, two-thirds of the remaining private firms with capital of £3,000,000 or more in 1951 have no identifiable controlling group of owners,[88] and the strength of trade unionism and practice of personnel management, with regular recruitment and promotion procedures, has everywhere increased. Since the education Act of 1944 admission to grammar schools, the gateway to the higher professions, has coincided as nearly as selection techniques will permit with whatever qualities pass under the name of intelligence. Grants covering full fees and maintenance are available under a means test to all students entering universities. It is also possible today to mobilise public opinion against discrimination against coloured or other minorities in a way that does not seem to have been found when Irish immigrants first poured into the country in the middle of the nineteenth century.[89]

But in many ways the advantage or disadvantage of belonging to a particular family or race remains. Commonwealth and Irish citizens can enter the British labour market freely, but foreigners, since the first World War, only under strict limitations. On arriving in the country immigrants, even the more conspicious of them (notably the coloured) can find jobs and get promotion if they persist in acquiring the necessary skills, and are ready to fit in with the local way of life. But they are likely to have to work harder for it. One firm may accept coloured workers or promote them: another next door may not. Eastern and Southern European workers have been banned by many lodges of the National Union of Mineworkers. Coloured workers have traditionally suffered more from unemployment than white. In 1951 15% of the coloured workers in Stepney and 12% of those in Merseyside were out of work: the 3% to 4% of white workers unemployed on Merseyside ran as high as 75%.[90] In general, foreigners are likely to be employed subject to some such explicit or implicit condition as 'all who are foreign citizens shall be the first to be selected' for dismissal when demand falls.[91]

Among British natives, the chances of a boy obtaining a job in a different class from his father, and notably in a higher class, were actually less if he reached the age of 21 in 1941–50 than if he had reached it in 1911 or earlier: though it seems to have been distinctly greater than the corresponding chance of a boy born in France, Italy, or the United States. The chances of a boy whose father was in the professions or high administrative work getting a job in that grade were 14 times as good, for boys reaching 21 in 1941–50, as for a boy from another grade. The chances of a boy whose father was a manager or executive entering the managerial or executive grades himself were 9 times as good as for a boy from another class. At the end of the 'fifties the chance that a boy whose father was in either the managerial or the professional grade would reach one of these grades was estimated at 4½–5 times the chance of a boy from another grade; but this estimate has still to stand the test of experience. In so far as there has been a recent increase of mobility into these grades, it has been associated more with an expansion of the numbers in the grade than with the displacement of sons of professional and managerial fathers. The proportion of sons of such fathers who entered professional and managerial work was 40% among those who became adult in the first World War, 41% of those who reached the same age in 1941–50, and is estimated at 38% for boys aged 18–25 at the end of the 'fifties.[92]

Direct heredity still plays an important part at all levels of the British economy. 75% of Manchester dock workers in 1950–1 were the sons of dock workers, and another 10% came into the business by marrying docker's daughters.[93] 81% of the farmers of England and Wales in 1944 were the sons of farmers, and 76% of their children, if they had made up their minds at all, expected to live their lives as farmers or farmer's wives.[94] Of a sample of directors of British firms with over £1,000,000 capital in 1950, 17% had succeeded their fathers as the third or higher generation in the same firm and 11% as the second generation; altogether 28% of hereditary business leaders. A similar study in the United States found 34% of "heirs" among leading business men born from 1891 to 1920.[95] A substantial number of leading figures in British financial institutions are linked by kinship (blood or marriage) as well as by school, college, and social background.[96]

But what is more important today than direct heredity is the indirect link heredity–education–job. The road to the top lies more and more through education (Table 25), and especially through favoured forms of education (Table 25(d)): though it is not clear how far it is the case that an Oxford or Cambridge arts degree is a passport to the top, or alternatively that those who already have passports to the top take Oxford and Cambridge degrees.* The road to the top in education is today formally open to all who have the ability. But it is still first and foremost the children of those already at the top who take advantage of it. An intellectual home background increases the chance that a boy or girl will qualify in the competition to enter a grammar school. Social background also affects prospects after admission. In the years just after the Second World War, of two boys actually admitted to a grammar school, the one whose father was a professional man or manager had seven times as good a chance of reaching the sixth form as the one whose father was a labourer: the ratio for girls was the same. By 1956–8 the

* See also Reference 96.

TABLE 25

Industrial Status and Educational Level, Great Britain, 1948–54

(a) Per cent of industrial supervisors (all levels, but 61 % Level B) who had the following educational qualifications, 1948–50:

General education	
elementary only	88½
beyond elementary	11½
Technical education	
evening classes, etc., no certificate	40
National Certificate, City and Guilds, etc.	5
None	55

(b) Managers in British organisations (including nationalised industries) employing 10,000 or over, 1954.

Date of reaching age 21	Per cent who started work as: Manual worker	Clerk	Management trainee, senior specialist	Per cent who are: Graduates	Professionally qualified
1916–20	25	35	7	10	13
1926–30	20	33	14	14	17
1941–5	12	26	22	34	19
All				19	
Top executives only				33	

(c) Sample of all adult men, England and Wales, 1949.

Man's present grade	Per cent in each grade who had attended: Grammar school	Further education (beyond grammar school level)
	%	%
Professional, managerial, etc.	63	44
Inspectorial, supervisory, etc.:		
Higher	26	19
Lower	16	9
Skilled manual, routine non-manual	9	5
Semi-skilled and unskilled manual	4	1

TABLE 25 (*Continued*)

(d) Large organisations employing 10,000 or over. Index of advantage to managers in having certain qualifications.

Index of 1 = all holders of that qualification are in top management.
0 = all in middle management
–1 = all in junior management.

Qualification: School	Qualification: Degree or qualification	First Job	Index
	Arts: Oxford or Cambridge		+.68
Major public			+.64
	Non-technical qualification		+.56
		Trainee	+.47
	Arts: other university		+.46
	Higher degree		+.43
	Science: other university		+.31
Lesser public			+.23
Grammar			+.20
	Technical qualification		+.13
		Technical or senior clerical	+.13
Ordinary secondary			–.16
		Clerical	–.17
		Manual	–.21
		Lab. assistant, sales	–.24
Elementary			–.44
	Has been foreman		–.52

From National Institute of Industrial Psychology, *The Foreman*, Staple (1951), pp. 128–9: Acton Society Trust, *Management Succession*, 1956, pp. 28–9, 91–2: D. V. GLASS (ed.), *Social Mobility in Britain*, (Routledge and Kegan Paul) pp. 294–7.

position had improved; 15–25% of the sons and daughters of unskilled and semi-skilled manual workers who reached grammar schools were staying to age 17 or 18, against around 60% of the children of professional or managerial workers. The proportion of boys and girls staying on at school continues to rise. But it rises slowly, and it may well be a generation or more before even approximately equal opportunity in education is achieved.[97]

For natives of the United Kingdom other forms of discrimination in access to jobs are today not very important. One that deserves a mention is religious discrimination. This is found notably in Northern Ireland and in one or two towns in Great Britain with a heavy Catholic Irish immigration. But in Great Britain as a whole it has little importance.

2. The Indirect Wage

Conditions of work are of many kinds, and in a sense all of them are relevant to a discussion of that part of the payment for work which does not come to the worker directly in relation to work done. But a discussion of pay, taken strictly, need concern itself with conditions of work only in so far as they give rise to cash expenditure or to benefits commonly valued in terms of cash. Strictly also, the discussion here should be concerned only with what are commonly known as industrial or occupational fringe benefits, that is with benefits paid for by employers or employees as such. But it will be necessary to refer also to benefits provided in other ways, and especially through State social services, for no firm line can be drawn between the responsibilities of the State and of industry. Services which come under the State in one country may be industrial in another. In 1951 the United Kingdom, Ireland, and Scandinavia charged 50–80% of their statutory health and social security expenditure to the State, that is the general taxpayer, whereas the countries of the European Economic Community, together with Austria and Switzerland, charged only 15–40% in that way. Employers' contributions for social security and paid holidays in 1952–6 in the second group of countries added (except for Switzerland) 20–40% to wages, and in one country as much as 68%: whereas in the Anglo–Scandinavian group they added only 5–15%.[98] Even within one country the line between State and industrial benefits or purely private provision fluctuates: it is changing fast in Britain now.

In the previous section it was possible to speak of established relationships or of long-term trends. But industrial fringe benefits are in full evolution and their whole picture is changing. In several very important ways principles are still unsettled, and it is not at all clear what the trend will be. In this shifting pattern there are three main themes:

(1) improving the adequacy of the services themselves.

(2) the shifting boundary between State, industrial and private provision.

(3) the closing of the differential in benefits between white-collar and manual employees: or rather the advance towards a situation in which the cost of indirect payments will bear the same relation to the cost of direct pay in the case of manual as of white-collar staffs.

The benefits to be examined fall into three groups.

(1) free time benefits: paid holidays and shorter working days or weeks.

(2) services incidental to the contract of employment: initiation, stabilisation, termination.
(3) income-disposal benefits (spending the worker's income for him) which can in turn be divided into:
  (a) provision for current needs:
    (i) on the job – canteens, music-while-you-work, industrial health.
    (ii) away from work: clubs, sports fields, houses.
  (b) provision for future contingencies:
    (i) away from work: family allowances, sick pay, insurance against medical costs, retirement pensions.
    (ii) on the job: saving and investment for production.

a. *Free Time Benefits*

The pattern of hours of work in Great Britain is traditionally mushroom-shaped. Up to a point, the greater the skill, the higher the pay; and the whiter the collar, the shorter are the hours. Adult male manual workers usually have today a standard working week of around 42 or 42½ hours and an effective week averaging about 48 (Table 26(2)). But within this average skilled men way work two or three hours less than unskilled and pieceworkers an hour or two less than timeworkers.[99] There is a general correlation between high pay (and presumably high skill) in manual work and short hours.[100] Supervisors may or may not work the same hours as the men under them: they will certainly complain if asked to work longer.[101] Clerks, the Office Management Association comments, probably average about eight hours a week less than manual workers.[102] The Royal Commission on the Civil Service thought in 1955 that 37 actual working hours in London and 39 outside would make Civil Servants' hours compare fairly with those of other clerks and managers.[103] But at the level of senior management hours may mushroom out again. American and Swedish studies suggest that top executives' working hours may typically be 55–60 a week; there is no reason to suppose that the situation is different here.[104] The death and breakdown rate from overwork in the higher Civil Service makes being a Permanent Secretary a true occupational risk.[105]

Over the last seventy years the differences between the hours of skilled and unskilled and of manual white-collar workers have become much less: the base of the mushroom of hours has become much narrower relative to its middle levels. The Webbs commented in the 1890's on the spread between the poorly organized laundry and chain and nail workers,

TABLE 26

Hours of work

(1) London

(a) 1890's. Number of manual trades in which hours were:

48 or less per week	13
49–53	51
54–59	84
60–71	29
72+	29

overall range from under 40 to over 100 hours. The shorter hours tended to be in the more skilled trades such as plumbers, shipwrights, bookbinders, engravers.

(b) 1886–1928

(i) Full normal weekly hours in a sample of trades:

1886	46½–72 (mostly 48–60)
1928	47 –48 (one at 44)

(ii) manual workers' normal weekly hours, 1890–100

	1886	1890	1914	1920	1928
skilled	102	100	98	90	90
unskilled	102	100	100	84	84

(c) Civil Service and clerks

(i) Civil Service (including lunch break):

1874	36 (most usual)
1910	38½ and 35 (alternate weeks)
1920	38½
Second World War	51
1955	44–45½
1956	42

(ii) other clerks (including lunch break)

1874	insurance	36–39
	banks, railways	48
	(Bank of England	42)
	solicitors	48–54
1929–30	large firms	38½–9
	railways	48
	cashiers and other retail	49–54

(2) National – manual workers

(i) commonest standard working week:

1920–45	48 hours
1947–59	44 or 45 hours
current	42—42½ hours

TABLE 26 (*Continued*)

(ii) actual average hours worked

		Adult men	Adult women
October	1938	47.7	43.5
July	1943	52.9	48.0
October	1947	46.2	41.7
October	1950	47.5	42.1
October	1955	48.7	41.8
October	1958	48.0	41.2
October	1960	48.0	40.5

From CHARLES BOOTH, *Life and Labour in London*, Series II (Industry), Vol. 5, pp. 182–3, 185, and 201 ff.: H. S. SMITH (ed.), *New Survey of London Life and Labour*, Vol. I, pp. 117, 134–5, and 284: Report of the Royal Commission on the Civil Service (1955) Cmd. 9613, pars. 191–8: G. ROUTH, "Civil Service Pay, 1875 to 1950", *Economica*, (August 1954) p. 202–3.: Ministry of Labour, *Time Rates of Wages and Hours of Labour*, Ministry of Labour Gazette.

working 70 or 80 hours a week, and the highly skilled and well-organised Fling Glass workers on 33 hours or Northumberland miners (face-workers) on 37.[106] In London the spread of hours was between less than 40 and more than 100; broadly, the more skilled workers had shorter hours and the less skilled longer (Table 26(1)1a)). But by 1928 hours for London and indeed all other manual workers were tending to standardise round 48 a week. The main change came just after the first World War, and the least skilled workers made the biggest gains (Table 26(1)(b)). Manual workers in general gained relative to clerks, (Table 26(1)(c)), though some clerical workers did also have their hours shortened. In 1945–7 (Table 26(2)) the standard working week for manual workers fell to 44–45 hours, and by 1949 some 105 out of 121 trades listed in the Ministry of Labour's *Time Rates of Wages and Hours of Labour* had standard weeks between 43½ and 45½ hours. In 1960–1 the standard week for many trades came down to around 42 hours. Civil Servants, admittedly once a highly privileged category, have had their hours actually lengthened over the period since 1874, especially since 1938 (Table 26(1)(c)).

The arrangement of hours matters as well as the number of them. Before the Industrial Revolution general public holidays, apart from Sundays, averaged about one a fortnight, and in 1761 Bank Holidays were at the rate of 47 a year. By 1834 these 47 holidays were reduced to four.[107] But a counter-attack then began. Between 1840 and 1875 the builders and engineers won a Saturday half-holiday by collective bargaining and the textile workers by law. In the Civil Service the Saturday half-holiday "began creeping into the Service" in 1876, and was fairly general by 1886.[108] In due course it became universal. After the second World War a powerful move began in favour of the five-day week. This has now become common for manual workers, some of the key agreements dating from 1946 and 1947; though a 5½ day week also remains common, and some public service occupations retain a week of six days or six shifts. The Royal Commission on the Civil Service noted that the 5-day week "is now fairly generally adopted" for office staffs, and that Civil Servants had a grievance in still being on 5½ days. They recommended a 5-day week for Civil Servants, and this has become the general rule. But the Commission took care to note that senior Civil Servants not only were but must remain liable to be called back to the office at week-ends, let alone any work they might take home with them.[109]

The scales of paid holidays usual in recent years are shown in Table 27.

TABLE 27

Paid Holiday Scales in Great Britain, late 1955

	Commonest scales
Manual workers	2 weeks plus public holidays
Clerical and managerial	
Clerks and junior management	2 weeks plus public holidays, rising to 3 weeks according to rank and length of service
Middle and senior management	3 weeks plus public holidays, rising to 4 weeks
Directors	4 weeks and public holidays
Civil Service (1953–5)	
Manual (Post Office engineering)	2 to 3 weeks plus public holidays
Typing and clerical	3 to 4 weeks, according to grade and service, plus public holidays and 3 "privilege" days at Xmas, Easter and the Queen's birthday
Executive and administrative	6 weeks plus public holidays and privilege days. Nominally 8 weeks for highest grades: but this is not allowed in practice

From Ministry of Labour, *Time Rates of Wages and Hours of Labour*; and Report of the Royal Commission on the Civil Service, Cmd. 9613 (1955) pars. 220, 228, 255, British Institute of Management, length of Holidays for Director and Executives, 1955.

Paid holidays for some white-collar workers date back to the nineteenth century. A banking correspondent in 1854 was indignant at the suggestion that many bank clerks had had only one holiday in years, at the Great Exhibition of 1851. The custom, he said, was to give clerks two weeks "if they deserved it".[110] By the end of the nineteenth century local government officers were catching up, and even manual workers in local government service might get holidays. Of 34 London vestries in the 1890's:

1 gave its manual workers no paid holidays
2 gave 2 or 3 days
7 gave 4–8 days
5 gave 9 or 10 days
16 gave 12 days
} including public holidays

In 1910 an Order in Council fixed the scales for clerical and executive Civil Servants at 2 to 4 weeks, and those for the Administrative Class at 6 to 8 weeks. But for the general run of manual workers, and for many clerical workers outside government or local governement service, paid holidays were unknown.[111]

Gradually, white-collar and a growing minority of manual workers obtained paid holidays. By 1929–30 "the great majority" of London clerks had a fortnight's annual holiday. By 1938 some 40% of all manual and lower-paid clerical workers in the country as a whole had paid holidays. In that year a Holidays with Pay Act empowered statutory wage-fixing authorities to require holidays with pay. In the next ten years paid holidays for manual workers became general: at first one week plus public holidays, then, in the 'fifties, two weeks[112]. There remain, as Table 27 shows, fairly wide differentials. But they are much narrower than in the past, and some are narrower than they seem. Civil Servants, grade for grade, have longer nominal leave than other employees. But where a private employer might for a special reason give a day off over and above ordinary annual holidays, a Civil Servant would usually have to take a day out of his annual leave.

The incidence of casual days off, as apart on the one hand from regular holidays and on the other from enforced absence through sickness and accident, is hard to determine. A survey of manufacturing firms in 1960 showed that men were taking an average of 2–2½ days off in a full working year for reasons other than sickness or accident, and women nearly 5 days. There is evidence that a part of what is formally recorded as sickness or accident absence –probably a rather small part, of the order of one day per employee per annum, though varying with such factors as sex, skill grade, size of plant, and job satisfaction– is actually casual absence without medical justification.[113]

b. *Services Incidental to the Contract of Employment*

The median cost of replacing a manual worker who left a British manufacturing firm in 1959, excluding severance pay and redundancy benefit but including advertising, training costs, scrap and other loss of production during training, overhead costs in the personnel and medical department, and any incidental loss of profit or extra payment for overtime, seems to have been about £20. Individual firms' returns ranged from £5 to no less than £330. The median figure, assuming that it applies equally to men and to women –the survey for which it is taken did not differentiate– was equivalent to 2.8% of adult men's average annual rate of earning in October 1959 and to 5.4% of adult women's. Adjusting for the different rates of turnover of the two sexes, it was equivalent to about 2½% of the average earnings of all adult women employed and 0.7% of the earnings of all adult men. The training costs included in these figures, referring as they do only to the training of recruits, would of course normally constitute only a fraction of the total training costs incurred by a firm. These might amount, according to another survey of manufacturing firms in 1957, to up to 7% of total cash remuneration, with an apparent median of 1.2% and a true median probably much higher.[114]

For managers and technologists earning £1.000 a year or over –roughly, that is, all those paid above the rate for a level B supervisor– median advertising costs and interview expenses in 1961 were about £150–£160 for each appointment made, though again with a wide spread from firm to firm. Firms which used management selection consultants quoted fees and expenses from £415 to £770 per appointment.[115] Typical costs, one firm suggested, were:

	per cent of the annual salary of each post filled	
if the firm conducts its own advertising:		
junior and middle level appointments	8	
senior appointments	13	
if a consultant is used (senior appointment only):		
consultant's fee	10	20
advertising	10	

The strictly administrative cost of administering pay contracts, once made, is comparatively small. The median cost of wage and salary departments in manufacturing firms, according to the 1957 survey just quoted, was 0.77% of total renumeration, with a spread from 0.3% to 1.6%. But other costs arising out of administering the contract can be substantial, and in particular that of ensuring its security and stability.

Security of employment is traditionally the most important differential between manual and white-collar workers. A clerks' place, wrote John Stuart Mill "is generally a place for life". Even in the nineteenth century manual workers were protected to some extent by the custom of the trade (especially in skilled trades) or by collective agreement. Limitations on entry, such as control of the intake of apprentices, refusal of admission to a grade while men in that grade were unemployed, or (generally informal) seniority rules helped to adjust the supply of labour in the better-paid grades to the demand. Work flow control through limits on output and overtime, manning scales, work sharing, and in one or two trades guaranteed time rates, helped to steady the flow of work and incomes. Unions organised for their members transfer provisions, to smooth the passage between jobs and if possible prevent arbitrary dismissal: unemployment pay, labour exchange service, in rare cases a guaranteed week. But "none of these regulations," wrote the Webbs, "secures, or even attemps to secure, to the workmen a full week's work or a full week's wage for every week in the year."[116]

Since the time of Mill and the Webbs the contrast of the secure clerk and the insecure manual worker had become less marked. Clerks are perhaps rather less secure than they were: though, as F.D. Klingender points out, their position even in Mill's time was less happy than the quotation above suggests. But they have remained remarkably secure, even, as yet, in face of the threat of automation of clerical work. A study by the Institute of Office Management points out that the automation of clerical processes has been used largely to make new types of analysis, not to substitute for work already being done, and is for the moment coming in too slowly to involve any widespread risk of dismissal of existing staff; though recent American studies indicate that this view may be too optimistic as regards the somewhat more distant future, and that insecurity may now be on the way.[117]

But meantime manual workers have been catching up. Some classes of worker have benefited from more limitation of entry: seniority rules, in particular, are now more commonly or perhaps more formally used to protect established employees. Of 236 company redundancy policies studied by the Ministry of Labour in 1961, 57% specified length of service, usually in combination with efficiency, as a factor in selecting workers for dismissal in case of redundancy.[118] The control of the flow of work and earnings has been improved. Guarantees of minimum hourly or daily earnings have long been taken for granted, and guaranteed weekly earnings became general during the seond World War. In 1941 the Essential Work Orders set up the general principle that a worker has a right to at least his minimum time rate for any week in which he is at an employer's disposal. After the war a similar provision was widely incorporated into collective agreements and statutory wage-fixing procedures. At the same time labour has been becoming both expensive and, in conditions of full employment, scarce, and this has put pressure on firms to utilise it more continuously. It is estimated that from the 1870's to 1924–38 the cost of labour doubled relative to that of capital, and that from 1930 to 1950 it doubled relative to that of electric power. These measures still however fall well short of what is needed to make manual workers' earnings as stable as those of white-collar staff. Weekly guarantees are commonly based on time rates, not on earnings including supplementary payments, and many still guarantee only 2/3 to 4/5 even of time rates.[119] The week–to–week and longer term fluctuations noted above (pp. 29–30) continue, in spite of the stabilisation measures so far taken.

The greatest transformation has been in what were called above "transfer" procedures. This has come about in two stages. The first, from the 1880's to around 1949 or 1950, was concerned with the organisation of the labour market as a whole, largely by the State. The second, which is proceeding today, is concerned with measures at the level of the firm and industry. The two stages together have produced hitherto five main changes.

First, the chances of losing a job or failing to find a new one have been reduced by control of the overall level and geographical distribution of employment. In 1944 the three main political parties pledged themselves to make a "high and stable level of employment" a major objective of State policy. Unemployment still falls proportionately more heavily on manual than on white-collar workers, and on the unskilled than on the skilled.[120] But its incidence on any one class is much smaller than in the 'thirties: a maximum of perhaps 5–5½% of the work force as a whole during the worst postwar recession, and usually much less –1% to 2%– as against upwards of 12%, on the same basis, on the average of 1930–8 and 16½% in 1932.[121]

Secondly, periods of notice have been lengthened. The wartime Essential Work Orders laid down that a worker has a right to a week's notice of dismissal as well as to a minimum weekly rate: as with the weekly minimum, this was incorporated after the war into collective agreements and statutory wage-fixing procedures.

Since 1950 a movement has developed [122] to extend the period of notice and gave at least the more senior manual employees –usually after two to ten years' service– the right to a month's notice. In the cement and glass industries senior employees have a right to 10 and 13 weeks notice respectively. Some firms offer still more, in a few cases up to six months. The extreme is represented by Thomas Hedley, the soap manufacturers, who guarantee employees of two years' service and over 48 weeks of work a year till death or retirement. It is also commoner today than it was to find procedures protecting workers against dismissal except for cause, with a regular right to appeal; and a great deal of effort is commonly made to avoid redundancy by limiting recruitment, work-sharing, downgrading without loss of pay, absorbing redundant workers in other departments, or transferring them (often at the employer's cost) to another of a firm's branches.

Thirdly, since just before the first World War insured employees have been entitled to State unemployment benefit on a flat rate plus dependents' allowances. It is at present equivalent for a married worker (no children) to 30–35% of an average adult male operative's earnings. Some unions also continue to pay unemployment benefit. To these sources of income for the unemployed many undertakings, both public and private, have begun in the last few years to add (Table 28) severance pay or supplementary unemployment benefit on their own.[123] The most generous schemes, those of the nationalised industries and a few private firms, offer supplementary unemployment benefit on a scale that raises unemployed workers' income to 2/3 of normal wage rates (in one case a maximum of 75% of normal earnings): or else up to six months' severance pay, and in a few cases more. More usual rates in private industry would be one to six weeks' pay or, say, £2 per year of service.

Fourthly, the labour exchange service formerly supplied by the craft unions to their own members is since 1909 supplied by the State to employees of all classes and grades. Three-quarters of the 236 private firms in the Ministry of Labour's survey offer redundant employees help (including time off with pay) in seeking new jobs.

Finally, opportunities for movement to a new job have improved. Opportunities for short-distance mobility, that is for finding a new job without moving house, have increased thanks to the improvement of local transport. It is commonly found that employees regard a journey to work of up to 20–25 minutes as convenient and up to 40 minutes as tolerable.[124] These periods of time represent very different distances to the nineteenth century worker on foot, his twentieth century successor on bus, train, or bicycle, and to the increasing number of men who run their own car.

TABLE 28

Severance Pay and Supplementary Unemployment Benefit Great Britain, 1958–9

(1) Nationalised industries	Payments to employees dismissed through redundancy, 1959:
National Coal Board	After two years served. Two-thirds of the minimum wage, less unemployment benefit, until other work found or up to 26 weeks. Paid weekly
Railway Workshops	Two-thirds of rates of pay, less unemployment benefit, from a fortnight after three years' service up to 13 weeks after 40 years' service, whether other work is found or not. Payments continue for double these periods if no work is found
Gas	After five years' service. Two-thirds normal weekly wage for each year of service up to 13 weeks' maximum. For those over 45, two-thirds of weekly pay for each additional year of service over 45. Usually lump sum
British Road Services	Two-thirds of claimant's current net emoluments, less two-thirds of any current benefits and less unemployment benefit for 13 weeks with an extra week for every year over 45 to a maximum of 13 additional weeks
Civil Service and Ordnance Factories	Unestablished employees. After five years' service. One weeks's pay for each year up to five, two for each year between five and 10, four for each year after 10, subject to a total maximum of one year's pay
London Transport Garages	Those with more than seven years' service get a lump sum equal to 14 weeks at their basic rate; those with more than 15 years' service got 26 weeks at their basic rate
(2) Private industry	
(a) Industries with specially rapid contraction in employment, 1959	
Cotton	One week's pay for a worker aged 21 to 30 weeks for a worker of 65 or over
Tinplate	Grants based on points system, one point for each year of service under 46 years of age; two points for each year over 46. Highest-paid workers get £ 3 a point, labourers £ 1.10.0. a point, women £ 1.4.0 a point.

TABLE 28 (*Continued*)

(2) Private industry (*cont.*)

(b) General sample, 1958. The Acton Society Trust summarise the position as follows:

Of the 200 firms whose procedure has been analysed, one-quarter pay some form of compensation. The remaining three-quarters do not mention such payments, so that the presumption is that they do not pay them, though the information about them was gathered in such a way as to be inconclusive. Included in the examples which are given below are also other cases we met in the course of the enquiry. Payment is made (i) in terms of weeks' pay, (ii) in terms of cash, (iii) in terms of making-up the national insurance benefit.

(i) In terms of week's pay:

We analysed the 39 firms, about which we have adequate particulars, which give compensation in this form. Seven of these pay uniform amounts, five giving one week's pay, and two giving two weeks' pay as compensation to all employees regardless of length of service. The remaining 32 relate the amount of compensation they pay to length of service, in sachemes of which the implications are set out in the adjoining Table. It will be seen that the majority of these make a simple distinction and pay one week's compensation to fairly short-service or medium-service employees (however defined), and two weeks' compensation to long-service employees. A number give one week's pay per year of service after a minimum of two, three or five years, with a maximum of 26 weeks' pay. One or two of the more elaborate (to which we shall refer again) give up to a maximum of one year's pay on an age-combined-with-length-of-service basis.

Compensation Payments Based on Length of Service

Amount of dismissal pay (in week's pay)	One mth.	One yr.	2 yrs.	3 yrs.	5 yrs.	10 yrs.	15 yrs.	20 yrs.	Selected points over 20 years' service
Agreements analysed: 32									
Less than 1 week's pay	1	2	—	—	—	—	—	—	—
1–and less than 22 weeks' pay	8	12	9	16	9	—	—	—	—
2–and less than 3 weeks' pay	2	6	9	4	11	12	11	10	10
3–and less than 4 weeks' pay		1	2	8	1	4	5	3	2
4–and less than 6 weeks' pay		1	3	2	7	5	1	3	4
6–and less than 8 weeks' pay		—	—	2	2	—	4	—	—
8–and less than 10 weeks' pay		—	—	—	—	—	—	1	—
10–and less than 12 weeks' pay		—	—	2	6	—	3	—	2
12–and less than 16 weeks' pay		—	—	—	—	3	6	1	2
16–and less than 20 weeks' pay		—	—	—	—	—	2	—	—
20–and less than 26 weeks' pay		—	—	—	—	1	—	7	3
26–and less than 32 weeks' pay		—	—	—	—	—	2	1	4
32–and less than 42 weeks' pay		—	—	—	—	—	—	1	3
42–and less than 52 weeks' pay		—	—	—	—	—	—	—	2
	11	22	23	32	31	31	30		

TABLE 28 (*Continued*)

(ii) In terms of cash

The following are typical examples:

(i) £40 for skilled men diminishing to £10 for under 21– after 12 months' service.

(ii) £5 under 1 year up to £10+£3 per year of service at 10 years – with age adjustment and minimum of £20.

(iii) £15 if notice worked.

(iv) £16 men and £12 women per year of service.

(v) £8 up to 3 years' service up to £14 at 10 years – plus £2 per year over 10.

(vi) £2 per year of service (plus extra if worked to end).

(vii) £45 for 30 years' service plus £2 per year over 30.

(viii) £50 man and £15 woman to those remaining as long as required.

(ix) £2 per year of service.

(x) £1 per year of service.

(xi) £8 for every 2 years' service, £3 per year from 5 to 10 years' service up to £12 per year for 40 to 50 years' service.

(xii) £8 up to 3 years' service: £12 from 3 to 10 years' service: £14 for 10 years, £2 per year over 10 years.

(iii) In terms of make-up of State unemployment benefit

One firm states that men with 2 years' service have unemployment benefit made up to basic wage for 13 weeks.

Two other firms pay two-thirds normal pay plus amount of unemployment benefit, total not to exceed average earnings (one for 13, the other for 6 weeks).

From *The Times*, 8.6.59, and Acton Society Trust, *Redundancy*, 1958.

Men moving over longer distances benefit from the increasing prevalence of large organisations and readiness of these organisations to pay removal costs for existing, and much more rarely for new, employees. The Ministry of Labour also offers transfer allowances, though the seare little used. Re-training facilities have also improved in the last generation, though they are still inadequate for adults wishing to retrain in a skilled craft.[125] The Ministry of Labour offers maintenance allowances during retraining at Government training centres at rates above that of unemployment benefit though below those of unskilled labourers.

These improvements in transfer provisions for manual workers are important, but still fall far short of giving them as much security as workers in white-collars. Unemployment reached, probably, about a million in the winter of 1958–9, allowing for those who escape the net of official statistics. It still gives rise to deep fear and hatred on the part of manual workers, particularly the less skilled workers on whom it chiefly falls. A great deal of it, in an economy where the level of demand is maintained and the location of industry controlled, arises during ordinary job changing. The most effective way to reduce it would be to carry the trend towards longer periods of notice to the point where all manual workers, including the unskilled and the less senior, were entitled to notice of not less than a month. For most of those affected by it, unemployment still means a sharp drop in the standard of living. Severance pay and supplementary unemployment benefits are not yet widespread enough to prevent this. Three-quarters of a sample of 200 firms examined by the Acton Society Trust in 1958 and 61% of those examined by the Ministry of Labour in 1961 — the two figures are not necessarily comparable — made no mention of payments of this kind.[126] Training and mobility provisions are still in many ways inadequate, though not necessarily more so for manual than for white-collar workers. But under all these heads proposals for reform are at present under active discussion.[127] Taking limitation of entry, control of the flow of work and earnings, and transfer provisions together, it is safe to predict that the present trend to improve the employment security of manual workers will be carried during the next generation to the point where they enjoy as much of it — or as near as makes no difference — as workers in white collars.

c. *Income-Disposal Services*

Of the four types of income disposal service, provision for current expenditure away from work had attracted the least interest in Britain. The tradition of British industrial relations is that employers:

> "Should make no attempt to organise lives outside the factory: rather shall they provide conditions which enable the individual to build his own interests and live his own life among friends of his own choosing." [128]

A personnel department may provide a counselling service, advising employees, where they so wish, on personal affairs. It is part of such a department's business to be aware of what is available locally in the way of clubs, sports or holiday facilities, housing or lodgings, or voluntary and statutory social services, and to provide employees with such information about these things as they may want. On occasions a firm may make a grant or loan for employees' housing, or provide or join in providing a club or sports field. It is very likely to supply its own products to employees free or below cost: the miner's coal, the railwayman's or busman's pass, the motor-worker's right to buy his car at a reduced rate. In exceptional cases firms may go much further. The National Coal Board still owns a mass of housing dating from the time when, if mineowners in remote coalfields did not build houses, no one else was likely to do it for them. The mining industry had an extensive welfare programme before nationalisation, and still has. Farm workers often receive a cottage as part of their wages, and no one is surprised if a building firm provides a hostel in a remote district, or firms operating overseas provide housing, recreational facilities, or educational grants.[129] The Forces provide married quarters, appropriately graded by rank: a brigadier, notes a report on Army housing at München-Gladbach, gets running water in every bedroom, a full colonel in every bedroom but one.[130] But the general opinion in British industry is shown by the fact that in a sample of five manufacturing industries in 1955 employers' outlay for current provision away from work was equivalent to only $\frac{1}{4}$% of their wage and salary bill. The Truck Acts restrict the payment of wages otherwise than in cash to the point of putting difficulties in the way of the provision of normal occupational benefits, though recently it has been proposed that this control be relaxed.[131]

This general impression does however cover up what is happening at one important level, the payment of higher executives. The Royal Commission on the Civil Service noted in 1955 that such tax-free amenities as "the use of company cars, interest-free loans for house purchase, entertainment allowances and similar matters"[132] have come in recent years to form an important and increasing part of private executives' pay. The Commission recommended that in the public service entertainment allowances and the use of official cars should be less tightly controlled, though not to the point of matching private firms. Public service standards are strict, and nationalisation has in a number of cases meant a loss of perquisites formerly paid under private enterprise. Coal Board officials no longer enjoy, as some of their predecessors did under private enterprise, tax-free perquisites worth £1.000 or £2.500 a year, or double this at the prices of today.[133] The superintendent of a mental hospital now pays for the vegetables that used to come from the hospital garden free.

On a long-run comparison, it is quite possible that the perquisities of senior executives in private firms have not increased. In the nineteenth century to the senior employee of a big firm such as the East India Company might be given a house, with lighting and firing, as well as the chance to trade on his own account.[134] But there is no doubt that what has been happily called "company generosity"[135] has increased since the second World War, though irregularly, and much less in big firms than in medium and small. It is not so sure that it will increase further, for many managers dislike it, and in so far it is a tax-dodging device the Inland Revenue keep a close eye on it.

Whereas provision for consumption off the job has had only a limited and specialised extension, provision for on–the–job welfare–safety, sanitation, canteens, cloakrooms, washing facilities, works medical services, music while you work - has advanced steadily since early in the nineteenth century. Basic standards of safety and sanitation were laid down under the original Factory Acts for textiles from 1819 to 1853 and for industry generally by 1878. From then until 1937 further provision was made against industrial disease and, increasingly, for amenity. These developments were consolidated in the Factory Act of 1937. During the second World War amenity provision, including such things as canteens, took a great leap forward, and this has been maintained since. In 1955 employers' contributions to on–the–job welfare averaged, for the industries covered in Table 29(a) about $1\frac{1}{4}\%$ of the wage and salary bill.

TABLE 29

Employers' Contributions to Fringe Benefits, Unweighted Average of Seven Industries[a], United Kingdom, 1955

	Contribution as per cent of total cash remuneration	
	staff	operatives
State insurance	2.1	2.7
pensions	7.5	0.9
accidents	0.0	0.3
sick pay and "other social security"[b]	1.1	0.2
holidays	7.3	6.2
Total	18.0	10.3
Welfare (expenditure for maintenance of current standards)[c]:		
on the job	1.2	
off the job	0.5	

[a] iron and steel, shipbuilding, machine tools, cotton, shoes, coal-mining, railways.
[b] mainly sick pay and contributions to sickness insurance. Also includes severance pay, family allowances, etc.
[c] as apart from provision for future contingencies such as sickness or old age.

Ministry of Labour Gazette, August 1957.

TABLE 29 (*Continued*)

(b) Employers' Contributions to Fringe Benefits in Two Further Industries, 1957

	Contribution as per cent of total cash remuneration, staff and operatives together	
	food	engineering
State insurance	2.5	2.4
pensions	5.1	2.8
common law insurance	0.2	0.3
sick pay	1.6	0.6
holidays	5.5	4.7
welfare:		
on the job	2.7	1.0
off the job	0.3 [a]	0.2 [a]
Total	17.9 [a]	12.0 [a]

[a] plus housing: food (average of 3 firms) 1.5 %, engineering (average of 7 firms) 0.15 %.

From W. DURHAM, *The £.s.d. of Welfare in Industry*, (Industrial Welfare Society, 1958) p. 19.

(c) Families where, on the Last Occasion when an Earner drew Sickness Benefit, his Money was Made up at Work. Greater London, 1957.

	% of all families in each class
managerial and professional	90
supervisory, technical, and clerical	74
operative	45
all	56

P.E.P. *Family Needs and the Social Services*, (Allen and Unwin, (1961)) pp. 161–163. The sample is of families with children under 16.

One effect of these developments has been to narrow the gap in respect of on–the–job welfare between manual and office workers. It is difficult to generalise here, for on both sides conditions vary vastly. A miner does not have or expect the same conditions of safety and amenity as the operative in a modern hosiery factory, and offices, even for senior managers, vary from the spacious and oak-panelled to those of which the National Coal Board's Committee on Organisation wrote that:

> "Many of the colliery offices are not conducive to efficient work. They need cleaning, washing, dusting, and painting. Often they need to be properly equipped with such things as filing cabinets for plans, documents, and records."[136]

But the general tendency has certainly been, while raising the standard of amenity in both office and works, to narrow the gap between them to the point where clerks may today be working under worse conditions than the manual workers in the plant outside.[137] Distinctions remain. The manager still has his private room, supervisors are still likely to have separate cloakrooms,[138] and a firm may have several grades of dining-room or canteen. But these distinctions start from a steadily rising basic minimum, and operate, so far as cost is concerned, within a narrower range from top to bottom. A distinction such as separate lavatories or wash-places, for example, may under modern minimum standards of provision mark a distinction of ranks without involving any significant extra cost at all.

The third type of income-spreading service, provision for future contingencies away from work, has long been important in British firms and public services and is becoming more so. In 1955 (Table 29(a)) employers' contributions to pensions and sick pay added 8.6% to the salary bill and 1.1% to the wage bill in typical industries. In addition, employees contributed to occupational funds, often at a high rate –5% or 6% of salary under many pensions schemes, for example– and employers contributed to State insurance. This is one of the most confusing areas to describe, for lines are neither clear nor fixed: neither what services are to be provided, nor which should be provided as an occupational basis, nor whether they should be provided equally for staff and operatives.

British employers rarely provide family allowances, whether alone or in cooperation with others. The only industry-wide scheme is that in the Universities, where academic staff are paid £50 a child. State provision is more substantial. Under the combined effect of State family allowances and income tax allowances the father of three children in 1957–8 could expect to have about 25% mote net income than a single man if he were an average operative, and about 21% more if he were on the margin between lower and middle management.[139] Even this provision, however, is modest compared with that made by employers and the State together in many countries of Western Europe.* State aid to families increased sharply during the second World War, but has tended to diminish since

* See Reference 98.

1947. A typical operative with three children had about 25% more income than a single man, after tax and State allowance, in 1957 as in 1947. But the cost of living had risen about 6% more for him than for his childless colleague, largely as a result of changes in State policy.[140]

The movement for equal pay in the public services has caused much dissatisfaction among married men, particularly in teaching, and it seems likely that before long there will be a drive for either or both of improved State provision or occupational family allowances. Both were in fact recommended by a Royal Commission in 1948.[141] But at the time of writing this movement has reached the point only of preliminary rumblings.

Sick pay and health insurance, on the other hand, are and have long been of great importance, though the responsibility for them has changed from time to time. So far as the general run of wage-earners is concerned, three stages can be distinguished. In the nineteenth century the basic means of provision was through insurance with trade unions and friendly societies. Five of the twelve million manual workers and clerks brought into National Health Insurance at its start in 1911 were in friendly or union benefit schemes. 73% of friendly society benefit expenditure in 1905 was for sick pay, and 28½% of trade union benefits.[142]

TABLE 30

Benefits under Statutory Social Insurance Schemes, Great Britain, 1897–1959

	Married man, no children,				Weekly rate	
	Old age sh.	Unemployment sh.	Sickness sh.	Industrial injury sh.	disablement industrial sh.	disablement non-industrial[d] sh.
1897	—	—	—	20/–[a]	20/–[a]	—
1911	10/–[c]	7/–	10/–	20/–[a]	20/–[a]	5/–
1938	20/–	26/–	15/–	30/–[a]	30/–[a]	7/6
1955	65/–	65/–	65/–	92/6	132/6[b]	65/–
1958	80/–	80/–	80/–	115/–	165/–[b]	80/–
1961	92/6	92/6	92/6	132/6	190/–[b]	92/6

[a] Maximum weekly rates under the Workmen's Compensation Acts. Payments were related to the worker's earnings in the previous 12 months (or shorter period under the same employer) and must not exceed 50 % of them: raised to 75% from 1923 for lowest paid workers. In certain cases lump sums of a greater capital value than the weekly sums named could be recovered.

[b] Total disablement and unemployability

[c] Subject to a means test

[d] I.e. not due to an accident at work or to a recognised industrial disease.

TABLE 30 (*Continued*)

	as percentage of average earnings of adult males in industry:					
1897	—	—	—	ceiling at 50% of earnings		—
1914	32	22	32			16
1938	29	38	22	44	44	11
1955	29	29	29	41	59	29
1961	31 [d]	31	31	44	63	31

earnings per week in 1961	pension in 1961	on retirement after maximum period of contribution related to level of earnings named
£	per cent of earnings	
9	44	44
13	31	41
15	27	40

All rates are flat, irrespective of earnings, except those marked [a]. In some cases (all cases, 1955–8) children's allowances are payable in addition.

e Under the National Insurance Act of 1959 State pensions include a flat-rate element and an element based on contributions calculated as a percentage of earnings above £9 a week and not exceeding £15. The amount of the graduated element depends on the amount and period of contributions paid in this way. In April 1961 average earnings of adult male operatives were £15.1.4. A man who earned £15 a week for a little over 45 years would receive on additional £2 a week graduated pension from age 65, giving him a total pension of 44% of his previous earnings.

From Report on Social Insurance and Allied Services, Cmd. 6404 (1942). Appendix B: Ministry of Pensions and National Insurance, *Guide to National Insurance* (1955): *The Times* (7.11.57) and Cmd. 588 (1958)

In 1897 and 1911 the State took a hand. 1897 is the effective start of the Workmen's Compensation Acts. From then till 1948 a man injured at work had a right to compensation for the loss of his earning power, up to a maximum of 50% of his earnings (75% for the lowest paid workers after 1923) and subject also to a cash limit (Table 30) In 1911 was introduced National Health Insurance. This provided a small flat-rate sickness benefit equal for a married employee to 20–32% of average adult manual workers' earnings (Table 30), and also the right to family doctor service for the employee himself: though not for his dependents, nor to hospital or other specialist service. Since State benefits were so limited, firms, unions, and friendly societies, or other voluntary bodies went on providing insurance for both sick pay and medical treatment. In 1947, just before the next main revision of national insurance, "most firms which do not pay wages to lower rated employees during illness have a contributory sick club,"[143] and this was often associated with a hospital contributory scheme.

In 1948 came into force the National Health Service. The State now guaranteed comprehensive provision of medical aid, and provision by contributory schemes largely ceased: though it has lately shown signs of reviving. Workmen's compensation was revised at the same time: henceforward title to benefits would depend not on past earnings but on the degree of disability, and benefit would be at a flat rate rather higher, relative to usual wages, than the previous ceiling rates (Table 30). National Insurance was also revised, but State sick pay as a percentage of earnings remained actually rather below its level of 1914. Firms therefore went on organising contributory schemes or, increasingly, paying even manual workers their wages during sickness. In a sample of 40 firms in 1954 (Table 31) 18 insured to their manual workers the

TABLE 31

Analysis of 40 Company Sick-Pay Schemes for Operatives and Similar Grades, 1954

(a) Period of service or contribution required to benefit

Under 2 months	2
2 months – 1 year	22
3–15 years	7
unspecified	9
	40

(b) Maximum period of benefit

1– 4 weeks	1
5–13	12
14–26	16
27–52	5
No limit, or whole period of contract	2
unspecified	4
	40

A common provision is that no benefit is paid for the first 3 days (or up to 2 weeks) of illness, or that benefit will be paid for those days only if illness lasts beyond a certain period, usually 2 weeks.

TABLE 31 (*Continued*)

(c) Type and amount of benefit

Fixed cash benefit	10
Percentage of earnings or of basic rate	6
Full earnings or basic rate	13
Part full, part percentage	5
Part percentage part cash	1
Unspecified	5
	40

(d) Fixed cash benefits (maximum rates for adult men)

	Number of schemes
10/– — £1 per week	3
21/– — £2	3
41/– — £3	2
over £3	2
	10

For comparison:

average weekly earnings of adult male operatives, October 1954	204/5

(e) Percentage rates of benefit (where the maximum rate of benefit for part or all of the benefit period is less than 100% of normal rates or earnings)

20–45	1 scheme
25–50	2
50	4
30–60	1
66.2/3	1
40–75	1
60–90	1
Unspecified	1
	12

It is not clear from the survey in how many cases or to what extent, National Health Insurance benefits are deducted from the benefits paid by firms. The original study covered 45 firms, but of these 5 made no regular or fixed provision for sick pay for operative and similar staff.

(f) Method of finance

Non-contributory	25
Contributory	5
Mixed	10
	40

From Institute of Personnel Management, "Company Sick Pay Schemes", (*Occasional Bulletin* No. 8. November 1954).

equivalent of full normal earnings or base rates during sickness for at least part of a period of, usually, three or six months. The rest offered at least a partial contribution. It is not clear in which cases State benefit, or any part of it, would be deducted from the amount contributed through the firm. 5 of the 40 schemes were financed purely by employees' contributions and another 10 partly by them: 25 were financed purely by the employer.

TABLE 32

Staff Employees' Entitlement to Sick Leave, 22 British Firms, 1957

	Number of firms or public corporations allowing a maximum of a given number of weeks' sick leave to staff with a staff service of:			
	1 year		25 years	
	full pay	reduced pay (additional to full pay leave)	Full pay	reduced pay (additional to full pay leave)
(a) Weekly paid staffs				
0 weeks	0	9	0	7
1– 4	8	5	2	1
5–13	7	2	3	3
14–26	1	0	6	4
27–52	0	0	5	1
Discretionary or mainly discretionary	5	5	5	5
Total	21	21	21	21
(b) Monthly paid staffs				
0 weeks	0	7	0	7
1– 4	4	4	0	1
5–13	8	0	2	1
14–26	2	3	8	5
27–52	0	0	4	2
Discretionary or mainly discretionary	8	8	8	6
Total	22	22	22	22

In some cases discretionary leave may be allowed beyond the maximum stated.

From British Institute of Management, "Staff Sick Pay", *Information Survey* (No. 33, 2nd Ed., February, 1957).

Extra sick pay – or simply sick pay – is a traditional benefit for staff, including clerks and supervisors, and though the gap between provision for staff and manual workers has grown smaller this is still true today. In Table 29 sick pay and related benefits add 1.1% to salaries but only 0.2% to wages. The Industrial Welfare Society found in 1957 that, whereas full payment for periods of sickness would have added 6% to employers' labour costs, actual figures in a sample of firms ranged from 0.1% to 3.35%, with a median of 0.9%, and the deficit (Table 29(b) covers two of the industries surveyed) was chiefly on the manual workers' side. In a Political and Economic Planning survey in 1957 it appeared that in London 45% of manual workers had their pay made up by their employers during sickness, but 56% of white-collar workers in supervising, technical and clerical grades and 90% of managers and proffesional workers (Table 29(c)). In Table 32 it appears that all staff in the firms examined could qualify for at least some sick leave on full pay, whereas Table 31 shows that this would not be the case for manual workers: the period of benefits would also usually be longer for staff. Also all benefits in Table 32 are non-contributory.

The public services have long been particularly well provided in matters of sick pay. As far back as the 1890's 28 out of 31 London vestries paid something, usually half pay, even to manual workers.[144] Established Civil Servants, the Royal Commission noted in 1955, enjoy conditions decidedly more favourable than are usual in outside employment: up to twelve months' sick leave in any four years (including up to six on full pay in any one year), and the chance to retire on full or part pension if disabled for work after ten years' service.[145]

Retirement pensions, the third main income-spreading service, are today in the most rapid evolution of all. Here too the main provision in the nineteenth century was through friendly societies, unions, or private savings and insurance.[146] But superannuation played a smaller part than sick pay in the work of unions and friendly societies. The Civil Service and Forces had superannuation schemes. But, in contrast to the position over sick pay, only one of 34 London vestries in the 1890's had a superannuation scheme for its manual workers, and then only if they were members of a friendly society as well.[147] A survey of the banks in the 1880's showed that the great majority had no pension scheme, and several of the few which did have them were foreign.[148]

In 1908 was introduced a small State pension, at a flat rate equivalent for a married man, from then till 1954 (Table 30), to 30–35% of an average adult operative's earnings. From the first World War onwards, the sections of the public services not yet covered added to this State provision or rather (under the then rules of insurance) substituted for it occupational schemes of their own: the teachers in 1918, the police and fire service in 1925, local government officers at various dates from 1922 to 1953. Pension arrangements in the voluntary social services struck an enquirer as chaotic as late as 1947, but by 1951 both coverage and transferability between services were greatly improved.[149]

Private enterprise, so far, had lagged. As late as 1929–30 "only a small minority" of London clerks – let alone manual workers – had occupational pensions, and these were mostly in the public services. But during the 'thirties superannuation began to spread through private enterprise, beginning with staff but going on to operatives. By 1936 (Table 33) 1½ million industrial and commercial employees were covered. By 1953 there were 4,600,000, of whom a third to a half would be supervisors and white-collar workers. Including the public services, the number of employees covered reached 8¾ million in 1957 and about 10 million early in 1961. This included over half the adult male work force. Averaged over the whole retired population, occupational pension schemes, public or private, added in 1953 about one-third to the amount paid in State pensions. But this greatly underestimates the importance of these schemes for coming generations of pensioners, since many of them had grown up too recently to have many members actually retired and drawing benefit.

TABLE 33

Persons Earning Rights (i.e. Excluding Those Already Drawing Benefit) under Occupational Pension Schemes, Great Britain, 1936–1957

	1936	1953		1956	1957	1961
Public services			2.5	2.3 } 3.8	3.75	
Nationalised industries	}	{	1.5	1.5 }		
Other industries	} 1.5	4.6 {				
Own schemes	}	{	1.4 }	4.3	5.0	
Insurance companies' schemes	}	{	1.7 }			
			7.1	8.1	8.75	c.10
Total occupied population			23.3			

From Report of the Committee on the Economic and Financial Problems of the Provisions for Old Age, Cmd. 9333 (1954) par. 218. (Phillips Committee), and statements by the Minister of Pensions, *The Times*, 12th October 1957, and 29th March, 1961, and *Occupational Pension Schemes*, a survey by the Government Actuary, HMSO, (1958).

The proportion of white-collar staff with superannuation rights continues to be higher than that of manual staff. In the industries covered by Table 29(a) employers' superannuation payments added 7½% to salaries but less than 1% to wages. Also superannuation schemes at all levels are patchy. Table 34 quotes some examples from private firms from the mid-fifties. The benefits paid are in addition to the State benefits shown in Table 30. Few if any occupational schemes, whether in public or private employment, are inflation-proof, and many have suffered severely through inflation since 1939.

TABLE 34

Benefits Payable under Typical Firms' Superannuation Schemes, 1935, Great Britain

Non-contributory schemes

(1) 12/– per week (10 years' service) to 52/– (50 years)

(2) related to average earnings in last ten years of service. Suppose these to be £8 a week, then:
24/– per week (10 years' service) to 48/– (30 years or over)

Contributory schemes

(3) related to earnings. A man earning say £8 a week earns a pension of £5 a year for each year he is at that salary level. A typical case might be a clerk entering the scheme at age 22, rising to £600 a year at age 65, and earning a pension of £149.10.0 p.a.

(4) £1.6.0 a year pension for every year as a contributor. E.g. £52 a year after 40 years.

Related to average earnings in 1954	Operatives	Clerks, Grade E
	sh.	sh.
Average weekly earnings of men	204/5	196/–
Above pensions as % of earnings	%	%
(1)	6–25	6–26
(2)	12–23	12–24
(3)		25 (% of final salary)
(4)	10	10

From R. R. HOPKINS, *A Handbook of Industrial Welfare*, (Pitman, 1955).

At the time of writing a general review and coordination of all pension schemes, State or private, is being made by both main political parties. The Conservative scheme, embodied in the National Insurance Act of 1959, came into force in 1961. It intends that the main provision of pensions for men shall be through occupational schemes or personal saving; the State scheme is to provide merely a floor and standard of comparison. Employees earning £9 a week or less pay under the Act a flat rate of contribution, divided between employer and employee and with an Exchequer supplement, and receive in due course a flat rate pension with a supplement for a wife and provision for a widow. Those earning £9 to £15 pay a percentage of the difference between their actual earnings and £9, and will in due course receive a correspondingly increased pension. For a married man who earned £15 a week regularly throughout his working life the maximum pension, including the flat rate element and wife's allowance, would be around 45% of his previous earnings. No provision is made for contributions or increase of pension in respect of earnings above £15. For comparison, in April 1961 average earnings for adult male operatives were £15-1-4 a week. All employees must contribute towards the flat rate pension, but employers can contract their employees out of the scheme for graduated pensions. To be approved for contracting out an occupational scheme must guarantee to all contracted-out employees benefits equal to the maximum obtainable under the State scheme (exclusive of widow's provision). It must also guarantee that an employee who changes his job shall carry with him pension rights equal to the maximums under the State scheme.

Provided that the terms of the Act are adhered to – this of course in a State scheme means gambling on the future of British politics, as well as on economic factors such as price stability or inflation – employees earning upwards of £12 a week (age 18 in 1961) or £15 (age 30 to 40) are likely to get better terms from an occupational scheme than from participating in the State scheme, in the sense both of a higher percentage of earnings in return for a given premium and of a pension related to higher earnings. Of the 10,000,000 members of occupational schemes in the spring of 1961, 4,200,000 were contracted out by the end of March of that year. The scheme carries no formal guarantee against inflation. But it has in fact been the consistent policy of Conservative governments to raise basic pensions at least in line with the rise of prices, and to revise other pensions paid from public funds by smaller amounts.

The Labour scheme on the other hand, published in 1957, puts the accent on State provision. Benefits under a revised State scheme would include a flat-rate element; 1/6 d a week for every year worked, with provision for a widow, and, temporarily, a dependent wife. The Labour Party proposes eventually to abolish pensions for wives not earned by their own paid employment. In addition State benefit would be related to earnings up to, not ordinary manual workers' levels, but the margin between middle and senior management. They would amount (including the flat-rate element) to from 50% of normal earnings near the bottom, with a maximum of 75%, to 35–40% at the top. State pensions would be guaranteed to keep pace with advances in the cost of living whether before or after the date of retirement, and with the rise in real incomes in the country as a whole until that date. It would be possible to contract out of the graduated though not the flat-rate part of the State scheme. But this could be done only if the alternative private scheme offered benefits as good as the State scheme, including presumably the guarantee to keep pace with the cost of living and advance of real incomes. An individual would be free to join the State scheme even if his employer or industry contracted out: this is not the case under the Conservative act of 1959.[151]

The future of occupational schemes, it is clear, will depend very much on whether the Labour or the Conservative plan is in the end victorious.

The fourth type of income-disposal service, provision for the future by way of saving and investment for production, has traditionally been handled with little reference to employees. Employees do not on the whole save or invest enough to provide the capital needed to support their own incomes. This is instead done either by the very rich as individuals or through levies by corporate bodies: by the State through taxes and by firms through profits in excess of the amount needed actually to satisfy the suppliers of borrowed capital. Many firms have in the past operated savings schemes for employees. Some (Table 13) have operated combined schemes for profit-sharing and employee investment: bonuses have been distributed in shares or otherwise invested in the firm. But till recently the effect of these schemes was small.

Since 1953 there has been a sudden explosion of interest in schemes for helping employees not merely to save but to invest, and in particular to invest in industry, whether their own firm or any other. Some of these operate outside industry and are not relevant here: as for instance the plans for the over-the counter sales of unit trust certificates operated by the Bank Insurance and other groups, and various plans for buying shares by instalments or through endowment insurance.[152] But others operate on an industrial basis. In 1953–5 there was a crop of employee shareholding schemes by firms such as Imperial Chemical Industries, Courtaulds, Rolls-Royce, A.E.I., and Rugby Portland Cement. One of the most striking was that of I.C.I. Under this shares are distributed to employees of all grades on a basis related to the company's profits. To the end of 1958 60% of the shares issued in the first three years of the scheme (1954–7) were known to have been retained by those who received them.* In 1957–59, when the unit trust movement was developing fast, various proposals were made for linking this movement to employee savings arrangements and for tying both up with profit-sharing. Aims of Industry

* Information from I.C.I.

Ltd. began in 1958 to sell special equity share certificates from shops in factories. Firms began to be pressed to use the existing machinery of employee savings schemes to promote investment in unit trusts. The Conservative Political Centre proposed in 1959 a special type of Industrial Investment Certificate suitable for sale in this way: The Liberal Party in 1958 proposed the creation of special Employee Accounts, income deposited in which would become liable to income tax only when withdrawn. The Liberal scheme also proposed that firms should be relieved from profit and income tax on 110% of any part of their profits used to give employees shares in the firm, or to supplement savings made by employees and invested in the firm.[153]

It is too early at the time of writing to say what will come of these movements. But they are now seriously on the agenda of British industry and are still far from their full development. Methods used in other countries, notably Germany, Holland, the United States, and France, are still by no means fully exploited in Britain. Further developments are to be expected, though, as in the case of provision for contingencies, subject to political factors. Employee investment, through occupational schemes or otherwise, has a natural attraction for Liberals and Conservatives, whereas Labour is more inclined to press investment by the State; the prospects of employee investment therefore depend on the political trends of the next few years.

d. *Conclusion*

Of the three lines of development of indirect pay – the improvement of services, the closing of differentials between manual and white-collar workers, and the adjustment of the boundary between the State and occupational or other private provision – two run fairly clear, while one has been and is confused. Services have been improved in the last two generations all along the line. Though the improvement has gone to white-collar as well as manual workers, it is manual workers who have gained most. These trends show every sign of continuing.

But about the division between the State and occupational schemes it is difficult to be so positive. The boundary has fluctuated. The most striking case is that of pensions. Occupational and other voluntary pensions schemes at first had the field to themselves: then the State stepped in as a major participant: then the importance of occupational schemes grew again: and now it is disputed whether this trend should go on or the State's share should increase. That there will be bigger and better pensions is certain, but who will provide them is not certain at all. This uncertainty runs through the whole range of income-spreading. Are there to be State or occupational sick pay, State or occupational family allowances, State, or employer-controlled, or employee investment?

The issue is in part a technical one. What method of supplying pensions or other services will best meet the needs of employees? But it is also heavily influenced by outside factors, of which three are particularly important.

One is political bias. There is as has been said a natural tendency for Socialists to prefer State plans and Liberals occupational plans, with Conservatives inclined to the Liberal side. To an important extent, in a field which the State is so heavily engaged, what happens is likely to be determined not on the specific merits of each issue but on grounds of general political and social policy.

Secondly, the balance of forces would be drastically changed if the British manual workers' unions began, as there are signs that they may do, to interest themselves in occupational benefits as vigorously as British white-collar unions or as American unions in general. In the practice of British wage-determination hitherto, terms of employment such as pension schemes, sick-pay provision, and profit-sharing or co-ownership:

> "Are the subject of company policy decisions, and although some of them may be the subject of negotiation, the majority are subjects for consultation and discussion rather than negotiation."[154]

They have not, like issues concerning the direct wage, been major centres of union interest. Powerful as the recent drive towards occupational benefits has been, it has fallen far short of what it might have become had there been full-scale trade union pressure behind it. Here again political attitudes have been at work. The slowness of the British manual workers' unions to enter this field has been due not simply to backwardness but to a heavy previous commitment to a socialist and State-centred approach.

Thirdly, recent discussion has underlined that there is a connection between the choice between State and occupational benefits and general economic policy. It has been argued that the general West European custom of charging social provisions mainly to industry rather than to the taxpayer makes industry more aware of the true and full cost of employing labour and increases the pressure on employers to economic labour and accelerate technical advance. The argument is a forceful one, for in 1955, whereas employers in Germany, France, Belgium, and Italy were paying in employers' contributions from 50% to 85% of the cost of social security, employers in Britain were paying no more than 27%.[155]

3. A Comment on Procedure

The most immediate impression to emerge from an overall review of a pay structure, even when the review is confined, as here, to factors that differentiate between employees within their firms and refers only incidentally to differentials according to region, industry, or size of firm, is one of complexity and bewilderment. There are three reasons for this.

The first is the sheer number of factors of which pay has to take account. A craftsman in Britain may normally expect to earn about 25% more than a labourer; compared to the craftsman, the labourer's coefficient is 0.8. But suppose that the craftsman is in the prime of life, whereas the labourer is an elderly man whose working capacity has fallen off (coefficient 0.85), and that the craftsman is on overtime or nightshift and on an incentive rate, whereas the labourer is not (coefficient in each case, say, 0.8); then the labourer's rate compared to the craftsman will be not 0.8 but $0.8 \times 0.8 \times 0.8 = 0.44$. This is to say nothing of the indirect wage – it would not be surprising today if the craftsman had, whereas the labourer had not, the right to a pension, to guaranteed sick-pay, and to extended notice – nor of sex differentials, nor of regional, industry, or size-of-firm differentials not covered here. It may equally of course happen that the various differentials, instead of supplementing each other, go in different directions, so that in particular cases labourers may actually be paid more than craftsmen in the same shop.*

Secondly, the significance of the various factors is often blurred because the means of measuring and weighting them are imprecise. Even in a relatively straightforward case such as that of adjusting the rate of one group of workers to those of other comparable groups, all rates other than the one adjusted being taken as given, the margin of error accepted as tolerable may be anything up to 10%.

Thirdly, the various elements in pay – time wages, incentives, overtime premiums, the various elements in the indirect wage – do not each serve a unique purpose. Good pensions or other occupational benefits may within limits be a substitute for high direct wages. Incentive or overtime payments, rightly or wrongly, are not always a supplement to time rates on account of extra effort or inconvenience. They may instead be used, without actually securing any extra quantity of production which could not have been secured under time rates in normal working hours, to make up an inadequate time rate to a level that matches the market.[156] Pay as a whole, however constituted, and whether direct or indirect, can to

* See Reference 15.

some extent be substituted for other conditions of good industrial relations, and *vice versa*. The level of pay pressed for and secured is for instance likely to vary according both to the accuracy with which workers' jobs are matched to their abilities and to the general policy of firms and the economy as a whole in such matters as prices, profits, and co-responsibility.[157]

With so many factors, uncertainties, and possibilities of substitution to consider, it is not surprising that pay structures prove hard to keep in control. Recent discussion has brought out that control of the British pay structure is in fact unbalanced in several respects. There are many technical rules for dealing with particular aspects of the pay structure; rules for introducing incentive schemes, actuarial rules for pension plans, rules for combining direct market valuation with job evaluation in assessing the payment for skill or responsibility. Disregarding these, there are six main general rules to be observed if a complex pay structure is to be controlled, and British practice in respect of these has been uneven. The difficulty of keeping order in a complex structure has been underestimated, and the structure has become confused because not all the right procedural lessons have been drawn.

a. *Reasonable Agreement*

The first rule, which is well understood in British practice, is that since pay decisions are in any case subject to a margin of error, and must be to that extent arbitrary, they should be a matter of reasonable agreement rather than of precise judicial interpretation. Rights, in matters of pay, cannot be exactly ascertained and enforced, at any rate until an initial arbitrary decision has cut through the web of uncertainty and laid down, as in a collective agreement, definite working rules. Since the initial decisions must be arbitrary, they have to be approved or rejected on the ground of their motive rather than their merit. This implies that all who are expected to accept them need to be able to check, and to that extent to participate in, the process, including both grounds and procedures, by which they are brought about. Where there are precise criteria for judging a decision, there may be little reason to insist on participating in it; those who make such decisions can be judged by results. But where the decision is arbitrary participation is indispensable for control.

b. *Simplicity*

The second rule is that, with so many factors to keep in balance and so many possibilities of error, cross-purposes, and confusion, clarity is better than casuistry even if it means only rough justice. If confusion and waste of time and effort are to be avoided, a pay structure needs to be rugged, capable of operating efficiently without continual tinkering and, often, under management of something less than the highest skill. Included under this rule is what may be called the rule against substitution. It is true, as has just been said, that to some extent different elements in pay can be substituted for one another, and that pay and other conditions of employment can also be mutually substituted. But to do this more than marginally creates confusion. Standardisation and simplification of the conditions of employment, like standardisation and simplification in other fields, avoids confusion, saves the scarce resources of time and effort, and in these ways accelerates action and ensures more accurate and predictable results.

This rule has been less well observed in recent British practice than the last. D. J. Robertson's *Factory Wage Structures and National Agreements* brings out particularly well the confusion and cross-purposes that can and do arise at plant level out of an over-complicated wage structure with a great deal of substitution; for example when overtime premiums or incentive bonuses are used to achieve results which might have been obtained in ordinary working hours on straight time rates. The reform of the wage structures of the National Coal Board and of Vauxhall Motors * arose out of similar considerations.

c. *Differentiating Tactical from Strategic Issues*

The main lines of a pay structure like that of Britain remain remarkably constant from one decade to another. A particular group of workers may climb up the ladder of differentials as their skill and responsibility develops,** but the rungs of the ladder itself tend to remain the same distance apart. During the last hundred years the percentage differentials for skill and responsibility appear to have changed markedly only in and just after the two world wars, and then for reasons which had little to do with the value of efficiency of labour.*** Marked customary or conventional elements can also be found in payments related to age and sex and in incentive, overtime, and shift rates, as well as in the insecurity – the more or less casual nature – of certain employment and in provision for contingencies such as old age, sickness, or family needs.[158]

Behind this there lie two factors. One is the immense power of conven-

* See table 2 and p. 10.

** See p. 8.

*** See p. 12 fg.

tion and custom; the bias is always in favour of the status quo, particularly where it is bound up with such powerful interests as established class relationships. The other is the fact that a market of any kind, and a labour market in particular, can work in either of two ways. One is to offer a certain supply on the market and to let the price adjust itself to the balance between this given supply and an equally given demand. The other is to predetermine a price and to regulate supply and demand so as to yield this price. Labour markets, particularly at the more skilled levels, tend to be regulated markets of this kind. The intake into training grades in the professions, the Civil Service, or management, even more than in manual crafts, is regulated according to the numbers needed in higher grades given a pre-determined scale of differentials. Sometimes, as in medicine and some crafts, the regulation is deliberate; elsewhere it is customary and carried on without deliberate thought. Women's work, in the same way, is often demarcated so as to force women into lower-paid areas of employment and to reduce the pressure of competition in areas of more interest to men. Action may also sometimes be taken to expand demand so as to absorb a rising supply of qualified workers without upsetting the established pay structure.

Since market pressures alone cannot be relied on to correct customary biases of this kind, deliberate, strategic decisions are needed to do so. Such decisions may arise at any level, that of the plant, the industry, or the economy as a whole. There are some interesting examples of them in recent British practice, notably the action taken during and just after the second World War to decasualise dock labour and the decision in 1955 to establish equal job rates in the public services.* On the whole, however, the tendency of British pay determining agencies has been to concentrate on short-run, tactical decisions and to leave customary biases uncorrected. A sharper distinction needs to be drawn between day to day or year to year procedures, concerned with detailed issues, and a separate set of decisions at longer intervals – probably five to ten years – on the main lines of the pay structure.[159]

d. *Differentiating Plant, Industry, and National Decisions*

A common and justified criticism of British wage determination in recent years is that it has concentrated too much on bargaining at the level of the industry.[160]

This is not to say that industry-level bargaining is unimportant or should be abolished. Action at the level of the industry is for instance

* See p. 60.

essential when attacking self-perpetuating biases, such as unequal job rates for men and women or the tendency, not dealt with here, for certain firms or sub-industries to become permanent areas of low or exaggeratedly high pay. It can be useful in planning and administering at least some of the occupational benefits which make up the indirect wage, and in rationalising a wage structure. In Britain as elsewhere, the main lines for some of the most successful recent plan for rationalising wage structures have been laid down from industry level.

But when this has been said, it does seem to be the case that recent British practice has unduly neglected decisions both above and below the level of the industry. Much of the confusion and complexity of firms' wage structures has arisen through failure to allow enough weight to plant bargaining or to devise satisfactory procedures for it. At the other end of the scale, effective procedures have still to be devised for establishing and enforcing the public interest in pay and, in particular, for settling the relation between pay increases and the increase of the national income and for making the view arrived at effective at the level of the industry and the firm.[161]

e. *One Problem: Pay, Prices, Profits, Economic Growth*

Factors such as prices, profits, and human relations have of course always affected pay claims. What is new in recent years is the growing appreciation that these factors, together with the newly emphasised factor of economic growth, cannot be allowed for adequately within the ordinary framework of a pay dispute, focussed as it is on a change in wages or salaries alone. The change in wages or salaries will no doubt indirectly affect these other elements as well as being affected by them. But they do not enter into consideration directly, and the conclusion of the wage or salary negotiation does not include any decision about them.

It does not follow that every wage or salary negotiation should be extended to include these other factors directly and explicitly. What seems to be required is rather that, at each level where considerations of this kind arise – the plant, the industry, and the national economy – there should be procedures in which all these issues will be taken into account together and guide lines will be laid down. The questions of specific rates of pay, or profit margin, or investment and rate of growth, can then be dealt with separately through machinery appropriate to each case, using the guidance given. Pay determination, it might be said, needs to be preceded by and to follow from more general co-responsibility.[162]

f. *The Need for Basic Principles*

In reaction against the narrowly micro-economic wage theories of the past, useful so far as they went but encompassing only a fragment of the problem of pay, the practitioners of pay determination in most countries have tended to an empirical outlook. This is particularly true of Britain by contrast, for example, with the Netherlands or Sweden.

Empiricism is valuable and even essential up to a point. In a complex and changing field like that of wage determination it is all to the good that practitioners should be ready to feel their way, to experiment, and to discover and concentrate on what actually works. But to enter into a maze as complex as this without the guidance of any basic principles at all is to reduce oneself rapidly to the state which David Riesman has labelled "other-direction".[163] Individuals and groups model their decisions on those already made by others. The resulting complex of decisions may evolve in a favourable direction, but there is no *a priori* reason why it should. It may equally lead to mounting confusion, as has happened in the wage structure of certain British industries, or to a recurring cycle of decisions in which a problem is always by-passed and never solved. At one time the characteristic example of such a cycle would have been the trade cycle. Today it is the cycle of wage increases and inflation.

Part of the answer no doubt lies in separating off strategic or macro-decisions and ensuring that they are taken at appropriate intervals by procedures specially designed for the purpose. But even strategic decisions are unlikely to be taken accurately unless they are guided by sound basic assumptions about the ends to be attained and the general type of procedure most likely to secure them. The assumptions needed are not working rules, giving definite answers to immediate practical problems. They are rather standards to which reference can be made to find the direction in which practical decisions should lead. Theorising about the substance and procedure of the Just Wage has been out of fashion for a good many years. Practical consideration of the complexity of modern pay structures and the need for guidance through them is bringing it back today.

References

1. E. Jaques, "An Objective Approach to Pay Differentials", *the New Scientist*, (3rd July 1958). See also his *Measurement of Responsibility*, (Tavistock and Harvard 1956) and *Equitable Payment* (Heinemann, 1961). The existence of the "equitable work payment scale" is confirmed in Hilde Behrend, "The Effort Bargain", *Industrial and Labour Relations Review*, (July, 1957). The 10% margin is confirmed in two recent official reports on industrial disputes: The Report of

the Royal Commission on Doctors' and Dentists' Remuneration (Cmd 939 (1960) and the Report of the Railway Pay Commission, (1960)). In each case the point of explosion proved to be when deviations approached the 10% level.

2. K. G. J. C. Knowles and T. P. Hill, "On the Difficulties of Measuring Wage Differentials," *Bulletin of the Institute of Statistics,* (Nov.–Dec. 1954).
3. cf. L. G. Reynolds and G. H. Taft, *The Evolution of Wage Structures,* (Yale, 1956) p. 270.
4. E.g. on goods porters 'earnings as compared with drivers' *in Ministry of Labour Gazette* (January 1957) and see K. G. J. C. Knowles and D. J. Robertson, "Differences between the Wages of Skilled and Unskilled Workers, 1880–1950," *Bulletin of the Institute of Statistics* (April, 1951) p. 121.
5. K. G. J. C. Knowles and D. J. Robertson, "Earnings in Shipbuilding," *Bulletin of the Institute of Statistics* (Nov.–Dec., 1951).
6. G. Routh, "Civil Service Pay, 1875–1950," *Economica,* (August 1954) p. 212.
7. E. Younghusband, *Employment and Training of Social Workers* (Carnegie Trust, 1947) p. 12 and Institute of Personnel Management, *Personnel Management Salaries* (1957). For scientists see especially the White Paper on the Scientific Civil Service, Cmd. 6679 (1945).
8. B. C. Roberts: see Table 2.
9. Manchester Guardian, 10.6.'59. For further data see H. A. Clegg and others, *Trade Union Officers* (Blackwell 1961) pp. 55–60, 66–67, 209–216.
10. H. A. Turner, *Trade Unions, Differentials, and the Levelling of Wages,* (Manchester School, Sept., 1952) pp. 252–254.
11. W. H. Scott and others, *Technical Change and Industrial Relations* (Liverpool University Press, 1956) pp. 196 and 215–216.
12. K. G. J. C. Knowles and Ann Romanis, "Dockworkers' Earnings," *Bulletin of the Institute of Statistics,* (Sept.–Oct. 1952) and Liverpool University, Dept. of Social Science, *The Dock Workers,* (Liverpool University Press, 1954).
13. J. W. F. Rowe, *Wages in Practice and Theory,* (Routledge, 1928), p. 27–28.
14. National Coal Board, Annual Report for (1947), par. 89.
15. T. P. Hill and K. G. J. C. Knowles, "The Variability of Engineering Earnings," *Bulletin of the Institute of Statistics,* (May, 1956).
16. British Employers' Confederation, evidence to the Royal Commission on the Civil Service, (1953–5), Minutes of Evidence, Appendix II.
17. Board of Trade (1913) and Ministry of Labour (Current) *Time Rates of Wages and Hours of Labour.*
18. Reference in note 16, p. 81, pars. 14–15.
19. A. L. Bowley, *Wages and Incomes in the United Kingdom Since 1860* (Cambridge, 1937) p. 48.
20. E. H. Phelps Brown and S. V. Hopkins, "Seven Centuries of Building Wages," *Economica* (August 1955).
21. Civil Service data from G. Routh, "Civil Service Pay, 1875–1950, *Economica* (1954). Wage data from A. L. Bowley, op. cit., pp. 46 and 50–51, and Routh.
22. Routh, *loc. cit.*
23. A. L. Bowley, *Studies in the National Income* (Cambridge 1942) pp. 92–93.
24. The fullest discussion of the trend of managerial and professional salaries to 1955 is in the Minutes of Evidence and Report of the Royal Commission on the Civil Service, Cmd. 9613 (1955). The quotation is from the same source as Table 6.

25. Royal Institute of Chemistry, "Remuneration Survey 1956," *Journal of the R.I.C.* (Sept. 1956). Some data for 1956–60 are summarised in M. P. Fogarty, *The Just Wage* (Chapman 1961) pp. 80–81, including notably figures from The Royal Commission on Doctors' and Dentists' Remuneration, the British Institute of Management (sales executives) and the Institute of Physics. The general impression indicated here is broadly confirmed in an unpublished survey by G. Routh for the National Institute of Economic and Social Research.
26. See the example in Acton Society Trust, *Management under Nationalisation*, (1953) p. 37.
27. National Coal Board, Annual Report for 1947, pars. 111–118.
28. Figures in Minutes of Evidence of the Royal Commission on Doctors' and Dentists' Remuneration, Introductory Memoranda, and *The Times* (24.12.'58).
29. Special article in *The Times* (20.11.'57).
30. R. K. Kelsall, *Higher Civil Servants in Britain* (Routledge and Kegan Paul, 1955) p. 198.
31. G.H.Copeman, *Promotion and Pay for Executives* (Business Publications, 1957) p. 36.
32. Acton Society Trust, *Management Succession* (1956) pp. 91–2.
33. Report of the Committee on Scientific Manpower, H.M.S.O. (1956).
34. J. Vaizey, in a paper to a conference of the NIESR and Institute of Personal Management, 6th June 1962.
35. See *Early Leaving* (Ministry of Education, 1954); 15 *to* 18, (*the Crowther Report*), Ministry of Education 1960; C. F. Carter and B. R. Williams, *Industry and Technological Progress* (Oxford, 1957), ch. 9. There is probably also a reserve of people who missed their educational opportunity in the past but could still be retrained; J. L. Gray and P. Moshinsky, *Ability and Opportunity in English Education*, (in L. Hogben (ed.)), *Political Arithmetic* (Allen and Unwin, 1938).
36. Hilde Behrend, "The Effort Bargain," *Industrial and Labour Relations Review*, (July, 1957).
37. Figures in Royal Commission on Doctors' and Dentists' Remuneration, Minutes of Evidence, Introductory Memorandum (1957).
38. Figures from 1st January (1959). *The Times* (24.12.'58).
39. E.g. the illustration (cooperative grocery branch managers in London) in Ministry of Labour, *Industrial Relations Handbook*, (1953) ed., p. 189. The recent survey is by the British Institute of Management for (1955–1960).
40. Cf. the comment on Civil Service practice in E. S. Hiscocks, *Laboratory Administration* (Macmillan, 1956), p. 281: also pp. 86 ff. on practice in other countries.
41. Ministry of Labour Gazette (August 1957).
42. Ministry of Labour, *Time Rates of Wages and Hours of Labour* (1959).
43. Ministry of Labour Gazette (April, 1958) pp. 127 ff.
44. N. C. Hunt, *Methods of Wage Payment in British Industry* (Pitman, 1951) pp. 83, 90, 95: See also the findings of the Birmingham study referred to in Table 16(a).
45. Report of a Court of Enquiry into a *Dispute Between the Iron and Steel Trades Employers' Association and the National Joint Trade Union Craftsmen's Iron and Steel Committee*, Cmd. 9843 (1956).
46. E. g. K. G. J. C. Knowles and D. J. Robertson, "Earnings in Shipbuilding," *Bulletin of the Institute of Statistics* (Nov.–Dec. 1951).
47. cf. the American study quoted in W. F. Whyte, *Money and Motivation* (Harper, 1955) p. 21.

48. A. D. Roy, "The Distribution of Earnings and of Individual Output'', *Economic Journal* (Sept. 1950). For some typical curves see R. Tiffin, *Industrial Psychology* (Prentice-Hall, 1947) pp. 6. 8. For somewhat mixed situations in engineering and shipbuilding see Robertson, op. cit. pp. 42, 54, 87.
49. National Institute of Industrial Psychology, *The Foreman*, (Staples 1951) p. 132.
50. Ministry of Labour, *Time Rates of Wages and Hours of Labour* (1956).
51. On the tendency for less skilled workers to work longer hours see K. G. J. C. Knowles and D. J. Robertson, "Earnings in Engineering" 1926–48, *Bulletin of the Institute of Statistics* (June 1951), p. 189, and "Earnings in Shipbuilding," ibid. (Nov.–Dec. 1951).
52. H. A. Turner, "Wages: Industry and Workplace Rates," *Manchester School* (May 1956) p. 113.
53. Based on Ministry of Labour, *Time Rates of Wages and Hours of Labour.*
54. D. J. Robertson, *Factory wage structures and National Agreement,* Cambridge 1960: Shirley Lerner and Judith Marquand, *Workshop Bargaining, Wage Drift and Productivity in the British Engineering Industry*, Manchester School, January 1962.
55. For a fuller discussion on the theory underlying this see M. P. Fogarty, *The Just Wage* (Chapman, 1961) chs. 1 and 2 and Appendix.
56. Lerner and Marquand, loc. cit.
57. See note (63).
58. See e.g. the brief summary in P. W. S. Andrews, *Manufacturing Business,* (Macmillan, 1949) pp. 215–229.
59. H. A. Turner, "Wages: Industry Rates, Workplace Rates, and the Wage-Drift," *Manchester School* (May 1956).
60. Ministry of Labour Gazette; (April 1959): Report of the Working Party on Boots and Shoes, H.M.S.O. (1946) p. 87; and T. P. Hill and K. G. J. C. Knowles, "The variability of Engineering Earnings" *Bulletin of the Institute of Statistics* (May 1956).
61. Turner, *loc. cit.*, p. 105.
62. Report and Minutes of Evidence of the Royal Commission on Doctors' and Dentists' Renumeration, Cmd. 939 (1960). Fogarty, op. cit., p.p. 86–89.
63. *National Institute of Economic and Social Research*, "Economic Review" (May 1959) pp. 18–20. Organisation for European Economic Cooperation, *The Problem of Rising Prices* (1961) p. 425–43.
64. For the very long run see n. 20. For the nearer past see E. H. Phelps Brown and S. V. Hopkins, "The Course of Wage-Rates in Five Countries, 1860–1939" *Oxford Economic Papers* (June 1950) and G. Routh (see note 20(a)).
65. H. A. Turner, "Employment Fluctuations, Labour Supply, and Bargaining Power" *Manchester School* (May 1959).
66. S. W. Ostry, H. J. D. Cole, and K. G. J. C. Knowles, "Wage Differentials in a Large Steel Firm" *Bulletin of the Institute of Statistics* (August 1958); University of Liverpool, *The Dock Worker* (Liverpool 1954) p. 159; Sheila Cunnison and T. Lupton, "The Cash Reward for an Hour's work under Three Piecework schemes," *Manchester School* (Sept. 1957). Robertson, *op. cit.* p. 50.
67. Robertson, *op. cit.* passim, esp. chs. 7–9; notably at pp. 55–54. See also Fogarty, *op. cit.* p. 77 and 107–110.
68. See e.g. the figures for engineering, building and printing apprentices in Ministry of Labour, *Standard Time Rates and Hours of Labour* (1929).

69. G. H. Copeman, in "Business" (Dec. 1959) and (Dec. 1960). See also The Royal Institute of Chemistry's Remuneration Survey for 1959, showing a tendency for older men to be 10% passed over.
70. For a good account of practice in one trade see University of Liverpool, *The Dock Worker* (Liverpool, 1954), especially pp. 156 and 166. See also F. le G. Clark, *Ageing in Industry* (Nuffield Foundation, 1955); and Institute of Office Management, *Clerical Salaries Analysis* (1952).
71. For the background of this statement and the history of women's rates to 1946 see the Report of the Royal Commission on Equal Pay, Cmd. 6937 (1946).
72. Hansard, "House of Commons Debates" (25th January 1955) Cols. 31–2.
73. Report of the Royal Commission on Equal Pay, Cmd. 6937 (1946) chapter 12.
74. Report of the Working Party on Social Workers, H.M.S.O. (1959) pp. 352 and 354.
75. The correction is by the Office Management Association, *Clerical Salaries Analysis* (1956) p. 15.
76. Cmd. 6937, par. 247.
77. (1909–10): See Table 5, (1956): Office Management Association, *Clerical Salaries Analysis*.
78. Routh, *loc. cit.*, p. 212.
79. K. G. J. C. Knowles and H. J. D. Cole, "Rates and Earnings in London Transsport", *Bulletin of the Institute of Statistics* (August 1953).
80. Statutory rates as supplied by the T.U.C. to B. McCormick and H. A. Turner, "The Legal Minimum Wage – An Experiment," *Manchester School* (Sept. 1957), pp. 293–294. General rates: Ministry of Labour Gazette and the Manchester School index.
81. Cmd. 6937 (1946) pars. 224–226.
82. K. L. Little, *Negroes in Britain* (Routledge and Kegan Paul, 1948); see also A. H. Richmond, *The Colour Problem* (Pelican, 1955) p. 234 ff.
83. As summarised in H. A. Turner, "Wages: Industry and Workplace, Rates", *Manchester School* (May, 1956) p. 103.
84. S. and B. Webb, *Industrial Democracy* (Longmans, 1902) ed., p. 455.
85. *ibid.*, p. 458.
86. See also the account in F. Williams, *Recruitment to Skilled Trades*, (Routledge and Kegan Paul, 1957).
87. *The Times*, special article, (20.11.'57).
88. P. S. Florence, *Ownership, Control and Survey of Large Companies* (Sweet and Maxwell, 1961) p. 185.
89. J. Hickey, *The Cardiff Irish Community*, unpublished M. A. thesis (University of Wales, 1959).
90. Richmond, *op. cit.*, p. 47 and 238, and M. Banton, *The Coloured Quarter*, (Cape 1955), p. 133; and references in the bibliographies of these books and Little, *op. cit.* See also L. Stephens, *Employment of Coloured Workers in the Birmingham Area* (Institute of Personnel Management, 1956).
91. From an agreement by The Glacier Metal Co., reported in "Employee Security" *British Institute of Management Information Note* 139 (January 1957).
92. D. V. Glass (ed.), *Social Mobility in Britain* (Routledge and Kegan Paul, 1954) pp. 186, 201, 262–263. 15 *to* 18 (*The Crowther Report*), Ministry of Education (1961) Vol. 2, p. 164.

93. UNIVERSITY OF LIVERPOOL, *The Dock Worker* (1954) pp. 49–50.
94. Reported in M. P. FOGARTY, *The Farming Life*, cyclostyled (Nuffield Foundation, 1952) Table XXXa.
95. G. H. COPEMAN, *Leaders of British Industry*, Gee (1955) p. 97; and R. BENDIX, *Work and Authority in Industry* (Wiley, 1956) p. 229.
96. T. LUPTON and G. S. WILSON, "The Social Background and Connections of Top Decision Makers," *Manchester School* (January 1959).
97. MINISTRY OF EDUCATION, *Early Leaving* (1954) p. 38; 15 *to* 18, Vol. 2, p. 17, 132.
98. POLITICAL AND ECONOMIC PLANNING, "Free Trade and Social Security," *Planning*, (15.7.'57). See also *International Labour Review* (December 1957) p. 567.
99. See note 52, and ROBERTSON, *op. cit.*, pp. 32, 62, 84.
100. B. WOOTTON, *Social Foundations of Wages Policy* (Allen and Unwin, 1955) pp. 56–58.
101. WOOTTON, *op. cit.*, p. 136 (railway supervisors): and note the interest created by the fact that American supervisors at Fawley in (1949–51) worked as long hours as their men: A. P. GRAY and M. ABRAMS, *Construction of Esso Refinery, Fawley* (British Institute of Management, 1954).
102. *Clerical Salaries Analysis* (1956).
103. Cmd. 9613 (1955) pars. 206 and 207.
104. FORTUNE, *The Executive Life* (Doubleday, 1956) pp. 63–65, and S. CARLSON, *Executive Behaviour* (Strombergs, 1951) p. 75.
105. Editorial in Public Administration (Summer 1951): see also Cmd. 9613 (1955) pars. 237 and 374–375.
106. S. and B. WEBB, *Industrial Democracy* (Longmans, 1902) ed. p. 583.
107. *The Times*, (8.8.'57).
108. S. and B. WEBB, *loc. cit.*, pp. 352–353, and ROUTH, *loc. cit.*, p. 203.
109. Cmd. 9613 (1955) pars. 371–376.
110. Quoted in F. D. KLINGENDER, *The Condition of Clerical Labour in Britain*, (Martin Lawrence, 1935) p. 10.
111. For local government and general conditions see C. BOOTH, *Life and Labour in London*, Series II (Industry), 4.41. For the Civil Service see Cmd. 9613 (1955) par. 224.
112. H. SMITH (ed.), *New Survey of London Life and Labour* (1937) 8.284. MINISTRY OF LABOUR, *Industrial Relations Handbook* (1944) ed. pp. 163 ff.: and *Time Rates of Wages and Hours of Labour*. See also *Ministry of Labour Gazette*, (March 1959).
113. BRITISH INSTITUTE OF MANAGEMENT, *Absence from Work* (1961): N. WALKER, *Morale in the Civil Service* (Edinburgh, 1961), ch. 6: *Woman, Wife and Worker*, (D.S.I.R., 1960): *Retirement*, (Acton Society Trust, 1960) ch. 5 and appendix.
114. BRITISH INSTITUTE OF MANAGEMENT, *The Cost of Labour Turnover* (1959): labour turnover figures from MINISTRY OF LABOUR GAZETTE (October 1959): W. DURHAM, *The £.s.d. of Welfare in Industry* (Industrial Welfare Society, 1958).
115. INDUSTRIAL WELFARE SOCIETY, "Vacancy Advertising and Interview Cost," (Information Survey no. 88, 1961).
116. MILL as quoted in KLINGENDER, *op. cit.*, p. 3. The account of 19th-century practice is based on S. and B. WEBB, *op. cit.*, II, chs. 9, 10, 11: also their *History of Trade Unionism* (Longmans, 1920 ed.) pp. 444–471. The quotation is from pp. 442–443.

117. O.M.A. as reported in *The Times* (17.8.'59): IDA RUSSAKOFF HOOS, "When the Computer Takes over the Office," *University of California* (Reprint No. 148, 1960).
118. Security and Change, Ministry of Labour (1961) p. 8.
119. White Paper on Employment Policy, Cmd. 6527 (1944).
120. Adjusting official prewar to official postwar statistics in accordance with the chance in the proportion of the work force covered: and adjusting postwar statistics to allow for the increased number of "secondary" workers not covered by the official statistics, as argued in H. A. TURNER, "Employment Fluctuations, Labour Supply, and Bargaining Power," *Manchester School*, (March 1959).
121. *Ministry of Labour Gazette* (November 1956).
122. The fullest survey is by THE ACTON SOCIETY TRUST, *Redundancy* (1958). See also BRITISH INSTITUTE OF MANAGEMENT, "Employee Security" (January 1957); *The Times*, (8.6.'59): "Security and Change," p. 16–17.
123. *ibid.*
124. D. CHAPMAN, *Convenience* (Human Relations 1950) I., p. 77.
125. ACTON SOCIETY TRUST, *Redundancy* (1958): BRITISH INSTITUTE OF MANAGEMENT, *Company Housing Policy* (1960) (covers also removal expenses): G. WILLIAMS, *Recruitment to Skilled Trades* (Routledge and Kegan Paul, 1957) pp. 39–42.
126. Acton Society Trust, *op. cit.*, p. 36.
127. See for example the comprehensive proposals in THE LIBERAL PARTY's *Redundancy* (1958).
128. B. J. COHEN and M. M. TOWY-EVANS, *Working Conditions and Employee Services*, (Institute of Personnel Management 1947) p. 7.
129. BRITISH INSTITUTE OF MANAGEMENT, "Financial Assistance for Education of Employee's Children," Information Note, 133 (Sept. 1956).
130. *The Times* (8.6.'59).
131. The five industries and those included in Table 32 (a): source as for that table. For the Truck Acts see the Report of the Committee on the Truck Acts (1961).
132. Cmd. 9613 (1955) pars. 371–376.
133. National Coal Board, Report for (1947) par. 113.
134. R. K. KELSALL, *Higher Civil Servants in Britain* (Routledge and Kegan Paul, 1955) pp. 184–185.
135. G. H. COPEMAN, *Promotion and Pay for Executives* (Business Publications, 1957) ch. 14. The Inland Revenue regulations of business expenses were sharply tightened up in (1961). See the INLAND REVENUE's *Notes on Expenses Payments and Benefits for Directors and Certain Employees.*
136. NATIONAL COAL BOARD, Report of the Advisory Committee on Organisation, (1955), par. 296.
137. Report of the Committee on Health, Welfare, and Safety in Industrial Employment, Cmd. 7664, 1949, pars. 7–70. The Committee point out that in many ways the conditions of work of office workers are liable to fall short of those of the Factory Acts.
138. National Institute of Industrial Psychology, *op. cit.* p. 132.
139. K. R. HUTCHINGS, *Prices, Taxation, and the Family*, cyclostyled, (1959).
140. HUTCHINGS, *op. cit.*
141. Report of the Royal Commission on Population, Cmd. 7695 (1949) ch. 17.
142. W. BEVERIDGE, *Voluntary Action* (Allen and Unwin, 1948) pp. 94 and 332.

143. Cohen and Towy-Evans, *op. cit.*, p. 43.
144. Booth, *op. cit.* (1891) Series 2, 4.41.
145. Cmd. 9613 (1955) par. 279.
146. Report of the Committee on the Economic and Financial Problems of the Provision for Old Age, Cmd. 9333 (1954) par. 11.
147. Booth, *loc. cit.*
148. Kilingender, *op. cit.*, p. 16.
149. Cmd. 9333, par. 16, and E. Younghusband, *Employment and Training of Social Workers* (Carnegie Trust 1947), p. 15, and *Social Work in Britain* (1951), pp. 13–14.
150. Cmd. 9333, p. 28.
151. Labour Party, *National Superannuation* (1957). On the comparison of the Conservative State Scheme with commercial insurance benefits see Life Offices Association and Associated Scottish Life Offices, *National Insurance Act 1959 – Inter-relation with Occupational Pension Schemes*, (1959).
152. References to some of the main developments will be found in *The Times*, 13–15 (11.'58), (25.3.'59), (24.4.'59), (29.4.'59), (5.6.'59). For the general thesis of this section see Fogarty, *op. cit.* ch. XI.
153. R. Wainwright, *Own as you Earn* (Liberal Publications Dept., 1958).
154. G. R. Moxon, "Collective Bargaining – National and Local," *Institute of Personnel Management* (December 1960) p. 229.
155. Political and Economic Planning, "The Promotion of Economic Growth", (Planning March 1961).
156. Robertson, *op. cit.*, chs. 7–9.
157. J. C. Dow and L. A. Dicks-Mireaux, *The Determinants of Wage Inflation*, (JRSS 1959), pt. 2: C. Argyris, "The Organisation – What Makes it Healthy?," *Harvard Business Review* (November–December 1958).
158. Fuller analysis in Fogarty, *The Just Wage*, chs. 5–7.
159. Fogarty, *op. cit.*, esp. ch. 13.
160. E.g. Robertson, *op. cit.*
161. Fogarty, *op. cit.*, ch. 12.
162. *loc. cit.*
163. D. Riesman, *The Lonely Crowd* (Doubleday, 1954).

Chapter 2

WAGE-STRUCTURE AND ORGANIZATION-STRUCTURE

J. L. MEY

Department of Business Economics, State University, Groningen, The Netherlands

Considering the wage-structure within the company, the wage-pyramid of those engaged in it, we must be aware of the relationship between wage-structure and organization-structure, in this context to be defined as the formal and informal relationships between the members of the company's personnel.* There are two reasons for this. First and generally, the wages earned by people are a factor in determining their status within the firm. The latter is one of the factors decisive for their mutual relations and for the way they communicate with each other.

More specifically, however, the wage-structure also shows how each job, that is, each point in the organization-structure, is evaluated. We, therefore, can see the internal wage-structure as the value-dimension of the organization-structure.

Its wage-structure, however, is not determined only by the company itself. External circumstances exert their influence. This might give rise to a conflict, because the external factors determining wages need not be in line with the interests of the company. The same can be said of fringes and other conditions on which people are engaged by the firm. Here also from the point of view of the latter, external influences may work against the firm's interests.

External influences on the internal wage-structure originate from government policy as well as from union activities. The union challenge to management control, of which Chamberlain spoke, is for a large part a *challenge to* the control of the company's wage-structure and other working-conditions.[1]

The influence of the unions and the relationship between internal and external wage-structure will be treated thoroughly in other chapters of this volume. Nevertheless in considering the relationship between organ-

* Apart from the organization-structure in the sense of the relationships between the personnel members, one may distinguish the organization-structure as the subdivision by departments and the relationships between them. Often both are mixed up. We will concentrate on the concept of organization-structure as defined in the main text.

ization-structure and wage-structure we cannot wholly eliminate the problem of the union challenge.

1. Organization Structure and its Function within the Company

Organization structure, as we defined it, is a result of a distribution of tasks over the people in a company. The goal of the company as a whole is split up again and again into sub-goals. In this way the task of each member of the enterprise is determined by delegation by those responsible for the goal of the company as a whole. The task of everyone is part of the goal the firm as a whole wishes to reach.

Organization-structure presupposes, therefore, an analysis of the goal of the firm and consists in a distribution of its parts among the workers on different levels. Everyone is held responsible for the fulfilment of his task, that is for the reaching of his sub-goal. Task-distribution is therefore, at the same time, responsibility-distribution. Since without the necessary authority one cannot be held responsible, task-distribution must also be accompanied with authority-distribution.*

Distribution of task, authority and responsibility has a qualitative and a quantitative aspect. The former only says what the task is the performer is held responsible for; it does not answer the question what must be done to fulfil the task and how far the responsibility of its performer reaches. This is the quantitative aspect.

Every distribution of task, authority and responsibility needs not only a qualitative indication or circumscription but also a quantitative fixation. This is accomplished through budgets and standards expressed in quantities of raw material, hours, etc., or in money. Only by saying how far resources may be used for the fulfilment of a task, has the delegation a real meaning. Only then can the performer be held responsible for it.

A third element of the organization-structure is the time allowed to elapse before the delegate has to report to his delegator on the way he has completed his task e.g. whether it is an hour, a day, a week and so on.**

* Nevertheless there need not be automatically a balance between task-distribution and authority-distribution. A task may be delegated without the necessary authority to fulfil it, this is a mistake often made by those who delegate parts of their tasks. It seems easier to delegate a task, than the authority necessary to fulfil it.

By delegation, the remaining task of the delegator is diminished, but his responsibility is not. As before, he is responsible for the whole task. Moreover he can be held responsible for the delegation as such and for the choice of the delegate.

** I am not inclined, as Eliott Jaques is, to see this as the only measure of responsibility. In my opinion responsibility is multi-dimensional and therefore must be measured in different directions. See reference 2.

By analyzing the goals of the enterprise and sub-dividing them accordingly into sub-goals, the organization-structure creates the system of relationships, information and communication-channels to take the decisions which are necessary to direct and co-ordinate all the company's activities. This is the second function of the organization-structure which is complementary to the first. It determines how the organization-structure can be used as a tool for management and for completing managerial activities. Particularly the organization can be considered as a means for taking decisions in structured management-problems.[3]

The organization structure cannot fulfil its functions, if the wage-scales for the different jobs in the company are not in line with their position, in the company.

One of the most important problems of company wage-policy therefore is how to keep the internal wage-structure in line with the organization structure. Lack of adequacy of the internal wage-structure is a cause for many tensions and many grievances and in last resort for low productivity.

2. Internal Wage-patterns and their Determining Factors

With regard to the internal wage-pattern it seems convenient to distinguish between functional and personal patterns. The functional pattern consists of the evaluated functions or jobs to be fulfilled within the company.

The personal patterns or the personal deviations from the functional pattern depend on two factors viz. the way the workers actually fulfil their jobs and on their personal qualities which might make them available also for the performance of other tasks.

It is the functional wage-structure that can in the first place be considered as a dimension of the organization-structure. Regarding the personal deviations the question must be raised whether or not they disturb the organization-structure or at least form an obstacle to the performance of its function.

From the functional wage-pattern it follows what distances exist quantitatively between the different jobs and functions in the company. It does not tell us that a supervisor stands on a level above the laborers, but how far this level lies above the labor-force under him.

What is said here can be easily illustrated by putting a wage- or salary-scale into an organization-chart.

Sometimes the wage-levels do not correspond with the levels in the organization. The work of higher paid performers can be supervised by lower paid supervisors or coordinated by lower paid managers. There are cases where this seems inevitable, for instance, if the performance needs very high skill or rare qualitites, as in the case of airline pilots being obliged to report to an administrative officer at headquarters; clinical specialists at a University-hospital being supervised by a non-medical managing director. In both cases the coordinator or supervisor need not have the skill and experience of those whose work he is directing and, therefore, he may be paid at a lower scale.

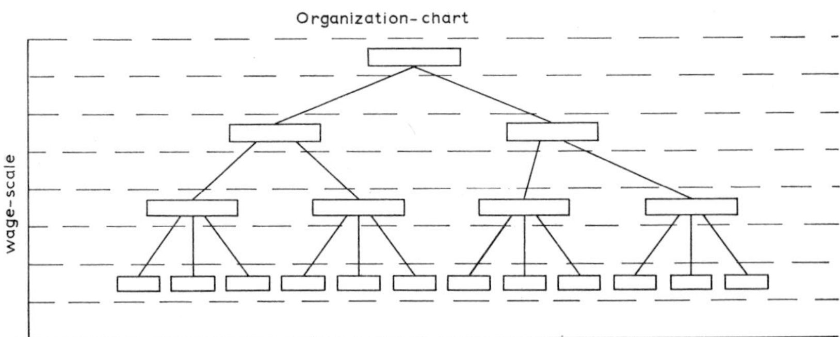

It might be questioned, however, whether it is not wise to attract higher paid people for such functions. Though they do not need the technical experience of those supervised, they must have qualities in respect to human relations, that may be equally rare.

In any case, if the wage-pattern does not correspond with the organization-structure, possibilities for tensions and difficulties arise.

Perhaps one of the most serious difficulties lies in the fixation of promotion-rules. One cannot be promoted to a higher position in the organization and at the same time be paid less or the same as before. At least in our society such a promotion would fail to have a real meaning. In the cases mentioned above, there are indeed separate promotion-scales for the pilots and the headquarter-officers of the airline; for the hospital-physicians and for its managing personnel. Apart from other reasons, the harmony between organization and wage-structure is necessary to give people entering the company the opportunity for promotion and to build up a satisfying career.

The labor-market for most enterprises does not furnish a wage-structure that can be brought in line with the organization-structure. This would only be the case if there was an uniformity of demand by all or large groups of companies for labor for different functions on one hand

and sufficient supply of such labor on the other. Only where there is need for labor on a craft-basis, such a situation might exist.

Present day development in industry makes the markets where labor is demanded and supplied on a craft-basis less important. In our days not the craft-aspect but the industrial aspect is most important. Firms are asking for different categories of labor of different skill and experience, which for the greater part can only be acquired by working in the company or in the industry itself. This is not only the case for managing and supervisory personnel but also for the operating labor.

For the latter, wages are largely determined by collective bargaining. As a result of these changes in the demand for labor most unions are no longer organized on a craft-basis. The industrial union, representing the labor-force of the firms belonging to the same industry, has become the dominant type. One can even say that, what is to be considered as an industry for the purpose of wage-negotiations, often depends largely on the way unions are structured, in other words on union-policy and union-organization.

This remarkable change has had serious consequences for wage-negotiations. They are valid now for a wide range of occupations or jobs. One can hardly speak of a market for each job because demand and supply, if any, are very small and incidental. There is still a tendency to increase the number of jobs originating from the technological development as well as from the application of new principles of organization. The contents of the jobs not only differ from industry to industry but even from company to company and from plant to plant.

Trade-unions as well as employers or their unions therefore are forced to negotiate whole sets of wages including the whole labor-force within the company or the industry. Subject of negotiation therefore are not wages, but wage-structures.

Thus companies on one side and unions on the other are confronted with the problem of the internal wage-structure, may either be for companies or plants individually, or for the industry as a whole.

If wages are controlled by government, as is the case in many European countries, the authorities concerned are also confronted with this problem. The company has to search for a wage-structure that is in harmony with its organization-structure. The union has to negotiate on the basis of a structure that will satisfy its members belonging to different occupational groups in its industry. Government wage-authorities have to prevent wage-structures that can give rise to an increase of the whole wage-level in an industry or in the country. All three are obliged to look for a wage-structure that is adequate in a certain respect. This, however, may differ for each of them. In any case it is understandable that they are interested in means to classify the different jobs. Thus several systems of job-evaluation have been introduced.

Job-evaluation was developed in the first place as a means of giving functions or jobs their proper place within the hierarchy of an individual plant or company. Gradually it got a broader significance, being not only a device for personnel policy of an individual company but also a method to create adequate wage-relationships in companies, in industries or even in the country as a whole.

We need not give here a detailed description of the different systems of job-evaluation now in use. We only wish to mention some points that can help us to judge job-evaluation in its meaning for the internal wage-structure.

Job-evaluation tries to replace price-determination for different categories of labor by an evaluation of different qualities or requirements needed for the fulfilment of that labor. There is no market for those qualities, whatever they may be. Therefore the evaluation of these qualities must be effected in some other way.

Generally this is done by formulating the elementary qualities of each type of labor and then trying to reach an agreement upon the evaluation of these qualities by those interested in the evaluation-procedure.

A better way is to deduct the evaluation of these elementary qualities from wages for labor for which a market still exists, where we have sufficient substantial supply and demand. In practically every industry there are such categories of labor. One can take also those jobs on which union- and employers bargainers agree that the wages paid for them are fair. It always seems easier to agree upon the fairness of the wage-rate for some category of labor than upon the fairness of the evaluation of qualities necessary for the performance of that and other kinds of labor.

Thus the significance of job-evaluation is as a device to bring the wages paid for all other jobs into line with the first mentioned ones. In other words, if the wages of some categories of labor are determined in any other way, job-evaluation is a method to attain consistent wages for all categories. In any case careful job-descriptions are necessary to state in which quantities the qualities already evaluated are present.[4]

The question now arises: can we get a satisfying internal wage-structure by means of any system of job-evaluation? What we can accomplish is perhaps a wage-structure that is consistent in itself, i.e. that all wages are in line with the wages we used as our starting-points. Is there also consistency with the organization-structure of the individual company or plant? This does not seem to be sure.

If the wages we use as our starting-points relate to labor performed in the same company we may at first sight suppose so. In that case it seems that these wages will correspond with the responsibilities of the function in the organization-structure and that they give a fair representation what their value is to the company.

We cannot be convinced of this if these wages are determined by negotiation on an industry-wide or on a craft-basis and the functions to be performed are not wholly uniform from company to company.

There is, however, still another difficulty in this respect. Are the elementary requirements or qualities necessary to fulfil a certain job the same as those needed for the performance of others? Unfortunately we cannot answer this question in the affirmative.

Knowledge, for instance, is used in most evaluation-systems as a requirement or quality. But knowledge is not the same thing for a trucker, a spinner, a supervisor or boss and a cost-clerk. Moreover knowledge has more dimensions so that superficial knowledge of a large number of facts is not comparable with thorough knowledge of a few and cannot be brought under the same denominator.

The same thing can be said of other qualities or requirements. As John T. Dunlop has rightly pointed out, we have to distinguish job-clusters or job-families,[5] being groups of jobs with related contents. In a company several job-clusters are to be found. At first sight, a classification of jobs within a cluster seems to have no serious difficulties. The requirements for jobs within each cluster are comparable. Nevertheless even here the difficulty of evaluation of the requirements arises. We need also comparisons with wages paid for other jobs, possibly belonging to other clusters and here we might meet the difficulty of incomparability of the requirements themselves. Strictly speaking, only if there are enough wages already determined for jobs within a cluster to be able to evaluate the requirements for these jobs, can we build up a satisfactory system of job-evaluation, but only for that cluster. Thus the incomparability of the different requirements turns out to be an obstacle for the comparison of different jobs with regard to these requirements as well as for the evaluation of these requirements themselves.

The conclusion from our analysis can not be very optimistic. Even the most refined point-rating cannot be considered better and is not supposed to give better results than the more simple and intuitive job-ranking.

What job-evaluation is trying to do is to bring the wage-pattern into line with the contents of the functions resulting from the organization-structure. Unfortunately the contents cannot be measured exactly.

Can we measure requirements quantitatively and evaluate them only roughly, always the results obtained must be scrutinized by our own judgement. This is a managerial task.

The best environment for measurement and evaluation is the individual plant or a group of homogeneous plants. If we try to extend job-evaluation to a wider field, the results will prove to be less convincing.

The merit of job-evaluation is that it demonstrates the necessary link between wage-pattern and organization-structure.

We will now turn from the functional to the personal wage-pattern. Given the functional wage-structure the personal pattern may show more or less substantial deviations. Therefore there is reason to distinguish the personal pattern from the functional.

One of the most important reasons for deviations consists in the use of wage-incentives. It is clear that whatever sort of incentive may be used, deviations from the functional wage according to the premiums earned by the individual workers will arise. The important question to be dealt with is how far those deviations can disturb the functional structure in such a way that it is no longer in line with the organization-structure.

At first sight it seems that, as incentive wage-systems pay higher remunerations according to higher productivity or efficiency, the position of the function in the wage-structure is raised, as it is fulfilled better. This need not disturb the harmony between the organization-structure and the internal wage-structure. Nevertheless there are elements in wage-incentives that actually make it difficult to keep this harmony intact.

Most of the incentives relate to the quantity produced in a unit of time or, to state it in reverse the units of time needed for a given quantity of product. The quantity produced, however, need not be the only measure of the efficiency of the laborer. The volume of raw material he uses or the degree he influences costs of repair and maintenance, because of his using machines and other durable means of production, may be more important. If a wage-incentive based on the quantitative achievements of the workers is applied, while the real efficiency of the performance lies elsewhere, the personal deviations from the functional structure tend to make the latter inadequate and no longer in harmony with the organization-structure. A worker whose efficiency in the process of production is lower may be paid more, while one whose efficiency is higher may be paid less.

Another factor making the incentive a disturbing element for the functional wage-structure is the fact that these systems are not applicable to all sorts of labor. Often very large groups of workers can only be paid on an hourly rate. Since the functional structure is also defined by wages per hour, deviations between those earning hourly wages and those working under incentive-systems will arise, notwithstanding the fact that their tasks and the way they fulfil them remain the same.

Also the gap between the higher and lower classified workers in the organization-structure may diminish in regard to the wage-structure if the higher classified workers, for instance supervisor or bosses, are paid on a hourly basis, whereas the laborers are working under an incentive-system. In such cases even the lower classified worker may earn more while the higher classified one earns less. For this reason supervisors' functions sometimes are less attractive. The laborer because of the incentive-system has a chance to earn more than a supervisor or a boss. To prevent this one can limit the premium to be earned; the significance of the incentive as a means to stimulate the worker to higher efficiency, however, will diminish in that case.

Sometimes there are more possibilities to earn a premium in one function than in another though the functions are classified as equal. Here too deviations from the functional pattern arise, which may disturb the harmony between wage-structure and organization-structure.

Apart from other objections, wage-incentives, because of the deviations from the functional wage-pattern originating from their application, form a serious obstacle to keeping the wage-structure in line with the organization-structure.

Productivity-premiums for the whole plant do not derogate from the functional wage-structure. They bring the whole wage-system only on a higher level without disturbing the relationships between the individual wages.*

Personal deviations from the functional wage-structure also may be brought about when applying a system of merit-rating. Nevertheless it has still other consequences than wage-incentives based on achievements of any kind. Merit-rating in our opinion, is not in the first place a wage-system but a system of judging personnel. Therefore it need not have any consequences for the remuneration of personnel. Nevertheless

* Sometimes a premium is already given before the normal level of performance is reached, for instance above 75 or 80 per cent efficiency. At or below the indicated level the workers are paid according to the hourly wage-rate. This, too, means a deviation from the functional wage-structure.

the results of the judgement are often used to award appropriate premiums.

What are the merits why a premium is paid for in that case? Not for the way the function is performed by the worker. The premium is granted after a certain period and is independent of the quantity of product or other achievements of the worker at the moment the premium is paid. The work actually done by the workers is not the only thing that interests the company. With regard to some workers it is obvious that we do not hope they will come into action at all. Here we need not only think of fire-divisions, first-aid-brigades, repairershifts, etc. which we hope we shall never have to use.

To large groups of workers it is not only and not in the first place of interest what they achieve but for what they are available. Though in the slack season they do not work at all or only part-time laborers are paid fully because of their availability in the busy season. In periods of depression we find the same thing.

For the same reason the availability of specific qualities or acquired experience, though not necessary for what the worker is doing at a given moment, can be of interest as circumstances change. We think of personal qualities making a man available for promotion to a higher level when there is a functionary to be replaced, of broader experience or skill that will make it possible for some workers to take over when necessary the work of their comrades of other departments or shifts and perhaps even of the loyalty of workers in cases of conflict.

In the labor force there is always a more or less large amount of potentialities which the company may need if circumstances change. Merit-rating wishes to rate the qualities that are of particular significance to its activities and its particular environment and to pay for them in order to keep them available for situations in which they will be needed. The most preponderant among them are changes in technology, fluctuations in demand, promotion and cases of emergency.

Technological development and, in present days (especially) automation will increase the importance of availability compared with actual productive services. Automation raises human labor to a higher level. The laborer becomes a supervisor, who has to watch a group of machines just as the boss in the non-automated factory watches a group of men. We need the boss because there must be someone available to give directives in cases of difficulties. The bosses are paid not for what they actually do, but for their availability.

Wages based on availability of particular qualities will more and more replace achievement-wages. What are the consequences of this development for the internal wage-structure?

A wage-structure based on merit-rating, though it may show personal deviations from the functional wage-structure based on normal performance, can, in principle, always be kept in line with the organization-structure.

This holds good also in case the only or principal reason we need laborers lies in their availability. In such circumstances the job is evaluated according to the requirements necessary for its normal fulfilment. Merit-premiums can be paid for possessing more qualities or the required qualities in a higher degree. It is only rational to pay for them if the availability of these qualities is worthwhile for the company.*

We have to distinguish the capacities or qualities necessary for the fulfilment of the workers' job and additional capacities. Only the latter present a problem, for the functional wage-structure will be based on the necessary requirements for the job. Paying for additional qualities, however, does not derogate from the functional wage-structure, though it may cause personal deviations. The premiums paid for additional qualities are to be considered apart from the functions actually fulfilled. They have no connection whatever with the tasks the workers have to perform in the existing processes of production.

3. The Link Between Organization-structure and Wage-structure and Union-policy

As already stated, in our opinion organization structure and wage-structure are linked together very closely. The wage for each job must be in line with the task, that is the volume of work, to be fulfilled normally and the authority and responsibility connected with it. These latter, tasks, authority and responsibility, follow directly from the organization-structure. The functional wage-structure therefore can be deducted by evaluating the contents of the job being determined by the organization-structure.

If we assume that the design of the organization-structure is a task of management, the same is true for the wage-structure. Thus job-evaluation, in this connection, is a managerial function. Personal deviations from the functional wage-structure as a consequence of wage-incentives do not

* We do not wish to propose that merit-rating is to be identified with availability-rating. If the achievements of the workers are still important for the company merit-rating might be applied. We only wish to say that the "rational" for merit-rating lies in available capacity and not in achievement.

disturb the harmony between organization-structure and wage-structure if every worker can be paid more or less in proportion to the performance of his task. Often this condition is not fulfilled and cannot be fulfilled either. Therefore there is a real danger that in practice incentives will cause inadequacies in the wage-structure. Management has to decide whether and in how far it will accept these inadequacies in exchange for a change for higher productivity.*

Premiums for specific capacities or qualities not necessary for the performance of the job, but considered as individual merits of the worker, do not derogate from the functional wage-structure.

Though the maintenance of an adequate wage-structure is a managerial task, management will not always be able to perform it correctly. Difficulties may arise first from market-conditions if wages are fixed, whether by collective bargaining or otherwise, on an occupational basis.

In this situation the individual company has no choice but to adapt its whole wage-structure to these market-rates and to accept a possible inadequacy in its structure.

If only some wages are fixed by market supply and demand, there is the possibility to create for the whole company or plant a consistent wage-structure (in relation) to these market-wages. This structure may not be in line with the organization-structure.

An other way is to create consistent wage-structures in the clusters round the hiring-jobs, the jobs for which a market exist, and to accept inadequacies between the clusters. The whole wage-structure will then also be inconsistent to a certain extent.

Collective bargaining on an industry-wide basis also gives rise to difficulties. They originate from two different causes. First the wage-structure accepted by the bargainers for the industry as a whole, will seldom be in harmony with the organization-structure of each individual company, unless there is a large degree of uniformity among the companies and plants.

Technological development, increasing managerial knowledge, growth by acquisition or merger, all are tendencies favoring the generation of more or less substantive differences among companies and even plants belonging to the same company. These developments are more advanced in some companies than in others and therefore functions, though indi-

* One of the crucial points in the fixation of incentives is that it is very difficult if not impossible to reckon with the different aspects of the performance as, for instance, quantity and quality of the product, repair, and maintenance, use of raw material, etc., in such a way that an optimal performance might be expected.

cated by the same names, may have different contents in a more technologically advanced plant or in a larger one than in a more backward or medium-sized one.

Moreover, as was already said, industry is not an exactly defined concept and therefore what is called an industry for collective bargaining purposes may comprise enterprises of a substantially different character. What collective bargaining brings forward therefore, can only be somewhat averaged job-contents, which are not characteristic for any company at all.

There is still an other reason that causes deviations of the adequate wage-structure for a company from that agreed upon by collective bargaining. These deviations originate from the objectives the unions are striving after. If unions are concerned with wage-structures as in the case of industry-wide bargaining they have other aims than management. The same is true even if they are bargaining on a company-wide basis. In general there is but little difference as regards the results the unions are trying to reach in industry-wide as compared with company-wide bargaining. In both cases their goal is to get equal pay for equal work and at the same time the highest possible pay. They are prepared to bargain with individual companies if they think they can get better results from one company than from the other. In the long run, they try to force the less advanced firms to pay the same wages as the more prosperous ones.

This principle of equal pay also operates against the aim of management to get a satisfying internal wage-structure. It seems already difficult to agree upon the question: what is equal work? Even where there are labor-markets for specific crafts or occupations and wages are fixed on that basis, the position in the organization-structure of the craftsman may differ from one company to the other. In bargaining on wages for specific crafts and occupations equal work seems to be more interpreted as equal skill acquired before entering the company, than as equal tasks within the company.

Equal work in industry-wide or company-wide bargaining on wage-structure, from what has been said about the differences in the contents of functions in various companies, will have an other meaning for unions than for different companies or plants. The more refined differences in function-contents originating from the way the activities and responsibilities in a company are subdivided cannot have much significance for a union seeking equal pay for broad groups of its members.

Specific difficulties may arise for geographically decentralized companies. Management may be interested in keeping its wage-structure in line with the organization-structure of the company as a whole whereas the union is interested to prevent differentials in the wages paid for work they consider to be equal in the same area.

Moreover the equal-pay principle may raise controversies between unions and management regarding the personal deviations of the functional wage-structure. Generally speaking, unions are somewhat reluctant regarding wage-incentives as well as with regard to merit-rating. They are eager in any case to have a say and if possible a decisive one in the introduction of incentives and the way they are applied. As we have already pointed out, wage-incentives mostly have a tendency to disturb the consistency of the wage-structure with the organization-structure to a greater or smaller degree. Therefore incentives, though inevitable or at least preferable in several circumstances and for several reasons are always difficult for management to handle.

According to their equal-pay concept, unions are inclined to require that every worker must have the same opportunity to earn a premium on their hourly rates. Therefore they not only wish to decide or at least to co-determine what normal performance is, they also require that premiums are to be awarded already at a level pretty far below normal performance; moreover that in any case the hourly wage-rate is guaranteed whatever the performance may be and finally that the maximum premium-percentage that can be earned is limited at a sometimes relatively low level above the hourly rate. Thus the equal-pay concept as it is handled by the unions does not only relate to the quantity – and eventually the quality – of work completed by the worker but also to his function in the related industry.

Unions usually have further objections with regard to merit-rating. This is understandable because in the case of merit-rating differentials in wages are not due to the quantity – and eventually the quality – of work completed nor to the functions performed, but to qualities available. Thus merit-rating contradicts the principle of equal-pay. Workers are paid unequally for the same work and for the same functions.

Men may have a specific idea of their social and industrial status, that may no longer be in line with the actual significance of their jobs. As unions represent the opinion of their members a conflict with management's efforts to create a wage-structure consistent with the organization-structure may arise. In times as ours with their rapid technological developments the task of the worker may change and accordingly his place in the organization-structure; his opinion of his status will presumably not change at all.

Much more could be said about the impact of union-policy on the internal wage-structure. This will be treated in detail in a separate chapter. Our aim is only to draw the attention to the difficulties of management to create and maintain a-wage-structure in line with the organization-structure.

4. Concluding Remarks

A few words may be said to conclude this short survey of internal wage-structure.

Though the determination of the internal wage-structure is in our opinion an important managerial task it is far from easy. Therefore it is not astonishing that in practice more or less satisfying solutions have for the major part only been achieved along the arduous road of trial and error.

Difficulties arise in the first place from the fact that, though functions can be described and ranked in an organizational system, it is very difficult to translate this system into a system of money-wages in a satisfying manner. Methods developed for job-evaluation may be helpful in this respect but they cannot have the last word. The requirements for each function can hardly be measured; still more difficult is it to evaluate their importance. Maintenance of a satisfying wage-structure seems to be equally difficult if by means of wage-incentives or merit-rating personal deviations from the functional structure arise.

Whereas these difficulties are internal, still more serious are those coming from the company's environment, the market-conditions for different categories of labor and the policy of the trade-unions.

We do not believe, at least up to now, that there are means to evade these difficulties. Regarding the inside ones we have to accept the fact that there will always remain – as far as organizations in themselves remain human – certain relationships that cannot be measured exactly and with full objectivity.

It seems to be doubtful, however, whether our society has developed hitherto a satisfying system of labor-procurement and of determining labor-conditions. If it is true that the wage-structure is a part, or better a dimension, of the organization-structure and therefore its fixation a task of management, it may be questioned whether the creation of wage-structures by collective bargaining through industry-wide organized or at least industry-wide oriented unions is the most adequate method.

We are far from denying that workers ought to have a say about the conditions under which they have to fulfil their jobs. We are only doubtful whether collective bargaining – though it might have worked satisfactorily in the past – in our days is the best way of dealing with the interests of the workers.

As technological developments create more and more different functions to be fulfilled in production and as the organization of labor within the company becomes more and more "tailor-made", adapted to the needs of the particular plant or company, the outside labor-market as a means of procuring people for various functions and as a means for wage-determination will become less and less important.

As the creation of the wage-structure is to be considered as a task of management, the solution must be sought in letting labor participate in management.

The task of organized labor is to protect the worker and his conditions of living. In the future it will have to concentrate more on the workers in the individual companies and less on the supply on the labormarket. Protecting the worker from inside that is via the company's own institutions will become more important.

The union's future task can be seen more in organizing the participation of labor in management than in collective bargaining. The extend to which the unions will be obliged to reorganize and alter their present behavior will not be discussed here.

References

1. NEIL W. CHAMBERLAIN, *The Union-Challenge to Management Control* (New York, 1948).
2. ELLIOTT JAQUES, *Measurement of Responsibility* (London, 1956).
3. HERBERT SIMON, *The New Science of Management Decision* (New York, 1961), is right when he states that apart from experience and standards the organization-structure is one of the means of solving structured managerial problems.
4. Descriptions of systems of job-evaluation are given by several authors. A classification of these systems is to be found in PATTON and SMITH, *Job-evaluation* (Homewood, Chicago (Ill.), 1950).
   These authors distinguish four main groups viz: job-ranking methods, pre-determined grading methods, factor comparising methods and point-rating methods. In essence all methods are factor comparising because they compare the requirements for the performance of the jobs subject to classification.
5. *New Concepts in Wage Determination*, edited by GEORGE W. TAYLOR and FRANK G. PIERSON (New York, 1957).

CHAPTER 3

THEORY OF WAGE FORMS

E. KOSIOL

Institut für Industrieforschung der Freien Universität, Berlin-Dahlem, Germany

A. Principles and Fundamentals of Wage Determination

I. *Basic Concepts and Measures*

Wages, in the widest sense of the word, are understood to mean any remuneration paid to a working person. They also include family allowances, relief pay, financial support, and other social benefits. The work or *performance wages* proper, however, represent a remuneration for individual labour performance. They are the object of this study.

The *material* wage problem, the question of the absolute wage level, is an external problem of the different wage rates between the enterprises. The *formal* wage problem to be discussed here, the question of wage rating, and of the relative wage level, represents an internal problem within the enterprises.

To clarify the wage problems it is necessary to distinguish between two completely different categories of human labour.

Technical labour is performed by mental and physical actions (operations) upon an intangible or tangible matter (object) according to a certain technological procedure. This includes not only the labour performed by order of higher-placed persons, but also the supervisory and leading labour regulating the work of all other co-workers, insofar as technical decisions are concerned. It comprehends both the work of the engineers and, to a large extent, that of the businessmen. For these technical performances work or performance wages are paid. These also contain the entrepreneur's wages.

Economic performances, on the other hand, are entrepreneurial activities consisting of economic decision making as a choice between alternatives. They weigh the various technical possibilities against each other from an economic point of view. In particular, they determine, for example, what kinds and quantities of goods are to be procured, manufactured or marketed and in what way this is to be done. Thus, decisions are made and integrated into an economic plan. For these economic performances no wages are paid in the sense described above. However, they are matched by the prospect of profit, which again is closely linked to the risk of loss. Hence, profit sharing is excluded from this investigation.

In *technical performances* there is further to be distinguished:

1. The work performance as a technical *process* of operation, i.e. the physical or mental act of working on a tangible or intangible object;

2. The work performance as the technical *outcome* of the process of operation, which results from carrying out the act of working on an object.

The object of the remuneration is always, in some way or another, primarily the work operation and secondarily its result. The difficulty degree of the work is ascertained by job evaluation and paid for on the basis of an appropriate wage rate. The work result must also be considered either in the wage rate by performance evaluation (merit rating) or by the choice of an appropriate wage form. The scales for measuring the quantitative work result are quantity or time units.

II. *The Principle of Equivalence and its Implementation*

The wages being a cost component of an enterprise, they shall be tailored in such a way that a rise in performance creates a situation favourable to cost and output. On account of this, the wages must give equivalent compensation for the work done.

The search for wages which adequately pay for the work done indicates that the wages must be commensurate with the technical work performed. This general principle of the equivalence between wages and performance comprises two sub-cases:

1. *Equivalence of Wages and Degree of Difficulty.* In the first place, the work performance is determined by the different degrees of difficulty of the work required for the individual operations. Therefore, they must be considered in the wages.

2. *Equivalence of Wages and Degree of Performance.* Furthermore, the work performance is determined by the quantitative-qualitative result which the individual worker achieves by his working method. This output is affected by the rate of performance of the workman involved. Therefore, it must likewise be considered in the wages.

The relative level is given by the structure of *wage differentiation*, i.e.

(1) by fixing the wage rates (*wage rate* differentiation),
(2) by selecting the appropriate form of wages (*wage form* differentiation).

Consequently, there are two methods to implement the principle of equivalence with respect to wages:

(1) *Wage Rate Differentiation*

Wage rate differentiation is applied for operations of varying difficulty. The fundamental principle for determining the degrees of difficulty is *job evaluation*. The interrelation of the wage rates within the enterprise shall be in accordance with the varying requirement characteristics (principle of the equivalence of wages and degree of difficulty). Wages giving adequate compensation for each category of work will promote the rate of performance of the workmen by their stimulating effect.

(2) *Wage Form Differentiation*

When establishing the wage rates on the basis of the various requirement characteristics, a standard performance is proceeded from, in principle. Individual deviations from the standard performance must be considered in accordance with the principle of the equivalence of wages and degree of performance. This purpose is served by the wage forms which stipulate the remuneration according to the respective rate of performance. The most suitable basis for ascertaining the rates of performance is a determination of *standard rates* (in Western Germany, for example, mostly by REFA). Different rates of performance can, in the long run, also be considered in the wage rate, through *merit rating*. A favourable wage form and wage rate differentiation, as a rule, leads directly to a performance increase.

With respect to the principle of equivalence and its implementation, we arrive at the following systematic survey:

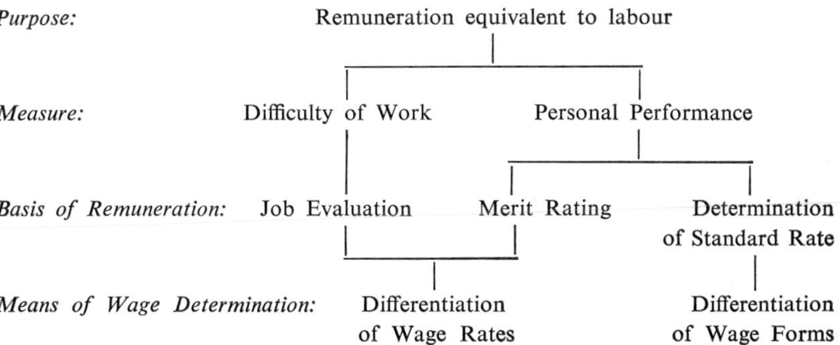

The possibilities to structure the wages as a remuneration for work after the principle of equivalence – i.e. to give it the shape of a performance compensation – are in accordance with the double-sided complex of wage differentiation within the enterprise. In the differentiation according to the difficulty of work the structurization of the wages is done only by differentiation of the wage rates within the enterprise. When differentiating according to the personal performance, both wage rates and wage forms are used as a means of structurization. The differentiation of the wage rates considers both the difficulty of the work and the personal performance. In the differentiation of the wage forms the rating basis is only the personal performance.

Viewing the wage structure from the angle of the working person, we can speak of an inter-personal and intra-personal wage structure. The *inter-personal* wage structure may be marked, in principle, by its differentiation both as to the difficulty of work and as to the rate of performance. The *intra-personal* wage structure mostly comprises merely a differentiation of the remuneration according to the rate of performance.

The general principle underlying every internal wage structure is that of wage differentiation through which the actual differences in performance are to be regarded. In this connection it becomes evident that neither the consideration of work difficulty nor that of personal performance, in their own right, can lead to an adequately compensating remuneration. It is always both elements of achievement which must be taken into account.

III. *Problems and Outline of the Investigation*

The following explanations deal with the differentiation of wage forms, as the problem of wage rate differentiation, based upon a job evaluation, is discussed at another place of this book.

The search for the best wage method, for a wage form specifically adapted to the performance, appears as part of the problem in the comprehensive task of rationalizing the work performance. The choice of a certain wage rating means, at the same time, the institution of a certain working method and work organization. With the aid of performance wages an increase in performance shall be achieved. This leads to the establishment of measures for an economic judgment of the remuneration methods, of criteria for the efficiency of different forms of wages.

The increase in work performance, in the first place, presents an objective and a subjective element.

Viewed *objectively*, four facts can be distinguished:

1. the *quantitative* performance increase,
2. the *temporal* performance increase,
3. the *qualitative* performance increase,
4. the *permanency* of the performance.

It must be admitted that both quantitative and temporal performance increases principally come down to the same thing in actual practice. Not only can the quantity of performance be fixed for a given period of time, but also the space of time can be ascertained for a given task. In either case we come to the same conclusion, economically, however, viewed from different angles. In spite of this it is purposeful and necessary to make a theoretical difference between the two cases, because they are expressed in different figures and the calculation of the premiums (whether on a piece or a time basis) will lead to fairly considerable differences.

If it is considered desirable to express the objective of the increase in performance in a concise form, we could say that it can be characterized as an endeavour to achieve much, rapid, good, and permanent work performance. The wage method must be selected in such a way that it formally tends to bring about an increase in performance and automatically realizes this tendency.

The *subjective* side of economizing labour comprises all psychophysical conditions which must be inherent in the workman to guarantee the desired increase in his performance. Insofar as they are considered in the abstract wage form and insofar as this form can affect their development and consolidation these elements can be collectively regarded as subjective incentives towards top performance. The enterprise, from its point of view, has to consider the rightful personal interests of the workman and create the strongest possible stimulus for his will to work by an appropriate wage form.

When the principle of the equivalence of wages and degree of performance is viewed from a mathematical-calculatory standpoint, the objective side of the increase in work performance is reflected in the amount of the *labour costs*, the subjective side in the amount of the *hourly earnings*. The influence of the principle of equivalence, with rising performance, manifests itself, in principle, by a decrease, at least by non-variation of the labour costs and by an increase in the hourly earnings. On account of this, both figures are used as a basis for a mathematical treatment of the problem. These conceptions will later be dealt with in a more suitable form and more extensively.

From the explanations given so far it may already be observed that there is no universally applicable wage method fully complying with the principle of equivalence. The search for the best wage form is, in itself, an absurdity. Properly speaking, every kind of performance is in conformity with its specific wage form. Practically, and also theoretically, however, it is an impossibility to pay for each single performance individually. Consequently, it appears necessary to work out certain methods to fix, in a schematic and compulsory manner, wages for regular performances agreed upon for a longer period of time. Given the fact that many different kinds of work performances lend themselves to being brought under larger categories with kindred peculiarities, we come to a certain number of typical wage methods, forms of remuneration which are characteristic for work performances with certain features. In practice, a series of such wage forms has actually been drawn up. We shall now have to verify to what extent they do justice to the basic principle of equivalence. The criteria of the objective and subjective increase in performance serve as the *guiding principle*. The result will be that the wage methods which have developed in practice, partly consciously, partly unconsciously, are tested for their labour-economic value and are explored with regard to their importance for enterprises.

In this way the *objective* of the investigations is marked by a clearly outlined problem. The formal wage problem, viewed from the angle of enterprise economics, shall not be dealt with in every detail and down to all consequences. Neglecting special circumstances and practical particulars, the internal, mathematically tangible structure of the various wage forms shall be outlined in a general theoretical way, and its economic efficiency be made clear. The *basic queries* in this investigation are: What is the inner structure of the various wage forms? What is its economic sense? How and to what extent is the equivalence principle structurally worked out?

With the answers to these questions, however, the scientific interest does not end. It is rather the idea that the multitude of the various wage forms be brought under a closed *system*. Also here it should be said, in principle, that no generally applicable system exists, but that more than one system is possible according to the principle of classification. On the other hand, however, we may not overlook that, for an examination of wage forms on a structural basis, only a system can be considered which elevates the kind of *wage structure* to a classifying principle.

B. Investigation into the Structure of Wage Forms

I. *Pure Wage Forms*

1. *Wages as a function of time*

a) *Time Wages.* The most frequent and perhaps the oldest form of wages brought down to us through the ages are the time wages, in special cases called hourly wages, shift wages, daily wages, weekly wages, decade wages, monthly or annual salary. Here a certain amount of remuneration is fixed for a given period of time. This does not mean that the time itself is to be paid for. Time wages, like any work remuneration, rather represent the countervalue of a *performance* of work. This becomes evident from the fact that in many cases in actual practice the breaks during working time are not paid for. Before everything, the wage rates are attuned to the kind and the difficulty of the work to be performed.

In the event of time wages a standard performance by the workman is taken as a basis. The time within which the required labour is performed merely serves as a yardstick for this work. Hence, the time wages could very well be denominated as *indirect* performance wages.

Now to examine the time wages as to their inner structure, the mathematical approach is used. The basis of the investigation is a fixed quantity of work, i.e. a unit of output, which should for short be called piece. Now, let s be the variable earnings per hour, s_0 the fixed hourly wage rate, further l the variable labour costs and t the variable time. We then obtain the following simple formulae for the time wages:

$$l = s_0 t \tag{1}$$

$$s = s_0. \tag{2}$$

In words:

The *labour costs* are found by multiplying the fixed wage rate by the time used. The *hourly earnings* equal the fixed hourly wage rate. This is illustrated by Fig. 1.

The curves represent straight lines. The earnings curve runs parallel to the time axis, i.e. the hourly earnings are independent of the time used or constant. The cost curve, on the other hand, rises evenly, i.e. the labour costs are proportional to the time expended.

With the labour cost curve as a function of time it is only the temporal performance increase as an objective element of the equivalence principle that can be examined.

The quality of the performance needs a special examination as does its permanency which cannot very well be gauged by numbers (for instance, by measuring on a physiological basis). If quality indices are introduced as independent variables, the influence of the wage form on the qualitative performance increase is directly to be put in evidence.

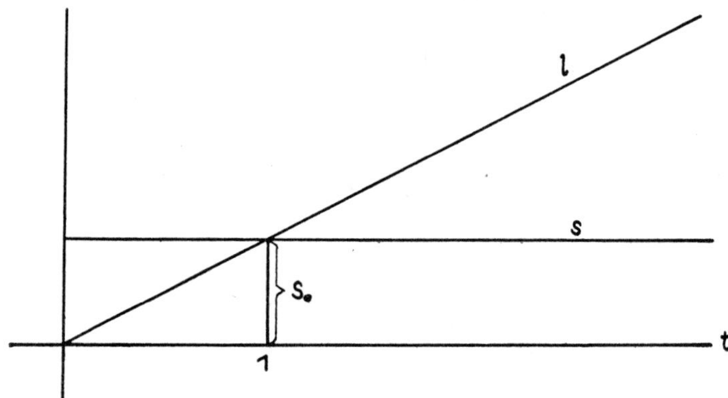

Fig. 1. Time wages.

The quantitative performance increase is left out of account for the time being. The quantity of work performed is in no way considered in the formulae.

A *temporal* performance increase is not present, either, in spite of the dominating influence of time. Certainly the labour costs decrease in proportion to time, so that evidently in the event of a decrease of time a rationalization would be warranted. Since, however, the hourly earnings remain constant in spite of a larger time saving, every subjective incentive is prevented. Therefore, we can obviously speak of a frustrated temporal increase of performance. It should be pointed out that this includes an indirect impediment to the *quantitative* performance increase, too.

On the other hand, the *qualitative* performance increase is effective to some extent as a result of this frustration of temporal-quantitative rationalization. Since no incentive to promote rapidity of work is established, there is an indirect, stronger tendency towards quality performances.

Furthermore, this is closely related to the possibility of *permanent* performances. Because of absence of overtiredness or exhaustion of the worker, because of this securing of his normal strength, continuous performances are safeguarded for a longer duration of time.

The *subjective* element of the performance increase, the stimulus towards top performance, is almost completely lacking in time wages, as is clearly evident from the constancy of the hourly earnings. On the other hand, it must be said that, given this promise of a fixed pay, the foundation is laid for a more regular progress, of a certain evenness in the performance.

On this account, the result of the investigation of the time wages proper is that time wages are appropriate for performances for which the *continuing lapse of time* is the best yardstick. This is work which requires an even amount of time and shows a constantly equal progress of work which can only be evaluated or measured in proportion to time, for instance, routine office and administrative work, which is not purely mechanical, but demands attention and mental activity. A strong incentive towards speed would in this instance endanger the safety and the correctness of the work. It may generally be said that time wages are appropriate wherever tempo versus the painstaking and conscientious execution versus the quality of the work performance is of subordinate importance. Further, in all cases where the quantity of work done cannot be measured or counted in any way, where the nature of the work is constantly changing, where difficult operations of an extraordinary nature are to be performed and where, finally, the continuity of the work is interrupted time and again. Here it is the time which presents itself as the only feasible yardstick for measuring the performance. This, too, goes especially for the highest-qualified productive-mental organizational brain work.

Seen from the viewpoint of the equivalence of wages and performance, time wages generally prove to be appropriate,

(1) when the personal performance shows a certain *constancy*, so that an adaptation of the wages to individual variations in achievement becomes *unnecessary* (time as the *best* measure),
(2) when the personal performance is *inconstant* to such an extent that a continuable adaptation of the wages is fundamentally *impossible* (time as the *only* measure).

So far the investigation has been limited exclusively to the wage form proper. In actual practice it is possible to carry out performance evaluation (merit rating) in addition to job evaluation, in order to create a *direct wage incentive* also for time wages.

The differentiation of the time wage rates on the basis of the difficulty of work is already a stimulating factor in itself, so that also with time wages it is possible to have a sound level of performance. Then it is of importance that an adequately exact *job evaluation* be applied and that the time wage rates are graded in accordance with the various degrees of difficulty of the job.

If the output of the time wage earner is to be directly stimulated on top of this, the individual performance must in some way be considered in the wage rate. This can be done with the aid of *merit rating*, which in modern times has led to a variable time wage formation. Attempts are being made to ascertain more or less accurately the personal output during a period of some length (say 3–6 months) according to different characteristics and to evaluate them by points (see other articles). The results of merit rating form the basis for a change (or no change) of the wage rates. The time wage earner has the opportunity to attain a higher wage rate by increasing his personal output. Hence, a direct wage incentive is offered which, in the event of a higher output, leads to a higher remuneration in a comparatively short time.

Merit rating does not mean the setting of an exact standard of performance. Its methods must rather be kept rigidly separate from those used for the *determination of standard rates*, as developed, for instance, in Western Germany as a basis for piece wages by the „Verband für Arbeitsstudien REFA e.V."

For the application of merit rating we can basically distinguish three cases:

1. The determination of standard rates *cannot be carried through* because no sufficient standards can be ascertained. In this case merit rating serves as a less exact substitute for the far more exact determination of standard rates.

2. Standard rates *need not be applied* because the work process has been rather cogently regulated (for instance, in the event of line production). Here, merit rating can include further important, non-cogent factors (for instance, co-operation within the workshop).

3. The determination of standard rates *is inadequate* to cover the personal performance completely, as it merely considers the measures of time and quantity. In this case merit rating serves as a supplement to the determination of standard rates, because it includes, for instance, the quality of the performance as well.

The introduction of job evaluation and merit rating in an enterprise tends to step up output also in the event of time wages. The latest development of these methods has therefore widened the opportunities to apply the time wage form.

Automation leads to a *shifting of the performance contents*. Instead of operations changing the state or location of the objects, it is preparedness, observation, supervision, control and other elements of performance that play an ever more important rôle. The more routine decisions are solved by means of the modern methods of data processing through programmed guiding and controlling machinery, the responsible performance due to *preparedness* will come further to the fore. Thus, the time wages gain completely new ways of approach.

b) *Piece Wages*. Unlike time wages, where a certain wage rate is set for a fixed unit of time, the piece wages refer to a certain amount of remuneration for a fixed unit of output. As a measure for the remuneration thus the performance serves itself (in units of quantity of the work performed), so that piece wages can be regarded as *direct* performance wages.

Piece wages may be based on a money contract or on a time contract. Both forms are equal in character, a formal difference only exists in the method of wage computation.

In the event of piece wages we start from standard hourly earnings which the workman has to attain by standard output. This *standard wage rate* must conform to the individual difficulty of work and, by so doing, consider the requirement characteristics as one component of human work performance (along with the rate of performance). Since a piece wage earner, as experience has taught, under the same difficulty of work shows a higher rate of performance than a time wage earner, the piece wage basis in Western Germany (Federal Republic), i.e. the hourly wage rate for piece work, called Akkordrichtsatz or briefly Richtsatz (base rate), normally lies 15 or 20% above the hourly wage rate for comparable time wage jobs.

We now have to take a look at the inner structure of piece wages.

Besides the aforementioned abbreviations, and on the same conditions, let l_0 be the fixed wage rate per piece, then we find the following formulae:

$$l = l_0 \tag{3}$$

$$s = \frac{l_0}{t}. \tag{4}$$

In words:

The *labour costs* equal the fixed wage rate per piece. The *hourly earnings* are found by dividing the piece wage rate by the time used. This is illustrated by Fig. 2.

The cost curve is a parallel to the time axis, i.e. the labour costs are independent of time or constant. On the other hand, the earnings curve represents a rectangular hyperbola with the co-ordinate axes as asymptotes, i.e. the hourly earnings are inversely proportional to the time expended.

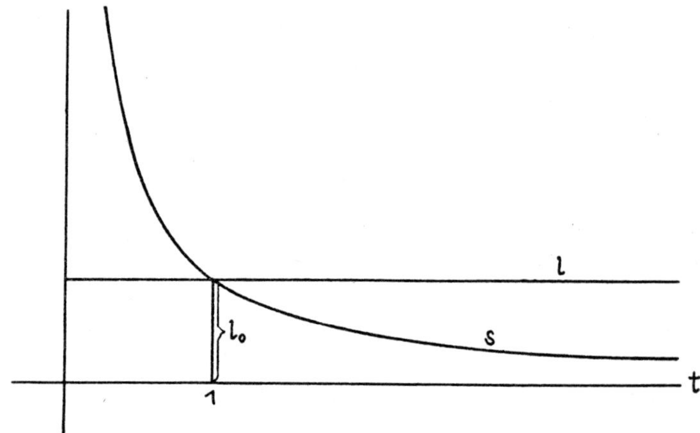

Fig. 2. Piece wages.

Now follows an explanation of the effects of the principle of equivalence in piece wages.

The *temporal* performance increase is considered in a prominent way. It is true that the labour costs themselves remain constant for each piece, even in the event of major time saving. Instead, it is the hourly earnings which are most closely adjusted to the amount of time used. It is the higher as the time expended on piece work is shorter. Consequently, contrary to time wages, we can speak of a promotion of temporal performance increase.

This is most closely related to the frustration of the *qualitative* performance increase. On account of the strong incentive towards a shortening of the time expended per piece a tendency towards negligence in point of quality arises. The worker becomes inclined to step up his hourly earnings at the expense of the quality of his work.

At the same time the *permanency* of the performance is jeopardized. In view of the higher earnings the worker will easily expose himself to overexertion and excessive fatigue, so that with this disturbance of his psychophysical balance continuous performances are no longer ensured for a long time to come.

The *subjective* element of performance increase is most strongly marked. When it is assumed that the worker, before changing over to piece wages, had fixed time wages s_0 per hour, the wage rate l_0 per piece is based upon a somehow fixed expense of time t_0 for each piece (standard time in hours). Formula (1) gives the mathematical relation between these three figures:

$$l_0 = s_0 t_0. \tag{5}$$

Then formula (4) would be:

$$s = s_0 \frac{t_0}{t} \tag{6}$$

and the increase σ in the earnings with piece wages, as compared with time wages, results from the formula:

$$\sigma = s - s_0 = s_0 \frac{t_0 - t}{t} \tag{7}$$

or, in words:

The *increase in the earnings* is inversely proportional to the time expended and directly proportional to the difference between fixed and actually used time. That is to say, the hourly earnings do not merely go up with the decreasing working time, but they also rise in proportion to the volume of time savings. The more the expended time differs from the fixed time, the more the earnings go up. Here we find the strongest effect of the equivalence principle, as the difficulty of performance increase augments as the time decreases and on this account a higher valuation of the additional output lies in the nature of the matter. Fig. 2 illustrates this in such a way that the earnings curve mounts more and more strongly as the time goes down, and finally rises beyond all proportions, which means that an increase in output becomes an impossibility.

When we give a graphic representation of the increased earnings according to (7), the resultant hyperbola (Fig. 3) crosses the time axis for $t = t_0$. If the expended time is equal to the fixed time, the worker does not achieve an increase in his earnings ($\sigma = 0$). In this case we disregard the fact that the base rate of the piece wage earner mostly is a few per cent higher than the hourly earnings of the time wage earner. If the worker needs more time, his earnings may even be lower ($t > t_0, \sigma < 0$). In realitity the wages can never fall below the guaranteed minimum wages, the amount of which is normally determined in collective agreements. Consequently, the worker can achieve a higher pay in piece work than in time work only in case he works more rapidly than required by the standard time $t_0 (t < t_0, \sigma > 0)$. Herein lies a strong subjective incentive to keep the amount of time expended down to a minimum.

Generally, for $t \lesseqqgtr t_0/2$ is always $\sigma \gtreqqless s_0$. For $t = t_0/2$, $s = 2s_0$; in this case the hourly earnings become twice as high as against the time wages.

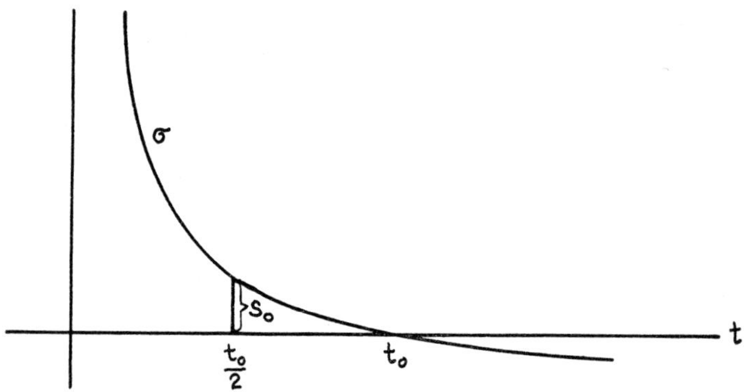

Fig. 3. Increase of the hourly earnings with piece wages.

In the first place, the *quantitative* performance increase is disregarded – at least directly – also in the event of piece wages, as the volume of work does not appear in the formulae. However, the tendency towards a subjective rise is inherent in piece wages on account of their mathematical structure. Because of the constancy of the costs per piece this stimulus to the greatest possible exertion results, together with a temporal performance increase, *indirectly* in a quantitative increase.

From these explanations it will be evident that piece wages are most suitable wherever the work is of a uniform and regularly repetitive nature, and is of a strongly mechanical character. They are operations for which the *quantity* of the work result represents the best measure. Work of this class includes, for instance, transportation and loading, collection and sorting, typified and specialized work, operations and parts thereof in mass production. Characteristic of these operations is that increase of output does not demand an essentially greater exertion, but is rather based upon an inner labour rhythm, an improved work technique, practice, training, and skill. The automatic compulsory adaptation of the earnings to the increased output directly urges the worker to improve and perfect these fundamental factors of performance increase.

Piece wages appear to be absolutely inappropriate as soon as the curtailment of time – beyond the principal waiving of certain quality requirements – leads to an unstinted exploitation of the production facilities. This fact is met in practice by suitable measures. The situation in case of danger to permanent performances is similar. The fact that in practice piece wages may lead and have led to a ruthless *exploitation* of the worker does not constitute a fundamental argument against the objective justification of this wage form. In most cases it is a wrongful handling, an abusive application of a – basically correct – method, which for the theoretical examination can be left out of account.

Of importance, however, is an internal difficulty, which adheres to the piece wage system on account of its structure. Formula (6) indicates that the hourly earnings are proportional to the relation between fixed and actual time. The *higher* the standard amount of time for the operation is fixed, the higher are the wages proper without the time actually used being essentially curtailed or the performance raised. The same is shown by formula (7), according to which the increase of the earnings in relation to the time wages comes out too high in case of the amount of time being appraised too high. The increase in wages is uneconomic in this instance, since it is not based on an increased performance; the principle of equivalence has been violated. In addition, the wage rate per piece, which on account of (5) has been rated too high, leads to unprofitable labour costs (3) and in the event of reduced competitiveness of the enterprise can no longer be maintained. Therefore, the piece wage system is rendered completely uneconomic and fails to reach its goal.

Further, it should be borne in mind that, conversely, after formula (7) and Fig. 3, a considerable *under*-estimating of the amount of time normally required for the performance makes it almost impossible for the worker from the beginning to obtain an increase over and above the time wages and that, as a rule, he will almost certainly stay below it. Also in this case the piece wage system will fall short of its economic purpose.

Of fundamental and decisive importance for the piece wages is, therefore, a proper and exact fixing of the *standard time* upon which it is based.

The incorrect appraisal or estimate of the standard time t_0 and, consequently, of the base rate l_0 in the event of a money contract, has in the beginning of piece wages resulted in a considerable *negative effect* of this wage system and caused the workers (and trade unions) to reject it. The understandable tendency of the workers to agree upon a high standard time which was advantageous to them, at the same time drew forth the danger of reducing the base rate. By way of countermove, the workers endeavoured to avoid a higher temporal quantitative performance increase or at least to reduce it, in order not to cause a reduction of wages through too high earnings. It was only by the setting up of objectivated, correct, and dependable procedures of *standard rate determination*, recognized by both parties, that these difficulties could be surmounted. These procedures are detailed in other articles of this book.

Recapitulating, we can ascertain as a result that from the viewpoint of wage equivalence the piece wages appear to be effective when the output is characterized by a numerical quantity, so that an adaptation of the wages is warranted only by the volume of output (quantity as the *only* and *best* measure).

The piece wage system does not in the last place owe its present extension to the systematic *time study*, which has contributed to overcome the earlier mentioned internal difficulties in the piece wage system to a large extent. One of the results obtained by an empiric enquiry held in 1952 among 84 West-German firms in various trades, together employing 95,121 workmen, was that 65 out of the 84 firms used some form of piece wage system.

2. *Wages as a Function of Quantity*

In order to penetrate further into the character of time and piece wages, both wage forms are subjected to a *joint* examination. For this purpose, it is essential that they be gauged and compared with the aid of an immanent measure, a unit based upon their inherent characteristics.

It must appear striking that the piece wages in our explanation only indirectly refer to a quantitative performance increase, whereas directly a temporal performance increase is attained. The reason is that, in the formulae, time acts as independent variable. Piece wages were measured on the basis of time – which is not congruent with its structure – instead of that of the quantity of output which conforms to it. Now it is the *quantity* of output which is introduced as an independent variable.

To obtain appropriate formulae and to make their analogy apparent, the *terminology* of the fundamental concepts – as practice has indiscriminately shaped it, and as it is still to be used hereafter – has first to be elaborated in a more suitable language. When talking about labour costs and hourly earnings, one proceeds from fundamentally different viewpoints, now from the viewpoint of the enterprise, now from the viewpoint of the workman. Seen from the angle of the enterprise, the expressions "*piece costs*" (labour costs per piece) and "*hour costs*" (labour costs per hour) shall be consistently used. The choice of the time unit "hour" explains the denomination "hour costs" instead of the general denomination "*time costs*" (labour costs per unit of time).

For time wages, therefore, the piece costs l for the quantity unit, which in the event of fixed hour costs $s = s_0$ is produced in t hours, has been computed in the formulae. When, similarly, we compute for *piece wages* the hour costs s for the time unit, in which, at the fixed piece costs $l = l_0$, q pieces are produced, the following formulae are found

(8) $$s = l_0 q$$

(9) $$l = l_0$$

or, in words:

The *hourly earnings* are found by multiplying the base rate by the number of pieces produced per hour. The *labour costs* per piece equal the fixed wage rate per piece.

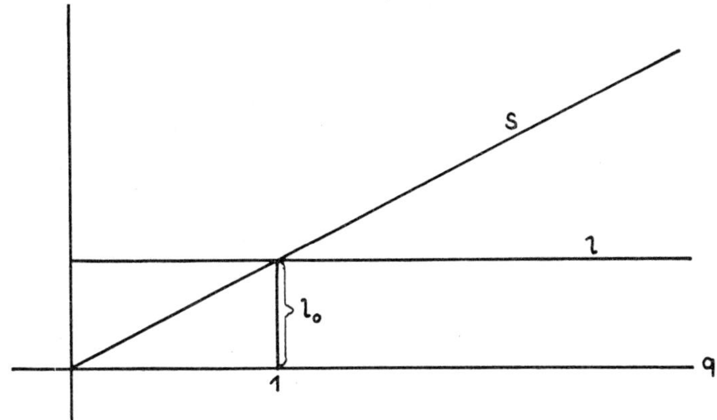

Fig. 4. Piece wages.

As independent variable – taking the place of the number of hours t per piece – the number of pieces q per hour now comes in. By exchanging the dependent variables s and l in Fig. 1 we find the fully analogous Fig. 4.

From this, we find the following result for the influence of the equivalence principle.

The *quantitative* performance increase has been considered to a large extent. The hourly earnings go up in the same proportion as the number of pieces produced. At first sight this result (8) appears to be contradictory to (4). As, according to (9), the earnings go up in the same proportion as the number of pieces q increases, i.e. rises in a straight line after Fig. 4, the earnings – according to (4) – are inversely proportional to the performance time t. With the time decreasing, it rises hyperbolically after Fig. 2, i.e. seemingly considerably more strongly. This difference is explained by the fact that with equal increases of the number of pieces the saving in time declines, but that on the contrary, with a constant decrease of time, the increase in pieces rises.

Intrinsically, therefore, both formulae have the same meaning. The formal advantage of formula (4) lies in the fact that the hyperbolic dependence of time can be directly observed. On the other hand, formula (9) has the advantage that it characterizes the piece wages by a direct increase of output.

The *subjective* element of the performance increase also becomes strongly apparent in formula (8). Let us determine with the aid of the formula

$$s_0 = l_0 q_0 \tag{10}$$

the somehow fixed quantity q_0, achieved within the unit of time, in which s_0 means the time wage rate per hour, we find:

$$s = s_0 \frac{q}{q_0}, \tag{11}$$

thus:

$$\sigma = s - s_0 = s_0 \frac{q - q_0}{q_0} \tag{12}$$

as an increase of the hourly earnings in case of piece wages as compared with time wages. Or in words: The *increase in earnings* is directly proportional to the surplus in output, the difference between actual and fixed quantity.

The graphic presentation shows a straight line, which for $q = q_0$ crosses the quantity axis (Fig. 5). Only then can the worker exceed the time wages by his earnings when he produces more pieces than fixed, it being disregarded that the base rate for the hourly earnings in the event of standard output lies higher than the hourly earnings for time wage earners. Even in case he falls short of his target, he has to expect a reduction in his earnings in respect of the time wages if no minimum wages are agreed upon or guaranteed collectively. In the correct appraisal of the *standard quantity* q_0 per unit of time, we have here the same inner difficulties already encountered in (7) and in Fig. 3 for the ascertaining of the standard time t_0 per piece.

That the increase in earnings is linear and not hyperbolic, as in Fig. 3, is based on the same connection which was set out above for the increase of output.

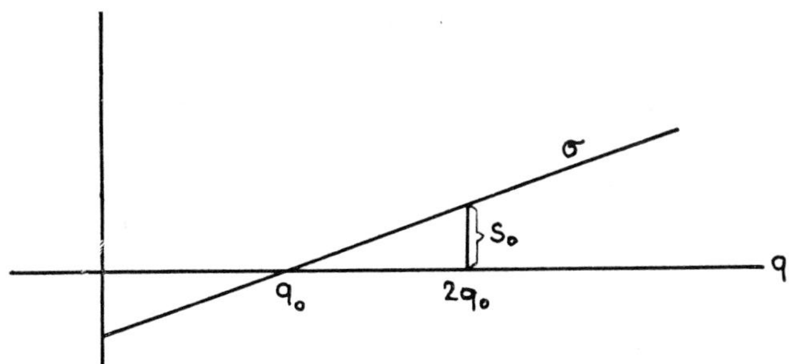

Fig. 5. Increase of the hourly earnings with piece wages.

Upon comparison of the formulae (5) and (10) we find the *fixed relation* between the two standard figures, the standard time t_0 per piece (unit of output quantity) and of the standard quantity q_0 per hour (unit of performance time):

$$t_0 = \frac{1}{q_0}, \qquad q_0 = \frac{1}{t_0}, \qquad t_0\, q_0 = 1. \tag{13}$$

The *temporal* performance increase, however, is left out of account in the new presentation, as the time spent on the performance is in no way considered in the formulae. On the other hand – contrary to the above – in view of the constancy of the piece costs and on account of the subjective impetus towards maximum output, an indirect temporal increase of performance can be spoken of. Whether the quantitative or temporal increase manifests itself as an indirect or a direct one depends upon the fact in what independent variables (whether in t or q) the formulae and graphs are expressed.

For the qualitative performance increase and the permanency of performance there are no further viewpoints.

The fact that by the introduction of the quantity q as an independent variable we can find the formulae for piece wages which are fully analogous to those pertaining to time wages, suggests the idea of applying the same changes to the *time wages*. The result obtained is as follows:

$$s = s_0 \tag{14}$$

$$l = \frac{s_0}{q}. \tag{15}$$

In words:

The *hourly earnings* equal the fixed wage rate per hour. The *labour costs* per piece are found by dividing the fixed wage rate per hour by the number of pieces produced per hour.

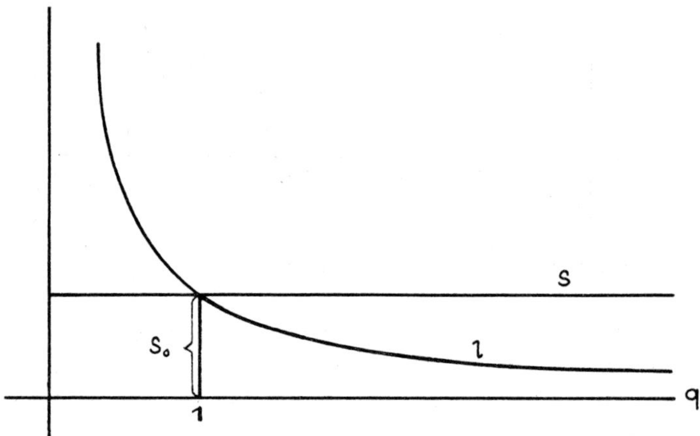

Fig. 6. Time wages.

We obtain a graphic presentation in Fig. 6 by exchanging the dependent variables s and l in Fig. 2. For the validity of the equivalence principle there is nothing really new to be found.

In case of guaranteed minimum time wages there is a *combination* of the two Figures 4 and 6. Curve s, representing the earnings, first runs in accordance with Fig. 6 for $q \leqq q_0$, parallel to the x-axis, and then after Fig. 4 for $q \geqq q_0$ with a linear ascent. In the point $(q_0, s_0 = l_0 q_0)$ the two sections of the curves meet. The cost curve l first goes down hyperbolically after Fig. 6 and then continues after Fig. 4 parallel to the x-axis. Also here the two sections of the curves meet at the corresponding point $q_0, l_0 = s_0/q_0$. The same ideas go, accordingly, for the combination of Fig. 1 and 2 in regard to the standard time t_0, since the time is here taken as a variable.

3. *Wages as a Function of Time and of Quantity*

In the mathematical presentation of the two wage forms one can go a step further and comprise two separate systems of formulae in t and q into a *unitary system* in both variables. Therefore, let – in a wider meaning than hitherto – q be the quantity of pieces produced within the corresponding amount of time t. Then we find the following general formulae for *time wages:*

$$l = s_0 \frac{t}{q} \tag{16}$$

$$s = s_0 \tag{17}$$

and for *piece wages:*

$$s = l_0 \frac{q}{t} \tag{18}$$

$$l = l_0. \tag{19}$$

In words:

For *time wages* the hour costs (time costs) are constant; the piece costs are obtained by multiplying the constant wage rate per hour (time unit) by the duration of performance and dividing it by the number of pieces worked upon during this period.

For *piece wages* the piece costs are constant; the hour costs (time costs) are found by multiplying the constant wage rate per piece (base rate) by the number of the pieces produced and dividing it by the amount of time used.

TABLE 1

Original Wage Forms	Time Wages	Piece Wages
constants	time costs s_0	piece costs l_0
variables	piece costs l	time costs s
time scale	directly proportional t	inversely proportional t
quantity scale	inversely proportional q	directly proportional q
temporal increase	impeded	enhanced
quantitative increase	impeded	enhanced
qualitative increase	enhanced	impeded
permanency	secured	endangered
subjective incentive	lacking	strongly pronounced
performance type	time performance	piece performance
characteristics	negative quality wages	positive quantity wages

The internal relationship of the two wage forms, based upon a *correlation* of the notions hour (time unit) and piece (performance unit), can now be observed. Both formulae pass over into each other if one replaces duration, time wage rate and number of pieces, in the same sequence, by number of pieces, piece wage rate and duration. The formulae used earlier appear as special cases. They are obtained by inserting first $q = 1$ and then $t = 1$.

The clear contrast between the two wage forms is shown by Table 1, which gives the essential elements. Here the piece wages are characterized, economically, as *positive quantity wages*, since they aim directly at a quantitative performance increase, and the time wages as *negative quality wages*, because they indirectly enhance the quality of the performance by the absence of a subjective incentive towards an increase in quantity.

Time and piece wages are the *original forms* of any wage determination. All conceivable wage forms ultimately proceed from these two elements. They are merely economic *combinations* of time and piece wage systems to balance the two extremes quality and quantity while securing the possibility of permanent performances.

II. *Gain Sharing Plans*

1. *The Halsey Wage Plan*

Inasmuch as time wages are primarily suitable for qualitative time performances and piece wages for quantitative piece performances, the practice of remuneration has worked out a number of *intermediate systems* to pay for the numerous actually occurring performances. The opinion, held even today, that both time and piece wages should have inherent disadvantages, must, however, be denied. The way the matter lies is rather that the two wage forms are tailored to two clearly outlinable, fundamentally different categories of performances. The remark that the drawbacks of the time wages are the advantages of the piece wages, or the reverse, only emphasizes that here we have two diametrically opposed wage forms. The numerous endeavours to set up new methods do not, therefore, aim at an improvement of these original forms, but are rather indicative of a search for a wage form adapted to a given kind of performance. However, all these wage methods, insofar as they are founded on time and quantity, must necessarily move between those two extreme pillars of the entire remuneration technique.

To arrive at such an intermediate wage form it suggests itself that the difference in hourly earnings, which arises when one and the same performance is now paid in time wages, now in piece wages, must be taken into account with a fraction, after the wage plan originally developed by F. A. Halsey and H. R. Towne. Also here it is again pre-supposed that in the event of standard performance the equal wage amount be paid either as piece wages or as time wages.

When first considering time as independent variable, this means, fundamentally, remuneration on a basis of time, with a certain additional pay, the so-called *premium*, which is found with formula (7):

$$\sigma = \kappa s_0 \frac{t_0 - t}{t}. \tag{20}$$

In this formula the *premium measure* κ is a positive fraction. Halsey considers $\kappa = \frac{1}{3}$ and Towne $\kappa = \frac{2}{3}$ as the best premium measure. Weir uses a premium measure of $\kappa = \frac{1}{2}$. An easy computation then supplies the two basic formulae:

$$s = s_0 + \sigma = s_0 + \kappa s_0 \frac{t_0 - t}{t} \tag{21}$$

$$l = s \quad t = s_0\, t + \kappa s_0 (t_0 - t). \tag{22}$$

In words:

The *hourly earnings* are equal to the fixed hourly wage rate increased by the premium which is computed with the aid of a fixed fraction of the

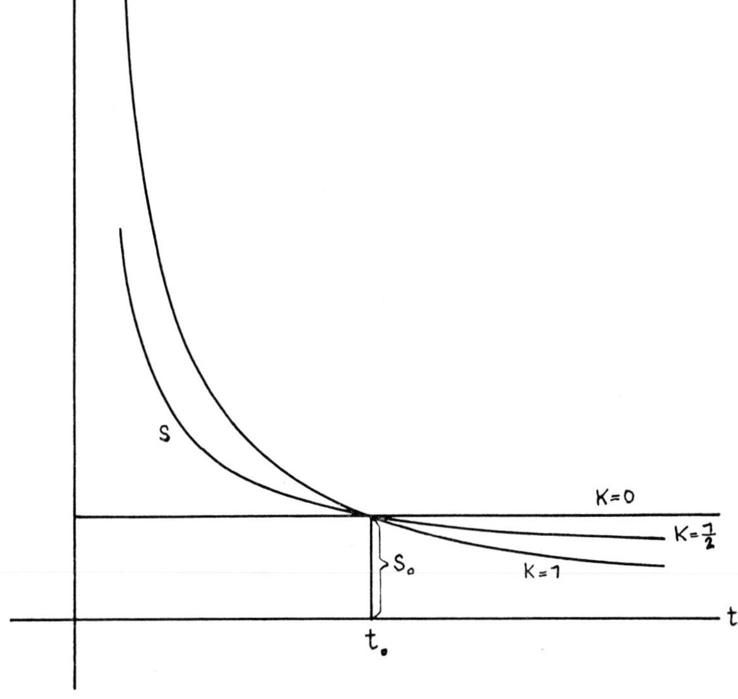

Fig. 7. Halsey wages.

relation between the time saved and the time actually used. The time saved is given by the difference between the standard and the actual time. The wage rate must principally be laid down on the basis of the work difficulty.

The *labour costs* are found by multiplying the hourly earnings thus computed by the time actually used. They equal the sum of the time wage costs and a fraction of the labour costs saved against the standard time.

For $\kappa = 1$, (20) becomes (7), and thus we find the pure *piece wages:* The total difference of the hourly earnings is paid. When κ is allowed to become smaller and smaller, ultimately $\kappa = 0$ causes $\sigma = 0$ and we have the pure *time wages:* No premium is paid. Both original forms prove to be special kinds or, mathematically, extreme cases of the general Halsey wage plan. In between we find for $\kappa < 1$ the entire scale of the widest variations in *premium wages.*

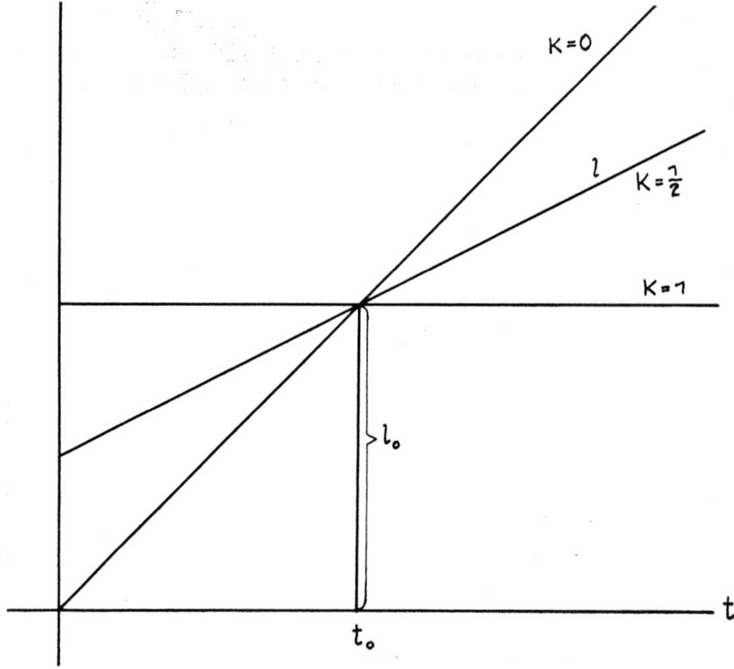

Fig. 8. Halsey wages.

When the two extreme cases are added, the graphic presentation leads to Figs. 7 and 8. In point $t = t_0$ all the (hyperbolic) earnings curves and also the (linear) cost curves cut each other for any κ. In this case the premium disappears. All the earnings and cost curves consequently form each a bunch of curves and straight lines with a point of intersection in t_0.

When, instead of the time actually used, we choose the number q of pieces produced as independent variable, we find according to (12):

$$\sigma = \kappa s_0 \frac{q-q_0}{q_0}. \tag{23}$$

Thus we find the following formulae:

$$s = s_0 + \sigma = s_0 + \kappa s_0 \frac{q-q_0}{q_0} \tag{24}$$

$$l = \frac{s}{q} = \frac{s_0}{q} + \kappa s_0 \frac{q-q_0}{q_0\, q}. \tag{25}$$

In words:

The *hourly earnings* are equal to the fixed hourly wage rate, increased by the premium computed with the aid of a fixed fraction of the relation

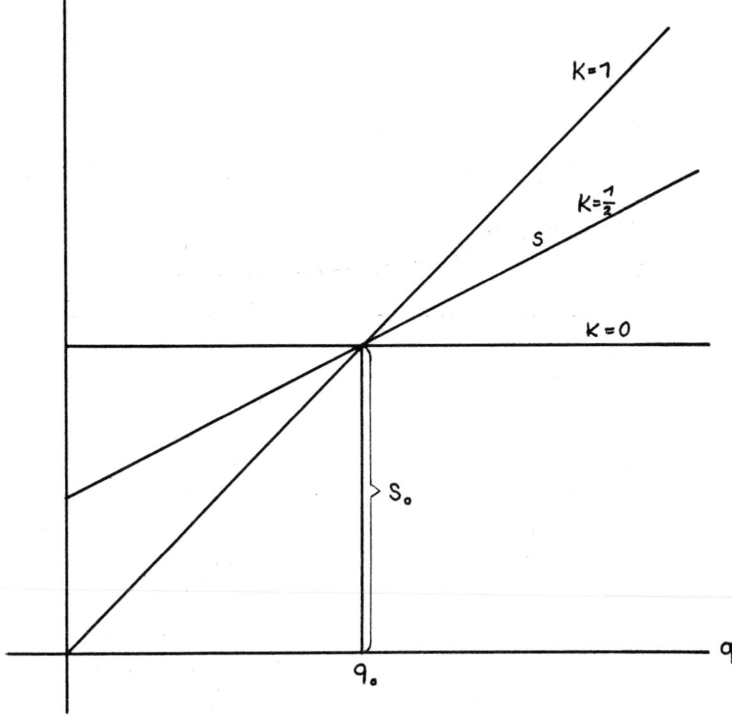

Fig. 9. Halsey wages.

between the surplus of pieces produced (based on a standard quantity) and the standard quantity.

The *labour costs* are found by dividing the hourly wages thus computed by the number of pieces produced.

Also in this presentation, for $\kappa = 1$ or $\kappa = 0$, respectively, we find the piece or the time wages, respectively, as extreme cases. In point $q = q_0$ all the curves cut each other as shown by Figs. 9 and 10.

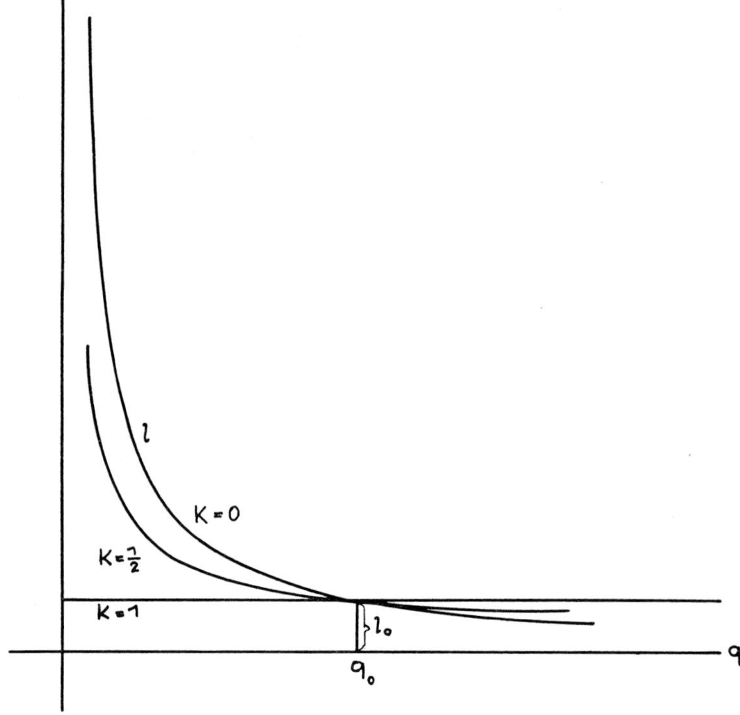

Fig. 10. Halsey wages.

When we now examine the Halsey wage methods after the principle of equivalence of wages and performance, we come to the following result.

The *temporal* performance increase is indicated by the fact that, as time decreases, also the labour costs per piece show a linear descent, but the hourly earnings show a hyperbolic line of increase. The degree in which the labour costs fall is lower than in the event of pure time wages. The degree to which the hourly earnings go up is smaller than for pure piece wages. The magnitude of these gradual differences is governed by choice of the fixed figure κ.

If κ is sufficiently small, the danger that, in the event of a performance standard fixed at too low a level, the wages mount up unjustifiably high is not so great as in case of pure piece wages. Here the mistake does not manifest itself in its entirety, since it merely affects the hourly earnings by a fraction (mitigated hyperbola).

When the performance exceeds the fixed amount of time ($t > t_0$), the earnings do not really go down so much as in the case of pure piece wages, but still below the time wages. In this case the piece costs exceed the estimated costs in proportion to time. Halsey himself applies a modification to the extent that he guarantees to the worker the time wages as minimal wages even in case the worker does not reach his target. This measure, however, is not in the nature of this premium wage method. The bottom limit is at present formed at any rate by the guaranteed minimum wages under collective agreement. In case of a guaranteed time wage rate the curves for the time wages ($\kappa = 0$) go for the Figs. 7–10 till t_0 and q_0 respectively; only from there do the hourly earnings and the labour costs follow the Halsey curves for $\kappa \neq 0$.

The *quantitative* performance increase lies in the fact that the hourly earnings go up as the number of pieces produced increases, but the labour costs drop. Also here the increase remains below that of the piece wages in the first instance, and below that of the time wages in the second instance. The degree of the change is indicated by fixing the premium measure κ. Also here the earnings go down below the time wages (as far as the amount of the guaranteed minimum wages) as soon as the performance remains under the fixed number of pieces ($q < q_0$).

The *qualitative* performance increase becomes manifest – albeit to a smaller extent – by the fact that, because of a suitable establishing of the premium measure, the subjective incentive towards an excessive temporal-quantitative increase of performance is mitigated, through which, indirectly, a better quality of performance can be attained.

At the same time a *permanency* of performance is guaranteed up to a certain degree.

The *subjective* element of performance increase does not become fully manifest as in the case of pure piece wages. But it can be used by appropriate determination of the premium measure, depending upon the nature of performance, to an optional extent for the attainment of the highest temporal-quantitative increase of performance. On the other hand, an appropriate cutting of this subjective incentive may indirectly lead to a certain quality of performance.

Recapitulating, we can say that the Halsey premium wage plan aims at achieving *both* an increase in *quantity* and better product *quality*. It will prove to be effective for those kinds of work which, while laying strong emphasis on the quantitative view, demand a certain attention to quality. As the qualitative side of performance gains a little more prominence the proper premium measure will be selected. It need not be emphasized that also here it can, in principle, only be used in mass production or repetitive operations with a strongly quantitative character. A more definite, generally valid, quantitative determination of the *premium measure* cannot be deduced from a purely theoretical angle. Here, extensive practice should supply the required experience.

It should be observed that the most exact determination of the *standard rates* is also of fundamental importance for the Halsey wage plan. On this point, the plan shows the same inherent difficulty as was already explained for piece wages. Since, however, it works out to a much smaller extent in case of a suitable choice of the premium measure, the Halsey wage plan was to serve originally as a *substitute* of the pure piece wages, so as to avoid the forcing-down of the contract wage rates which often occurred in former days. The structural character of the Halsey premium wages, however, is to be found, in the first place, in the fact that in case of strongly quantitative performances the quality, too, is taken into consideration. To separate this, we have to abstract the human fallibility in ascertaining work standards.

Nowadays, the Halsey wage plan is frequently recommended and used – though under *different names*. With due consideration of the collective agreement regulations, the Halsey wage plan can, by a correct selection of the premium measure be eminently utilized in influencing performances to the desired extent.

2. *The Rowan Wage Plan*

Another intermediate form between time wages and piece wages, which nowadays is known under various denominations, is arrived at when the premiums are fixed in a different form. The Halsey premium increases both with the growing time saved and with the decreasing time used. Contrary to this, James Rowan chooses as premium the relation between the time saved and the time fixed, thus:

$$\sigma = s_0 \frac{t_0 - t}{t_0} \tag{26}$$

i.e. the bonus goes up only in case of increasing time saving. Thus the following two formulae are found:

$$s = s_0 + \sigma = s_0 \frac{2t_0 - t}{t_0} \tag{27}$$

$$l = st = 2s_0 t - \frac{s_0}{t_0} t^2. \tag{28}$$

In words:

The *hourly earnings* are equal to the fixed wage rate per hour, increased by the premium which is computed on the basis of a percentage of the time saved. The *labour costs* are found by multiplying the hourly earnings by the time used. There are three *special cases.*

For $t = 0$ (i.e. 100% time-saving) $s = 2s_0$ and $l = 0$; the hourly earnings reach their maximum value, double the underlying time wage rate; the labour costs disappear.

For $t = t_0$ we find $s = s_0$, $l = s_0 t_0 = l_0$; the Rowan wage plan goes over into pure time and piece wages at the same time.

For $t = 2t_0$, $s = 0$ and $l = 0$.

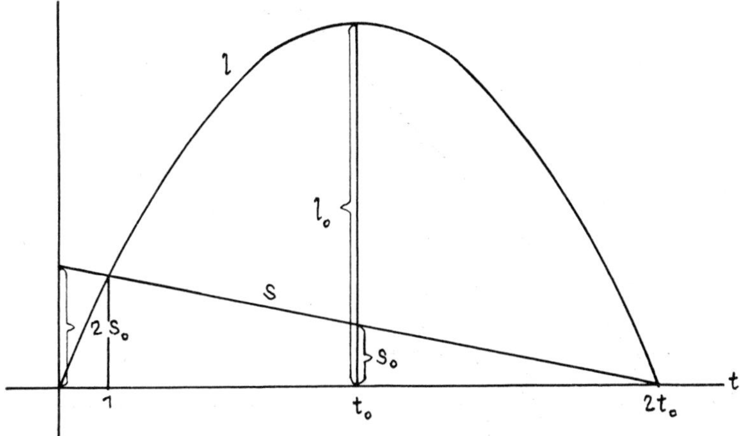

Fig. 11. Rowan wages.

The graphic presentation is given in Fig. 11. The earnings curve is a straight line through the two points $(0, 2s_0)$ and (t_0, s_0). It cuts the time axis at the point $t = 2t_0$. The cost curve is a parabola with the main axis $t = t_0$. It reaches its maximum at the point (t_0, l_0) and cuts the time axis at the point $t = 0$ and $t = 2t_0$.

When using the *quantity q* as independent variable, the Rowan premium can be determined in the following way:

(29) $$\sigma = s_0 \frac{q-q_0}{q}.$$

Then the following formulae are obtained:

(30) $$s = s_0 + \sigma = s_0 \frac{2q-q_0}{q^2}$$

(31) $$l = \frac{s}{q} = s_0 \frac{2q-q_0}{q^2}.$$

In words:

The *hourly earnings* are equal to the fixed wage rate per hour, increased by the Rowan premium. The *labour costs* are found by dividing the hourly earnings thus computed by the number of pieces produced.

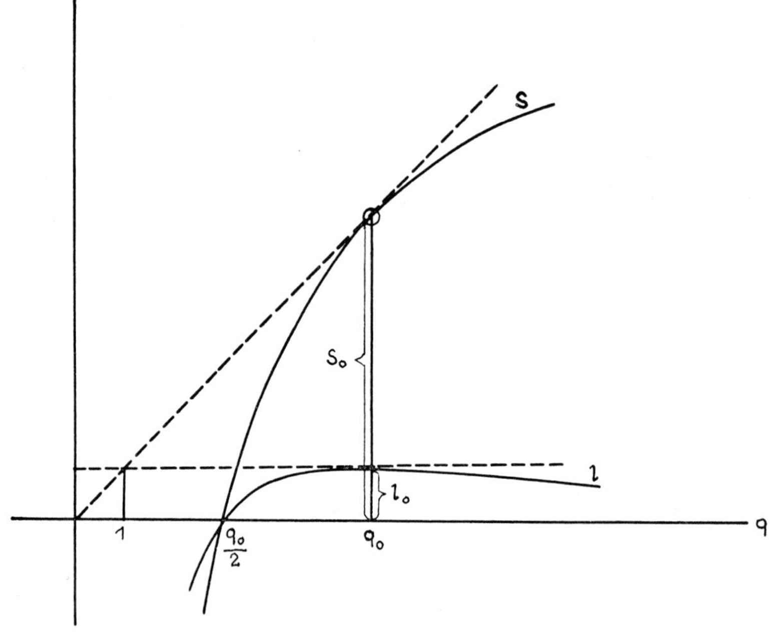

Fig. 12. Rowan wages.

Also here there are three *special cases*. In case $q = q_0/2$, $s = 0$. For $q = q_0$ we find $s = 2_0$, $l = l_0$. As a limit $q \to \infty$ we find $s = 2s_0$, $l = 0$. The graphs are shown by Fig. 12.

The earnings curve is a hyperbola which cuts the q-axis at $q = q_0/2$ and does not reach its maximum value $s = 2s_0$ before infinitity. The tangent at the point (q_0, s_0) goes through the origin and represents the pure piece wages $s = (s_0/q_0)q = l_0 q$.

The cost curve is a hyperbola of a higher order through the point $(q_0/2, 0)$, which attains its maximum value $l = l_0$ at the point $q = q_0$. The tangent at the point (q_0, l_0) runs parallel to the x-axis and represents the pure piece wages $l = l_0$.

Now we are to examine the value of the equivalence principle of wages and performance for the Rowan premium wages.

The *temporal* performance increase appears in such a way that, with decreasing time $t \leq t_0$ the piece costs go down parabolically, i.e. slowly at first, more rapidly later. When the standard time $(t > t_0)$ is exceeded, the costs go down likewise, so that also in this case the output becomes cheaper. Further the hourly earnings go up as time decreases, namely in a linear way up to a (practically unattainable) maximum value, which can never be exceeded. On the other hand they go down as soon as the fixed time t_0 is exceeded; ultimately they disappear when the time used equals double the standard time. In practice, however, the limit for the decrease of the earnings lies where minimum wages are guaranteed.

The *quantitative* performance increase becomes apparent from the fact that the piece costs, proceeding from the standard quantity, decrease both with increasing and decreasing quantity. The earnings go up with the increasing quantity to the top limit of $2s_0$.

This *top limit* of $2s_0$ is a characteristic feature of the Rowan wage plan. Its special meaning lies in the fact that in case of the standard quantity q_0 being fixed too low (as in the case of too high an estimate for the standard time t_0) the hourly earnings cannot go up to any level dangerous to the enterprise. Erroneous estimates in the standard rates become apparent to a far smaller extent than in the Halsey wage plan. The danger of the base wage rate being forced down is almost completely eliminated. In formula (26) this becomes evident by the fact that in the case of too high a value for t_0, the numerator, but at the same time also the denominator become too high, so that the change in the value of σ is only a small one.

The *qualitative* performance increase has been considered insofar as the increase in the earnings, which becomes smaller with the number of pieces produced, sets no impulse to the highest quantitative intensification of performance. The same is evident from the hourly earnings which go up only in a linear way as the time decreases, although the difficulty of increase in performance goes up progressively.

For the same reason there is no serious danger for the *permanency* of performance.

The *subjective* impetus to achieve top output has already been emphasized with the different elements of the objective increase of performance. Let us take another brief look at the premium.

Formula (26) graphically represents a downward line, which for $t = t_0$ intersects the time axis. In the limit case $t = 0$, σ is s_0. Generally speaking, however ($t > 0$), $\sigma < s_0$, i.e. the premium always remains below the fixed time wage rate. If the time used is equal to the fixed time, the premium disappears ($t = t_0$, $\sigma = 0$). For the rest, in case $t \gtrless t_0$, σ is always $\gtrless 0$. Also here, a wage reduction occurs as the output falls short of the target. It is not an essential feature of the Rowan wage plan that Rowan himself practically guarantees the time wage rate.

As a *final result*, it can be ascertained that the Rowan (like the Halsey) premium wages are suitable for those performances where, besides numerical *quantity*, also the *quality* of the performance is important. Generally speaking, it can be said that in case of the Rowan wage plan the quality is emphasized a little more strongly, whereas the quantity of the output finds a less pronounced emphasis. A further explanation of the special kinds of performance is theoretically impossible. To this end an accurate knowledge of the production process as well as ample practical experience are required.

The Rowan wage plan may be particularly important in those cases where the management is interested in manufacturing a *standard quantity* which, for reasons of sales policy, shall not be exceeded. Given the fact that on account of the wage structure the incentive towards higher output disappears more and more in the event of excess of the standard output, the wage form favours the production of a more or less limited standard quantity.

It should be pointed out that for the practical application of the Rowan wage plan certain *conditions* have to be fulfilled if the wage method is to meet the modern conceptions of the equivalence of wages and performance. This comprises the guarantee of the minimum wages which the worker must have when the output falls short of the standard performance through no fault of his own. Further, in the event of standard performance the base rate must be paid, which corresponds to the difficulty of work and the normal working intensity customary under this wage plan.

The starting point for the adoption of the Rowan wage plan is basically time wages which are augmented by the Rowan premium. The objection that the Rowan wage plan – contrary to pure piece wages – does not fully remunerate excess output is not valid, seeing that not the piece wage but the time wage method forms the starting point and because the Rowan wage method as such represents a fully independent form of wages tailored to special kinds of performance.

If a wage form is to be applied to mitigate the drawbacks of *unprecise performance standards*, the Rowan wage plan is to be preferred to the Halsey plan, inasmuch as in the former plan mistakes in the estimating of standard rates become least apparent. Here, before everything, performances are meant that can hardly or not at all be appraised, for instance repair work.

Just as the Halsey wage type, in a more general way, can be regarded with any value of premium measure κ, the Rowan premium plan also allows for many *modifications*, only part of the premium being awarded. This is put down as follows.

$$\sigma = \kappa s_0 \frac{t_0 - t}{t_0}. \tag{32}$$

Then we find for hourly earnings and labour costs:

$$s = s_0 + \sigma = s_0 + \kappa s_0 \frac{t_0 - t}{t_0} \tag{33}$$

$$l = st = s_0 t + \kappa s_0 t \frac{t_0 - t}{t_0}. \tag{34}$$

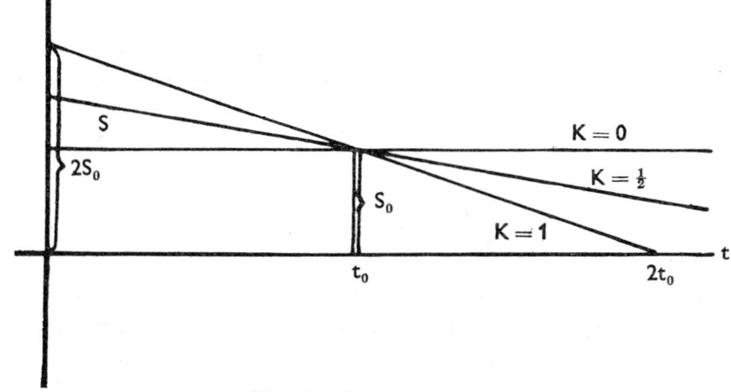

Fig. 13. Rowan wages.

The graphic presentation (Figs. 13 and 14) shows for all values of κ straight lines as earnings curves and parabolas as cost curves.

For $t = 0$, $s = (\kappa+1)s_0$ and $l = 0$. For $t = t_0$, $s = s_0$ and $l = l_0$. For $t = t_0(\kappa+1)/\kappa$, $s = l = 0$. All earnings curves run through the point

(t_0, s_0) and all cost curves through (t_0, l_0). Either of them forms (as in the general Halsey wage plan) a bunch of curves or straight lines, intersecting each other in t_0. The earnings reach their top value for $t = 0$, the costs for $t = t_0(\kappa+1)/2\kappa$. For $\kappa = 1$ we find the special Rowan wage, $\kappa = 0$ gives the time wages as a limit case.

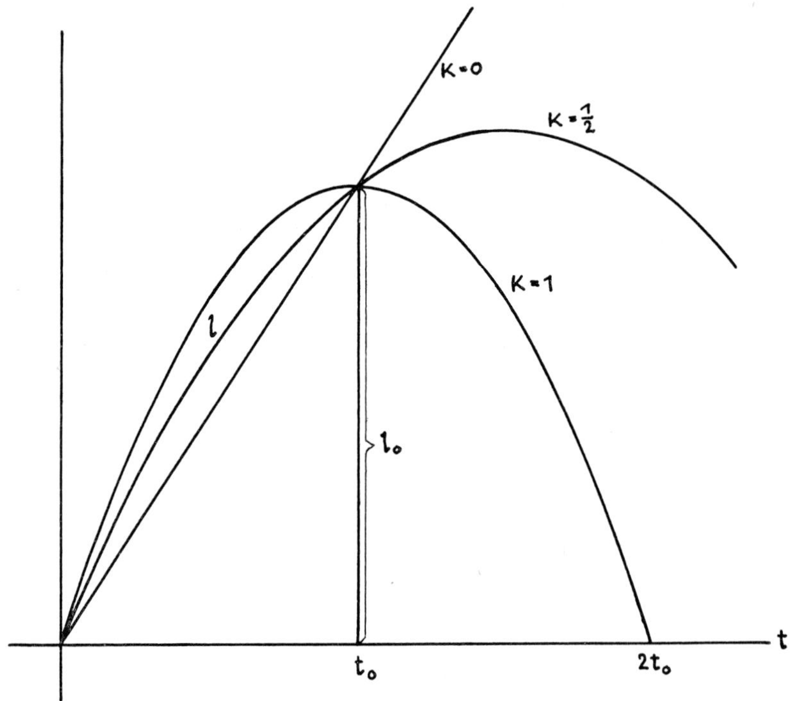

Fig. 14. Rowan wages.

The smaller the premium measure κ, the smaller the increase of hourly earnings under diminishing time. Likewise, the costs fall the more rapidly, the smaller the premium measure κ is chosen. The variation of the premium measure permits a certain adaptation to the various performances of the enterprise. The economic structure shown for the special Rowan wages is essentially also a property of the general form.

We shall refrain from giving a more detailed explanation of the modified Rowan wages as a function of the *quantity q*, since the relative formulae can be found without difficulty:

(35) $$s = s_0 + \sigma = s_0 + \kappa s_0 \frac{q - q_0}{q}$$

(36) $$l = \frac{s}{q} = \frac{s_0}{q} + \kappa s_0 \frac{q - q_0}{q^2}.$$

Also for the Rowan wage plan, with a guaranteed time wage rate, in all Figs. 11–14 occurs a *combination* with the relative time wage curves, in which first the time wage curves ($\kappa = 0$) are valid and, only from point t_0 or q_0, respectively, the special or general Rowan curves ($\kappa \neq 0$).

3. *Comparative Study*

Both premium wage forms studied so far, viz. the Halsey and the Rowan wage plans, can be designated as *gain sharing plans*, as they try to find an intermediate form between the two extreme wage forms, the time and the piece wages. Of the "premium" which is behind the piece wages in respect of the time wages, only a certain share is paid to the worker, whereas the rest comes to the benefit of the enterprise.

With the *Halsey wage plan* this portion is calculated as a fixed fraction (20) of the full amount of the difference which, once established, remains *constant* throughout the total production process. In other words: The share paid to the worker stands to the undiminished piece wage surplus as $\kappa : l$. This proportion is equal to the *premium measure*. The magnitude of the share in the excess output, therefore, is fixed beforehand.

This is different under the *Rowan wage plan*. Here the premium (26) equals

(37) $$\sigma = s_0 \frac{t_0 \,.\, t}{t_0} = s_0 \frac{t_0 - t}{t} \frac{t}{t_0}.$$

It is *variable* within the same production process, namely the undiminished piece wage surplus stands to the paid-out share of the worker as $t_0 : t$, i.e. as the standard time stands to the actual time. The share in the surplus output therefore depends upon the extent of this surplus output itself. The worker receives a percentage equal to the time he uses. Strictly speaking: The more time the worker saves, the less he participates – relatively – in the full piece wage surplus. In the absolute sense, the share of the worker, under otherwise equal circumstances, is first larger under the Rowan wage plan than under the Halsey plan; then, however, the Rowan share falls considerably behind the Halsey share. The Rowan earnings curve is a tangent to the piece wage earnings curve in the point $t = t_0$. Similarly, the labour costs under the Halsey plan decline more sharply than in the Rowan plan; in the event of higher time savings, however, they sink considerably more deeply with this wage form than with the other one.

Both wage methods thus show a gradual, steady increase of the hourly earnings, connected with an equally steady reduction of the labour costs. When we place this general property of the gain sharing wages in a *comparative relation* to time and piece wages, we come to Table 2.

TABLE 2

Time as Scale		Hourly Earnings		Labour Costs
time wages	↓	constant	↑	proportional
Rowan wages		linear		convex-parabolic
Halsey wages		slightly concave-hyperbolic		linear
piece wages		strongly concave-hyperbolic		constant

An increase of the rise of the hourly earnings in the direction time wages → piece wages, and an increase of the fall of the labour costs in the reversed direction piece wages → time wages is easily recognized. On account of this, the Halsey wages can be characterized as an intermediate wage form with a stronger increase of the hourly earnings, the Rowan wages as an intermediate wage form with a stronger decrease of the labour costs. In other words: The Halsey wages are gain sharing wages with ultimately a higher *subjective* increase of performance, the Rowan wages are gain sharing wages with ultimately a stronger *objective* increase of performance.

The same result is arrived at when the *quantity* q is utilized as independent variable. The Halsey premium is obtained from (23). The Rowan premium, according to (29), amounts to

$$\sigma = s_0 \frac{q-q_0}{q_0} \frac{q_0}{q}. \tag{38}$$

The former is a fixed fraction of the full piece wage surplus, the latter is variable as q stands to q_0. The more the worker raises his output quantitatively, the smaller the premium becomes in relation to the pure piece wage. In this way we find Table 3.

From the comparative study comes a result which has already been brought forward in another way: The Halsey wages place the emphasis more on the *quantity*, the Rowan wages more on the *quality* of the performance. I should like to formulate this idea in a different way. The Halsey wages are qualitative quantity wages, the Rowan wages are

TABLE 3

Quantity as Scale	Hourly Earnings	Labour Costs
time wages	constant	strongly concave-hyperbolic
Rowan wages	convex-hyperbolic	strongly convex
Halsey wages	linear	slightly concave-hyperbolic
piece wages	proportional	constant

quantitative quality wages. In this connection it should be noted carefully that the increase of the quantity is reached *positively* (directly), the increase of the quality, however, is achieved only *negatively* (indirectly). Thus we come to the following classification:

I. *Positive quantity wages:*
 a) pure quantity wages (piece wages)
 b) qualitative quantity wages (Halsey wages).

II. *Negative quality wages:*
 a) pure quality wages (time wages)
 b) quantitative quality wages (Rowan wages).

4. *Modifications of the Gain Sharing Plans*

The wage forms originally developed by Halsey and Rowan have, in course of time, given rise to a large number of similar wage forms.

A practical variation of the Halsey wages is, for instance, the wage plan by Willans and Robinson, in which for each of unit quantity produced a certain wage sum is established as a base rate ($l_0 = s_0 t_0$), which in case of time savings amounting to half the labour costs saved is added to the time wages:

$$s = s_0 + \tfrac{1}{2}(l_0 - s_0 t) = s_0 + \tfrac{1}{2} s_0 \frac{t_0 - t}{t} \tag{39}$$

$$l = s_0 t + \tfrac{1}{2} s_0 (t_0 - t). \tag{40}$$

Here we have Halsey wages with the premium measure $\kappa = \frac{1}{2}$. In actual practice Halsey wages are applied generally with a wide variety of premiums, the value of which is adapted to each case.

In point of structure and labour economy the Willans wage form runs closest to a modification of the Halsey wage type examined by B. Schiller, where the standard time t_0 is fixed one third too high. A strong conformity becomes apparent from the fact that Schiller bases his wage plan also on different standard times for different time wage rates, so that the products from either of them remains as equal as possible. Also the method of Ross is set up in the same way.

The Manit wage plan by Hasbrouck H. Haynes can likewise be regarded as a special form of the general Halsey wages. This is a wage system which grants time wages to which a premium is added. The premium is calculated on the basis of half the time saved in relation to the standard time. Therefore, we have also here Halsey wages with a premium measure $\kappa = \frac{1}{2}$. However, also other premium measures are apparently used. Since, besides the workers, also the supervisors are granted a premium, the method is very much like the one by Bedaux. The *Manit method* has got its name from the fact that the standard output is gauged by a special unit, the manit (= man-minute). A manit is the normal work produced in a worker-minute and serves as a basis in wage computation.

William Baum's wage plan is characterized by the fact that the hourly earnings, upon attaining certain output stages $q_1, q_2, q_3, \ldots$, go up by jumps and that between these output stages the form of the Halsey wages is effective. Consequently, it is a combination of Halsey wages and the step wages which will be discussed later.

Whereas the Baum method recognizes more than one (2–5) output stages, the Hugo Diemer wage plan has only one jump. Up to the attainment of the standard output Diemer grants time wages, pays a 20% bonus on time wages in the event of standard output and in case of surplus output applies the Halsey wage form, so that here we have a further modification of this wage form.

Frequently, Halsey wages appear under *different denominations:* under-proportional piece wages, mixed piece wages, mixed wages, partial piece wages, flat piece wages, or simply premium wages (Rummel, Peter, Motalik, Görres). The Rowan wages appear as decreasingly rising piece wages (Rummel). Cp. also the combinations on p. 185–186.

Both gain sharing wage forms have lately been used also as group or collective premium wages, which include particularly the *proportional wages* (salaire proportionnel) developed in France, for the first time in 1936, by the industrialist E. Schueller. The fact that the amount of the wages ascertained is later distributed over a group, is of no importance for the wage structure proper. Therefore, the problem of group remuneration cannot be dealt with here any further. Still, the incentive to cooperation shall be mentioned which evolves from a well-thought-out and equitable group remuneration.

An obvious *misconception* has to be pointed out. The Halsey wages were denominated as gain sharing method, since here the full premium is shared between worker and entrepreneur. Viewed from a purely mathematical angle, this is undoubtedly right, but seen from the angle of labour economy, it is confusing and may easily lead to misconceptions. Basically, the Halsey wages – according to the usual approach – are founded on time wages, to which a premium is added. It is not as if the labourer works on piece wages and receives only part of the earnings. In reality we have here, on the basis of a specific wage form, a fundamentally different, peculiar labour organization. Economically, the Halsey wages are a wage form which is fully independent of piece wages and a form in its own right. They can be calculated mathematically both from time wages and from piece wages. Economically, however, the Halsey and Rowan wage plans are fundamentally based on time wages and show up their difference by the relation of the premium to the surplus output.

Also the Bedaux wages can be regarded as a type of general Halsey wages; however, from literature this cannot be clearly concluded, because various explanations are given.

The premium measure granted originally amounts to $\kappa = \frac{3}{4}$, a minimum pay being guaranteed. For this we refer to the Figs. 7–10, combined with time wages ($\kappa = 0$), and with break points at t_0 and q_0, respectively.

Later on, Bedaux has – apparently for optic reasons – chosen the form of pure piece wages, but has reduced the base rate at the same time. Sometimes a premium measure of $\kappa > 1$ is used, also, so that we then have premium piece wages.

The Bedaux wage plan has become known less because of its wage form than because of its special remunerative principles. For, besides the special wage form, it also comprises a special job evaluation and determination of standard rates. Moreover, the system covers a special organization of wage computation and similar measures, as, for instance, the – psychologically not unimportant – daily publication of the performance results in the enterprise.

III. Premium Wages

1. *Types of Premiums*

A premium does not refer to wage differences on account of diverging degrees of difficulty or discriminations between various wage plans; even less does it refer to fringe benefits. The denomination *wage premium* is to denote rather a (fixed or variable) additional pay to certain basic wages, which is related to a performance in return that answers the purpose of the extra pay. It is clear that also here the full weight of the equivalence principle shall be aimed at.

According to the specific basis of additional pay for the premium we can further distinguish the *hour premium* (more generally: the *time premium*), where the extra pay is awarded on the hourly earnings (generally, hour or time costs) and the *piece premium*, added to the piece costs (labour costs per piece). It can be seen that each hour premium (time premium) brings with it a very definite piece premium, and the reverse. Nevertheless, it appears efficaceous to make this difference in meaning, because practice knows both methods of establishing the premiums.

a) *Basic Premiums.* Basic premiums are generally known by the fact that they are based *directly* on the units *time* or *quantity*, therefore structurally change the underlying wages (time or piece wages) and so create another, economically *autonomous* wage form. They aim at a direct increase of performance. We distinguish between

a) *Quantity premiums*, granted for a quantity of pieces produced over and above a standard quantity.

b) *Speed premiums*, gauged after the difference between actual time and standard time (time saving).

It should be observed that in the final labour-economic result quantity and speed premiums, in principle, come down to the same thing.

The following classification of the *basic premium wages* can then be made:

1. *Premium time wages*, based upon time wages, to which a basic premium is added.

2. *Premium piece wages*, basically to be regarded as piece wages, to which a basic premium is added.

Thus, the basic premium wages have already been characterized from the viewpoint of structure labour-economics. In principle, they show a tendency to a temporal-quantitative performance increase over their basic wages. This is naturally attended by a (relatively different) drag on the qualitative performance increase and endangers the permanency of performance. On the other hand, the subjective element of the equivalence principle becomes manifest insofar as the payment of a premium represents a (more or less) strong incentive towards top output. Certainly this personal impetus works on the one side in the temporal-quantitative direction, whereas upon the other elements it has a plainly dragging effect.

b) *Additional Premiums.* The additional premiums have as their objective a very definite partial effect (therefore also called *partial premiums*) and are granted for quality, savings, punctuality, attentiveness, accuracy, permanency of employment, etc. They are tailored to a specific particularity and are in each case established more or less individually.

Premiums are not always paid in the form of special one-time grants, but special patterns for premiums have been developed which stipulate certain *functional connections* between appropriate indices, quality degrees or savings quotas, and wage amounts. Thus, we arrive at wage forms which, however, cannot be regarded as independent wage forms. In many cases, they are regularly used for certain work categories, which proves the growing importance of additional premiums which, in former days, were often granted only in individual cases as remunerations established more or less arbitrarily.

That the additional premiums *cannot* exist as *independent* wage forms becomes clear when we study the forms in which they occur.

A premium for punctuality, attentiveness or permanency of employment would be absurd when paid by itself. These premiums are meaningful only when based upon a certain output in a certain time. They are paid in addition to the basic wage form for corresponding performances.

No more can a premium for quality be thought of as an independent wage form, even when a certain functional connection between several degrees of quality and the wages is established, so that, outwardly, we see the picture of a wage form in its own right. Quality cannot be separated from the quantity produced during a certain time. That is why quality premiums, too, must essentially be additional payments to a basic wage form. The same goes for cost saving premiums. There can only be a saving in costs when a performance is completed. The achievement of a quantitative performance within a given time is here also conditional for the use of cost saving premiums.

Time and quantity are the original scales for the measurements of wages All premiums based directly upon these scales change the elementary forms of time and piece wages in their structure and create the independent premium wage forms. These are the basic premiums. All the other premiums are founded on *different scales* and do not affect the original wage pattern. They are additional remunerations which, it is true, may outwardly give the impression of a wage form in its own right, but *cannot* really *alter* the original wage stucture. They are added to a wage form and can, therefore, appropriately be designated as additional premiums.

When trying to arrange the numerous forms of additional premiums, two large *groups* can be distinguished first:

1. Additional performance premiums.
2. Cost saving premiums.

Both premiums are eventually based on technical standards of a quantitative or qualitative nature. The additional performance premiums aim especially at a temporal-quantitative or qualitative *performance increase*, whereas with the cost saving premiums the viewpoint of *minimizing costs* comes into prominence. It is not possible to make a clearly marked distinction between the two kinds of premiums, since also the cost saving premiums ultimately come down to a relative increase of performance based upon quantity or quality. For example, the quantitative and qualitative result of the production process has to be improved by the greatest possible reduction of wastage when using raw materials, by the best possible utilization of power, coal and oil, by drastic reduction of rejects and re-working and by the best and most economical use of machinery and equipment.

The division of the additional premiums into the groups of additional performance premiums and cost saving premiums must, however, be maintained since it appears to be workable in practice. In the first case an absolute increase of quantity and quality of performance has been thought of when granting the premium, in the second case the idea has rather been that a certain quantity and quality of performance shall be attained at the lowest possible costs (input). The group of the additional performance premiums can be further subdivided into additional quantity premiums and quality premiums.

The following additional premiums can, in practice, be regarded as *quantity premiums:* the punctuality premium, partly the accuracy premium, the attentiveness premium, especially the supervision premium, the permanency or loyalty premium, and the premium on the prevention of accidents.

Premiums for *punctualty* are paid to further a starting of the work in time and to avoid disturbing breaks and stops. Such premiums are by no means granted because of the punctuality itself. It is rather the idea to ensure the desired output through regular starting and carrying out of work. The purpose of the premium for punctuality is, therefore, directed at the quantitative performance increase. Punctuality only serves indirectly as a means to achieve a desired output. Premiums for punctuality are thus to be regarded as additional quantity premiums.

Many additional premiums cannot be rigidly arranged under one of the premium groups. This is the case, for example, with the premiums for *accuracy* and for *attentiveness*. They can be quantity as well as quality premiums, aiming in one case at a temporal-quantitative, in the other case at a qualitative performance increase.

Premiums for *permanency* of employment or for *loyalty* have the intention to form a skeleton group of labourers who have been employed for a long time and are well-trained. In this way training expenses can be saved and the enterprise will benefit by the relatively higher performances of trained labourers. Also here it is essentially the desired rise in output which is strived after through these premiums. Therefore, they may be designated as additional quantity premiums.

The economic idea of premiums on the *prevention of accidents* is to obtain an uninterrupted and regular flow in the working process by avoiding accidents (due observance of the safety regulations), in order thus to ensure the desired performance. For this reason these premiums can be regarded as an additional quantity incentive.

Quality premiums are always additional premiums, since they always pre-suppose a quantitative performance and are paid in addition to the basic wages. Therefore, the longer denomination "additional quality premium" can be replaced by the shorter term of quality premium, which is not possible with the additional quantity-premiums. The quality premiums are now extensively used and are met with in various forms. They are to be recommended wherever the worker is inclined to neglect the quality of his performance, as is the case when, for instance, the piece wage pattern is employed. The simple non-payment for performances of bad quality does not always ensure the degree of quality desired. For that reason, special quality premiums have often to be granted, offering a direct stimulus to the qualitative increase. They can, however, only be applied when the worker can really influence the quality of his performance.

An essential premise for the introduction of quality premiums is the gauging, or better still, the valuation of the quality, since an accurate gauging of the quality is not always possible. The point of departure for the consideration of the quality of performance is, in principle, the *standard quality*, which for each job has to be established in a different way (for instance with the aid of a statistical gauging of errors). The relation of the effective to the standard quality of performance is the *degree of quality*. To the degrees of quality attained each time the amounts of the wages (quality premiums) can then be assigned.

Quality premiums are mostly graded after the degrees of quality attained (graded premiums).

Also with the cost saving premiums, the second group of the additional premiums, the payment of wages founded upon time or quantity is in some way conditional. The basis for the evaluation is either a technically established, physical input of goods (e.g. weight units of lubricants) or a cost amount in money, comprising a certain quantity of goods. The idea of the cost saving premiums is to achieve a quantitative reduction of costs, i.e. to raise the physical efficiency (technicity) of the production. They should, therefore, be kept rigidly separated from the real profit sharing, which is built up on economic decisions.

Cost saving premiums likewise occur in many forms. There are premiums which are supposed to affect the magnitude of a certain kind of costs only, and those which, on the basis of an extensive internal profit and loss account, aim at a general reduction of costs. Also the form of the cost saving premiums is different. Frequently graded, but also constant forms of premiums are used.

A well-known example for cost saving premiums, based upon cost amounts in money, comes from N. T. Ficker who has developed the so-called *machine cost saving system.* Here a certain machine cost rate is worked out, a premium being granted when a worker goes below that rate. It consists of half the machine costs saved. The Ficker plan occurs in two forms. One form is founded on the Halsey wage plan with a premium measure $\kappa = \frac{1}{2}$, to which is added the cost saving premium. The second variety consists in piece wages as basic wages, to which comes the cost saving premium.

In modern times it is those cost saving premiums that have especially gained in importance which are based on a correspondingly developed internal cost accounting system. Within the framework of the plan cost accounting a premium pattern can be applied on the understanding that, as a basis for the premium, we take the degree of approximation of the actual costs to the lower planned costs or the decrease below the higher planned costs.

As an essential feature for the additional premiums we should once more point out the fact that they are not directly based upon the (quantitative) measures of time and quantity and, therefore, do not create wage patterns insofar as their measures cannot be united with the time and quantity measures already incorporated in the basic wages, to form a uniform measure and, consequently, the additional premiums cannot be merged with the basic wages to form a uniform combined wage pattern. They come in addition to wages of a certain form as special supplementary remunerations.

According to their character the wage patterns, under the viewpoint of their independence, must be divided into:

1. Autonomous wage forms (time and piece gauging), which occur as functions of the time or quantity of the performance;

2. Dependent wage forms (additional premium wage forms) which can at the utmost be expressed as functions of other measures.

Many additional premiums do not take the shape of a (dependent) wage form. By way of example the punctuality premiums are mostly paid as one-time premiums. This goes also for many other additional premiums which occur in practice. Consequently the additional premiums can be classified as follows:

1. Additional premiums in the shape of a (dependent) wage form, acting as a function of certain measures (but not of time or quantity);

2. Additional premiums in the shape of one-time premium payments.

For the premiums of the first group a fixed functional relation between premium basis and premium amount is established from the outset, which is always taken into account when the wages are paid out and goes for several or all conceivable stages of the premium base. This is not so with the additional premium of the second group. For reasons of special performance they are mostly given as one-time payments without showing any further graduation or regularity.

Whereas the additional premiums in the shape of a dependent wage form can be regarded as a means in wage policy and technique, a delimitation against the wage rate differentiation is necessary in the shape of one-time premium payments (based upon the individual performance). In the wage rate differentiation a wage rate increase, on account of higher individual performance in the past, is made for a certain future period; the new wage rate is then effective for the whole of this limited time. In case of the one-time payment of the additional premium, however, the wage payment is made on the basis of the work done, without the higher remuneration being regularly paid from then on.

The additional premiums have latterly attained more practical importance everywhere. Generally, they can be characterized by the fact that they show a tendency towards a certain performance increase which agrees with the changing basis of gauging the additional premium. Thus, quality premiums lead, for example, to a qualitative performance increase. In that case we have a positive quality premium contrary to the pure time wages, which are characterized as negative quality wages insofar as they show a qualitative tendency because of the absence of a quantitative production increase. Cost saving premiums aim at a rise in savings performance. The extent of the effect of the additional premiums depends upon their individual structure, especially the amount of the premium. Under certain circumstances, high incentive effects of the additional premiums may endanger other aspects of performance. When applying additional premiums it should be borne in mind that the additional premiums do not mar the envisaged effects of underlying autonomous wage forms. It is the idea to find a sensible optimum combination of basic and additional premiums in accordance with the specific performance situation.

2. *Premium Time Wages*

a) *Bonus and Graded Wages.* In the premium time wages there is, as mentioned previously, a double possibility of the establishment of premiums depending upon whether one issues from a fixed work quantity (pensum, task) or from a fixed working time.

In the first case ($q =$ constans) a *maximum standard time* t_0 is established. When this is reached or understepped, a certain percentage of the hourly wages is added as a premium (speed premium). When we denote the fixed additional percentage by p_0, the following general formulae result for the hourly earnings and the labour costs *on time basis:*

$$s = s_0 \qquad t > t_0 \tag{41}$$

$$s = s\left(1+\frac{p_0}{100}\right) = s_0+\sigma_0 \qquad t \leqq t_0 \tag{42}$$

and

$$l = s_0 t \qquad t > t_0 \tag{43}$$

$$l = s_0 t\left(1+\frac{p_0}{100}\right) = (s_0+\sigma_0)t \qquad t \leqq t_0. \tag{44}$$

In words:

As soon as the time used on the performance reaches the standard time or remains below it, the hourly wages multiply themselves by a *premium factor* (formed analogous to the interest factor of the compound interest computation). At the same time the labour costs multiply themselves by the same factor.

The graphic presentation is shown by Fig. 15. Here we have interrupted discontinuous curves, showing a jump point $t = t_0$. For the rest they run like the curves of the pure time wages in Fig. 1.

In the second case (t = constans) a certain *minimum standard quantity* q_0 is prescribed. When this is reached or exceeded, the percentage p_0

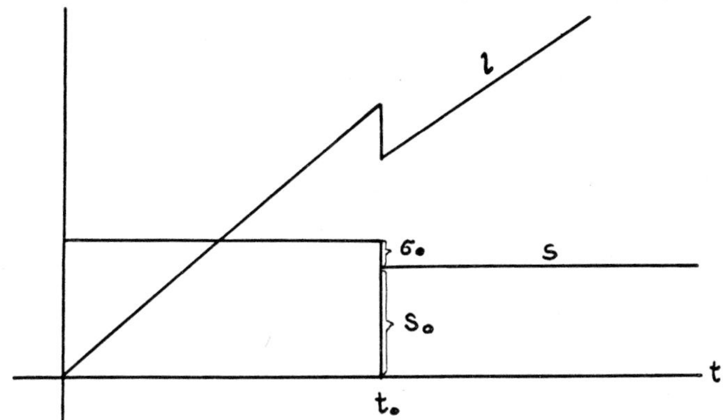

Fig. 15. Bonus wages.

(quantity premium) comes in addition to the hourly wages. On this account the following formulae are found *on piece basis:*

$$s = s_0 \qquad q < q_0 \tag{45}$$

$$s = s_0\left(1+\frac{p_0}{100}\right) = s_0+\sigma_0 \qquad q \geqq q_0 \tag{46}$$

$$l = \frac{s_0}{q} \qquad q < q_0 \tag{47}$$

$$l = \frac{s_0}{q}\left(1+\frac{p_0}{100}\right) = \frac{s_0+\sigma_0}{q} \qquad q \geqq q_0. \tag{48}$$

Fig. 16 shows the corresponding broken curves, which (otherwise analogous to Fig. 6) are discontinuous at the point $q = q_0$.

Premium time wages of this kind are called *bonus wages* according to H. L. Gantt. At the jump point, characteristic for these bonus wages, the quantitative element of the equivalence principle becomes apparent. As long as the time or quantity targets are not attained, it recedes as in the pure time wages. Not until the accomplishment of the target are the wages adapted to the performance. The premium has to agree to a performance accomplished in a shorter time or with a larger quantity, respectively. Contrary to a regularly proceeding, continuous agreement we have here a later and discontinuous adjustment of wages and performance. At the *jump point* the labour costs, coinciding with rising performance, go up suddenly for a moment, to go down again later. The premium may not be chosen too high, as otherwise it would be more economical for the enterprise to work with a smaller performance quantity, but with lower labour costs. The unsteadiness in the shape of a "limping" premium is of much influence on the subjective element of the performance increase.

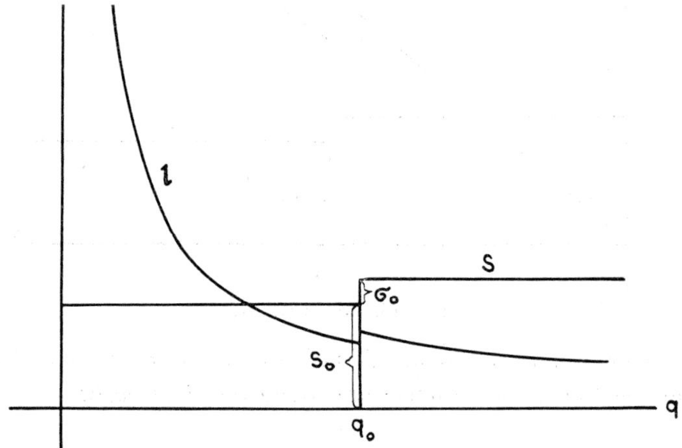

Fig. 16. Bonus wages.

The premium loses its stimulus as soon as the attainment of the desired higher performance, on account of an incorrect estimate of the standard rates, proves to be impossible or the premium appears to be too low and unequal to the work increase. The result of the bonus wages, therefore, depends essentially on the economically correct establishment both in the standard rates and in the additional premium. Since Gantt has afterwards worked out a piece wage system as a link-up with Taylor's, the one-stage premium time wages are also designated as Gantt I.

It is endeavoured to avoid the big danger of the ineffectiveness, which is comprised in this establishment, by a previously inserted transition premium or a formal *graduation* of the premiums. Several time stages $t_1, t_2, t_3, \ldots t_n$ are fixed, with which very definite percentages $p_1, p_2, p_3, \ldots p_n$ are in agreement, so that the following formulae can be made up for the time wages with graded premiums *on time basis:*

$$(49)\quad s = s_0\left(1+\frac{p_n}{100}\right) = s_0+\sigma_n$$

$$(50)\quad l = s_0 t\left(1+\frac{p_n}{100}\right) = s_0+\sigma_n t \qquad (t_{n+1} < t \leqq t_n,\ n = 1, 2, 3, \ldots).$$

The graphic presentation produces time wage curves showing "breaks" in several places. The *points of discontinuity* (generally) lie on some given curve. To do Gantt credit, such unsteady premiums are generally designated as bonus premiums. We also speak of a *bonus principle* in the sense of a principle of discontinuity of the wage curves.

Two methods of premium graduation with a *constant premium rate* are of great importance, theoretically. In the first place the time stages are established in equal periods whose length is immaterial. The premium can be granted either as a percentage of the *originally* valid hourly earnings or as a percentage of the hourly earnings obtained *each time.* In the former case they are termed arithmetically graded, in the latter case geometrically graded premium time wages.

In the event of *arithmetical graduation,* by substitution of:

(51) $$p_n = np$$

the following formulae are obtained:

(52) $$s = s_0\left(1+\frac{np}{100}\right)$$

$$(t_{n+1} < t \leqq t_n,\ n = 1, 2, 3, \ldots).$$

(53) $$l = s_0 t\left(1+\frac{np}{100}\right)$$

For the *geometrical graduation* we find:

(54) $$s = s_0\left(1+\frac{p}{100}\right)^n$$

$$(t_{n+1} < t \leqq t_n,\ n = 1, 2, 3, \ldots).$$

(55) $$l = s_0 t\left(1+\frac{p}{100}\right)^n$$

The premium relative to the original hourly earnings can be computed after a somewhat complicated formula. Not much simpler is the expression for the extra pay, based upon the hourly earnings attained each time. On the other hand the *quotient* of two consecutive hourly earnings is constant, viz.:

(56) $$\frac{s_{n+1}}{s_n} = 1+\frac{p}{100}.$$

The graphic presentation of both graded wages is supplied by the Figs. 17 and 18. The points of discontinuity lie on a certain continuous curve. In the event of arithmetical graduation the earnings curve is a straight line (s_{n+1}—$s_n = 0.01\ s_0 p =$ constans), the cost curve is a parabola.

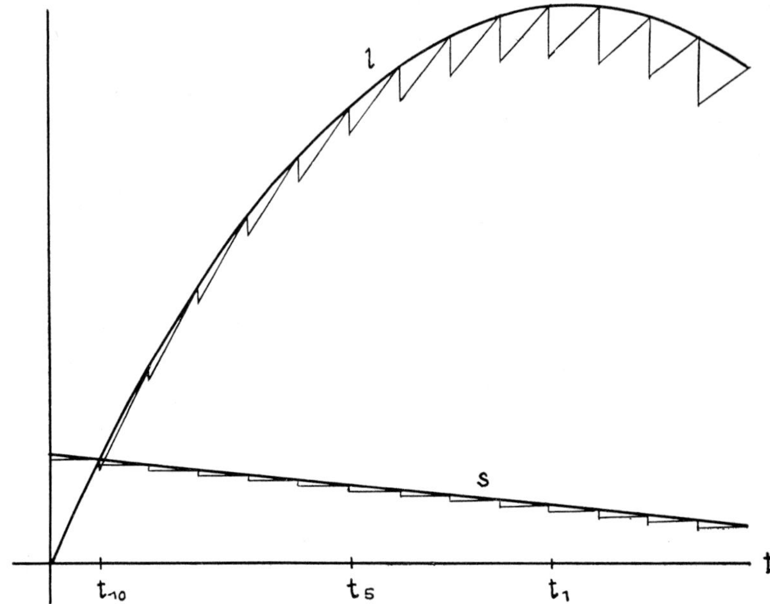

Fig. 17. Arithmetical graduation.

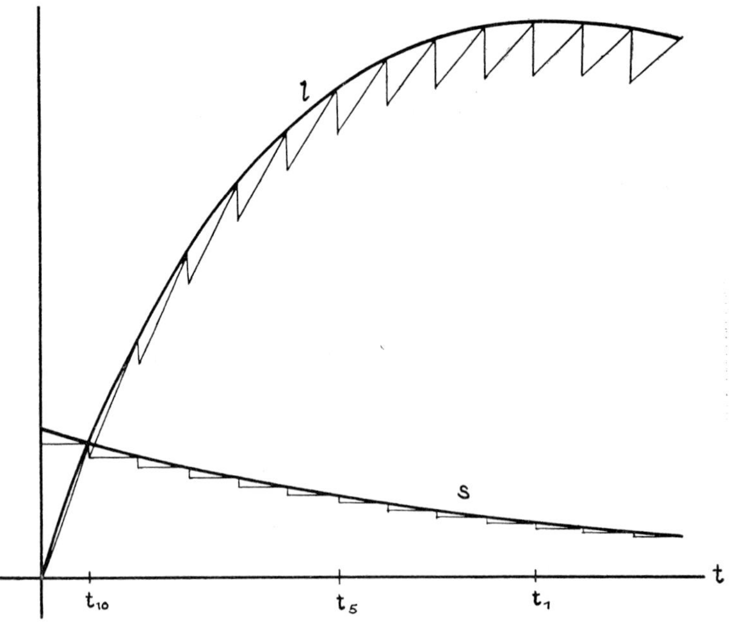

Fig. 18. Geometrical graduation.

In case of geometrical graduation we have transcendent curves, and the earnings curve is an exponential curve $\left((s_n+1)/s_n = 1+0.01\,p = \text{constans}\right)$.

For the validity of the equivalence principle the following result is obtained.

For the two graded wages the hourly earnings are a finite quantity at the limit $t = 0$, i.e. at this point they are in agreement with Rowan wages and pure time wages, as opposed to Halsey wages and pure piece wages. This top limit, in case of too high an estimate of the standard time t_0, lowers the danger of an over-payment of the performance (cp. Rowan wages). Whereas in the event of arithmetical graduation, however, the hourly earnings increase in a linear way, they rise more slowly at first under geometrical graduation, but after that considerably more rapidly. Correspondingly, the labour costs decrease in both graded wage forms. It may be said that the geometrical graduation better answers the actual excess performance, i.e. subjectively represents also a stronger impetus towards work increase. On the other hand, the arithmetical graduation is in order where the performance is deliberately kept below a certain limit.

If, in the graduation of the premiums, one starts out from a fixed working time, various quantity stages $q_1, q_2, q_3, \ldots q_n$ and related percentages for additional pay $p_1, p_2, p_3, \ldots p_n$ are established. It is not required to carry out the calculation of these graduations, especially of the arithmetical and geometrical ones, *on piece basis*, since the result can be easily obtained. We find analogous formulae and curves. Therefore only the formulae for the arithmetically graded premium time wages shall be given:

$$(57)\quad s = s_0+\sigma_n = s_0\left(1+\frac{np}{100}\right)$$

$$(q_n \leqq q < q_{n+1},\ n = 1, 2, 3, \ldots).$$

$$(58)\quad l = \frac{s_0+\sigma_n}{q} = \frac{s_0}{q}\left(1+\frac{np}{100}\right)$$

The special graded wages under review are of much theoretical importance since they give the evidence that the bonus wages do not represent some ineffective premium wages which are not equal to the extra performance, but – on the contrary – can be worked out with no economic shortcomings and with any desired amount of accuracy.

The premium time wages dealt with so far are based on an *hour premium* (*time premium*) as the bonus σ_n is paid in addition to the hourly earnings (time costs) s_0. When, however, the premium is added as a *piece premium* λ_n to the labour costs, we obtain the following general formulae:

For a *speed premium* ($q=$ constans):

$$(59)\quad s = s_0 + \frac{\lambda n}{t}$$

$$t_{n+1} < t \leqq t_n, \quad n = 1, 2, 3, \ldots.$$

$$(60)\quad l = s_0 t + \lambda n$$

For a *quantity premium* ($t=$ constans):

$$(61)\quad s = s_0 + \lambda_n q$$

$$q_n < q \leqq q_{n+1}, \quad n = 1, 2, 3, \ldots.$$

$$(62)\quad l = \frac{s_0}{q} + \lambda_n$$

In this connection it should be noted that the piece premium – unlike the hour premium – cannot be expressed as a percentage of the labour costs per piece, since the latter would then change during the periods, i.e. between the points of unsteadiness. We only wish to point out that also here we can set up special premium time wages with arithmetical and geometrical graduation.

From the formulae the *structural difference* between hour premium and piece premium is clearly apparent. According to (49) the *hourly earnings* between the premium stages remain constant, whereas after (59) with the piece premium they rise hyperbolically with decreasing time. Correspondingly, according to (50), the *labour costs* per piece go down within each graduation stage in proportion to the time, i.e. more strongly than in the preceding period, whereas with the piece premium after (60) they diminish evenly within each graduation stage in a linear way with decreasing time. Or, in other words (always pre-supposing a finite premium): In the hour premium the hourly earnings always remain finite, whereas the labour costs per piece eventually disappear. With piece premiums the hourly earnings ultimately grow to an infinite degree, whilst the labour costs never completely disappear. These conditions are schematically shown by the Figs. 19 and 20.

When comparing the graduation on a time basis (i.e. on the basis of a speed premium) with the graduation on a piece basis (i.e. on the basis of a quantity premium), it must be emphasized that the two methods differ essentially in their results. In point of structure, they are fundamentally different things, whether a premium is paid for the smaller amount of time used or for the higher quantity produced. Both methods lead to equal premiums only when the unit of quantity is produced exactly within the unit of time. But if t hours are needed for the quantity unit, the premium on piece basis is not graded in the same way as that on time basis. When, conversely, q pieces are produced within the time unit, the graduation after time is not equal to that based upon the number of pieces.

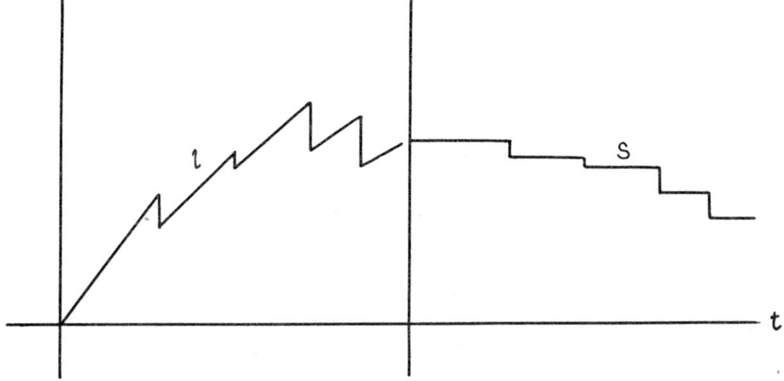

Fig. 19. Time premiums.

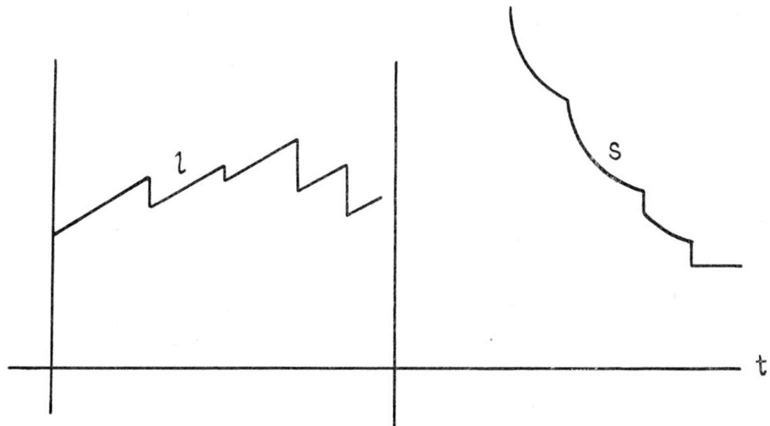

Fig. 20. Piece premiums.

b) *Regular and Continuous Premium Wages.* We can speak of *regular* premium wages when the points of discontinuity lie on a definable curve. This is already the case when the intervals between the various performance stages and the percentages to be added are chosen in accordance with a certain law. In this way, the time stages t_n and the quantity stages

q_n are established in arithmetical order, i.e. in the order of the values of 1, 2, 3, ... in the special graded wages under discussion. By way of example also the geometrical order 1, 3, 9, ... or any desired systematic progression can be chosen. The jump points would always be on a certain curve. I, therefore, suggest a sub-division into regular and irregular premium time wages.

The *irregular* premium time wages comprise the one-graded and most of the multi-graded premium time wages. Besides the systems of Gantt I, Baum and Diemer we should, for example, refer to the premium pattern by Parkhurst. Originally, Parkhurst I has modified Gantt I's pattern in such a way that the bonuses to the time wages, depending upon the kind of work performance (simple operation of machine tools or assembly which requires special skill) are measured at different values. Later, Parkhurst II has made his pattern more conform to piece wages. At 60 % of the standard performance a bonus to the value of 7 % of the original wage rate is granted, then the hourly earnings run in a linear (but under-proportional) way up to a break point at standard performance, where they pass over into the form of the (proportional) piece wages.

An irregular course is taken also by similar wage patterns originating from Anglo-Saxon countries, like for example the premium systems by H. Emerson, C. E. Knoeppel, Carle M. Bigelow and E. K. Wennerlund. These wage patterns are distinguished from one another by only minor differences and have been developed for special circumstances within enterprises.

Between 67 % and 100 % of the standard output, H. Emerson grants a gradually rising premium on basis of a worked-out bonus plan. Upon reaching the standard performance the time premium amounts to 20 % of the time wage rate. From that point onward the worker receives piece wages at the original time wage rate, so that the form $s = l_0 q + \sigma$ of premium piece wages ($l_0 = s_0 t_0$ and $\sigma = 0{,}2\, s_0$) is obtained, which runs under-proportionally. The patterns by C. E. Knoeppel and Carle M. Bigelow are derivatives of the Emerson wage plan. With Knoeppel the premiums are slightly higher, to which another 5 % premium is added at standard performance. With Bigelow the hourly earnings go up under-proportionally as from the standard performance after the shape of the Halsey wage plan, i.e. by an increase which is smaller than that of the piece wage curve. The wage pattern by E. K. Wennerlund is very similar to that of Emerson as far as the standard performance, and from then on – as it passes over into the pure piece wages – it concords with the Parkhurst wages. The premium systems of Wennerlund and Parkhurst consequently represent transitions from time wages to ultimate piece wages as from the standard performance.

All these wage forms represent *combinations* of the continuous Halsey wages (at different premium measures) and of the pure piece wages with the time wages and with the one- or multi-graded bonus principle, so that *broken connections* arise from continuous components (wage form branches) which are joined either by break points or by jump points.

The premium time wages further comprise the *gain sharing wages* already amply discussed above. Under the Halsey and Rowan wage plans the time wages are basic wages.

Under the *Rowan wage plan* the worker receives, according to (26), a percentage of his basic wages as a bonus, which is equal to the percentage of time he saves. This can therefore clearly be designated as a premium time wage. In the *Halsey wage plan* this is still doubtful at first. When studying formula (23), however, it becomes evident that the worker receives a multiple of his basic wages as a premium, which is equal to a fixed fraction of the pieces produced in percent over and above the target. This is based on the fact that, besides time, also the number of pieces as an independent variable is used in the investigations. In this way, however, the Halsey wages are likewise characterized as premium time wages.

The listing of the Halsey wage plan under the premium time wages introduces a completely new viewpoint into the approach. Now it is possible also to regard the *piece wages* as premium time wages. For in his piece wages the worker receives as a premium a percentage of his basic wages equalizing the percentage by which the number of pieces is surpassed. The concept of the premium must in this case be extended a little, by regarding the premium (7) so far called "apparent" as a real one. It is still undecided whether this view is effective both from a structural and systematic point of view. A point in its favour is, at any rate, that every establishment of a piece wage rate is founded on a time wage rate, which, however, is not manifested until multiplication by a fixed period of time.

If, however, one follows the new point of view, the gain sharing methods can be explained in a much more general form.

In formula (20) the value of the premium measure κ is to denote a positive fraction. If this limitation $\kappa < 1$ is dropped, we find as a *general Halsey premium*

$$\text{(63)} \qquad \sigma = \kappa s_0 \frac{t_0 - t}{t} \quad \text{or} \quad \sigma = \kappa s_0 \frac{q - q_0}{q_0}, \text{ respectively,}$$

in which the premium measure κ can be any positive rational number.

The case $\kappa < 0$ is fundamentally excluded, as then we no longer have premium time wages. Practically, a top limit for $\kappa > 0$ is also given when the extra costs are no longer in an economic proportion to the extra performance. For $\kappa < 1$ we find the intermediate forms obtained so far; for $\kappa > 1$ we have new wage forms which, in their economic effects in the direction of the quantitative side, exceed the piece wages. They are also designated as *progressive piece wages.* For $\kappa = 1$ the piece wages no longer appear as a limit case, but as a special case "in the middle", as so-called proportional piece wages. The Figs. 7–10 can easily be completed with $\kappa > 1$.

Likewise the formulae (26) and (29) can for the Rowan wage plan be substituted by the *general Rowan premium*

$$\text{(64)} \qquad \sigma = \kappa s_0 \frac{t_0 - t}{t_0} \quad \text{or} \quad \sigma = \kappa s_0 \frac{q - q_0}{q} \quad \text{respectively,}$$

in which the premium measure κ can again be any positive rational number. For $\kappa < 1$ we then find the intermediate forms used so far. But for $\kappa > 1$ we obtain wage forms which, in their economic effect, exceed the special Rowan wages $\kappa = 1$. While, however, for $\kappa \leqq 1$ the labour costs decrease for every case of $t < t_0$, since $t_0(\kappa + 1/2\kappa)$ is always $\geqq t_0$, the piece costs for $\kappa > 1$ first rise for $t_0(\kappa + 1/2\kappa) < t < t_0$ (the more strongly, the larger the premium measure κ of the premium), after which they also decline after a maximum for $t = t_0(\kappa + 1)2\kappa$. It should not be difficult to complete the Figs. 13 and 14 correspondingly.

Now the *question* arises: How are the gain sharing wages distinguished from the other (structurally different) premium time wages? A more profound study reveals that this difference is to be found in the form of the premium.

In the other premium time wages the premium is an always fixed invariable additional pay to the hourly earnings or to the labour costs, respectively, which remains unaltered also in the event of further saving of time or higher quantity performance until the next stage is reached. Even when the intervals between the stages are put down to the lowest value, when for instance the premiums progress from piece to piece, the premium proper still remains independent of the target performance. It is simply constant or *fixed.*

In the gain sharing wages, however, the premium is, from the outset, a certain function dependent upon the performance, which goes uniformly for the total continuous course of the independent value (time or quantity). It is simply variable or *functional.*

Consequently, we can distinguish *two groups* of premium time wages:

1. Time wages with constant, fixed or independent premium
2. Time wages with variable, functional or dependent premium.

Either of the two groups can be adjusted both to a time basis (speed premium) or to a piece basis (quantity premium). Either of the two premiums can figure both as an additional pay to the hourly earnings (time premium) and as an additional pay to the labour costs per piece (piece premium).

It can be observed that the premium time wages with simple dependent or functional premium can be rightly termed *continuous*, since we have here a strictly steady course of the curves. Correspondingly, the other premium time wages are termed *discontinuous*. The related curves run in grades steps, i.e. in a broken form with jump points (points of discontinuity).

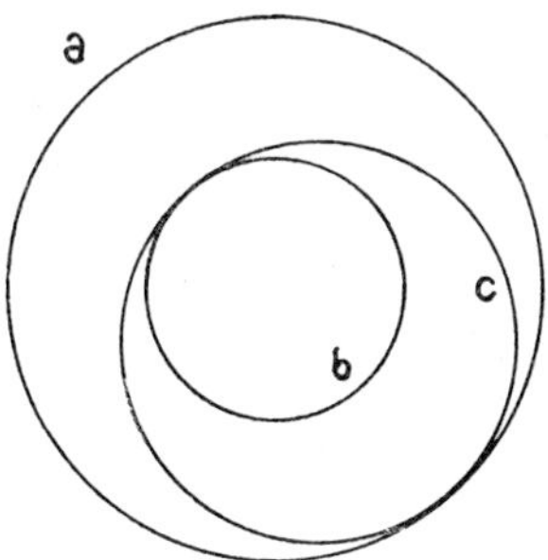

Fig. 21. Symbol of the premium division.

How does this division into continuous and step premium time wages compare with the former division into regular and irregular premium time wages?

Continuous premiums are always regular, and irregular premiums are always stepped. On the other hand, step premiums can be both regular and irregular, and regular premiums can be both stepped and continuous. The following scheme (Fig. 21) is to illustrate these concept relations.

The large circle *a* denotes the totality of all premiums. The small concentric circle *b* represents the continuous premiums and the middle circle *c*, which is tangent to the two others, represents the regular premiums. Then the circle ring *ab* contains the step premiums. The larger half-moon *ac* denotes stepped irregular and the smaller half-moon *bc* stepped regular premiums. The more comprehensive image contains in each case the more comprehensive concepts.

In this way we obtain the following *classification* of the premiums:

1. *Irregular premiums:* $\sigma_n = c_n$.

   The premium is established arbitrarily and without any rule. It comprises all one-graded bonus wages and most of the multi-graded step wages (graded or step wages).

2. *Regular premiums:*

$$\sigma_n = \varphi_{(n)}, \quad t_n = \psi_{(n)}, \quad \text{or} \quad \sigma_n = f(t_n).$$

The premium is established according to rule.

a) *Regular step premiums* (regular graded premiums):

$$t_n \neq t \quad \text{or} \quad \sigma_n \neq f(t), \text{ respectively.}$$

The premium is established periodically. The premium function only goes for certain times t_n. For these the hourly earnings and the labour costs each lie on a determinable curve. Between them both follow the curves of the pure time wages. The times t_n themselves are points of discontinuity (jump points) within the course of the curves. Cp. Figs. 17 and 18: Arithmetically and geometrically graded wages.

b) *Continuous premiums:*

$$t_n = t \quad \text{or} \quad \sigma_n = f(t), \text{ respectively.}$$

The premium is established continuously. The premium function goes for each time t. The connecting curves mentioned before pass over into the curves of the hourly earnings and of the labour costs themselves. The Halsey and Rowan wages belong here.

The same classification is arrived at under appropriate changes if, instead of the time, the number of pieces is chosen as an independent variable, or if eventually, instead of a time premium, we proceed from a piece premium. The following *connections* should be observed: Every regularity or function of the premium based upon time entails a corresponding relation to the quantity, and the reverse, whilst the reciprocal values

$$t_n \rightarrow \frac{1}{q_n} \quad \text{or} \quad q_n \rightarrow \frac{1}{t_n} \tag{65}$$

are substituted. Every time premium entails a certain piece premium, because we always have the relation:

(66) $\lambda_n = \sigma_n t$ or $\sigma_n = \lambda_n q$, respectively.

Generally speaking, the premium time wages are marked from a labour-economic angle by the fact that they add a basic premium to the non-quantitative (i.e. indirectly qualitative) time wages, in order to achieve in this way a temporal quantitative increase of the work performance. With the one-graded bonus wages the achievement of a fixed pensum is aimed at by means of a strongly retarded premium, whilst the graded wages aim rather at a fundamental performance increase in each point of the continuous flow of the work process, at any rate, however, at certain stages. The closest adaptation to the performance is made possible by the use of continuous premiums. Before everything, they are appropriate when the work process is susceptible to considerable fluctuation which cannot be avoided. We can hardly say more, generally, on the economic structure of the premium time wages. They are too strongly differentiated for each premium, so that the common properties are of quite an elementary nature, whilst the subtle differences come into prominence in a decisive manner. This goes also for the subjective stimulus towards the temporal quantitative performance increase and the indirect thwarting of qualitative labour, as well as for the guarantee of permanent performances.

By the appropriate selection of the premium function, by the effective establishment of the stage periods, by the use of continuous premiums and, finally, by the purposeful determination of the premium measure (for instance for Halsey and Rowan wages) an almost unending multitude of *variations* can be achieved, to adapt the premium time wages to the existing work procedure. In this, every desired course of hourly earnings, as well as every envisaged movement of the piece costs (whether it be with a constant, rising or falling tendency) can be attained. Further subtle details in wage planning are possible through the selection of the point of issue, depending upon whether they are founded upon a speed or quantity premium or a time or piece premium, respectively. In this way forms of the premium time wages can be obtained, which in the development of their earnings and costs not only approach the pure piece wages, but also far exceed their economic effects.

The classification of premiums set up is of *general validity*. It not only refers to basic premiums, i.e. to premium time wages and the premium piece wages (to be dealt with later), but also to the additional premiums discussed earlier.

c) *Sales and Success Premiums.* At the beginning of the study of premium wages the concept of the premium as a *wage premium* was limited to the case of a conditioned extra wage pay as a compensation for a special work performance conditioning it. Thus, generally speaking, gratuities, remunerations, extra pay, profit and revenue sharing, etc. were excluded. This limitation should be examined a little more closely.

While from the outset the wages were also understood to be a function of the performance quantity, they were generally measured by the number of pieces produced, and the *piece* was taken as a unit of performance. Thus, the case of the industrial worker's wages came into prominence as a typical example for reasons of simplicity and greater clarity. For the salary, the wages of the commercial and technical employee, circumstances are different. Here, the purely quantitative number of pieces cannot always serve as a yardstick for the performance. Instead, it is frequently necessary to select a unit based on *value*. Of course, there is nothing against designating it merely as a "piece" again in the sense of the unit of performance. This leads to the question of *sales commission.*

As a unit of performance let us assume a sale of DM 100.—. Then a sale of, say, DM 100,000.— equals 1,000 units of performance. If now the fixed monthly salary be taken as s_0, and u be the monthly sale, correspondingly $q = 0.01\ u$ the number of performance units (sales units) and p_0 be taken as the fixed rate of commission (a percentage of the sales u), we find the following formulae for the monthly earnings (= time costs) and the labour costs per unit produced (= piece costs):

$$s = s_0 + p_0 q = s_0 + p_0 \frac{u}{100} \tag{67}$$

$$l = \frac{s_0}{q} + p_0 = \frac{100 s_0}{u} + p_0 . \tag{68}$$

In words:

The *time costs* equal the fixed monthly salary plus the sales commission. The *piece costs* are equal to the fixed monthly salary as a percentage of the sales plus the fixed rate of commission.

It is recognized that the sales commission represents a *continuous* wage premium. It is a fixed piece premium p_0 or a time premium $p_0 q$ directly proportional to the quantity produced and must be designated as a special *sales premium.*

The usual achievement of sales acts can, from an angle of economics and organization, be compared simply with the technical work performance done by any worker in the workshop. For that reason, the extension of the *concept of quantity* (as a volume) to performance units expressed in money (e.g. sales values) can be defended. Insofar as, in the sales sector, no real economic decisions which influence the profit are concerned, the activities connected with sales can be regarded as those of a *technical* nature.

The wage character of a compensation, which is determined by the sales, is not lost until the sales values only represent the measure for a participation in the profit on the basis of entrepreneurial decisions.

For the usual sales commission one can proceed from the fact that the time wages (salary) granted pre-supposes a certain sales quantity and that the surpassing of this leads to a certain premium. Since the gauging of the wages is here founded on the sales quantity per unit of time, the sales commission has the character of a basic premium.

The *manager's commission*, which is gauged after the internal performance profit, can also be designated as a wage premium, because it is also a compensation for the performances within the scope of *technical* rationality. It aims at a minimizing of costs in the sense of technical efficiency (technicity) and appears as an additional premium (cost saving premium), because it is an addition to wages (time wages, piece wages or basic premium wages) and has a different basis of gauging (internal performance profit) from basic wages.

Whilst the extension of the quantity concept as a performance volume to sales activities of the kind indicated can be defended in this connection and, therefore, the sales commission represents an autonomous wage form, an extension of the quantity concept to units of the internal performance profit is not possible. Here it appears more sensible to proceed from the idea that in the first place time and quantity (in a narrower sense) provide the measure for gauging the wages. Thus, the manager's commission appears in the shape of a *dependent* wage form.

To represent the manager's commission, the internal performance profit can best be taken at DM 100.— for a unit of performance. Then a profit of, say, DM 10,000 equals 100 units of performance. If we now let the fixed monthly salary be s_0 again, the monthly profit e, the number of performance units correspondingly $q = 0.01\ e$ and the commission rate (as a percentage of the profit e) p_0, the following analogous formulae are found:

(69) $$s = s_0 + p_0 q = s_0 + p_0 \frac{e}{100}$$

(70) $$l = \frac{s_0}{q} + p_0 = \frac{100 s_0}{e} + p_0.$$

In words:

The time costs equal the fixed monthly salary plus the monthly commission. The piece costs are equal to the fixed monthly salary as a percentage of the profit plus the commission rate.

We can observe that also the manager's commission represents a continuous wage premium, viz. a fixed piece premium or a time premium which is proportional to the performance quantity. It is to be designated as a special *result premium.*

Sales and result premiums are genuine wage premiums only in the sense of the terminology used so far if the completed performance actually represents the measure for the gauging, when therefore the sales or the result are measures for the work performance. Normally, the sales will, for the salesman or sales manager, be in positive correlation to his work performance, even though often the limits set up here are practically narrow. This relation of dependence, however, is very doubtful in the usual computation of the manager's commission. In practice, we can only speak of a real wage premium when a monthly profit (as opposed to an enterprise profit as per balance-sheet) is calculated which is to a very great extent the measure for the internal performance of the manager in the sense of technicity.

It should be pointed out that sales and result premiums may also occur as discontinuous one- and multigraded *step premiums* (graduation of the premium percentages after the magnitude of sales and results). For instance, for sales premiums:

(71) $$s = s_0 + p_n q = s_0 + p_n \frac{u}{100} \quad \text{for} \quad u_n \leqq u < u_{n+1}.$$

As constant *time premiums* they occur as salary increases in the event of rising sales or results, e.g.

(72) $$s = s_0 + \sigma_n \quad \text{for} \quad u_n \leqq u < u_{n+1}.$$

Finally, let us observe that sales and result premiums can also be chosen as *speed premiums* (on time basis) with fixed sales or result, for instance:

(73) $$s = s_0 + \sigma_0 \quad \text{for} \quad t \leqq t_0 \quad \text{and} \quad u = u_0.$$

3. *Premium Piece Wages*

a) *General Classification.* For the premium piece wages we find the same classification as for the premium time wages: irregular, regular, graded and continuous premiums.

The general formulae for graded time premiums are on piece basis:

$$(74) \quad s = l_0 q + \sigma_n$$

$$q_n \leqq q < q_{n+1}, \quad n = 1, 2, 3, \ldots$$

$$(75) \quad l = l_0 + \frac{\sigma_n}{q}$$

and on *time basis:*

$$(76) \quad s = \frac{l_0}{t} + \sigma_n$$

$$t_{n+1} < t \leqq t_n, \quad n = 1, 2, 3, \ldots$$

$$(77) \quad l = l_0 + \sigma_n t$$

In the first case of a *quantity premium* we have a fixed period of time. As soon as the prescribed performance stage q_n is reached, the hourly earnings suddenly increase by the premium σ_n. Between two performance stages q_n and q_{n+1} they go up linearly. The labour costs per piece rise at the jump points, in between they go down hyperbolically.

In the second case of a *speed premium* a fixed work quantity is given. As soon as the prescribed time stage t_n is arrived at, the hourly earnings increase here, too, by the premium σ_n. Between two time stages t_n and t_{n+1}, however, they decrease hyperbolically. The labour costs per piece go up at the jump points, elsewhere they fall linearly with the duration of time without ever disappearing completely.

The general formulae for *graded piece premiums* are on *piece basis:*

$$(78) \quad s = (l_0 + \lambda_n) q$$

$$q_n \leqq q < q_{n+1}, \quad n = 1, 2, 3, \ldots$$

$$(79) \quad l = l_0 + \lambda_n$$

and on *time basis:*

$$(80) \quad s = \frac{l_0 + \lambda_n}{t}$$

$$t_{n+1} < t \leqq t_n, \quad n = 1, 2, 3, \ldots$$

$$(81) \quad l = l_0 + \lambda_n$$

In both cases the hourly earnings increase at the jump points, in between them they run as in the case of pure piece wages. The labour costs per piece go up by steps, but within the stages they remain constant.

When discussing premium time wages we pointed out that – following the conception that the pure piece wages only represent a special case of the premium time wages – the *Halsey* and *Rowan wages* can be generalized to comprise the cases where the premium measure $\kappa > 1$. Then, in their economic effect they surpass that of the pure piece wages. In this connection the general Halsey and Rowan wage plans for $\kappa > 1$ can be characterized as *premium piece wages.*

If, in the Halsey wage pattern, we substitute the premium measure κ by $\kappa = \kappa^*+1$, we arrive at the formula:

$$s = \frac{l_0}{t} + \kappa^* s_0 \frac{t_0-t}{t}, \quad \kappa^* \geqq 0. \tag{82}$$

The Halsey premium appears as a time premium of premium piece wages. For $\kappa^* = 0$ we come to the pure piece wages.

In the Rowan wage plan a simple changing of the equations is not possible, as there are no piece wage curves to be found among the bunch of Rowan curves. Since, however, the curve of the hourly earnings of the special Rowan wages $\kappa = 1$ is tangent to the corresponding piece wage curve, all Rowan curves for $\kappa < 1$ are below it. In this case, therefore, the Rowan wages are decidedly premium piece wages. On the other hand, the Rowan earnings for $\kappa > 1$ lie first over the corresponding piece wage earnings, so that we have to do with genuine premium piece wages. In this connection it should certainly be noted that, starting from a certain $t < t_0$, the Rowan wages again fall below the pure piece wages.

Whilst the premium piece wages – based on time wages as basic wages – normally remain below the pure piece wages with respect to the *quantitative-temporal* performance increase, but in the event of the proper choice of the premium may also surpass them, the premium piece wages – from the viewpoint of labour-economics – are characterized by the fact that, fundamentally, they will raise the subjective element of the principle of equivalence above the effect of the pure piece wages. It was already observed earlier that here the hourly earnings grow proportionally to the number of pieces produced, and thus it was recognized a rigid adaptation to the performance. In this, it is overlooked, however, that under increasing performance the surplus performance becomes more and more difficult, so that ultimately even the proportionality of the hourly earnings is no longer an equivalent for the working effort. This leads to premiums being granted even on piece wages. Premium piece wages are particularly used in the event of work of an *extraordinarily urgent* nature, where – given a fixed limited number of workers – high working intensity is required. In such cases the strong rise in labour costs per piece is economically justified. It is accepted when, for instance, big losses and stagnation in production cannot be avoided in any other way. Connected with the very strong emphasis of the quantitative performance is the indirect neglect of quality. Even bigger than with the pure piece wages is the danger of inferior workmanship. It is only too obvious that labour of such extraordinary intensity cannot be done in the long run. The premium piece wages are nowadays often indicated as *progressive piece wages.*

As to the *piece premium* it should further be noted that the labour costs per piece fundamentally show up a rising tendency, whereas in the other premium wages we may have not only increasing, but also – under certain circumstances – decreasing labour costs. The piece premiums are additional labour costs from the very outset. The recognition of this fact is of great import, economically, since it only justifies *rising* piece rates, when under all circumstances, even with rising labour costs, an increase of the quantitative performance is decisive. It is not intended to aim at lower labour costs per piece, but rather at a rise in production at any price.

Finally, it should be pointed out that, after the aforementioned approach which does not regard the piece wages an as elementary wage form, but rather sees premium time wages in it, the premium piece wages can be regarded as *combined* premium time wages. Instead of a single premium, we have here a combination of various kinds of premiums. Under this aspect of the combination of premiums there arises yet another abundance of fresh possibilities for premium wages.

b) *Taylor Wages and Fundamentals of Compensation Technique.* In connection with his system of scientific management, Frederick Winslow Taylor – in 1884 – introduced a special wage pattern which is referred to as the differential piece wage plan and has been of the greatest importance for the development in the field of wage planning.

When proceeding from a *fixed performance quantity*, the working time required for this task is first ascertained by means of time studies. Taylor still aimed at a relatively high standard of performance, whereas nowadays an average standard is always proceeded from. By multiplying the standard time t_0 by the usual hourly earnings s_0, we find the standard piece wage rate

$$l_0 = s_0 t_0. \tag{83}$$

Then two other piece rates are established, one *increased* by $B\%$ and the other *decreased* by $b\%$. We now have two cases.

If the standard time is *reached* or even *remained under*, the pure piece wages with the increased rate apply:

$$(84)\quad s = \frac{l_0}{t}\left(1 + \frac{B}{100}\right) = \frac{l_0 + C}{t}$$

$$t \leqq t_0 .$$

$$(85)\quad l = l_0\left(1 + \frac{B}{100}\right) = l_0 + C$$

If the standard time is *surpassed*, the pure piece wages with the decreased rate apply:

$$(86)\quad s = \frac{l_0}{t}\left(1 - \frac{b}{100}\right) = \frac{l_0 - c}{t}$$

$$t > t_0 .$$

$$(87)\quad l = l_0\left(1 - \frac{b}{100}\right) = l_0 - c$$

There is yet a third case which, however, does not fit in the graphic representation: if the standard time is reached or remained under, but – on the other hand – the *quality* of the performance remains below standard, a still lower piece rate is applicable.

If a *fixed working time* is proceeded from, an appropriate performance quantity q_0 is ascertained first, based on work studies. The standard piece wage rate is found as follows:

$$(88)\quad l_0 = \frac{s_0}{q_0} .$$

Then, apart from any inferior quality of the performance, two cases are again possible.

If the standard quantity is *attained* or even *exceeded*, the increased rate applies:

$$(89)\quad s = l_0\left(1 + \frac{B}{100}\right) q = (l_0 + C) q$$

$$q \geqq q_0$$

$$(90)\quad l = l_0\left(1 + \frac{B}{100}\right) = l_0 + C$$

but the decreased rate applies to *below*-standard performances:

$$(91)\quad s = l_0\left(1 - \frac{b}{100}\right) q = (l_0 - c) q$$

$$q < q_0 .$$

$$(92)\quad l = l_0\left(1 - \frac{b}{100}\right) = l_0 - c$$

In older literature two viewpoints have generally been raised as characteristic of the Taylor differential wage plan:

1. The *establishing of standard rates* is not made by estimate, but is based upon profound and most possibly exact time or work studies by the method of the computation of elements.

2. Whereas under all other wage plans time wages are guaranteed as minimum wages in the event the target performance is not reached, a cut in wages set in under the Taylor system. The reduction of the piece wage rate has intentionally been chosen in such a way that the worker remains below the usual hourly earnings.

On the other hand, however, it can be said that both aspects are no specific characteristics of the Taylor wage plan. Neither the scientific determination of standard rates nor the cut in the piece wage rates in the event of unattained targets are incorporated in the structural nature of this wage form as such. It is rather to be noted that the Taylor wages are nothing else but one-graded step premium piece wages with fixed piece premiums.

At first sight this gives the impression of being a degrading of the differential piece wages. In exchange for this, however, two fundamentals of the compensation technique, effective for all wage forms, are gained:

I. The principle of the exact determination of standard rates.
II. The principle of the reduction of wages in the event of unattained targets.

In my opinion, Taylor has not created a new wage pattern, but has applied these two fundamental principles to an existing wage plan. And there is nothing against extending them also to the other wage patterns, generally. For, ultimately, the two fundamentals are more special cases of the principle of the equivalence of wages and degree of performance.

In former examinations of the various wage plans it was repeatedly pointed out of how basic importance is the most exact determination possible of standard rates. The piece wage rate can only be ascertained by means of a correct time study. The estimated standard time must agree to the actually required average time of an average worker. In the various premium wages these difficulties more or less strongly recur, but they exist in any case. As long as a practical-arbitrary estimate of the standard rates is made, the time wages are expressly guaranteed as minimum wages to avoid hardship. Consequently, it cannot be doubted that Taylor's exact method of the computation of elements is equally essential to all wage forms.

The principle of cuts in the wages is already met with in pure piece wages. When the actual achievement remains below the estimated standard performance, the piece wage rate lies below the corresponding time wages. In the examination of the gain sharing wages this possibility is taken into account from the outset, whilst it has been expressly emphasized that the guaranteeing of minimum wages does not form part of the character of these wage patterns. This guarantee is based only on a still inadequate estimating method to determine the standard rates. It is evident how Taylor's two basic principles interplay and influence each other. As soon as the exact determination of the standard rates is possible, there is nothing in the way of extending the cutting in wages on account of unattained targets also to other wage forms.

In all the cases where a deficiency in performance is to be imputed to circumstances which are no fault of the worker, *minimum wages* must naturally be paid, which is actually the case on account of existing collective agreements. The fact that frequently guarantee wages are granted for social-political reasons is left out of account here, since it does not form part of the problems around the performance wages, which is what we are dealing with exclusively here.

When judging Taylor's wage pattern from an economic angle, two things shall be kept rigidly apart: First the premium piece wages proper and then the two fundamental principles. These require – in my opinion – *unlimited recognition*, since the success of the Taylor system does not in the last place repose on their application. *Criticism* arises when one forms an opinion on the wage pattern itself. Without exception, it boils down, however, to a criticism of its practical application. Structurally the premium piece wage has already been characterized by its tendency towards the highest temporal-quantitative performance increase and the strong jeopardizing of the quality of performance. This Taylor meets effectively by a stringent system of intensive controls. When, on top of this, the adversaries have pointed to the brutality and rigour of the Taylor wage methods, which were said to lead to a *ruthless exploitation* of the workers, this is directed at a kind of application which is not based on sound economic motives, but private, purely egotistic aspirations. The answer to the *theoretic-scientific* question, however, whether the Taylor method of differential piece wages *must*, according to its character, lead to unlimited exploitation of human labour, is to be answered – after the preceding explanations – absolutely in the negative as long as the underlying principle is a real standard performance, based upon modern conceptions. The complicated and subtle problem of work mechanization, however – as a general problem of the utmost division of labour – does not belong to the special complex of structural and wage-technical questions.

Recapitulating, we can say the following:

1. The fundamental Taylor principles of the compensation technique merit the widest possible application to all wage forms from the viewpoint of enterprise economics. Seen as a whole, they have an absolute validity.

2. The premium piece wages can only be used for certain categories of performance where the quantity is of overriding importance and the quality can be accurately controlled. Like all other kinds of wages, it has its objective limits.

3. A serious word of warning should be given against a schematic transference of the Taylor differential piece wage system – which because of its limitation to a single premium stage represents the lowest wage form differentiation – if the circumstances have not been adequately investigated. The kind of performances, the psychological attitude of the worker and the actual organization are essential conditions for its introduction.

On the Taylor wage form a modification has been made by the wage pattern of Merrick. Whereas Taylor's plan has only one premium stage, Merrick introduces two such stages. The first is established at 83% of the standard performance, the second upon attainment of the standard performance. In either case the premium percentage amounts to 10% of the original base rate. Merrick's wage pattern may be regarded as two-graded step premium piece wages with fixed piece premiums.

Another modification to the Taylor wage plan has been adopted by his collaborator H. L. Gantt. This method, in literature also indicated as Gantt II, guarantees the time wages instead of a cut in wages in the event of unattained targets up to the standard quantity. When the time wage rate is s_0, it increases by a premium σ_0 (e.g. by $33\frac{1}{3}\%$) upon achievement of the pensum q_0. For performance quantities produced $q > q_0$ pure piece wages are granted with the increased piece wage rate $(s_0+\sigma_0)$: $q_0 = l_0'$.

4. *General Step Wages*

We now have to investigate generally the cost tendencies for the various premium periods for all graded premium wages (step wages).

First the *time* is chosen as an independent variable. In this connection it can be presupposed that always:

$$t_{n+1} < t_n, \quad \sigma_{n+1} > \sigma_n, \quad \lambda_{n+1} > \lambda_n. \tag{93}$$

Then a simple study of inequalities gives the following regularities:

a) *Step Premium Time Wages.* 1. The time costs show a tendency constantly going up from one step to another. Within the various step periods they remain unaltered with time premiums, whilst with piece premiums they rise hyperbolically.

2. The piece costs show a rising, constant or falling tendency at the beginning of each step:

With time premiums according as

(94) $$\frac{t_{n+1}}{t_n} \gtreqless \frac{s_0+\sigma_n}{s_0+\sigma_{n+1}} = \frac{100+p_n}{100+p_{n+1}}$$

with piece premiums according as

(95) $$s_n(t_n - t_{n+1}) \lesseqgtr \lambda_{n+1} - \lambda_n;$$

they show a rising, constant or falling tendency at the *end* of each step:

With time premiums according as

(96) $$\frac{t_{n+1}}{t_n} \gtreqless \frac{s_0+\sigma_{n-1}}{s_0+\sigma_n} = \frac{100+p_{n-1}}{100+p_n},$$

with piece premiums according as

(97) $$s_0(t_n - t_{n+1}) \lesseqgtr \lambda_n - \lambda_{n-1}.$$

Within the various step periods the piece costs take a linear descent, more strongly with time premiums than with piece premiums.

b) *Step Premium Piece Wages.* 1. The *time costs* show a tendency which goes up from step to step. Within the various step periods they also rise, but hyperbolically.

2. The *piece costs* increase with piece premiums from step to step and remain unchanged within each step period. With time premiums, however, it shows a rising, constant or falling tendency:

At the beginning of each step according as

(98) $$\frac{t_{n+1}}{t_n} \gtreqless \frac{\sigma_n}{\sigma_{n+1}}$$

at the end of each step according as

(99) $$\frac{t_{n+1}}{t_n} \gtreqless \frac{\sigma_{n+1}}{\sigma_n}.$$

Within the various step periods the piece costs drop slightly along a linear course.

For improved illustration the basic properties of the general step wages can be composed schematically in three Tables. The two Tables 4 and 5 each deal with the premium time wages and the premium piece wages as functions of the performance time; Table 6 shows both step wages as functions of the quantity produced. In the latter case no new insights will come forward, so that the text formulation can be abandoned. Only the differences in meaning in point of the dependence relations should always be borne in mind. Table 6 only gives the indications that differ from the other two tables.

TABLE 4

Premium Time Wages (Step Wages)	with Time Premium		with Piece Premium	
	time costs	piece costs	time costs	piece costs
equations in t	$s_0+\sigma_n$	$(s_0+\sigma_n)t$	$s_0+\frac{\lambda_n}{t}$	$s_0+\lambda_n$
criteria of irregularity	$\sigma_n = c_n$		$\lambda_n = c_n$	
criteria of regularity	$\sigma_n = f(t_n)$		$\lambda_n = f(t_n)$	
tendency at the beginning of the stage periods	increasing	increasing constant decreasing	increasing	increasing constant decreasing
tendency at the end of the stage periods	increasing	increasing constant decreasing	increasing	increasing constant decreasing
tendency within the stage periods	constant	decreasing	increasing	decreasing
curve within the stage periods	parallel to the time axis	straight line through the origin	hyperbola	straight line through $(0, \lambda_n)$
limit for $t = 0$	$s_0+\sigma_n$	0	∞	λ_n
schematic graph	Fig 21		Fig. 22	
subjective element of incentive	strongly pronounced	—	more strongly pronounced	—
objective element of cost reduction	—	strongly enhanced	—	slightly enhanced
permanency of performance	secured		attainable	

When we compare the various basic premium wages one with the other, the following recapitulating conclusion can be drawn for the *economic effect* of their structural character.

1. With a view to the *time costs* (or hourly earnings) and also in regard to the subjective impetus towards top performance the premium piece wages are superior to the premium time wages, and the piece premium is superior to the time premium, too. Therefore, it can be said, in general,

TABLE 5

Premium Piece Wages (Step Wages)	with Time Premium		with Piece Premium	
	time costs	piece costs	time costs	piece costs
equations in t	$\frac{l_0}{t} + \sigma_n$	$l_0 + \sigma_n t$	$\frac{l_0 + \lambda_n}{t}$	$l_0+\lambda_n$
criteria of irregularity	$\sigma_n = c_n$		$\lambda_n = c_n$	
criteria of regularity	$\sigma_n = f(t_n)$		$\lambda_n = f(t_n)$	
tendency at the beginning of the stage periods	increasing	increasing constant decreasing	increasing	increasing
tendency at the end of the stage periods	increasing	increasing constant decreasing	increasing	increasing
tendency within the stage periods	increasing	decreasing	increasing	constant
curve within the stage periods	hyperbola	straight line through $(0, l_0)$	hyperbola	parallel to the time axis
limit for $t = 0$	∞	l_0	∞	$l_0+\lambda_n$
subjective element of incentive	more than strongly pronounced	—	most strongly pronounced	—
objective element of cost reduction	—	hardly possible	—	impossible
permanency of performance	endangered		impossible	

TABLE 6

Step Wages as a Function of the Performance Quantity q	with Time Premium		with Piece Premium	
	time costs	piece costs	time costs	piece costs
criteria of irregularity	$\sigma_n = c_n$		$\lambda_n = c_n$	
criteria of regularity	$\sigma_n = f(q_n)$		$\lambda_n = f(q_n)$	
equations of the premium time wages	$s_0 + \sigma_n$	$\frac{s_0 + \sigma_n}{q}$	$s_0 + \lambda_n q$	$\frac{s_0}{q} + \lambda_n$
curve within the stage periods	parallel to the piece axis	hyperbola	straight line through $(0, s_0)$	hyperbola
limit for $q = 0$	$s_0 + \sigma_n$	∞	s_0	∞
equations of the premium piece wages	$l_0 q + \sigma_n$	$l_0 + \frac{\sigma_n}{q}$	$(l_0 + \lambda_n)q$	$l_0 + \lambda_n$
curve within the stage periods	straight line through $(0, \sigma_n)$	hyperbola	straight line through the origin	parallel to thepiece axis
imit for $q = 0$	σ_n	∞	0	$l_0+\lambda_n$

that the *subjective* element of the equivalence principle of wages and performance is very strong in premium time wages with time premiums, stronger in premium time wages with piece premiums, exceptionally strong in premium piece wages with time premiums, and strongest in premium piece wages with piece premiums. That this element – objectively – first comprises only the quantitative-temporal performance increase has been sufficiently emphasized.

2. In regard to the *piece costs* and thus with a view to a possible cost reduction through increased performance we have, in principle, the reversed order of things. Here we can correspondingly formulate that the *objective* element of the equivalence principle of wages and performance is strongly aided in premium time wages with time premium, less strongly aided in premium time wages with piece premium, that a cost reduction in the event of premium piece wages with time premium is hardly possible and practically impossible in premium piece wages with piece premium.

3. It can be seen that the premium time wages with time premium ensures the permanency of performance, which can also be reached with piece premiums through effective establishment; that, on the other hand, the premium piece wages with time premium jeopardize permanent performances, and even make them impossible as a rule with piece premiums.

4. It has already been recognized that basic premium wages in principle offer no ways to raise the *quality* of performance directly. This is done by additional premiums and other special remunerations.

IV. Classification of the Wage Forms by their Tendency to Cost Changing

1. *Step Approach*

We have to distinguish between the relation of the production increase to hourly earnings (in general: to *time costs*) and to labour costs (in general: to *piece costs*). Both relations are of fundamental importance from the angle of calculation and economic policy.

In general, I denote wages (like Schmalenbach) as (directly) *progressive*, *proportional*, *degressive* or *fixed* in regard to *time costs*, when the latter *rise* more strongly, in the same proportion, less strongly than the number of pieces produced or *not* at all. Instead of the expressions degressive and progressive it is also possible – here and later – to use the denominations *under-* and *over-proportional*.

Let q^* be any chosen base quantity and s^* the related time costs, then for $q > q^*$ always $s \gtreqless s^*$. Apart from the fixity $s = s^*$, progression, proportionality and degression of time costs are expressed by the corresponding *relations:*

$$\text{(100)} \qquad \frac{s-s^*}{q-q^*} = \frac{\Delta s}{\Delta q} \gtreqless \frac{s}{q} \gtreqless \frac{s^*}{q^*}, \quad q > q^*, \quad s > s^*,$$

$$\text{(101)} \qquad \frac{\Delta s}{\Delta q} = \operatorname{tg} \varphi_i \quad \frac{s^*}{q^*} = \operatorname{tg} \alpha \quad (i = 1, 2, \ldots).$$

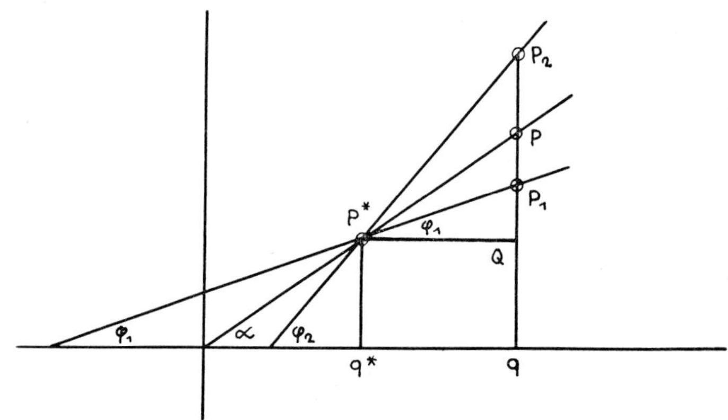

Fig. 22. Direct cost changing tendency.

As appears from Fig. 22, the *proportionality* of time costs becomes manifest by the fact that in this case the two points $P(q, s)$ and $P^*(q^*, s^*)$ lie on a straight line passing through the origin. At the *degression* in P_1 the angle of direction φ_1 is smaller, in *progression* at P_2 the angle φ_2 is larger than the angle of direction α of the straight line passing through the origin. Further, progression, proportionality or degression of time costs, after our definition of the formula (100) correspond with a rise, constancy or fall of related piece costs. In this connection it should be noted that to the fixity of time costs a (stronger) drop in piece costs corresponds, so that we can also speak of ultra-degressive time costs. The inference from the time costs to the piece costs is, therefore, not clearly reversible.

With the piece costs the conditions are more complicated than with time costs insofar as if $q > q^*$, then $1 \gtreqless 1^*$. Apart from the case of the fixity $l = l^*$ – to be anticipated also in this case – two cases can be distinguished.

Supposing $l > l^*$, we find an identical formation of concepts: In general I denote a wage as (directly) *progressive*, *proportional* or *degressive* in regard to the *piece costs*, when the latter *rise* more strongly, in the same proportion or less strongly than the number of pieces produced. The following formulae, analogous to (100) and (101), are found:

$$\text{(102)} \qquad \frac{l-l^*}{q-q^*} = \frac{\Delta l}{\Delta q} \gtreqless \frac{l}{q} \gtreqless \frac{l^*}{q^*}, \quad q > q^*, \quad l > l^*,$$

$$\text{(103)} \qquad \frac{\Delta l}{\Delta q} = \operatorname{tg} \varphi_i \quad \frac{l^*}{q^*} = \operatorname{tg} \alpha \quad (i = 1, 2, \ldots).$$

A special graphic representation appears superfluous.

In case $l < l^*$, we come to an analogous and appropriate conception through inverse transference: In general, I denote wages as *inversely* progressive, proportional or degressive in regard to the piece costs, when the latter *drop* more strongly, in the same proportion or less strongly than the number of pieces produced goes up. This can be expressed in the formula in the following way:

$$\text{(104)} \qquad -\frac{l-l^*}{q-q^*} = -\frac{\Delta l}{\Delta q} \gtreqless \frac{1^*}{q} \gtreqless \frac{l}{q^*}, \quad q > q^*, \quad l < l^*,$$

$$\text{(105)} \qquad -\frac{\Delta l}{\Delta q} = \operatorname{tg} |\varphi_i| \quad \frac{l^*}{q} = \operatorname{tg} |\alpha| \quad (i = 1, 2, \ldots).$$

Please note that now $l - l^* = \Delta l < 0$.

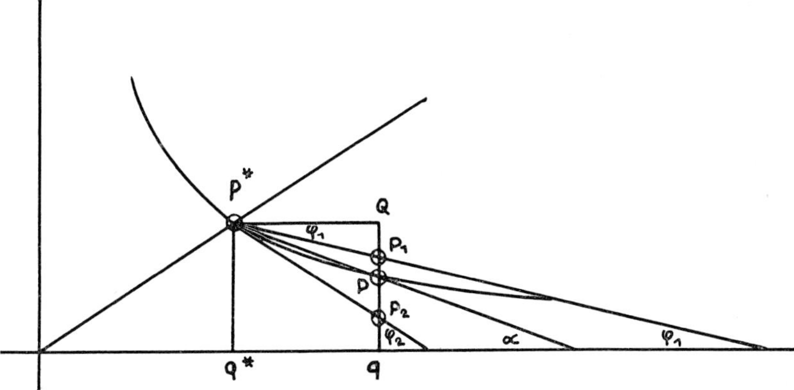

Fig. 23. Reverse cost changing tendency.

As is evident from Fig. 23, the inverse proportionality (reciprocity) is indicated by the fact that in this case the two points $P(q, l)$ and $P^*(q^*, l^*)$ lie on a certain guiding hyperbola (with the co-ordinate axes as asymptotes). Their equation is $lq = l^* q^* =$ constans.

The secant formed by the straight-lined connection corresponds to the straight line through the origin at the direct proportionality. In the event of inverse degression in P_1, the angle of direction φ_1 is absolutely smaller, with inverse progression in P_2, however, the angle φ_2 is absolutely larger than the angle of direction α of the comparison secant. In this connection it should be observed that all these angles have been regarded as negative (supplementary) angles.

In the sense of this definition the pure *time wages* indicate fixed time costs and inversely proportional (reciprocal) piece costs, whereas the pure piece wages have proportional time costs and fixed piece costs.

Another difficulty and obscurity remains unsolved, even in this conception. For it is undecided, from what *commencing quantity* q^* (base quantity) the production increase is to be calculated. It is true that this may be immaterial, but it can also be imagined that, depending upon the selection of the starting point, different results are obtained. When, for instance, the piece quantities q_1, q_2, q_3 are chosen, the wages may indicate progressive time costs with a rise from q_1 to q_2, and degressive time costs from q_2 to q_3, whilst proportional time costs result in a rise from q_1 to q_3.

For the Halsey wages with all modifications the cost changing tendency is independent of the commencing quantity of pieces. When substituting q by a multiple $\rho q^*(\rho > 1)$, we obtain from (24) after a simple calculation:

for $\kappa > 1$ progressive time costs,
for $\kappa < 1$ degressive time costs,
for $\kappa = 1$ proportional time costs.

The usual Halsey wage form ($\kappa < 1$) is therefore always degressive (underproportional).

Things are different with *Rowan wages*, where these conditions are much more complicated. According to (35) a lengthy calculation with inequalities leads to the result that the cost changing tendency depends upon the fraction

$$z = \frac{\kappa q_0}{q^* + \kappa q^* - \kappa q_0}. \tag{106}$$

For any value of κ we find the following classification:

1. $q^* \leqq \dfrac{\kappa}{\kappa+1} q_0$: Progressive time costs.

2. $\dfrac{\kappa}{\kappa+1} q_0 < q^* < \dfrac{2\kappa}{\kappa+1} q_0$: The cost changing tendency

depends upon ρ, i.e. upon the distance between the performance quantity q and the base quantity q^*.

a) $\rho < z$ or $q < \dfrac{\kappa q_0 q^*}{q^* + \kappa q^* - \kappa q_0}$: Progressive time costs,

b) $\rho = z$ or $q = \dfrac{\kappa q_0 q^*}{q^* + \kappa q^* - \kappa q_0}$: Proportional time costs,

c) $\rho > z$ or $q > \dfrac{\kappa q_0 q^*}{q^* + \kappa q^* - \kappa q_0}$: Degressive time costs;

3. $q^* \geqq \dfrac{2\kappa}{\kappa+1} q_0$: Degressive time costs.

We observe a rather complicated dependence of the cost changing tendency on the base quantity q^* as well as the value ρ of the production increase considered.

For the special Rowan wages ($\kappa = 1$) we arrive at the following classification:

1. $q^* \geqq q_0$: Degressive time costs;

2. $q^* < q_0$

   a) $q < \dfrac{q_0 q^*}{2q^* - q_0}$: Progressive time costs,

   b) $q = \dfrac{q_0 q^*}{2q^* - q_0}$: Proportional time costs,

   c) $q > \dfrac{q_0 q^*}{2q^* - q_0}$: Degressive time costs.

If, however, the standard quantity q_0 is chosen as a fixed point of departure, the following result (analogous to the Halsey wages) can be worked out:

1. $\kappa \leqq 1$: Degressive time costs;

2. $\kappa > 1$

   a) $q < \kappa q_0$: Progressive time costs,

   b) $q = \kappa q_0$: Proportional time costs,

   c) $q > \kappa q_0$: Degressive time costs.

It is only for $\kappa > 1$ that a dependence of the value ρ of the production increase exists. For the Halsey wages this special examination is superfluous, since it has already been considered in the general study. In the special Rowan wages ($\kappa = 1$), as always in the usual Halsey wages ($\kappa < 1$), the time costs for $q^* \geqq q_0$ are also degressive (under-proportional).

In the event of the *bonus wages* with *one* premium stage the concept of cost changing tendency is first completely "in the air", because a base quantity q^* for the production increase is lacking. To regard the increase of the hourly earnings upon reaching the standard quantity q_0 as progressive is not self-evident, since the relation to production increase is completely vague.

With the general *step premium time wages* we have to deal with the same relations which formerly were indicated as a tendency of the time and piece costs at the beginning, during and at the end of the various step periods and thoroughly characterized in Tables 4–6 of the step wages.

With the graded wages progressing *from piece to piece* with constant piece premium, for instance, conditions are simple. Two main cases can be distinguished:

1. The premium begins with the *first piece:* The time costs are always degressive, completely independent of the amount of the premium.

2. The premium λ starts from *a standard quantity* q_0: Let q_0 be the minimum quantity from which the first premium is paid, we find, after the amount of the constant piece premium, for

a) $\lambda > \dfrac{s_0}{q_0 - 1}$ Progressive time costs,

b) $\lambda = \dfrac{s_0}{q_0 - 1}$ Proportional time costs,

c) $\lambda < \dfrac{s_0}{q_0 - 1}$ Degressive time costs.

For *increasing piece premiums* no such simple relations can generally be set up, since it is the degree of premium increase that matters.

When we take the number of pieces produced in a stage as *a new unit* of production, the discontinuous time wages become continuous. Only the irregular (including the one-graded) premium time wages cannot be comprised by a systematic classification, since their cost changing tendency has to be investigated in each individual case.

For *premium piece wages* with one- or multi-graded time premiums the concept of cost changing tendency cannot be clearly defined, either. Depending upon the choice of the base quantity q^* the time costs can at the same place be progressive, proportional or degressive. In the event of regularly graded time premiums it appears appropriate that here, also, the steps should be taken together. In the first place it is essential that the cost changing tendency be made clearly noticeable at the points of discontinuity. But also in that case the ambivalence of the course of the time costs subsists.

With premium piece wages with *piece premium* (rising piece rate wages) we always find here a progression of time costs when the base quantity q^* lies in a preceding step period. This limitation does not go for step premium piece wages, when they are reduced to piece rate wages which rise up from piece to piece.

In the event the standard quantity q_n at the beginning of the period is uniformly taken for all *step wages* (whether regular or irregular) as the base quantity q^* for the time cost course within the step period, whilst at the points of discontinuity the corresponding quantity of the preceding step period is taken, we arrive at Table 7 for the changing tendency of time costs.

TABLE 7

Step Wages		Changing Tendency of the Time Costs		
		at the beginning of the step period	within the step period	at the end of the step period
Premium Time Wages	with time premium	progressive proportional degressive	fixed (ultra-degressive)	progressive proportional degressive
	with piece premium	progressive proportional degressive	degressive	progressive proportional degressive
Premium Piece Wages	with time premium	progressive proportional degressive	degressive	progressive proportional degressive
	with piece premium	progressive	proportional	progressive

A short remark should still be made on the basic premium wages tailored on *time basis*. Here the time saving first has to be converted into the surplus of piece output since these two are by no means identical. When a work piece is completed in 6 hours instead of 10, the time saving is $\frac{2}{5} = \frac{6}{15}$, the surplus of piece output $\frac{2}{3} = \frac{10}{15}$. If the fractions by which the hourly earnings exceed the time saving be $\frac{15}{15}$, $\frac{10}{15}$ or $\frac{9}{15}$, the time costs are, in succession, progressive, proportional or degressive. A conclusion from the temporal dependence to the piece-wise tendency of cost changing therefore, is out of the question.

2. *Continuity Approach*

For the continuous basic premium wages a special treatment appears to be in order. The afore-mentioned conception of the cost changing tendency is *discontinuous* since it refers to a base quantity q^* which differs from the output quantity q by a finite multiple. If, however, the factor ρ is allowed to tend to 1 in $q = \rho q^*$, so that in the limit the performance quantity q to be examined and the base quantity q^* coincide, a *continuous* concept of the cost changing tendency is obtained, under which each point of the time cost and piece cost curve is compared with its (infinitely near) *neighbouring point*. Instead of the cost changing tendency with regard to a preceding smaller base quantity, we then obtain the cost changing tendency in a point q or for the performance quantity itself. In the definitions of the formulae (100)–(105) the *difference quotient* $\Delta s/\Delta q$ or $\Delta l/\Delta q$ of *finite* differences passes over into the *differential quotient* $\mathrm{d}s/\mathrm{d}q$ or $\mathrm{d}l/\mathrm{d}q$ of *infinitesimal* changes. Besides the continuity, also the differentiability of the wage functions, i.e. the smoothness of the curves, is pre-supposed. This always applies when the break points are disregarded in the combination of several wage forms.

I generally denote the *time costs* or *piece costs* of wages for a performance quantity q as (directly) *progressive, proportional* or *degressive*, when the differential quotient at this point is *positive* and larger, equal or smaller than the relation of these costs to the performance quantity:

$$(107) \qquad 0 < \frac{\mathrm{d}s}{\mathrm{d}q} \gtreqless \frac{s}{q} \quad \text{or} \quad 0 < \frac{\mathrm{d}l}{\mathrm{d}q} \gtreqless \frac{l}{q},$$

$$(108) \qquad \frac{\mathrm{d}s}{\mathrm{d}q} = \operatorname{tg}\varphi, \quad \frac{s}{q} = \operatorname{tg}\alpha \quad \text{or} \quad \frac{\mathrm{d}l}{\mathrm{d}q} = \operatorname{tg}\varphi, \quad \frac{l}{q} = \operatorname{tg}\alpha.$$

I generally denote the *piece costs* of wages for a performance quantity q as *inversely progressive, proportional* or *degressive*, when the differential quotient at this point is *negative* and its absolute value larger, equal or smaller than the relation of these costs to the performance quantity:

$$(109) \qquad 0 < -\frac{\mathrm{d}l}{\mathrm{d}q} \gtreqless \frac{l}{q},$$

$$(110) \qquad -\frac{\mathrm{d}l}{\mathrm{d}q} = \operatorname{tg}|\varphi|, \quad \frac{l}{q} = \operatorname{tg}|\alpha|$$

I generally denote the *time costs* or *piece costs* of wages as *fixed* when the differential quotient at this point disappears

$$\text{(111)} \qquad \frac{\mathrm{d}s}{\mathrm{d}q} = 0 \quad \text{or} \quad \frac{\mathrm{d}l}{\mathrm{d}q} = 0; \quad \operatorname{tg} \varphi = 0.$$

The secant through the points P and P^* (Figures 22 and 23) passes over into the tangent at point P. In case of fixity it runs parallel to the piece-axis, at direct proportionality it passes through the origin and at inverse proportionality it coincides at this point with the tangent of the guiding hyperbola.

Also in the sense of this new definition the pure time wages have fixed time costs and inversely proportional piece costs, whereas the pure *piece wages* have proportional time costs and fixed piece costs.

As first example the continuous general Halsey wages after (24) and (25) are chosen:

$$s = s + \kappa s_0 \frac{q-q_0}{q_0}, \quad l = \frac{s_0}{q} + \kappa s_0 \frac{q-q_0}{q_0\, q}, \quad \kappa \geqq 0.$$

Thus:

$$\text{(112)} \qquad \frac{\mathrm{d}s}{\mathrm{d}q} = \kappa \frac{s_0}{q_0} \geqq 0 \quad \text{or} \quad \frac{\mathrm{d}l}{\mathrm{d}q} = \frac{(\kappa-1)\, s_0}{q^2} \gtreqless 0,$$

and we have the division in Table 8.

TABLE 8

Halsey Wages		Time Costs	Piece Costs
$\kappa = 0$		fixed	inversely proportional
$0 < \kappa < 1$		degressive	inversely degressive
$\kappa = 1$		proportional	fixed
	$q < \frac{\kappa-1}{\kappa} q_0$		progressive
$\kappa > 1$	$q = \frac{\kappa-1}{\kappa} q_0$	progressive	proportional
	$q > \frac{\kappa-1}{\kappa} q_0$		degressive

The result is the same for the time costs as for the discontinuous cost changing tendency, because the latter is here independent of the choice of the base quantity q^*.

This is not the case with the continuous general Rowan wages after (35) and (36):

$$s = s_0 + \kappa s_0 \frac{q_0 - q}{q}, \quad l = \frac{s_0}{q} + \kappa s_0 \frac{q - q_0}{q^2}, \quad \kappa \geqq 0.$$

Here there is:

$$\text{(113)} \qquad \frac{ds}{dq} = \frac{\kappa s_0 q_0}{q^3} \geqq 0 \quad \text{or} \quad \frac{dl}{dq} = -\frac{(\kappa+1)s_0}{q^2} + \frac{2\kappa s_0 q_0}{q^3} \gtreqless 0.$$

We then arrive at the division according to Table 9.

TABLE 9

Rowan Wages		Time Costs	Piece Costs
	$q < \frac{3}{4} \frac{\kappa}{\kappa+1} q_0$		progressive
$q < \frac{2\kappa}{\kappa+1} q_0$	$q = \frac{3}{4} \frac{\kappa}{\kappa+1} q_0$	progressive	proportional
	$q > \frac{3}{4} \frac{\kappa}{\kappa+1} q_0$		degressive
$q = \frac{2\kappa}{\kappa+1} q_0$		proportional	fixed
$q > \frac{2\kappa}{\kappa+1} q_0$		degressive	inversely degressive

For the special Rowan wages $\kappa = 1$ this gives the corresponding classification in Table 10.

TABLE 10

Special Rowan Wages ($\kappa = 1$)		Time Costs	Piece Costs
	$q < \frac{3}{4} q_0$		progressive
$q < q_0$	$q = \frac{3}{4} q_0$	progressive	proportional
	$q > \frac{3}{4} q_0$		degressive
$q = q_0$		proportional	fixed
$q > q_0$		degressive	inversely degressive

For $\kappa = 0$ we find the pure time wages also here. The same result is obtained, when substituting $q^* = q$ for the discontinuous cost changing tendency.

The conceptions of the continuous cost changing tendency can be applied also to *step wages* within their continuity ranges and determined through differentiation of the cost function with respect to the performance quantity. Then we arrive at the extended scheme in Table 11 in agreement with the former Table 7.

TABLE 11

Step Wages		Time Costs	Piece Costs
Premium	with time premium	fixed	inversely proportional
Time Wages	with piece premium	degressive	inversely degressive
Premium	with time premium	degressive	inversely degressive
Piece Wages	with piece premium	proportional	fixed

For *regular* step wages the conceptions can further be applied to the points of discontinuity themselves. In this way the *tendency* of the costs can be rigidly comprehended by means of computation. We then arrive at the scheme of the relations previously set-up through differentiation of the cost functions.

In the investigations so far made into the cost changing tendency it was tacitly premised that the wage form is given as a function of the performance *quantity*. The changing tendencies (gradients) of the time costs s and the piece costs l were regarded as functions of the number of pieces q. There is no obstacle to carrying through all accomplished ideas, derived formulae and distinctions based upon them also to the dependence of the time and piece costs on the performance *time* t. Then it is a matter of the difference quotients or differential quotients, respectively,

$$\frac{\Delta s}{\Delta t} \text{ and } \frac{\Delta l}{\Delta t} \quad \text{or} \quad \frac{\mathrm{d}s}{\mathrm{d}t} \text{ and } \frac{\mathrm{d}l}{\mathrm{d}t}.$$

We refrain from details here, as no new structural viewpoints arise. Table 12 gives a composition of continuous premium wages, which uses *both gradients of the time costs* $\mathrm{d}s/\mathrm{d}q$ and $\mathrm{d}s/\mathrm{d}t$ one beside the other. The wage form of Carl G. Barth, which reposes on the *geometrical* mean of standard time and actually used time, represents a special case of the Rothert wage pattern for $\kappa = \frac{1}{2}$. Correspondingly, the Halsey wage for $\kappa = \frac{1}{2}$ can be expressed by the *arithmetical* mean of the two time figures.

To avoid misunderstandings it is sometimes necessary that the cost changing tendencies referred to so far be *more precisely indicated* as quantity-fixed, quantity-progressive, quantity-proportional or quantity-degressive and to oppose them, terminologically, to time-fixed, time-progressive, time-proportional or time-degressive time or piece costs.

Then, in the event of *time wages*, the time costs are to be regarded as time-fixed and quantity-fixed, but the piece costs as (directly) time-proportional and inversely quantity-proportional, whereas in the event of piece wages, the time costs are to be denoted as inversely time-proportional and (directly) quantity-proportional, but the piece costs as time-

TABLE 12

Continuous Premium Wages	Time Cost Formula	Gradient of the Time Costs
Linear Form after Rowan	$s_0 + \kappa s_0 \frac{t_0 - t}{t_0}$	$\frac{ds}{dt} = -\kappa \frac{s_0}{t_0}$
Linear Form after Halsey	$s_0 + \kappa s_0 \frac{q - q_0}{q_0}$	$\frac{ds}{dq} = +\kappa \frac{s_0}{q_0}$
Exponential Form after Schilling	$s_0 e^{\kappa \frac{t_0 - t}{t_0}}$	$\frac{ds}{dt} = -\kappa \frac{s}{t_0}$
Analogous Exponential Form	$s_0 e^{\kappa \frac{q - q_0}{q_0}}$	$\frac{ds}{dq} = +\kappa \frac{s}{q_0}$
Logarithmic Form	$s = \kappa s_0 {}^e\log\left(\frac{t_0}{t}\right)$	$\frac{ds}{dt} = -\kappa \frac{s_0}{t}$
Analogous Logarithmic Form	$s = \kappa s_0 {}^e\log\left(\frac{q}{q_0}\right)$	$\frac{ds}{dq} = +\kappa \frac{s_0}{q}$
Wage Form after Rothert	$s_0 \left(\frac{t_0}{t}\right)^\kappa$	$\frac{ds}{dt} = -\kappa \frac{s}{t}$
Analogous Parabolic Form	$s_0 \left(\frac{q}{q_0}\right)^\kappa$	$\frac{ds}{dq} = +\kappa \frac{s}{q}$

fixed and quantity-fixed. Correspondingly, for the usual *Halsey wages* ($0 < \kappa < 1$) the time costs are to be described as (directly) quantity-degressive and inversely time-degressive and the piece costs as inversely quantity-degressive and (directly) time-degressive.

Let us now recapitulate the results of our critical studies:

1. The cost changing tendency (in regard to the time costs) is not always independent of the initial quantity after which the production increase is gauged.

2. In these cases appropriately a uniform (though established by computation) base quantity is generally fixed.

3. In the event of regular basic premium wages with graded steps a collection of the steps into new production units is necessary, because otherwise the cost changing tendency remains completely non-uniform and an appropriate classification becomes impossible.

4. The strongly uniform concept of the continuous cost changing tendency can only be defined for continuous and then mostly differentiable basic premium wages and for step premium wages only within their continuity and differentiability ranges. But even then the cost changing tendency is not always distinctly clear for the same wages.

5. For irregular basic premium wages a systematic division of the cost changing tendency is, in principle, not feasible.

6. The classification after the cost changing tendency is unsuitable for wage form systematics.

V. Wage Form Systematics

When the total investigation into the various autonomous wage forms is collected into a synthesis, we first arrive at the setting-up of a structural system of the autonomous wage forms.

A. *Elementary wage forms* (Method of pure wage gauging; *pure* wage forms)

- I. Time wages (pure time gauging)
- II. Piece wages (pure piece gauging)

B. *Basic premium wages* (Method of premium gauging; *compound* wage forms)

- I. After the *basic wages:*
  1. Time wages as basic wages: Premium *time* wages
  2. Piece wages as basic wages: Premium *piece* wages
- II. After the *gauging scale:*
  1. Premiums on time basis (time gauging): *Speed* premiums
  2. Premiums on piece basis (piece gauging): *Quantity* premiums
- III. After the *addition basis:*
  1. Addition to the time costs: *Time* premiums
  2. Addition to the piece costs: *Piece* premiums
- IV. After the *premium form:*
  1. Step premiums
     - a) Irregular premiums
     - b) Regular step premiums
  2. Continuous (always (regular) premiums
     - a) Linear premiums
     - b) Non-linear premiums

This system of the autonomous wage forms is exclusively divided up according to the kind of *wage gauging*, i.e. built up purely structurally. As gauging scale performance time and performance quantity can be used. In this connection two fundamental methods of compensation can be differentiated in the first place: The *pure* wage gauging and the *premium* gauging.

Time wages and piece wages are pure wage forms, since a certain *gauging scale* is marked out in them: For time wages the time costs are independent of the performance quantity and for piece wages the piece costs are independent of the performance time. Further, they are *elementary* wage forms, since further wage forms can be evolved from them. Basic premium wages are composed from a pure wage form as *basic wages* and an addition, the *basic premium*. The addition must not always be a real addition, but may also be a multiplication (premium factor).

Depending upon the basic wages we distinguish premium *time* wages and premium *piece* wages. According as the premiums are established for a given performance time or for a certain performance quantity we can speak of *speed* premiums (on time basis) or of *quantity* premiums (on piece basis). Depending upon whether the addition is based on the time costs (hourly earnings) or upon the piece costs (labour costs per piece), it is referred to as *time* premium or as *piece* premium. According to the premium *form*, we can distinguish step (graded) or continuous premiums, regular or irregular premiums and linear or non-linear premiums (premium wages). Step premiums can also be designated as graded premiums. The graduation can be of one-graded, limited multi-graded or unlimited multi-graded structure.

In this way we obtain a logically self-contained, complete classification of *all* autonomous wage forms after gauging principles. In the basic premium wages each of the four classification viewpoints can be *combined* with each of the others, so that, when we distinguish for premium forms, we obtain a total of $2^3 . 4 = 32$ *basic types*. Basic premium wages are only defined clearly by all four features, for instance as premium time wages with regularly graded piece premium on time basis or as premium piece wages with linear time premium on piece basis.

Mathematically, the complete *disjunction* of the systematics has been *broken through* consciously in several places:

1. There are premium piece wages which can also be represented as premium time wages with corresponding premium measure, for instance Halsey and Rowan wages for $\kappa > 1$.

2. Every speed premium can be expressed by a corresponding quantity premium, and vice-versa, i.e. the analytical representation, in which the performance time is the independent variable corresponds with the similar representation with the performance quantity, and vice-versa. It is always possible to pass over from the consideration on time basis to

that on piece basis, and vice-versa. With the Rowan wages, for example, the time premium after (21) and (27) can be represented by a linear speed premium, with the Halsey wages after (18) by a linear quantity premium. However, we find a parabolic speed premium for the piece premium in the Rowan wage plan after (22) and (28) and a hyperbolic quantity premium in the Halsey wage plan after (19).

3. Every time premium corresponds clearly to a piece premium, and vice-versa. Either can be derived from the other by applying a simple rule:

$$\lambda = \sigma t \quad \text{or} \quad \sigma = \lambda q. \tag{114}$$

Because of this *ambiguity* in regard to the gauging scale (time or piece basis) and to the addition base (time or piece premium) each autonomous wage form can be described *in four ways*.

This fact might be called a disadvantage if purely *mathematical* viewpoints were used in a systematic division of wage forms. Since, however, *economic* connections must be decisive, the mathematically simplest method of expression will always be applied in concrete cases and it will not be felt suitable to work with the more complicated form merely for the sake of systematics. The system drawn up for autonomous wage forms thus gains a strong adaptability to the practical facts in enterprises by including division principles which, though mathematically *identical*, are *different* from an angle of economy. This, however, can only be advantageous:

1. Premium time wages are those premium wages which, in principle, issue from time wages as basic wages and can, as a rule, be ranged between time and piece wages, viewed from a labour-economic angle. This does not preclude that, formally, they exceed the piece wages through appropriate selection of the premium measure and thus become real premium piece wages. These, however, are premium wages which, fundamentally, proceed from piece wages as basic wages and thus, seen from a labour-economic angle, can never lie below it.

2. We have frequently referred to the economic difference between speed and quantity premiums, for example, between the graduation on time and on piece basis. Here the simpler form of expression will always be chosen.

3. The differentiation between time and piece premiums gains importance with step wages, since in this way the course within the stages is determined. On the other hand, it is unessential with continuous premium wages, but can, nevertheless, not be dispensed with.

A *complete disjunction* of the classification, however, is found in the division after the form of the premiums. It follows cogently from the conceptual pattern in Fig. 21. When we, therefore, fix the basic wages, the gauging scale and the addition base, all basic premium wages can be *clearly defined.* Thus, the premium form represents the essential characteristic of any form of premium wages. In addition to this, the subdivision into continuous, graded, regular and irregular premiums is independent of the other division principles. Their influence does not commence before the further sub-division of the premium forms. In this way we arrive at the following *absolute systematics* of all autonomous wage forms:

A. *Elementary* (*pure*) *wage forms*

1. Time wages
2. Piece wages

B. *Premium wages* (*compound wage forms*)

1. Irregular premium wages (always step wages)
2. Regular premium wages:
   a) Regular step premium wages
   b) Continuous premium wages.

Contrary to this are the additional premiums which, as partial premiums, leave the basic wages unchanged. On this account they do not belong to a system of autonomous wage forms. They can rather be added (as additions) to each of these wage forms, also to the premium wages. The classification of the additional premium wages after the gauging scale has been worked out on p. 219. Insofar as the additional premiums are paid in the form of a non-autonomous (dependent), but *functional* wage form, the systematics after the premium form go for them, too. It is to this extent that the absolute systematics generally comprise basic *and* additional premiums.

With the inclusion of the additional premiums into our considerations the system of the autonomous wage forms appears as a *partial system* of a *complete system* of the wage forms (in a broader sense) comprising the autonomous *and* the dependent wage forms. The heart of this wider system – based on actual conditions – is formed by the partial system of autonomous wage forms, with which the second partial system – of the additional premiums – is connected.

By combining the two partial systems the following classification of *all* wage forms is obtained:

A. *Autonomous wage forms*

I. *Elementary wage forms*
(Method of the pure wage gauging; pure wage forms)

1. *Time* wages (pure time gauging)
2. *Piece* wages (pure piece gauging)

II. *Basic premium wages*
(Method of premium gauging; compound wage forms)

1. After the *basic wages:*
   a) Time wages as basic wages: premium *time* wages
   b) Piece wages as basic wages: premium *piece* wages

2. After the *gauging scale:*
   a) Premiums on time basis (time gauging): *Speed* premiums
   b) Premiums on piece basis (piece gauging): *Quantity* premiums.

3. After the *addition base:*
   a) Addition to the time costs: *Time* premium
   b) Addition to the piece costs: *Piece* premium

4. After the *premium form:*
   a) Step (graded) premiums
      aa) Irregular premiums
      bb) Regular step premiums
   b) Continuous premiums
      aa) Linear premiums
      bb) Non-linear premiums

B. *Dependent wage forms:* Additional premium wages

I. *After the gauging scale:*

1. *Additional performance premiums*
   a) Indirect *piece* gauging:
      Additional quantity premiums
   b) Direct and indirect *quality* gauging:
      Quality premiums.

2. *Cost Saving Premiums*
   a) Indirect *piece* gauging:
      Special additional quantity premiums
   b) Direct and indirect *quality* gauging:
      Special quality premiums

II. *After the premium form:*

1. *Step* premiums
   a) Irregular premiums
   b) Regular premiums
2. *Continuous* premiums
   a) Linear premiums
   b) Non-linear premiums

The dependent wage forms are already defined as such by the underlying gauging scale and the chosen premium form. The determination factor of the basic wages mentioned with the basic premium wages cannot be referred to in this connection for the determination of the additional premium wages, as it does not affect its structure. As already observed, the additional premium wages can be added to the elementary wage forms and to the basic premium wages.

When dividing the additional premium wages after the gauging scale the *time scale* (indirect time gauging) could also be included; it would then appear beside the indirect piece gauging, to which it would be equivalent in the labour-technical effect. Then we have the same connections between performance time and performance quantity as previously explained with the basic premium wages. For reasons of simplicity, however, the time scale was not included.

The third division principle of the basic premium wages, the addition base, cannot be used, either, for the additional premium wages, since a structural connection between additional premium and time or piece costs does not directly exist.

Mathematically, there is nothing against regarding the *time wages* as the *only elementary* wage form. On account of this view we come to considerably different systematics of the wage patterns. All wage forms then appear as premium time wages, and the system of the wage forms is reduced to a system of premium additions.

It may be correct that the piece wages are always based upon a time estimate, but it is also correct that, conversely, the time wages often take into consideration the performance quantity. Above all it is not possible, however, to reduce the two gauging scales of time and quantity to one single basis. Hence, also the abolition of the distinction of speed and quantity premiums is only artificial and is in contradiction to the facts in practice. With the elimination of the piece wages as basic wages the gauging on the basis of quantity has by far not been abandoned yet.

The cogently occurring combined premiums render the systematics extremely complicated and obscure, whereas the differentiation into premium time wages and premium piece wages is clear and economically appropriate. Besides, a division into simple and combined premiums is not founded on the method of wage gauging, therefore it is not built up structurally, but follows the more outward viewpoint of complicatedness.

All in all, it can be said that the possibility to convert all wage forms into a *single* elementary form, which may appear attractive at first, proves to be structurally and systematically *inappropriate*. A reduced system of premium additions must therefore be *rejected*. As the only usable method remains the total system, set up here, of autonomous and dependent wage forms based on two elementary forms (time wages and piece wages).

CHAPTER 4

THE IMPACT OF TRADE UNIONISM ON INTERNAL WAGE STRUCTURES

H. M. DOUTY

Bureau of Labor Statistics, U. S. Department of Labor, Washington 25, D. C., USA

1. Introduction

It is most difficult to trace with precision the influence of trade unionism on the internal wage structures of firms and industries. This question, indeed, has been subject to little systematic investigation.

Trade unionism is a complex phenomenon. We are not concerned here with the political and other activities in which unions often engage, but only with the union as a vehicle for the representation of workers in decisions on wages and other terms of employment. This function is performed largely through collective bargaining and through the role of unions or related organizations (e.g., works councils) in the administration of collective agreements. Once established, collective bargaining is a continuous process, characterized by revision from time to time in the basic terms of agreements, and by the day-to-day application of these terms in the firms to which they relate.[1]

The influence of trade unionism on internal wage structures, therefore, obviously manifests itself over periods of time. Its effects will usually be gradual rather than sharp and dramatic. Moreover, there is no discernible point at which union influence cases, for wage structures must be adapted from time to time to changes in the occupational requirements of firms and to external or labor market conditions. In this process of adaptation, unionism clearly plays a role.

It is convenient, but misleading, to attempt to analyze "trade union policy" as though trade unions everywhere, and at all strages of development, exhibited the same characteristics. They do not. Even within a country, no single union is quite like any other. Each union reflects particular circumstances that condition its policies and activities. The most important factors tending to differentiate unions arise out of economic (market) and technological characteristics of the industries in which they function. For example, a steel mill, a shoe manufacturing plant, a coal mine, and a retail store each presents a somewhat different spectrum of wage structure problems. Uniformity of approach to these problems on the part of the unions concerned should not be anticipated.

The nature of union organization within a firm or industry may also affect the union approach to questions of wage structure. A union representing all of the manual workers in a plant may have attitudes on wage structure problems considerably different from those that would emerge if worker representation were divided among a number of unions. Again, the character of its membership may well affect a union's position. The question of occupational differentials, for instance, may appear in one light to a union with a predominantly unskilled membership and in a somewhat different light to a union with substantial proportions of workers at various skill levels.

If trade union organization, policy, and collective bargaining arrangements differ within countries, they differ even more strikingly among countries. These international differences express themselves in many ways. For example, trade union wage policy in the United States is reflected primarily in wage negotiations conducted directly with the individual employers or groups of employers immediately concerned. Industry-wide collective bargaining is prevalent in Great Britain, but British bargaining appears relatively decentralized in comparison with the arrangements that have developed in the Netherlands during the postwar period.[2] It has been stated that in France "the trade unions make their principal gains not through collective bargaining but through a kind of guerrilla warfare directed not so much against private employers as against the government."[3]

For these and related reasons, one should not expect to find uniform union policy on wage structure problems, either within particular countries or among countries. Union attitudes and objectives will be shaped by, and will reflect, a host of factors. Moreover, collective bargaining on wages is essentially a process of accommodation, and the results of bargaining typically reflect some measure of compromise between employer and union views. Finally, the fact must be stressed that at many points union and management views on wage structure problems may be in broad agreement, or at least the differences may be of degree and not of kind. The emphasis in this chapter is on union views and influence; this obviously should not be taken to mean that these are necessarily more compelling than the views and influence of management.

That much of the discussion in the present chapter relates to the United States reflects limitations in the knowledge of the author. At a number of points, however, reference is made to European experience and developments.

2. Elements of Wage Structure

For the purposes of this chapter, the term "internal wage structure" means the hierarchy of wage rates within a firm or establishment designed to compensate workers for their contributions to the productive process. But a definition in terms of wage rates alone is not sufficient in view of the growth of supplements to wages in recent years. These supplements may be required by law or may reflect practices agreed to in collective bargaining or instituted by employer personnel action. Wage supplements typically yield additional income, paid leisure, or security to workers; they involve expenditures by employers. In the United States, and certainly in most European countries, wage supplements now represent a significant item of pay-roll expense to most firms.[4]

In simple, the wage structure of a modern firm consists of a series of wage rates plus a variety of wage supplements. Supplements to basic wages may be divided into three broad groups: (1) *premium pay*, as for overtime, late shifts, or holiday work; (2) *pay for time not worked*, as illustrated by paid vacations or holidays; and (3) *social security benefits*, as represented by public or private programs for old-age pensions, unemployment insurance, compensation for industrial injuries, hospital and medical insurance and other forms of protection against loss of income.

The hierarchy of wage rates for an individual firm may be comparatively simple or quite complex, depending upon a variety of factors that affect occupational requirements, such as industry, size of firm, product diversification, and technology. The rate structure may consist only of time rates. Where time-rate structures are found, use may be made of single rates for jobs or labor grades, ranges of rates, or some combination of single rates and rate ranges. Or the structure may consist largely or in part of rates related to output. Other types of rates – minimum guaranteed rates, rates for "down time," and the like – are often associated with incentive rate systems. The rate structure of a firm may embrace minimum entrance rates, probationary job rates, rate progressions for apprentices, and, of course, a variety of premium rates.

3. The Establishment of Internal Rate Structures

a. *Union Wage Policy: The Standard Rate*

In their great work on British trade unionism, the Webbs wrote that "among trade union regulations there is one which stands out as practically universal, namely, the insistence on payment according to some definite standard, uniform in its application." [5] This concept was termed the "standard rate;" in the United States the term "union scale" is more widely used. We can usefully begin a discussion of union impact on wage structures with the aid of this concept.

The standard rate clearly retains its original meaning wherever work is conducted, and union organization is established, on a craft basis. For many years the United States Bureau of Labor Statistics has conducted annual surveys of union scales in building construction, printing, and several other industries. In these studies, the term is defined as the "minimum wage scales . . . agreed upon through collective bargaining between unions and employers. Rates in excess of the negotiated minimum, which may be paid for special qualifications or other reasons, are not included." [6] The union scale for carpenters in the building trades in Washington, D. C., as of July 1, 1958, was $3.50 an hour. A qualified union carpenter could not be paid less than this amount for the duration of the agreement by any employer subject to its terms. The employer could, however, pay more, and payments "above scale" were undoubtedly made to especially skilled, industrious, or reliable men.

The essence of trade union wage policy, as expressed through the standard rate, is to establish a uniform scale of pay for the workers in a craft or occupation. The scale may relate to a particular local labor market; in the building trades in the United States, union scales are typically negotiated on this basis, so that the standard rate for a craft in Washington may well differ from that in Pittsburgh. Or the scale may relate to a broader geographic area. In the case of the railroad industry, for example, wage scales are, for practical purposes, fixed on a nation-wide basis.

The union scale may be in terms of time rates (typically per hour or per day for manual workers) or in terms of piece rates or other forms of incentive pay. The actual earnings of individual workers may deviate upward from the scale. In occupations paid on an incentive basis, indeed, the dispersion of the earnings of individual workers may be quite wide, since the standard rate represents, in effect, simply the labor cost per unit of output. A significant measure of wage dispersion may also occur in time-rated occupations.[7] In general, however, the effect of a standard rate policy, especially for time-rated jobs, is to reduce differences in earnings among workers in the same occupation within the firm or industry to which the collective bargaining agreement relates.

The application of the concept of the "standard rate" to the wage structure of a modern factory is much more complicated than its application in industries (e.g., construction or printing) where the division of labor is along relatively clear-cut craft lines, or in industries such as longshoring, where the occupational structure is simple and the work comparatively unskilled. The wide variety of skills and, over large areas of work, the minute subdivision of labor in the modern factory present special problems. Many factory jobs are not "occupations" in the accepted sense of the term; they involve one or at most a few closely related tasks of a specialized nature. For personnel and other administrative purposes, however, specific job titles are typically assigned to these tasks. In the basic steel industry, for example, some thousands of job titles are required to account for the variety of tasks performed by the work force. This same development is evident in the large office, where work specialization, based partly on the increasing use of specialized office machines, has assumed significant proportions. The "general clerk" is virtually as obsolete in office employment as the "common laborer" in manual work.[8]

Under these circumstances, the trade union approach to the "standard rate" must take the general form of attempting to secure (1) equal pay for jobs of equal skill or difficulty; (2) a system of wage rate differentials that in some sense reflect the relative worth of the jobs, or groupings of jobs, within the enterprise. The achievement of this difficult task usually involves the simplification of the wage structures of firms and the development of consistent procedures for the administration of wages. Certainly in the United States, one consequence of the growth of trade unionism has been to focus management attention on the related questions of rationality in wage structures and on the requirements of sound wage administration. Wage administration, indeed, is rapidly becoming professionalized, and a vast literature is developing on the subject.

The fact should be emphasized that, in many cases, management has an interest in the simplification and rationalization of wage structures that tends broadly to parallel the trade union interest. As enterprises increase in size, as the job structure becomes more complex, and as labor force recruitment becomes a function of central personnel offices, the need for consistent and "defensible" wage rate structures becomes apparent. Trade union pressures to correct "inequities" in wage structures undoubtedly have contributed powerfully in many instances to management concern with the problem, and have stimulated the growth of formal procedures for the establishment and administration of wage rate structures.

There are various ways in which unions influence the internal wage structures of firms. These range from direct bargaining on rates of pay and the processing of grievances involving alleged inequities in rates for particular jobs to joint participation with employers in the rationalization of rate structures through job evaluation. Another type of union influence, which will be discussed at a later point, arises out of the way in which general wage changes are applied to wage structures.

b. *The Collective Bargaining Approach*

Most unions probably prefer to approach wage structure problems solely through the collective bargaining process rather than through joint participation in formal job evaluation schemes. Bargaining over job classification may assume several forms. The union from time to time may appeal the appropriateness of particular classifications through the grievance procedure. At the other extreme, management and the union may review the whole structure of jobs at one time. A fairly common practice in the United States is for the union, when a new contract is being negotiated, to press for the reclassification of certain jobs or groups of jobs on the ground that their rates are out of line with the rate structure as a whole.

Examples of this latter form of internal rate adjustment through collective bargaining can be given almost endlessly from United States experience. For instance, an agreement concluded in November 1958 between the United Automobile Workers and a plant of the Westinghouse Corporation provided for a general wage increase and certain other benefits; it provided also for upward "inequity adjustments" for jobs employing about 10 percent of the workers.[9] A two-year contract between the Hussmann Refrigerator Company and a number of union locals provided for inequity wage adjustments in certain job classifications in addition to an across-the-board increase.[10] Wage adjustments for particular jobs were provided for in a contract negotiated by a local of the Machinists' Union with Cutler-Hammer, Inc., a metal-working firm.[11] A new agreement with the North Carolina Pulp Company provided the occasion for inequity adjustments in a number of job classifications.[12]

These cases reflect employer-union agreement, when new contracts are negotiated, that rates for certain jobs should be adjusted to correct inequitable relationships with other job rates. In many contract negotiations, of course, this issue does not arise. In other negotiations, the issue may not be pressed by the union, either because its case is weak or other contract changes seem more important. In still other contract settlements, as in the case of a recent agreement involving the Minneapolis-Honeywell Regulator Company, the parties may agree to submit inequity claims to arbitration.[13]

The nature of the collective bargaining arrangement may largely determine the direction of trade union effort. In the British engineering (metal-working) industry, for example, national collective bargaining is carried on between the Engineering and Allied Employers' National Federation and the Confederation of Shipbuilding and Engineering Unions. Although the focus in bargaining is on general wage changes, minimum rates for skilled fitters and for laborers exist on a national and district basis. Derber points out that "the unions (in British engineering) are endeavoring to establish national minima for a number of intermediate jobs between the skilled fitter and the laborer on the grounds that this would lead to a more rational and simplified wage structure throughout the industry." [14]

This objective has not yet been achieved. Its purpose clearly is to establish greater uniformity than now exists in the wage rate structure of this highly diversified industry, and to provide a number of points in the job rate structure to which other rates could be related.[15] But the major problems of wage structure, as at present, would continue to be resolved at the individual establishment level between management and the representatives of the local unions concerned.*

The collective bargaining approach to wage structure problems will inevitably be affected by the nature of the union-management relationship at the level of the establishment or company. If a single union represents the workers, the possibility of working out reasonably systematic procedures for dealing with job rate relationships will be greater than if worker representation is divided among a number of unions. An employer and a single union can better consider the structure as a whole and its interrelationships, and develop, perhaps over a period of time, a mutually satisfactory rate structure within which adjustments required by such factors as changing technology, products, and work organization can be accommodated. The situation under multiple-unionism is likely to be more difficult because of the particularized job interests that the several unions represent and seek to protect.**

Satisfactory and viable wage structures can result from a purely collec-

* A PEP study contends that "although the whole (engineering) industry is unified in its negotiation procedure, its wage system is completely chaotic, with varying district rates, inadequate grading of semi-skilled workers and other problems."[16]

** The situation is probably even more difficult where, as in much of British industry, union organization is on the basis of geography rather than establishment, company, or industry, and where, within a given establishment, union interests are coordinated through a shop steward system.

tive bargaining approach to the problem. The absence of formal criteria for ranking jobs, as in job evaluation, does not preclude the exercise of knowledge and judgment on the part of management and unions. Much depends on the attitude of the parties and their willingness or ability to develop some sort of reasoned approach to job classification.

c. *Job Evaluation*

Job evaluation can be defined as a systematic method of appraising the "worth" of each job in relation to other jobs in an establishment or firm.[17] There are a number of well-recognized job evaluation procedures; these need not concern us here. All systems essentially involve the utilization of organized knowledge about occupations to arrive at informed judgments as to the relative worth of jobs. Job evaluation is not, in any rigid sense, scientific. Judgment clearly enters into the evaluation process. But it does provide a technique for the rating of jobs under a consistent set of criteria, and it tends to narrow the area of dispute with respect to claims of improper rating. Moreover, an evaluation program facilitates the introduction of new jobs into the rate structure, and the reappraisal of old jobs when their content changes.

Job evaluation may grow out of collective bargaining. Numerous grievances involving appropriate job classification may convince an employer, or an employer and union jointly, that the job structure needs systematic review. In some instances, an employer may spot a variety of jobs whose rates seem "out of line" and decide that a more rational structure is needed. In modern industry, the sheer complexity of a job rate structure and the problems incident to its administration may suggest the need for a comprehensive reappraisal of job relationships and simplification of the rate structure.

Job evaluation may be undertaken solely by management or jointly by management and the union or unions concerned. Some unions in the United States, as indicated below, are opposed in principle to job evaluation. Other unions, while not opposed to job evaluation as such, refuse to participate with management in the institution of plans, preferring to use the grievance procedure to protest particular job classifications and rates.

d. *A Joint Approach to Job Evaluation*: *The Case of U. S. Steel*[18]

Perhaps the most notable instance in the United States of union-management collaboration in rationalizing the wage rate structure of an industry is the well-known case of basic steel. It may be useful, however, to summarize this development, which resulted, after great effort, in the establishment in 1947 of uniform wage scales (except for a southern wage differential, since eliminated) for more than 40 plants of the United States Steel Corporation. The same system was then applied jointly by the United Steelworkers Union and other major steel producers. The achievement at U. S. Steel has rightly been called "an application of industrial engineering and collective bargaining without parallel in American industry." [19]

Internal wage rate inequities had long been a problem in the steel industry. When collective bargaining relations were established at U. S. Steel in 1937, the approach to this problem was a piece-meal adjustment of individual grievances without any broader program of rate review.* In 1942, the union and the company established a joint commission to seek agreement on a complete overhauling of the internal wage structure. This effort floundered. In 1944, the union asked the National War Labor Board, which administered the wartime wage stabilization program, to approve "equal pay for similar work throughout the industry" as a guide in collective bargaining for the elimination of wage rate inequities. This the Board denied. However, the Board ordered the company and the union to "negotiate the elimination of existing intra-plant wage rate inequities and reduction in the number of job classifications," and established a number of "guideposts" to facilitate the process. What the Board ordered, in effect, was the institution of a job evaluation plan. A commission was set up to oversee the project and resolve disputes.**

The joint union-management committee at U. S. Steel met for the first time in February 1945. Its work was completed two years later. Very briefly, agreement was first reached on descriptions for a sizable group of benchmark jobs. The parties then agreed on a manual for job evaluation, involving use of a point system in which each of 12 factors

* A union representative has written that "all of the many variations in rates were a constant source of irritation among employees and were the cause of countless work disturbances and grievances. Before the job evaluation program in the steel industry, over 90 percent of all grievances came from disputes over wage rates. The settlement of these grievances by raising certain rates created further inequities and dissatisfaction [20].

** National War Labor Board, Directive Order in case of Carnegie-Illinois Steel Corporation, et al., and United Steelworkers of America, November 25, 1944. This order applied to 86 steel companies and was later extended to 10 more. The special Steel Commission provided for in the directive order was continued after the abolition of the War Labor Board and was given power to make final and binding decisions. Actually, the company and the union reached all of their decisions by agreement.

was given a maximum weight.* Literally thousands of jobs were subsequently described and rated. A wage rate structure consisting of 30 job classes or labor grades was established, with rates rising by 3.5-cent increments from $1.09 to $2.25 an hour (agreement of January 13, 1947).** In 1948, the number of labor grades was increased to 32; in 1956, job class 1 (the lowest labor grade) was combined with job class 2. As of July 1, 1958, the rate structure at U. S. Steel, and for the great bulk of the basic steel industry, consisted of 31 labor grades, with rates rising by 6.7-cent increments from $1.96 to $3.97 an hour.***

The union-management installation of an evaluated wage rate structure in the basic steel industry in the United States was a tremendous undertaking, but there were a number of factors that were favorable to success. Although we are told that the initial atmosphere in the joint committee at U. S. Steel was one of "suspicion and distrust," [22] both sides clearly recognized the need to find a solution to what had become a most serious problem. This atmosphere changed as the work of the joint committee progressed. The fact that participation in the joint committee on the union side was at the national union level also contributed to the success of the venture. Tilove points out that "a typical local union may prefer elbow-room with which to accommodate its inevitable internal pressures; an international union dealing with U. S. Steel subsidiaries and endeavoring to set a pattern for the industry can hardly afford to give major consideration to local pressures. In other words, the level is high enough so that statesmanship, wholly aside from its own merits, also corresponds to good politics." [23]

e. *Union Attitudes on Job Evaluation*

As previously noted, probably most unions object on principle to the job evaluation approach to problems of wage structure. The International Association of Machinists, a highly important union in the metal-working industries in the United States, takes this position. It prefers a

* The 12 factors were as follows: (1) pre-employment training; (2) employment training and experience; (3) mental skill; (4) manual skill; (5) responsibility for materials; (6) responsibility for tools and equipment; (7) responsibility for operations; (8) responsibility for safety of others; (9) mental effort; (10) physical effort; (11) surroundings; (12) hazards. The heaviest weighting (53 percent) was given to the four responsibility factors.

** The rates in the structure represented the straight-time hourly rates for workers paid on a time basis and minimum hourly guaranteed rates for workers paid on an incentive basis.

*** Excludes cost-of-living bonus [21].

purely collective bargaining approach. In a *Manual* prepared for the use of its local representatives, the union states that "the use of job evaluation as a means of determining the relative importance of jobs has been viewed by our organization as a serious threat to free collective bargaining." [24]

The Machinists raise numerous objections to job evaluation. The union argues that job evaluation tends in various ways to limit collective bargaining over rate adjustments for individual job classifications; that it creates rigidity in the wage structure; that in rate-setting it fails to consider labor market and other forces; and that in other ways it adversely affects the wage position of the workers. The union also claims that job evaluation presents a threat to the stability of the union by hampering the efforts of local unions to establish uniform rates of pay on an area basis, strengthens management's opposition to union wage demands, and tends generally to place the union in a disadvantageous position. The backbone of membership in the Machinists' Union is made up of skilled craftsmen, and perhaps central to the union's attitude is its fear that job evaluation will "dilute traditional skills" and "discourage bona fide apprenticeships" and thereby reduce the reservoir of skilled workers.*

Where job evaluation plans do not exist, the Machinists advise their local officials to resist their introduction. "If the employer insists that a more 'equitable wage structure' be established, you must be ready to take the initiative and show him that the 'necessary adjustments' can be made through the give and take of collective bargaining, rather than through the installation of a formal job evaluation manual." [26] The union recognizes, however, that job evaluation already exists in many plants represented by the union and that ordinarily these plans cannot be eliminated. In such cases, local union representatives are urged to influence the plans to obtain "maximum benefits" for the workers. The union *Manual* also deals with situations in which the "negotiating committee finds it impossible to reject the company proposed job evaluation plan." In these situations, perhaps somewhat surprisingly, the union appears to recommend that its representatives participate as fully as possible in the installation and administration of plans. Detailed instructions are given on this point.[27]

The position of the Machinists' Union on job evaluation reflects the pragmatic approach of most American unions to collective bargaining problems. Although opposed in principle to this method of internal job alignment, the union nevertheless provides its representatives with guid-

* A job evaluation plan developed by the National Metal Trades Association is used in many plants organized by the Machinists. See Reference 25.

ance in those situations where job evaluation is already employed or where the local union is not strong enough or persuasive enough to prevent its introduction. The Office Employees International Union, to give another example, points out that it does not endorse "any job evaluation system, or the formalizing of job comparison through job evaluation methods." [28] However, the union provides its local representatives with material designed to enable them to participate more effectively in the installation or administration of job evaluation systems. It points out that "job evaluation is not something new. Job comparison in some form enters into all collective bargaining negotiations. It probably always will – it is up to us to drive a good bargain!" [29]

One close observer of American union attitudes toward wage structure problems has written that "union leaders almost unanimously take an extremely negative attitude toward all of the so-called scientific procedures employed in the administration of the internal wage-rate structure." [30] In a formal sense, this judgment has a large measure of validity. But as suggested earlier, union attitudes, which grow out of historic attachment to collective bargaining, *per se*, appear to adapt themselves to the concrete situations with which unions are confronted. Especially if management does not claim too much for job evaluation, and if unions are given a reasonable voice in policy and administration, a systematic approach to wage structure problems through some form of job evaluation can command union support in many situations. In a later study, the same author points to a growing accommodation of union and management attitudes in this area.[31] Another recent study concludes that "the resistance on the part of unions against formal job evaluation to a large extent is because of inadequate communication or misdirected educational activity on the part of management." [32]

f. *The "Standard Rate" Concept in Modern Industry*

It may now be useful to sum up the argument to this point. The traditional trade union objective of the "standard rate" in the usual sense of the term still has relevance in industries in which the labor force is employed (and unionized) on a craft basis. In industries in which the work is divided into numerous jobs or tasks, and where craft skills are possessed only by a small minority of the workers, the standard rate objective finds expression in the development of uniform rates of pay for jobs of approximately equal "worth," and the establishment of appropriate rate differentials among the different job levels into which the work force is divided.

The way in which this objective is approached varies greatly among companies and industries, depending in part on the nature of union organization and policy. It may be approached on a purely collective bargaining basis, either piece-meal or through a more comprehensive review from time to time. Formal job evaluation plans may be utilized, with the union participating jointly with management in the evaluation process or retaining the right to contest particular decisions through the grievance machinery. Collective bargaining, with or without job evaluation, undoubtedly has exerted substantial influence in creating and extending simplified and more uniform wage structures. Employers will usually take the initiative in pressing for wage structure rationalization. The employer objectives may include relief from union pressure for the correction of alleged inequities in wage rates. The union agreements at the United States Steel Corporation, in fact, contain a provision stating that "no basis shall exist for an employee, whether paid on an incentive or non-incentive basis, to allege that a wage-rate inequity exists and no grievance on behalf of an employee alleging a wage-rate inequity shall be filed or processed during the term of this agreement." [33]

The standard wage scale agreed to in collective bargaining may be expressed in terms of specific rates for each job classification found in the enterprise. This is still the practice in many situations. For example, a recent agreement between the Charleston plant of the West Virginia Pulp and Paper Company and the unions concerned sets forth basic rates of pay for more than 200 job classifications.[34] There were not, of course, that many different rates, since identical rates frequently applied to more than one job classification.

Increasing use is being made, particularly in large plants, of wage scales expressed as a series of labor grades. Reference has already been made to the case of the basic steel industry in the United States, which now has a wage structure composed of 31 labor grades, each with a single rate, and with a uniform increment between grades. Many companies operate on the basis of a smaller number of grades. Thus, an agreement entered into in July 1958 between the Winchester Arms Division of the Olin Mathieson Chemical Corporation and the Machinists Union provides for 12 labor grades, with a range of rates attaching to each grade.[35] The wage structure at North American Aviation, Inc., under contract with the United Automobile Workers, currently consists of 17 labor grades.[36] A range of rates attaches to each labor grade, with the width of the range varying among grades.

The use of a labor grade wage rate structure means that diverse job classifications must be slotted into the appropriate grades. At North American Aviation, for example, labor grade 15 includes such job classifications as grinders, machine tools and precision cutters; inspectors, final assembly-electrical, mechanical; instrument technicians, aircraft; mechanics, flight-line engine-checkout; mock-up men, wood.[37] These are all skilled jobs, but the decision as to whether each belonged in labor grade 15, or in a lower or higher grade, plainly involved either a formal or an informal evaluation process.

The 1958 collective bargaining agreement at North American Aviation, indeed, reflected dissatisfaction with the existing allocation of jobs among labor grades. The agreement provided for the establishment of a committee consisting of three representatives of the company and three of the union. The principal duties of this committee are to (1) "develop a system for determining the relative worth of each job classification in relation to each other job classification by measuring systematically the demands of such jobs on employees," and (2) "establish a basis for relating such determination of the relative worth of each job classification to rates of pay." In undertaking this task, the committee is instructed to "observe and give effect to the principle of equal pay for equal work" and to "observe and give effect to the right of the Company to make all work assignments, establish job classification requirements and describe such requirements to distinguish those of each job classification, when considered in its entirety, from all others." [38] The outcome of this effort is not presently known, but evidently a joint effort is being made to devise a new evaluation procedure for the conduct of a comprehensive review of existing job and wage rate relationships.

The "standard rate" policy of unions involves the creation of rate uniformity for comparable jobs over as broad an industrial and geographical area as possible. In companies with multi-plant operations, union effort to eliminate wage rate differences among plants of the same company is likely to be highly persistent. In the United States Steel Corporation, for example, a long-standing differential in wage rates had existed between its northern and southern facilities. This differential was erased in a series of steps between 1948 and 1954, under the terms of collective bargaining agreements.

In the basic steel industry as a whole, rate differences among companies have been very substantially removed in recent years through collective bargaining and the use of the job evaluation plan described earlier. But the union as recently as 1958 contended that not all differentials had been removed. It issued a detailed study showing company by company the differentials which, in its view, remain to be corrected. The Introduction to this study states that "the Steelworkers Union has repeatedly adopted Wage Policy statements calling for the complete and immediate elimination of all differentials" and that remaining differentials require serious consideration "if we are ever to achieve our goal of 'equal pay for equal work' throughout the properties of these basic and major producers." [39]

In the automobile assembly industry, to cite another example, a large measure of wage rate uniformity exists among the companies in the industry.[40] This has not been produced, as in steel, by the application of a common job evaluation plan. It reflects, rather, the results of company-wide collective bargaining with a union representing substantially all of the production workers in the industry.

It must not be assumed that unions can readily extend the "standard rate" concept (in the sense of relatively uniform job rates) in all, or even in most, industries. Much depends on the nature of the industry, on employer wage policy, and on the extent and character of union organization. In both basic steel and automobile assembly, a few large firms in the United States account for the bulk of the output, and in each industry a single union represents most of the plant workers. This is not true of most industries in the United States. Even industries, such as automotive parts or steel fabrication, that are closely related to industries in which substantial rate uniformity is found, exhibit considerable diversity in rate levels. In automotive parts manufacture, for example, about an eighth of the establishments reported entrance rates for inexperienced workers in July 1957 of less than $1.25 an hour, and about half of the establishments had entrance rates of less than $1.70.[41] At the same time, the minimum hiring rate in the plants of the motor vehicle companies was substantially above this latter figure.[42]

In the winter of 1957–58, the U. S. Bureau of Labor Statistics made a survey of wages in the nonelectrical machinery manufacturing industries in 21 labor markets.[43] These 21 areas contained more than 4,500 machinery establishments, each employing 20 workers or more. About three-fourths of the workers were covered by collective bargaining agreements. Although the workers in each unionized establishments are typically represented by a single union, a number of different unions function in the industry and there is no coordination of bargaining policy or strategy. Moreover, the firms in the industry differ greatly in terms of such factors as size, product, financial strength, and labor market position. Under these circumstances, rates of pay, even among firms in the same local labor market, exhibit considerable dispersion.

The importance of company wage policy shows up clearly in those multi-plant companies which, as a matter of policy, seek to relate wages in their plants to levels prevailing in the labor markets in which the plants are located. This policy is as defensible from some points of view as a standard rate policy is from others. The General Electric Company, for example, has plants located in many parts of the United States. The company has successfully resisted efforts of the unions concerned to establish wage rate uniformity among its manufacturing facilities. The operating subsidiaries of the American Telephone and Telegraph Company also relate the wages of their workers in an approximate way to labor market levels.* This general policy is not confined to private companies in the United States. The Federal government, by law, is required to compensate its manual or "blue-collar" workers on the basis of rates of pay prevailing in the areas in which they work.[44] This results in considerable dispersion in rates of pay for comparable job classifications. For example, the rates of pay among areas for labor grade 2 (light unskilled labor) in Army-Air Force installations ranged from less than $1.25 to more than $2.00 an hour during the first part of 1958.[45]

The trade union goal of wage rate uniformity by job classification, industry, and labor market is difficult of universal achievement for a variety of purely technical reasons. Two of these reasons are of particular importance. The first is that occupational structures and requirements differ widely among establishments. This is frequently true even among firms and establishments within the same industry. The differences reflect variations in such factors as work organization, technical processes, and product. For example, the occupational requirements for an assembler or fitter in one establishment may differ substantially from the requirements in another. How are these differences to be measured for pay purposes? One approach conceivably would be through the use of a uniform system of job evaluation. To a limited extent (as in basic steel), this approach has been utilized in the United States. But in many industries, particularly in those that are widely dispersed geographically and in which product competition is keen, the use of a uniform job evaluation plan appears remote. Agreement on uniform standard rates would be even more difficult to achieve.

The second technical reason is that occupational wage differences

* Multi-plant companies that base wages on those prevailing in local labor markets have a choice of policies, depending largely upon the quality of workers they seek to attract and retain. Thus, a company may aim to pay rates somewhat above the average prevailing in each market in which it operates.

among geographic areas or firms may well reflect underlying realities relating to labor market conditions, the profitability of firms, and other factors. Wage bargains tend to reflect these underlying conditions. Trade unions often concerned with the employment opportunities as well as the wages of their members, and the "employment preferences" of unions frequently provide a sanction for wage inequalities.

It was widely agreed at the end of the war that the rehabilitation of the Dutch economy, after five years of German occupation, would require a broad measure of centralized control, including control over wages.[46] Even before the end of the war, representatives of the leading trade union and employer federations, meeting in London, had agreed to establish a permanent joint body, the Foundation of Labor. This voluntary organization was to concern itself with a range of problems of labor-management relations, including wages. Legal responsibility for formulating and administering wage policy was placed in a Board of Government Conciliators (actually a board of wage control) appointed by the Minister of Social Affairs. This Board is required by statute to consult with the Foundation of Labor, and this consultation has been carried on most extensively. The Board must also operate within the framework of basic policy decisions taken by the Minister of Social Affairs. Finally, in 1950, the Netherlands government established a Social and Economic Council (composed of trade union, employer, and government representatives) for advice on basic problems of social and economic policy.

This elaborate structure for wage determination is not, as Roberts has pointed out, incompatible with collective bargaining and free enterprise "so long as it responds to the economic and political pressures that are generated in a free society." [47] Centralized wage determination may, as apparently in the Netherlands, alter the manner in which collective bargaining takes place. Bargaining, in effect, becomes national rather than sectional. The underlying goals of trade unions and employers, however, are not suddenly transformed; the struggle for their realization becomes transferred to a different plane.

In the Netherlands, one of the aims of wage policy was the "establishment of equitable and satisfactory wage differentials between different occupations." [48] The Dutch unions, writes Windmuller, have "striven for the attainment of a rational wage structure based, at the bottom, on a social minimum wage and supporting differentials principally by reference to differences in skills, living costs, and individual output." [49]

The initial step in the Netherlands was the establishment of a national minimum wage for unskilled adult workers at a level that would enable a man to maintain a family of four at a reasonable subsistence standard. The wages of semi-skilled and skilled workers were fixed at 10 and 20 percent, respectively, above this level. Later a commission was set up to develop a comprehensive plan for job evaluation and work classification. A point job evaluation scheme was adopted. The application of this plan was not made compulsory; its adoption was left to the voluntary decision of the unions and employers concerned. It has been, in fact, widely utilized in breaking down the broad categories of unskilled, semi-skilled, and skilled work into more refined occupational groupings. It should be noted that employers must comply with the basic wage rates (maximum as well as minimum) established in the wage control regulations. Changes in the wage structure resulting from use of the job evaluation plan, therefore, were required to be approved by the wage control agency (the Board of Government Conciliators).

It will be seen that this system of wage structure determination largely ignores the factors that were mentioned earlier as obstacles to the realization of a "standard rate" policy across industry, such as variations in profitability among firms and industries and differences in local labor market conditions. The Dutch system provides for socially determined wage limits, with job evaluation providing for some flexibility in the classification of occupations and their compensation within these limits. Since about 1953, with recovery from war dislocations and the return of more normal economic conditions, the rigidities of this system have become subject to criticism. Windmuller writes that what some of the trade unions (he refers specifically to the denominational unions) and the employer Associations "have demanded above all is the introduction of more wage flexibility between industries. Their combined pressure to include differences between industries as to profits, ability to pay, and productivity in the roster of wage criteria has been gaining ground, as the most recent round of wage increases demonstrated." [50] Windmuller concludes, however, that most proponents of greater wage flexibility in the Netherlands concede the need for continued government supervision of wage structure and trends.

In Sweden, a somewhat different road has been taken in an effort to extend the "standard rate" concept beyond the bounds of particular trades and industries. Beginning in the years prior to World War II, the Swedish unions attempted to give content to the idea of "solidarity" as at least one element of wage policy.

The precise meaning of the concept of "solidarity" is not altogether clear, despite the fact that the Swedish trade union movement is outstanding for the sophistication of its approach to wage problems. At least in the beginning, solidarity was conceived in terms of reducing wage differentials among industries or, even more simply, as "helping the worst paid groups of workers," principally those employed in agriculture and forestry.[51] Indeed, this is probably the most significant sense in which the term has been understood and applied. A 1953 report of the Swedish Confederation of Trade Unions states that, in earlier years, "the practical significance of the expression 'wages policy of solidarity' was relatively clear. Wage differences between different industries were so great that practically every reduction of wage gaps could be regarded as just and reasonable." [52] The report contends that interindustry wage differentials were so reduced between 1939 and 1950 that it is now difficult to conclude whether a differential for a given industry (presumably in average wages without regard to occupation) is too great.

The report suggests that there are now two ways to determine which of two industry groups, in terms of the solidarity principle, should obtain support for a wage increase above normal. "One is to carry out a detailed and systematic job evaluation, taking into account all the factors contained in the overhead expression 'nature of work,' which should affect wages in one job in relation to the other. The second method is to judge this question according to each industry's ability to recruit and retain manpower." [53] With respect to cross-industry job evaluation, the report concludes that "the introduction in Sweden of a general system of job evaluation as between jobs in different industries similar to that practiced in the Dutch trade union movement would not appear possible for psychological reasons." [54]

The Swedish trade union movement has tried to give concrete meaning to the policy of "solidarity." In the course of this effort, a rather highly centralized collective bargaining system has been created. Within this system, the Confederation "has constantly and consistently tried during and since the war to give prior consideration to lower-paid groups of workers – though it has not always defined who they were – and to women workers. For 1947, for instance, a successive closing of differentials between the sexes in accordance with the principle of 'equal pay for equal performance' was recommended." [55] It appears, however, that the effect on wage structures of the policy of solidarity has not been particularly impressive.[56] The underlying reason was expressed as early as 1936 in a motion adopted by the Confederation of Trade Unions to the effect that the trade unions alone could not secure wage equalization (for comparable work) among industries. Social policy would be needed to supplement trade union effort in view of differences among industries in their profitability and hence in their capacity to pay wages. It is worth quoting from a report on this problem prepared subsequent to the 1936 convention.

> Equalization of wages within a particular industry (the Report states) can probably be achieved by exclusive use of trade union action, but the resources of the trade union movement are inadequate for the purpose of eliminating wage differentials between different industries and sectors of the economy. In the last resort it is the profitability of the sectors which sets the limit to what the trade union movement can achieve. An industry with a stable market and a large demand can naturally pay better wages than a branch which is suffering a hard and often precarious existence. In the latter industry the workers do not, however, obtain better wages simply because their comrades in more favorable branches refrain from exploiting their opportunities to improve their position further. An equalizing wages policy can only be achieved here by means of social policy measures.[57]

Actually, as suggested earlier, variations in profitability among firms and industries is only one obstacle to the achievement of a "standard rate" policy throughout industry. It is, however, a powerful factor; in general, it is difficult to see how this and other obstacles can be overcome, in the absence of strong social measures relating to the wage structure. Such measures, in turn, might well have adverse effects on productivity and hence on real wages in the economy as a whole.

4. Special and Penalty Rates

The wage rate structure of a modern firm consists not only of a series of occupational or labor grade rates. It typically will contain also a variety of rates that must be paid under special circumstances. Many of these rates tend now to be taken for granted. In many instances, however, their incorporation into rate structures is comparatively recent. Their existence surely reflects, at least in part, the influence of trade unionism and collective bargaining. Changes in these rates, or the introduction of new types of rates, are frequently subject to collective determination.

Some special rates are confined to particular industries and reflect conditions peculiar to those industries. An example would be the penalty rates in stevedoring, which provide extra compensation for the loading or unloading of defined categories of dangerous or disagreeable cargo.

Where piece-rate systems of wage payment are found, a variety of *time* rates may exist to provide protection to the workers against loss of earnings, or unduly low earnings, arising from the operation of the incentive schemes. Most incentive systems of the bonus type, of course, are built on the basis of time rates, with extra earnings arising from production in excess of the level determined to be standard. But in straight piece-rate plans, this cushion of time rates is not built into the system, except to the extent that legal minimum wage standards are in effect. There is a clear tendency for unions in piece-rate industries to push for guaranteed rates of pay, which are usually set at levels below expected piece-rate earnings. Protection against loss of incentive earnings in the event of lost or "down" time is also a common safeguard found in union agreements. Such down-time may be caused by machine breakdown, lack of material, power failure, or other causes beyond the control of the workers.

Premium pay for work beyond standard hours – the concept of standard hours itself has a long and complicated evolution – is now very widely found in industrially developed countries. Even where premium pay for overtime work is provided by legislation, additional provisions liberalizing the legislative standard may be adopted through collective bargaining. In the United States, for example, employees covered by the Fair Labor Standards Act must be paid at the rate of time and one-half their regular rate of pay for all hours worked in excess of 40 in the *work-week*. Despite this legal requirement, a 1957 study of more than 1,800 major collective bargaining contracts found that specific provisions relating to overtime were incorporated in all but 6 percent of these agreements. The chief method by which the legislative standard was liberalized involved provision for "daily overtime rates or premium overtime rates for all work outside of the normal schedule. In addition, union agreements frequently define 'hours worked' for overtime pay purposes more liberally than the law requires (for example, by counting holidays as working time)." [58]

Other forms of premium pay rates may also figure in the rate structure of a firm. Extra pay for night-shift work was uncommon in the United States two decades ago; it is now a common practice. In 1958, about three-fourths of the major collective bargaining agreements in the United States provided for the payment of a rate differential for late-shift work. The amount of the premium varied considerably among industries, and was typically higher for the third than for the second shift. It is not uncommon in European industry for workers to be paid a premium when they are subject to late-shift work (e.g. on rotating shift), and an additional premium when they actually perform late-shift work. Premium pay for weekend work, when not part of the regular work-week, is also widespread. Under the impetus of collective bargaining, there is also a tendency to pay premium rates for Saturday, and especially for Sunday, work to employees who are regularly scheduled (notably in continuous process industries) to work on these days.[59] In basic steel, for instance, an agreement in 1956 provided for time and one-tenth for standard hours worked on Sunday during the first year of the contract; the rate increased to time and one-fourth during the third year.

Another form of premium pay widely found in American industry is for work on paid holidays. A 1958 study of major collective bargaining agreements points out that "most union contracts with paid holiday provisions also provide for the payment of premium rates to employees who may be required to work on holidays. Among the 1,465 agreements which provided such premium rates, 38 percent stipulated double time (i.e., holiday pay plus straight-time pay for hours worked); 7 percent, double time and one-fourth; 28 percent, double time and one-half; and 18 percent, triple time. The remaining 9 percent of the agreements with premium pay provisions contained other variations." [60]

It may well be that premium rates of one type or another would be found in the complete absence of unionism. A firm might find it necessary, for example, to pay a premium over straight-time rates in order to induce workers to accept late-shift work, to work on Sundays or holidays, or to work overtime. Moreover, some forms of premium pay, in their origin, were intended to perform a regulatory function. Thus, the overtime pay provisions of the Fair Labor Standards Act (1938) in the United States were certainly intended to discourage work-weeks in excess of 40 hours in the interest of spreading employment. Many overtime provisions in union contracts in the United States doubtless have the same objective. In Great Britain, on the other hand, premium pay for overtime in the postwar period seems designed primarily to increase the weekly pay packet rather than to shorten hours of work. It may be partly for this reason that the rate of premium pay is not as high as in the United States.

It is difficult to escape the conclusion, however, that unionism has exerted a strong influence on the creation of the structure of premium rates that now exists in modern industry. Collective bargaining experience in the United States clearly indicates that unions are alert to press for the introduction or liberalization of premium rates whenever the opportunity presents itself. There must be some rationale, of course, for the payment of premiums above straight-time rates of pay. This rationale exists whenever some disadvantageous aspect of employment, as compared with ordinary or normal conditions is found. When some such aspect is identified, unions will tend to seek recognition for the disadvantageous condition in the compensation system.

5. The Administration of Wage Structures

The wage structure of a firm is not fixed; it is subject to change from various forces that impinge upon it. Indeed, unless a wage structure is well administered, it will soon cease to serve as an adequate system of compensation. Wage administration is in the first instance a management function. Unionization, however, will influence the administration of wages at many points and strongly condition the nature of the internal adjustments that must be made from time to time. Unions will also influence, of course, the way in which general changes in wages are applied to the wage structure.[61]

What may be termed the *internal* forces making for changes in wage structures arise from technological innovations, new products, changes in methods and materials, and similar factors. Such changes, which tend constantly to occur in any dynamic industry, become reflected in changing occupational requirements for the firm. Some jobs become obsolete, new occupations are created, new production standards must be established, incentive rates require revision. In unionized firms, the decisions required cannot be made entirely at the discretion of management; at the least, they are subject to union scrutiny and review. The union may participate directly in some decisions; in others, management actions may be subject to appeal through a grievance procedure terminating, if necessary, in arbitration.

If a new job is created, the wage rate for that job must be determined. The appropriate rate may be by no means self-evident. It may be determined by direct bargaining. If the firm has a job evaluation system with union participation, the determination of the proper labor grade for the job presumably will be made within this framework. The determination may be made initially by management; in this case, the union, if it disagrees, may appeal the decision through the grievance procedure. If the content of an existing job is changed, the rate for the job, or its place in an evaluated job structure, may require consideration. Each decision of this nature may be comparatively small in itself, but the decisions have a cumulative effect. If they are not made well, the whole wage structure may in time get out of joint. Frequently changes in job requirements involve deep human relations problems and various methods of accommodation will need to be used.

This latter aspect of the problem is stressed in a careful study of collective bargaining experience with adjustments in pay, work standards, and work assignments in a number of companies in the United States. The study concludes that "in order to facilitate change and to solve problems without resort to arbitration, the parties may disregard the provisions and procedures of the collective agreement. In each of the four cases studied, the management has not, in the face of worker and union opposition, always insisted on the rates called for by job evaluation or the new production standards indicated by time study . . . To some, such readiness to compromise may appear to be unjustified temporizing and dangerous expediency. Experience, however, seems to indicate the need for flexibility and adaptation to particular circumstances; some departure from so-called objective criteria may be necessary to avoid work stoppages, slow downs, and continuing employee dissatisfaction."[62]

A most instructive account of some problems of internal wage administration under collective bargaining in Sweden, based upon interviews at 22 firms, has been presented by Professor Myers.[63] Derber touches upon the same problems in Great Britain.[64] The Tavistock Institute has provided us with a description in unusual detail of the problems encountered in a shift from one method of wage payment to another in a department of a British engineering firm.[65] The U. S. Bureau of Labor Statistics has traced over a five-year period the consequences of the introduction of technological changes at a large bakery, and the ways in which management and the union concerned sought to minimize the impact on the employees.[66]

In the United States, union participation in industrial engineering has become increasingly active. A study by the Bureau of Labor Statistics points out that —

> Union involvement with industrial engineering functions, whether through joint participation, negotiation, informal consultation, or the exercise of grievance and arbitration procedures, has become an important and often routine part of day-to-day plant operations. Instruction of union representatives and shop stewards in the techniques of industrial engineering and in ways of dealing with management on these matters are now fairly common features of union operations in those industries where industrial engineering methods are widely used.[67]

A number of American unions have established industrial engineering departments primarily to provide assistance to their local unions with problems of time and motion study, job analysis, and the setting of production standards and incentive pay rates. The training of local union officials is carried on. Manuals are issued. A notable example of the latter is the *Textile Workers' Job Primer*, issued by the Textile Workers Union of America primarily for the guidance of its shop stewards and business agents in the evaluation of work assignments arrived at by management engineers. The American Federation of Labor-Congress of Industrial Organizations nationally now employs industrial engineers to provide advisory services on request and to arrange training programs and seminars for union representatives.

Some collective bargaining agreements go so far as to provide that union industrial engineers shall have the right to study operations in dispute. One agreement, for example, provides that –

> In any case after a dispute between the parties involving a piecework rate or standard is appealed to the next to final step of the local grievance procedure (or earlier by mutual agreement), the employer will permit a time-study engineer approved by the union to enter the plant for the purpose of making studies of the rate or standard in dispute in order that the union may be in a position to properly present its case. An employer's time-study engineer shall be present during such studies or observations by the union time-study engineer.[68]

A word should be said at this point specifically on incentive wage systems. There is no consistent union position on incentive versus time methods of wage payment. Some unions in the United States are officially opposed to incentive methods of pay; others either approve or have a tolerant attitude. Official positions of the national unions do not always conform with those of subordinate bodies. Kennedy points out that "whatever the position of the international body as expressed in convention resolutions or in the opinions of officers, the study of individual cases reveals that in local plant situations in each industry departures from that position and differences in viewpoint on incentive methods occur ranging from bitter opposition to definite approval." [69] Slichter suggests that "there is some tendency for workers to prefer the system of wage payment under which they work and to which, in consequence, they are adjusted." [70]

Controversy has surrounded incentive systems practically from the beginning.[71] This has been particularly true of those bonus systems in which the earnings of workers do not increase in direct proportion to their output. Straight piece-work systems, on the other hand, may command wide union acceptance in those industries (e.g., the apparel trades) where individual or group output can be readily measured. Union opposition to the use of incentives may manifest itself especially in industries in which work is essentially machine-paced and where it is believed that incentives are used to speed up output unduly.

Union influence on the use of wage incentives takes two forms. First, the union may attempt to determine the method of payment to be used. This may take the form of attempting to obtain conversion of an incentive rate system to a time rate system; of preventing a shift from time rates to incentive rates; or, less frequently, of urging the substitution of incentive rates for time rates. Possibly the best known case in the United States of union pressure for the elimination of incentive systems occurred in the automobile assembly industry following its unionization in the late 1930's. The United Automobile Workers' Union was generally successful in negotiating time-rate systems in the plants of the major producers. It is probable that this outcome can be attributed in part to the conclusion by management that payment by results was no longer an effective incentive in this highly mechanized industry. In the automotive parts industry, organized predominantly by the same union, incentive systems are still widely employed.

The second form of union influence relates to the administration of incentive systems. As an I.L.O. report points out:

> "Probably the most common safeguard to be found in collective agreements with provisions relating to systems of payment by results is a guarantee against changes or cuts in existing rates during the life of the agreement except, in some cases, for such specified reasons as changes in job content or methods of operation, the introduction of new machinery, or to correct clerical errors. Such a safeguard is rendered particularly necessary by the fact that rate-cutting by employers in the past is one of the main reasons why workers are often suspicious of, or hostile to, systems of payment by results." [72]

The protection of workers against arbitrary rate cutting is undoubtedly one of the most important achievements of trade unionism in incentive situations. But important also is union action relating to the determination of the production standards on which incentive rate structures are based. Production standards can be determined in a variety of ways, but of growing importance, for both piece-rate and bonus systems, is the use of time study. This helps to explain the growth of union interest, as described earlier, in industrial engineering. Time study has been subjected to systematic analysis from a union point of view.[73] Within the limits of the personnel available, training is given to local union representatives in incentive industries in time study techniques. Unions sometimes participate jointly with management in the determination of production standards. In other cases, standards are set by management with the right of union appeal, if the standards are alleged to be improper, through the grievance procedure.

In brief, unions in some situations can influence the method of wage payment used, whether incentive or day work.* Where incentives are employed, unions typically have some influence on their administration, both by protecting workers against arbitrary reductions in incentive rates of pay and with reference to the determination of production standards.

Clearly the existence of effective union organization influences the day-to-day administration of plant wage structures. The precise impact of union influence, even on the administration of a wage structure in a specific plant, probably defies complete measurement. It undoubtedly ranges from highly beneficial to both workers and management in some cases to destructive in others. On the whole, union intervention appears to have improved wage administration, in the sense of providing needed protection to workers without adversely affecting necessary adjustment to changing conditions. Much depends, in concrete cases, upon union and management attitude and the extent to which mutual confidence and understanding have developed.

It is now necessary to deal briefly with what may be termed *external* forces that make for change in wage structures. The reference is to the way in which general changes in wage rates, reflecting adjustments to the general forces (cost of living, profitability, etc.) impinging upon wage levels, are applied to the wage structures of firms.

When a general wage increase (or decrease) is decided upon through collective bargaining or company action, the way in which the change is applied to the existing structure of job rates must be determined. The nature of the application will clearly affect the system of job differentials in effect in the firm.

General wage increases applied uniformly in money terms have the effect, of course, of preserving absolute but of lowering relative wage rate differentials among jobs. The application of a wage increase in uniform percentage terms has the effect of preserving relative differentials but of widening absolute differentials. General wage settlements can be applied nonuniformly to meet the objectives of the parties to the agreement. A union may insist, for example, on a larger increase (both absolutely and in percentage terms) for the lower paid workers. Many wage settlements in the United States in recent years have combined a uniform money wage

* In many situations, of course, method of wage payment is not an issue between unions and management.

increase with an additional increase – averaging, let us assume, two cents an hour – for the correction of "inequities" in particular job rates; or a flat money wage increase has been combined with an additional increase for a particular category of workers, usually the skilled.

The application of a general wage increase to workers on incentive presents particular problems. One device is simply to add the wage increase to incentive earnings, leaving the structure of piece or bonus rates unchanged. In essence, incentive earnings are thus supplemented by time payments. In straight piecework systems, the increase may be "factored" into the structure of piecework rates. This means that piece rates are changed so that the level of expected earnings will reflect the increase in wages agreed upon.

Clearly the way in which general wage changes are applied to the wage structures of particular firms will affect systems of job differentials. Job differentials may be increased or reduced in money or percentage terms, or specific wage structure objectives may be accomplished in the distribution of general wage changes. Under collective bargaining, unions obviously have influence on the ways in which wage gains are distributed. This is one of the important items subject to joint determination, and one on which there may well be differences of view from time to time between employer and union representatives.

There has been a distinct tendency in the industrialized countries for occupational wage differentials to decline, certainly in relative terms. Differentials tend to be wider in the United States than in Western Europe, but the relative decline in the United States has been marked.[74] Several underlying factors affecting the supply and demand for workers at different skill levels help to explain this decline in occupational wage differentials. These are principally an increase in the level of education and training of the working population and the mechanization of large areas of unskilled work. A special factor in the United States was the great decrease in immigration following World War I, which greatly curtailed the supply of relatively unskilled labor from abroad.

But the decline in skill differentials during the past two decades, certainly in the United States, has been more rapid than long-run labor market forces would appear to warrant. The following comments appear relevant:

1. The past two decades have been characterized largely by inflation. Wage increases have occurred in considerable measure simply to offset increases in living costs. Lower-paid workers tend to spend a larger proportion of their incomes than higher-paid workers for basic cost-of-

living items. Hence, they may, depending on relative price movements, experience proportionately higher than average increases in living costs. Uniform money wage increases, which are larger percentage-wise for the lower-paid workers, may therefore appear more equitable than uniform percentage increases.

2. It is probably politically easier, especially in an inflationary period, for union leadership to press for uniform money increases. All workers thus appear to be treated equally. In industrial or quasi-industrial unions, unskilled and semi-skilled workers typically make up a majority of the membership. Their political power within the union is bound to be an important consideration in formulating demands and in bargaining strategy. In these circumstances, only a strongly disciplined union with a conscious wage structure policy can readily agree to differential money increases.

3. Skilled workers, within limits, may be content with the maintenance of absolute wage differentials, even though their relative wage position is deteriorating.

4. Employers in many situations may, for a considerable time, be more concerned with the size of negotiated wage increases than with the form of their distribution. This probably reflects, in part, a reluctance by management to make an issue over the distribution of agreed-upon increases with unions that presumably reflect the wishes of their membership.

5. Many unions may themselves have no clearly formulated wage structure objectives. They may not visualize the impact of any particular form of wage increase application on the structure of job rates within a firm. In this sense, the substantial decline in skill differentials in recent years may be partly accidental.

6. Government wage control policy during the years of World War II and the postwar period, in the United States and elsewhere, has reenforced the tendency to grant wage adjustments, especially of the cost-of-living variety, uniformly in money terms.[75]

It should not be assumed that relative occupational wage differentials have uniformly declined in all firms or industries. At least in the United States, this has not been the case. Both unions and management in some industries have shown greater concern than in others for the effect on internal wage structures of the application of general rate increases. There is evidence that this concern is increasing. Myers points out that in Sweden the adverse effect of "narrow differentials on the incentive for a worker to qualify for a more skilled job is generally deplored in management circles . . . Some union officials admitted privately that they were concerned about this problem." [76] In the United States, the tendency for job differentials to narrow has been largely arrested in recent years.[77] Particularly under conditions of reasonable economic stability, the problem of proper job rate differentials is likely to command increased attention.

The "correct" wage structure for a firm or industry is a dynamic concept. Whether, for example, the rate differential between the top and bottom jobs in a particular structure should be 80 percent or 40 percent or 20 percent depends primarily on the nature of the jobs and of the labor market. Presumably in the short-run, job rate differentials need be no greater than are necessary to attract and retain the kinds of labor needed by the firm. In the long-run, however, the question of the size of differentials needed to induce training and the assumption of responsibility that goes with higher level jobs cannot be neglected.

6. **Wage Rates and "Fringe" Benefits**

Even thirty years ago wage structures in most advanced countries could be described largely in terms of straight-time rates (time or incentive). Penalty and special rates were not widely found. Sophisticated approaches (e.g., job evaluation) to rationality in wage structures were not extensively employed. The art of wage administration was in a rudimentary stage of development.

Today the worker's money income is a function not only of basic rates of pay and hours of labor or quantity of output; it may to some extent be augmented by premium payments for work at particular hours and by special rates for the performance of certain designated tasks. But in addition, the worker typically derives certain other benefits from his status as an employee, and those benefits involve cost to the employer. He may, for example, obtain time off with pay for vacation, holiday, sick leave, or other purposes. He may be covered by provisions, the cost of which is borne in whole or in part by the employer, for life insurance, hospitalization, and medical services, and for old-age pensions.

These benefits – called "fringe" or supplementary benefits in the United States – have become of substantial importance to workers and to employers. They may be provided by law or through collective bargaining or employer personnel action. Benefits provided by law may be supplemented or liberalized by private labor-management agreements. In the United States, for example, basic provision is made by law for old-age pensions and for unemployment insurance. But private pension plans, many negotiated by unions, now provide additional protection to millions of workers,[78] and there has been a more recent but significant development of private supplementary unemployment benefit plans.[79] In the case of paid vacations or holidays, there are no legal provisions in the United States insofar as private employment is concerned. However, a vast majority of employees in private industry do in fact receive paid holidays and vacations through collective bargaining or employer practice.[80]

A study by the International Labor Office has thrown light on the importance of supplementary benefits in the total wage costs in selected manufacturing industries in a number of European countries.* In the United States, these costs are now substantial and appear to be increasing, both absolutely and relative to the wage bill. The term "wages" now must be understood to include not only the complex of rates (including premium and special rates) that make up the wage rate structure of a firm or industry, but also a package of supplemental benefits, some legally required and others obtained through direct negotiation, that increase the real standard of life of the worker (paid leisure and protection against loss of income from old age, illness, and unemployment).

In the United States, fringe benefits in addition to basic wage rates enter widely into the collective bargaining process. The result has been the "package settlement," involving some stated adjustment in basic rates of pay plus changes in one or more fringe benefits. The total adjustment in these cases (in terms of its cost to the employer) presumably could have been realized in pay rates alone; the allocation of some portion of the increase to fringe benefits – perhaps an additional paid holiday, more generous vacations, or an increase in pensions – reflects union preference, and perhaps to some extent employer preference as well, for a different kind of distribution of the total wage increase.** Joint decision-making through collective bargaining undoubtedly influences greatly the way in which wage gains are allocated as between rates and benefits. In the absence of union pressure, it is almost inconceivable, for instance, that employee health, insurance, and pension plans would have spread with such rapidity in recent years in the United States.

Almost 70 percent of the major wage settlements concluded in the United States during the first half of 1959 that provided for increases in basic wages also provided for the establishment or liberalization of one or

* See Reference 4. Tables III-X of the ILO study are particularly illuminating.

** The 1955 collective bargaining settlements in the automobile industry in the United States included a general increase in basic wage rates, provision for correction of wage inequities, the inauguration of a supplemental unemployment benefits plan, and liberalization in pension, hospitalization, vacation, and premium pay provisions. See Reference 81.

more supplementary benefits. Activity was most marked in the fields of health and welfare plans, pensions, vacations, and holidays.[82]

To the extent that fringe benefits are jointly negotiated, the effect of their cost on the viable wage "package" can be taken account of directly in the collective bargaining process. This is also true, although somewhat less directly, in cases where new or improved benefits are secured through legislation. The 1959 wage negotiations in Sweden provide a clear example. The unions attached great importance during the wage talks to the pension plan that Parliament was expected to adopt (and in fact did so by a narrow margin). They realized that they could not get both a pension law and a substantial wage increase in 1959, since the pension bill called for sizable employer contributions to the pension fund. A relatively modest wage increase of 2 percent for time workers and 1.5 percent for piece-rate workers was agreed to.[83]

The wage structure of a firm, to conclude, needs to be viewed not only in terms of wage rates but also in terms of supplementary benefits. The structure of both rates and benefits is influenced by the collective views and pressures of workers as expressed through their trade unions. Indeed, the growth of supplementary benefits presents, in many respects, an exceptionally clear view of union influence in molding elements of the wage structure.

7. Summary

The analysis in this chapter of union influence on plant wage structures may be very briefly summarized as follows:

1. Union influence on internal wage structures, which is difficult to trace with precision, makes itself felt largely through the collective bargaining process and through day-to-day contract administration. In view of the dynamics of wage determination, there is no discernible point at which union influence ceases.

2. There is no uniform trade union "policy" on internal wage structures. Union attitudes and policies are shaped by a host of factors, some internal (e.g., the skill composition of its membership) and some external (e.g., character of the labor market) to the union.

3. Plant wage structures need to be viewed not only in terms of hierarchies of basic wage rates and of premium rates, but also in terms of supplementary benefits, representing cost to the employers and added income, leisure, or security to the workers.

4. As an aid in analyzing union wage actions affecting the structure of wage rates, the concept of a "standard rate," as developed by the Webbs,

still has usefulness. A standard rate policy means the establishment, or the attempt to establish, a uniform minimum scale of pay for the workers in a craft or occupation. Wherever work is conducted on a craft basis, a standard rate policy retains its original meaning.

5. The application of the concept of the "standard rate" to the wage structure of a modern factory is much more complicated than its application to industries (e.g., construction or printing) where the division of labor is along craft lines. In the modern factory, the trade union approach to the "standard rate" must take the general form of attempting to secure (1) equal pay for jobs of equal skill or difficulty; (2) a system of wage rate differentials reflecting the relative worth of the jobs, or groupings of jobs, within the enterprise.

6. Wage structure problems may be approached solely through collective bargaining, and viable wage structures may be produced through the bargaining process. Much depends on the attitude of the parties to the bargaining and their willingness or ability to develop some sort of reasoned approach to job classification. Another approach is through some sort of formal job evaluation program, undertaken solely by management (with the right of union protest through the grievance procedure) or jointly by management and the union or unions concerned.

7. Unions differ in their attitude toward job evaluation. A notable example of union-management collaboration in this field is found in the basic steel industry in the United States. On the other hand, some unions object on principle to the job evaluation approach to problems of wage structure. Even in these cases, a pragmatic attitude is often adopted by unions in the United States to the installation of evaluated wage structures.

8. The "standard rate" policy of unions involves the creation of rate uniformity for comparable jobs over as broad an industrial and geographical area as possible. There are, however, many factors that tend to limit the extent to which wage rate uniformity among firms can be achieved.

9. Modern wage structures consist not only of a series of basic rates (time or piece), but also of various special and penalty rates. It seems clear that unionism has exerted a strong influence on the creation of the structure of premium rates that exists in modern industry.

10. Wage structures are not fixed; they must be adapted from time to time to take account of the internal and external forces that impinge upon them. Although wage administration in the first instance is a management function, unionism will influence wage administration at many points.

11. The internal forces making for changes in wage structures arise from technological innovations, new products, changes in methods and materials, and similar factors. These become reflected in changing occupational requirements for the firm. Other wage administration problems grow out of method of wage payment, especially the use of wage incentive systems.

12. The external forces that make for change in wage structures arise from the labor or product markets and take the form of general adjustments in rates. The way in which general rate adjustments are made affects the structure of occupational differentials. In general, skill differentials have tended to narrow in industrially advanced countries, notably in the past two decades.

13. Benefits supplementary to wage rates have become an important part of wage structures. They may be provided by law or through collective bargaining or employer personnel action. Trade unions have played a significant role in shaping the system of benefits that now exists in advanced countries.

References

1. H. M. Douty, "Labor Status and Collective Bargaining", *Monthly Labor Review* (June 1956) pp. 1–7.
2. John P. Windmuller, "Postwar Wage Determination in the Netherlands", *Annals*, American Academy of Political and Social Science (March 1957) pp. 109–122.
3. Lloyd G. Reynolds and Cynthia H. Taft, *The Evolution of Wage Structure* (New Haven: Yale University Press, 1956) p. 225.
4. "Wages and Related Elements of Labor Cost in European Industry, 1955: A Preliminary Report", *International Labor Review* (December 1957) pp. 558–587; for the United States, see U. S. Department of Labor, Bureau of Labor Statistics, Bulletin No. 1186, *Problems in the Measurement of Expenditures on Selected Items of Supplementary Employee Renumeration: Manufacturing Establishments*, 1953 (Washington: Government Printing Office, 1956); *Fringe Benefits*, 1957 (Washington: Chamber of Commerce of the United States, 1958); American Federation of Labor-Congress of Industrial Organizations, "Costs of Fringe Benefits", *Collective Bargaining Report* (March 1956).
5. Sidney and Beatrice Webb, *Industrial Democracy* (London: Longmans, Green and Co., 1897) I, p. 279. See also David A. McCabe, *The Standard Rate in American Trade Unions* (Baltimore: The Johns Hopkins University Press, 1912).
6. U. S. Department of Labor, Bureau of Labor Statistics, Bulletin No. 1245, *Union Wages and Hours: Building Trades* (July 1, 1958) p. 1.
7. H. M. Douty, "Some Aspects of Wage Statistics and Wage Theory," *Proceedings*, Industrial Relations Research Association (1959) pp. 196–211.
8. For a general discussion of these developments see Harry Ober, "The Worker and

his Job", *Monthly Labor Review* (July 1950) pp. 13–22. The tremendous number of jobs and jobs titles in modern industry is illustrated by the *Dictionary of Occupational Titles* (Washington: Government Printing Office, 1949), 2 Volumes. This dictionary, prepared by the United States Employment Service, contains 22,028 defined jobs which are known by an additional 17,995 titles, for a total of 40,023 defined titles.

9. United Automobile Workers, *Solidarity* (November 24, 1958).
10. St. Louis *Post-Dispatch* (May 2, 1959).
11. *Wisconsin Journal* (April 2, 1959).
12. *Pulp, Sulphite and Paper Mill Worker's Journal* (October 1958).
13. *Minneapolis Star* (December 29, 1958).
14. MILTON DERBER, *Labor Management Relations at the Plant Level Under Industry-Wide Bargaining* (Urbana: University of Illinois, 1955) p. 41.
15. DERBER, *op. cit.*, pp. 53–58.
16. *British Trade Unionism* (London: Political and Economic Planning, 1955) p. 61.
17. The literature on job evaluation is extensive. A good basic work is JOHN A. PATTON and C. L. LITTLEFIELD, *Job Evaluation* (Homewood, Illinois: Richard D. Irwin, Inc., revised Edition, 1957). A useful exposition, with many references to United States publications may be found in DAVID W. BELCHER, *Wage and Salary Administration* (New York: Prentice-Hall, 1955) chaps. 6–10.
18. This chapter was prepared prior to the publication of the exhaustive study by JACK STIEBER, *Steel Industry Wage Structure: A Study of the Joint Union-Management Job Evaluation Program in the Basic Steel Industry* (Cambridge, Mass.: Harvard University Press, 1959). The interested readers are referred to this volume for a detailed account of the job evaluation program and its results.
19. ROBERT TILOVE, "The Wage Rationalization Program in United States Steel", *Monthly Labor Review* (June 1947) p. 967.
20. See JOE GOIN, "Job Evaluation in the United States Steel Industry," *Bulletin*, International Metalworkers' Federation (March 1953).
21. For a historical summary of wage developments under collective bargaining in the basic steel industry, see U. S. Bureau of Labor Statistics, Wage Chronology No. 3, *United States Steel Corporation*, 1937–48, and subsequent supplements.
22. GOIN, *op. cit.*
23. TILOVE, *op. cit.*, p. 972.
24. Research Department, International Association of Machinists, *What's Wrong With Job Evaluation* (Washington: 1954) p. 3.
25. *Ibid.*, pp. 4–5.
26. *Ibid.*, p. 71.
27. *Ibid.*, pp. 74–97.
28. Office Employees International Union, *Are You Confronted With Job Evaluation?* (Washington: 1947) p. 1.
29. *Ibid.*, p. i.
30. E. ROBERT LIVERNASH, "Wage Administration and Production Standards", in ARTHUR KORNHAUSER, ROBERT DUBIN and ARTHUR M. ROSS (editors), *Industrial Conflict* (New York: McGraw-Hill, 1954) p. 330.
31. E. ROBERT LIVERNASH, "The Internal Wage Structure", in GEORGE W. TAYLOR and FRANK C. PIERSON (editors), *New Concepts in Wage Determination* (New York: McGraw-Hill, 1957) p. 145.

32. Borje O. Saxberg and Donald L. Barklow, "Union-Management Attitudes Toward Job Evaluation," *University of Washington Business Review* (June 1959) pp. 9–10.
33. Agreement between Tennessee Coal and Iron Division, United States Steel Corporation, and the United Steelworkers of America (August 3, 1956) section 9(g).
34. Agreement between West Virginia Pulp and Paper Company, Charleston Plant, and International Brotherhood of Pulp, Sulphite and Paper Mill Workers and the United Papermakers and Paperworkers, effective July 1, 1958, pp. 54–63.
35. Agreement between Olin Mathieson Chemical Corporation (New Haven, Connecticut) and International Association of Machinists, effective July 29, 1958, p. 78.
36. U. S. Bureau of Labor Statistics, Wage Chronology No. 24, *North American Aviation*, 1941–51, and subsequent supplements.
37. Agreement between North American Aviation, Inc., and United Automobile, Aircraft, and Agricultural Implement Workers of America, effective May 19, 1958.
38. *Ibid.*, pp. 80–81.
39. Research Department, United Steelworkers of America, *A Study of Minimum Rate and Increment Differentials in Steelworker Organized Plants* (Pittsburgh, Pennsylvania, 1958) p. 3.
40. H. M. Douty, "Wages in the Motor Vehicle Industry, 1957", *Monthly Labor Review* (November 1957) pp. 1321–1329.
41. U. S. Bureau of Labor Statistics, Report No. 128, *Wage Structure: Motor Vehicles and Motor Vehicle Parts*, Table 8, p. 35.
42. For example, see U. S. Bureau of Labor Statistics, Wage Chronology No. 9, *General Motors Corporation* (1939–49) and subsequent supplements.
43. U. S. Bureau of Labor Statistics, Report No. 139, *Wage Structure: Machinery Manufacturing*, Winter 1957–58.
44. Toivo P. Kanninen, "Rate Setting by the Army-Air Force Wage Board", *Monthly Labor Review* (October 1958) pp. 1107–1112.
45. *Ibid.*, Table 2, p. 1111.
46. The writer knows of no detailed account in English of experience in the Netherlands with national job evaluation. The brief account above is based largely on John P. Windmuller, "Postwar Wage Determination in the Netherlands", *Annals*, American Academy of Political and Social Science (March 1957) pp. 109–122; and B. C. Roberts, "National Wage Policy in the Netherlands", *Economica* (August 1957) pp. 191–204.
47. Roberts, *op. cit.*, p. 203.
48. *Ibid.*, p. 193.
49. Windmuller, *op. cit.*, p. 116.
50. *Ibid.*, pp. 119–120.
51. T. L. Johnston, "Wages Policy in Sweden", *Economica* (August 1958) p. 214.
52. Swedish Confederation of Trade Unions (LO), *Trade Unions and Full-Employment* (Stockholm, 1953) p. 97.
53. *Ibid.*, p. 97.
54. *Ibid.*, p. 98.
55. Johnston, *op. cit.*, p. 220.
56. See ibid., pp. 227 ff.; also Reynolds and Taft, *op. cit.*, pp. 248 ff.
57. Cited by Johnston, *op. cit.*, p. 216, note 1.

58. Harry P. Cohany and Dena G. Weiss, "Hours of Work and Overtime Provisions in Union Contracts", *Monthly Labor Review* (February 1958) p. 134.
59. U. S. Bureau of Labor Statistics, Bulletin No. 1251, *Premium Pay for Night, Weekend, and Overtime Work in Major Union Contracts* (Washington, 1959).
60. U. S. Bureau of Labor Statistics, Bulletin No. 1248, *Paid Holiday Provisions in Major Union Contracts*, 1958 (Washington, 1959) p. 13.
61. H. M. Douty, *Wage Structures and Administration* (Los Angeles: Institute of Industrial Relations, University of California, 1954) for a laymen's guide to wage structure problems.
62. Richard A. Lester and Robert L. Aronson, *Job Modifications Under Collective Bargaining* (Industrial Relations Section, Princeton University, 1950) pp. 75–76.
63. Charles A. Myers, *Industrial Relations in Sweden* (Cambridge, Mass.: Technology Press, 1951) pp. 34 ff.
64. Derber, *op. cit.*, pp. 53 ff.
65. Elliott Jaques, *The Changing Culture of a Factory* (London: Tavistock Publications, 1951) pp. 73–105.
66. U. S. Bureau of Labor Statistics, Report No. 109, *Studies of Automatic Technology: A Case Study of a Large Mechanized Bakery* (Washington, 1956). Other studies in this series throw light on the problems of wage structure and employee adjustment to technological change.
67. "Union Industrial Engineering Activities", in U. S. Bureau of Labor Statistics, Bulletin No. 1225, *A Guide to Labor-Management Relations in the United States* (Washington, 1958).
68. *Ibid.*, p. 5.
69. Van Dusen Kennedy, *Union Policy and Incentive Wage Methods* (New York: Columbia University Press, 1945) p. 55.
70. Sumner H. Slichter, *Union Policies and Industrial Management* (Washington, D.C.: Brookings Institution, 1941) p. 284.
71. R. Marriott, *Incentive Payment Systems: A Review of Research and Opinion* (London: Staples Press, Ltd., 1957).
72. International Labour Office, *Payment by Results* (Geneva, 1951) p. 70.
73. See William Gomberg, *A Trade Union Analysis of Time Study* (Chicago: Science Research Associates, 1948); Bertram Gottlieb, "Predetermined Motion Time Systems in the U.S.A.", (paper prepared for the International Trade Union Seminar on Pre-determined Motion Time Systems, Dortmund, Germany, October 27–31, 1959). Mr. Gottlieb is the industrial engineering consultant to the AFL-CIO.
74. Reynolds and Taft, *op. cit.*, especially pp. 355–360; for the United States see Harry Ober, "Occupational Wage Differentials, 1907–1947", *Monthly Labor Review* (August 1948) pp. 127–134; Toivo P. Kanninen, "Occupational Wage Relationships in Manufacturing, 1952–53", *Monthly Labor Review* (November 1953) pp. 1171–1178; and James F. Walker, "Occupational Wage Relationships in 17 Labor Markets, 1955–56", *Monthly Labor Review* (December 1956) pp. 1419–1426.
75. H. M. Douty, "Union Impact on Wage Structures", *Proceedings*, Industrial Relations Research Association (1953) pp. 61–76.
76. Myers, *op. cit.*, p. 43.
77. H. M. Douty, "Postwar Wage Bargaining in the United States", *Economica* (November 1956) pp. 315–327.

78. Evan Keith Rowe, "Health, Insurance, and Pension Plans in Union Contracts", *Monthly Labor Review* (September 1955) pp. 993–1000; Walter W. Kolodrubetz, "Characteristics of Pension Plans Under Collective Bargaining", *Monthly Labor Review* (August 1958) pp. 845–853.
79. U. S. Department of Labor, Bureau of Employment Security, *Supplemental Unemployment Benefit Plans and Unemployment Insurance* (1957).
80. U. S. Bureau of Labor Statistics, Bulletin No. 1233, *Paid Vacation Provisions in Major Union Contracts*, 1957; Bulletin No. 1248, *Paid Holiday Provisions in Major Union Contracts*, 1958; Bulletin No. 1224–20, *Wages and Related Benefits*, 19 *Labor Markets*, 1957–58, Tables B-23 and B-24.
81. See "The 1955 Ford and General Motors Union Contracts", *Monthly Labor Review* (August 1955) pp. 875–881.
82. U. S. Bureau of Labor Statistics, *Current Wage Developments* (August 1959) Table 1.
83. U. S. Bureau of Labor Statistics, *Labor Developments Abroad* (August 1959) pp. 5–6.

CHAPTER 5

EXTERNAL INFLUENCES AND THE DETERMINATION OF THE INTERNAL WAGE STRUCTURE

GEORGE H. HILDEBRAND

Cornell University, Ithaca (N.Y.) USA

Probably the weakest area of modern economic theory concerns the determination of the internal wage structure of a plant, firm, or bargaining association. The conventional treatment of the problem reveals two main strands of thought.

One is to start from single-rate theory, in which competitive forces link the firm to the labor and product markets through a unique price for a homogeneous grade of labor. The next step is to modify the explanation, on the one side to allow for differences in personal efficiency, which lead in turn to differences in personal rates; and on the other to recognize broad skill grades, which give rise to a structure of market-determined rates that is adopted by the firm. These last are simply occupational averages, rather than job rates as such.

The other main approach is to disregard the problem altogether, as a question not for economic theory but for the practical arts of business administration and collective bargaining. The evasion may be convenient, but it will no longer do if we are not to surrender the whole field of wage determination for economic analysis. Surely abandonment would be an egregious blunder, for the design of internal wage structures is influenced by economics on almost every side.

At the very time that the competitive model of the labor market and of the firm entered upon its academic supremacy shortly after 1870, historical forces were already busily at work to make it grossly inadequate, if not downright obsolete, as a predictive and explanatory instrument for dealing with the formation and evolution of internal wage structures.

First, the rise of large organizations in business and in government now posed major problems concerning the organization of work – questions of job and wage structure, and of labor procurement, flows, and assignments.* Second, the emergence of business unionism and collective bargaining introduced another novel element to the making of the firm's wage and employment policies. The union has always been an organization with interests and objectives of its own, often of a different order from those of the firm. Naturally, it demands a voice in matters involving job structure, wage structure, and labor flows.

In the rationalistic industrial society of today, wages and employment are now part of a decision-system embracing the many interconnected parts of industrial relations within the firm. This system necessarily includes a whole cluster of policies affecting the occupational structure, the wage structure, the method of wage payment, overall wage compensation, and labor flows involving hiring, promotions, transfers, demotions, layoffs, and recalls.

Any approach to an understanding of particular systems must distinguish and relate the internal and external forces that go into their shaping. In all cases these forces include the influences exerted by the external labor and product markets, for these still survive, although in quite complicated form. Where relevant, they must also embrace unionism, collective bargaining, and statutory regulations.

Inquiry into these problems is still too new to yield a finished theory of wage determination. However, it should provide an enlarged appreciation of the strategic factors at work. Without this, no useful generalizations of any kind are possible.

1. The Nature of the Internal Wage Structure

a. *Inadequacy of the Labor Market as a Pricing and Grading Mechanism*

To some extent, there is an analogy between the actions of a buyer of a list of securities on the stock exchange and the employer who obtains the services of various types of labor. However, as with most analogies one can learn more from the differences than from the similarities.

The bourse offers the prospective buyer a clear-cut list of prices at which alternatives are then available. Each price is attached to a specific security. What is available is thus graded and identified by the market itself. The buyer's task is to select his personal list and the quantities he

* The first attempt to rationalize a job and pay structure was undertaken by the federal civil service, shortly after the Civil War. Frederick Winslow Taylor began his studies of job analysis and wage incentives at the Midvale Steel Company in the early 'eighties. Job evaluation got under way in primitive fashion by 1910, but did not become widespread and sophisticated until the resurgence of unionism in the nineteen-thirties.

desires, with an extensive body of information readily at hand to guide him. Admittedly, the information is incomplete, while the buyer must act despite uncertainty regarding future outcomes.

The employer of labor lacks most of these advantages. Usually the external market provides no single uniform price for each type of labor desired, hence no objective system of prices that the employer can adopt for internal use. The internal system is simply not given. It must be developed from within the employing unit itself.* Equally important, the external market offers no precise grading of labor services, while in practical life these are not abstract and general, but concrete and specific. To the employer, the services for which he pays wages are quite indeterminate until he determines them. In other words, labor services acquire specific economic meaning only in relation to the particular jobs to which they are attached. Development of the job structure thus fixes the requirements for skill, experience, and responsibilities that bound off the kinds of labor needed. Accordingly, the job system is important for the grading function, but it is not the whole of it, for what the employer ultimately seeks in employing a worker is his potential contribution to value product. Partly, this contribution is affected by the content of the particular job, particularly if it is highly mechanized. Partly, too, it depends upon the way in which workers are selected for staffing the job structure, for selection determines the quality of the workers obtained, by grading them for their ability and willingness to work.** Selection thus embraces all of the personnel movements connected with hiring, promotions, demotions, transfers, and dismissals.

The upshot of the discussion so far is that the inadequacies of the external labor market inevitably thrust a heavy burden of decisions upon the employer, beyond those of simple quantity-determinations as such. These

* There are exceptions: starting rates in some cases for manual and clerical jobs; statutory minimum rates; and standardized union rates. However, the latter two are not market-determined rates, although market forces may influence them.

Tacit recognition that the external market fails to provide a graded system of specific rates no doubt explains the tradition in wage theory of concentrating upon one grade of labor, with a single rate level for attacking the employment problem of the firm, despite the interest from Smith's time onward in the broader aspects of external wage differences. Thus Marshall: "The work done by the various classes of operatives in a boot and shoe factory is not all of the same difficulty; but we may ignore differences in the industrial rank between the classes, and suppose them all to be of the same rank."[1] Pigou and Hicks follow the same line, while Clark avoided the whole problem.

** Like the securities buyer, the employer faces some uncertainty of outcome here. However, the outcome will also reflect the influence of the product market, and the quality of equipment, organization and supervision within the firm.

decisions embrace pricing and grading activities that the labor market does not, and inherently cannot, provide. They are coupled inevitably to the larger task of formulating production plans wherein the external product market and wage and employment decisions are linked together. Even more, the whole corpus of these decisions is not determined once and for all, but demands continuous revision as market conditions, technology, and institutional influences undergo change. Here, however, the firm is not merely the passive respondent to outside forces. In all cases, its policies are creative acts by which choices are made in an uncertain world. All firms must innovate merely to operate at all. The failures, rather, are those that innovate only once and then fall into sleepy or rigid routines, or that innovate frequently but in ways that prove decisively unprofitable.

Within the narrower confines of labor policy, it is of interest that attempts to make knowledge more extensive and more systematic in matters of wage structure, wage payment, job structure, and personnel selection and control were not the work of economists in the central theoretical tradition, but instead were the contributions of more mundane experts in wage and incentive systems, job analysis, job evaluation and personnel management, aided more recently by students of modern collective bargaining. The reason is clear: while policies in these fields surely have economic implications of growing interest to some theorists, orderly thinking at the empirical level was inspired in those who were compelled to pay close attention to business practice – its nature and improvement. Latterly, the bargaining specialists, also with an often keen eye to the real world, have examined and interpreted unionism and its impacts in similar spirit. The task of higher generalization and systematization awaits some future theorist, hopefully one in the Marshallian tradition.

b. *The Internal Wage Structure as a Conceptual Construct*

What is an internal wage structure? Viewed in the large, it is a system of wages lying under the control of a common administrative authority. As such, it embraces wage rates on jobs, earnings from jobs, and a variety of wage supplements as well. Viewed more narrowly, it refers to a system of wage equalities and wage differentials, typically, relative job rates and occasionally personal rates, under a common unit of administrative control. Clearly, too, the development of an internal wage structure is inseparable from the development of a job structure to which wage differences normally apply.

What gives unity and coherence to this internal wage system is the wage-making authority to which it owes its existence and by which its outer limits are determined. What, then, is the nature of that authority?

Here distinction must be made between two main cases. If there is no union, management has full discretion in the exercise of its authority, limited only by market forces and statutory regulations. If the firm is a multiplant concern, the question of centralization versus decentralization enters, affecting the internal distribution of administrative power. Local plant managers require discretion for the conduct of daily affairs, but plant wage structures must be kept in line for reasons of competitive costs.

Under collective bargaining, management retains residual authority, but its freedom of action is necessarily circumscribed, by negotiated rules established through bargaining. These rules are both substantive and procedural. They define the job structure and establish the wage structure for the bargaining unit, although job content is usually not negotiated. Further, the rules may embrace a procedure for detailed bargaining over rates for new and changed jobs. Here management usually retains the right of initiative, but its acts can be challenged through the grievance procedure and arbitration.

The natural history of these systems of negotiated rules is for them gradually to embrace the entire employment relationship. Within such an evolutionary context, wages and employment become an integral part of a larger internal system of industrial relations. Moreover, wage and employment rules impart structure both to the labor market and to internal wages, regulating as they do accessions, movements, and exits of workers, together with rates on particular jobs. Thus the union reduces the scope of management authority, at the same time subjecting it to new external pressures. Matters become even more complicated with multiple unionism and bargaining units in a single firm, particularly where, as in aluminum, multiple-plant firms must deal with rival unions at different locations. Finally, where several firms bargain through an employer association, as in building construction and in longshoring, the association itself becomes a second authority, acting as decision-maker for certain wage and employment policies, to which the member firms are bound and through which the discretionary power of each management is further circumscribed. Since association contracts typically fix job rates, here is a case where the internal wage structure extends beyond the firm itself.

Even without collective bargaining, the modern firm must have a wage and employment policy, ranging well beyond that encompassed by the traditional competitive analysis. What collective bargaining does is to add a new set of outside forces, at the same time narrowing the freedom of management to administer the policies it wishes to follow.

Regardless of collective bargaining, although the internal wage structure arises and changes through the exercise of discretionary managerial authority, power in these matters is never absolute. Rather, it is always exercised relative to an environment of externally-imposed constraints, incentives, and imperatives. The environment encompasses the external labor and product markets, institutional organizations such as unions, government, and employer associations, and technological discoveries and improvements. These are the main sources of the stimuli and constraints to which management must respond in the development of its internal wage structure.

The freedom available to the firm may be either broad or narrow. To illustrate, the wage-paying ability of an oil concern is normallymuch higher than that of a textile enterprise, because gross profit margins in petroleum are far less sensitive to changes in labor cost, while product-market competition is much less acute than in textiles. Or, to cite another example, the availability of production workers to a basic steel mill is much less sensitive to changing conditions in the local labor market than is the case for stenographers or secretaries in a larger metropolitan community. In consequence, base rates for production jobs in steel could be set under the joint industry-union evaluation plan with little reference to any "going" rates in the local market.*

The evolution of internal wage structures depends upon the combined effects of three elements: The impacts of the environmental forces just noted, the range of administrative discretion afforded in each case, and the strategies and lines of action by which discretion is exercised.

Here the American industrial scene offers almost bewildering variety, reflecting the decentralized and pluralistic character both of the economy and of unionism. Yet some understanding of this diversity is essential for gaining greater comprehension of the ways in which internal wage systems are both determined and developed.

2. **Diversities in Job and Wage Structures**

a. *Tasks and Jobs*

The job structure in any line of activity takes its major outlines from

* See Reference 2. Total employment of production workers in basic steel has declined slightly in trend since 1947, permitting high turnover without many new entrants. Those "in" the force, either at work or on recall, are already attached, at very high average rates and, at times, earnings. Displacement of labor by technical improvements has provided an expansion joint, allowing most labor requirements to be met internally.

the activity itself – what is produced and the technology employed for transforming inputs into outputs. The structure is merely a synonym for the division of labor internal to the enterprise. Its content and meaning flow from the tasks made necessary by the products or services desired. In very small concerns, the structure often is ill-defined. Tasks are simply assigned to persons, repetitively or diversely, without recourse to formal job classifications. Today such practices are more anachronistic than they are typical.[3]

In essence, the creation of explicit job classifications is an effort to take greater advantage of specialization and to make the selection and control of personnel more systematic. By stabilizing clusters of duties to which prospective incumbents can be assigned with relative permanence, productive efficiency is increased. In spirit, such formalization expresses the functional rationality that pervades the whole of industrial society, vividly illustrated by the rise of mass production and the decline of the artisan and the petty tradesman. In fact, job formalization is the consequence of technological advance and of increasing scale of organizations, aided in laggard cases by the pressure of unions for the standard rate.

Job structures have taken shape from two kinds of forces, both typical of modern industrialism. One involves the differentiation of tasks as such, wherein the advantages of specialization are had without collateral requirements of particular knowledge, skill, or prior experience. Examples would include sweepers, filing clerks, stock clerks, machine feeders and tenders. Here vocational requirements are negligible beyond an aptitude for dexterity and adaptability to monotony. For such jobs, the notion of an "occupation" is purely honorific, lacking all substance.[4]* Quite commonly, they have arisen by decomposing traditional skill clusters, as was undertaken in the aircraft industry to overcome an acute wartime shortage of skilled machinists. By separation of tasks, often accompanied by mechanization, formerly required skills are eliminated, with only a "knack" at most required in their stead.

The other force affecting specialization and job structure is required knowledge and skill, either of the traditional sort or that made necessary by technological advance. Examples of the former would include the chef, the barber, the carpenter, and the bricklayer. Among the latter would be the electrician, the railroad engineer, and the refinery stillman. Here in

* From the honorific standpoint, one is reminded of the obituary for John O'Hara's streetcar conductor, which describes him as having decided "to enter the transportation field."

all cases the word "occupation" has meaning, shaping the external labor market accordingly. And here unionism serves not as a creator of skills but as a perpetuator of tradition.[5]

b. *Activities and Job Structures*

Job structures acquire their main characteristics from the nature of the production process. Here it is useful to distinguish factory work from other activities, such as craft trades and service industries.

Functionally considered, the work of a factory involves the main sequence of physical production, and supportive activities such as maintenance, sales, and accounting. The main sequence starts with receipt of incoming materials and parts; proceeds to processing and fabrication; continues with assembly, inspection, and storage; and ends with packing and shipping. Both the main sequence and the supportive activities usually lead to organizational separation by divisions and departments. Within each such unit there are subdivisions by technical functions, leading in turn to job families and clusters. In each job group there will normally exist a tier of jobs, ranging upward in level of vocational requirements. Mobility is easiest up and down these and closely related particular occupational ladders; less so among more remote job families; and least between departments and divisions. The primary labor flows are vertical within the given line of progression, rather than lateral or even diagonal within the larger confines of the plant. However, where the bulk of the production jobs represents simple subdivisions of tasks, rather than true differentiations by skill and required experience, lateral and diagonal moves can be much wider in scope, making departmental or even plant-wide seniority a workable principle. Thus in copper mining, where plant-wide seniority is often used, reductions of forces will involve extensive "bumping" by employees from the open pit mining division to the reduction works or even into repair and maintenance of equipment.

Factory job structure may be illustrated by an aluminum extrusion plant. The main sequence starts with the cast house, where ingots are received from primary aluminum plants, sawed up, and remelted in electric furnaces. After cooling, the metal is moved to the extrusion department, where it is converted to desired shapes- as sheets, tubing or channels. In the next stage, the product enters the finishing department, where it is cut, straightened, polished, and if need be, assembled. Following these operations, it enters storage. As incoming orders are filled, it is inspected and then packed for shipment.

Each main stage in the production sequence, and each of the principle supportive activities, embraces a collection of jobs and of particular job groups. Some jobs are purely menial and self-determined – loader, packer, shipper, or helper. Others require little skill and experience, embracing a wide range of machine operations. Some reflect genuine skills – extrusion press operator, millwright, plant physician, or salesman. Obviously, technological advance and simple subdivision of tasks both have gone into the making of this job structure, as would be equally true of a steel mill, an automobile plant, a brass foundry, or an oil refinery.

Vertical and functional segmentation of the factory job structure is inherent technologically. Technology makes certain jobs key positions from the standpoint of labor cost and as the strategic points for certain processes, around which other jobs become automatically grouped – for example, extrusion press operator and his helpers, or miner and mucker underground. By automatically invoking particular lines of job progression, technology also puts a premium upon accumulated plant experience, operating at the same time through mechanization and work simplification to downgrade former skills, while creating or preserving others in the upper tiers of each specific promotional sequence. In turn, the greatly increased importance of training on the job makes promotion-from-within a logical development of personnel policy, a practice that draws added support from the natural tendency of the vertically-oriented production worker to consider himself permanently "in the plant" once he has passed the probationary period. Refusal to "pirate" labor from nearby concerns has equally logical origins, reflecting as it does not an insidious monopsonistic conspiracy but recognition that turnover is needlessly costly, that plant experience adds to labor efficiency.[6] Codification of all this through collective bargaining, expressed in seniority rules, is but further recognition of the same principles, posing, however, new issues regarding freedom of managerial selection for promotions, demotions, transfers, and layoffs.

The factory job structure has important consequences for the labor market, as Clark Kerr has ably pointed out.[7] It leads directly to a division of the market into "outside" and "inside" segments. The outside sector supplies labor primarily for starting jobs in production, and for maintenance and clerical work. The inside one provides workers for the inner steps of the many promotional ladders. Since experience and adaptability count for more than skill in the usual case, the number of bidders normally will exceed the number of vacancies. Job price does not clear the market, so direct rationing is required – by selection or strict seniority, or some combination of the two.* Wages within and between ladders of promotion are interrelated, to be sure, but not because the jobs are substitutes for each other. Both within and among promotional sequences, there is relatively strict complementarity, imposed by the underlying technical process. Whatever marginal choices exist will be discrete and large, for example, whether to shut down a duplicate line, whether to add an overtime shift, whether to install new equipment.

Consider now by contrast a small housebuilder with a portable firm. His job structure, too, will be defined by a required technology, but largely it will rest upon traditional skills, powerfully enforced by firm trade-union rules. Since he will normally have to deal with the construction trades, each representing a traditional skill with its own bargaining unit, his job structure will be determined automatically for him, and a ready-made wage structure to go with it. Because his bargaining relations with the building trades will normally be conducted for him by an association of employing contractors, he finds himself in the position of the uncomplicated quantity-adjuster of simple competitive theory — except that at times he will have to pay his craftsmen overscale rates to keep them around.

Yet, as in California, where anything can happen, the forces of changing technology and of increased organizational size have made themselves felt even in construction, frequently altering the lot of the small custom builder, too. Very often he has become a big operator, building tract houses in volume, or undertaking major non-residential projects-developments that permit factory methods at the site, with breakdown of some tasks, specialization, mechanization, skill dilution, and relative permanency of job tenure. In addition, some site work has been shifted to the factory itself – wallboard for plaster, cabinets, prefabrication of frame lumber, and even whole houses. On the site, mechanical hoists replace laborers and hod carriers with operating engineers, while mobile crews of craftsmen now turn out repetitively items such as foundations, plumbing units, framing, flooring, and painting.

Turn, next to office work. In his study of banks and insurance firms in Boston, George Shultz has found considerable standardization of jobs – filing clerks, typists, stenographers, and secretaries, for example. Here, too, is a ready made job structure, imposed by the nature of the services rendered and by the tools for rendering them. While there is an order of progression for these jobs, the skills required at the higher levels are usual-

* The principle of seniority is the principal device for job control for an industrial union.[8]

ly acquired in high school or business college. Surprisingly, there is considerable market uniformity in salaries, so that, roughly speaking, the employer's internal wage structure is market-determined, rather than internally designed. The reasons are that clerical workers are quite mobile, while the clerical market is comparatively well organized through intermediaries such as school counselors and employment exchanges, and by systematic surveys by the employers themselves. There is no trade-union organization to structure the market or to reshape job rates. Some employers pay salaries below average as a deliberate tactic, accepting lower quality applicants and moving up their scales only as their competitors do. Others stress aggressive recruiting methods, including non-pecuniary benefits – cafeterias, attractive surroundings, and so on.

Here, then, is a job and wage structure largely given by the market – a special case that Hicks once thought to be general – where relatively pure competition truly is a powerful wage determining force.[9]

Finally, consider the railroads. Again, the job structure has emerged and changed under the impacts of technology – a technology that in its essentials came into being a long time ago. However, the structure can only be fully explained by recognition of the quite ancient craft system through which the railroad unions have organized the industry from their beginnings almost a century ago.

The production of railway services involves a complex of functions, part manual and part clerical, at both fixed and mobile locations. Technology has imposed an extensive array of tasks, most of which are distinct and inherently separable – for example, locomotive engineer, conductor, station agent, shop mechanic, rate clerk, and section foreman. For many of these tasks, skill is the distinguishing element. Separability of skills made logical the craft-union structure, although the latter mainly owes its origins to the dominance of craft-union principles at the time the railroad workers were first organized. Today there exist some seventeen railroad unions, representing the operating brotherhoods, the yard groups, the shop crafts, and the clerical organizations.

Despite many functional parallels between railroad and factory work, craft stratification of railroad employees has given the roads a system of industrial relations in many ways similar to that in the construction industry. Craft bargaining units have meant separate job jurisdictions and quite rigid rules for the separation and allocation of work. These have impeded vertical flows of labor along "natural" promotional sequences, also checking to some extent the decomposition of some skilled jobs into simpler forms of specialization. Craft separatism has also contributed to the perpetuation of traditional jobs, despite the eroding effects of changes in technology.* Finally, the craft structure makes for complex collective bargaining, conducted along national association lines by the roads, dealing separately in turn with functional groups such as the operating brotherhoods of the shop crafts. In consequence there has emerged an equally complex internal wage structure, having both industry-wide and system-wide characteristics. Further, the mobile nature of operating jobs gave rise long since to a dual system of wage calculation, in which time and distance both serve as factors, together with an array of special allowances to recognize excessive time in terminals, etc.[10]

Accordingly, the job and wage structure of the American railroads has taken its peculiar form not from the influence of technology alone, but from collective bargaining, particularly from the craft-structure of the bargaining units represented by the participating unions.

c. *Some Major Determinants of Job Structure*

These few examples will serve to indicate the great variety of job and wage structures extant in the American economy, although these divergent characteristics no doubt can be found in other advanced industrial economies. They also suggest the major causal forces that have gone into their making.

Obviously, one of these is technology, which both makes industrial products possible and defines the technical functions requisite to the production process. In the large, these functions are not limited to the transformation of materials and services, but necessarily include the entire array of specialized activities in any modern firm, from insurance to automobile manufacture – managing, record-keeping or selling, to name a few. Each calls for a complex of specific tasks that are the raw material of job structure. As technological advance makes available new products, processes, equipment, and tools, it alters both functions and tasks. Job structures are thus rarely static, unless social institutions make them so.

It would be both easy and also patently wrong to conclude that technology is the sole or predominant determinant of job structure. It is not. In the first place, management usually has a continuing choice among several particular technologies available for a chosen line of production

* The trend of increased labor productivity on the railroads has been high. However, it has been achieved mainly through new or improved capital equipment – more powerful locomotives, electronic classification yards, and automation of record-keeping – rather than through breakdown of traditional skilled jobs.

with the inception of operations and thereafter. Selection here is a matter of economics, not of technology alone. In the second, either acting alone or in company with a union, management has the task of translating technically required functions and tasks into specific jobs. Here broad discretion usually exists. Jobs can be made extremely narrow, by extreme specialization, or quite broad by contrast, a choice partly dictated by the firm's hiring policy and the tightness or looseness of the labor market. In the third place, competition in the product market compels frequent changes in technique and in work organization, constantly driving firms to create new jobs, abolish old ones, and change others. Under the lash of profit-and-loss economics, job structures are rarely static, while their specific form depends upon the way in which management uses the discretion available to it.*

Technology, therefore, does not impose a ready-made job structure. Moreover, while management erects and develops the structure, the labor union enters as an independent force. In craft industries, union bargaining units are based upon traditional skills. Here the pressure for organizational survival leads to perpetuation of the internal job structure, dividing it by established functions into distinct job-groups, each narrowly defined by the typical apprentice-helper-journeyman sequence. Thus, in the building and printing trades, the composite structure that the employer must accept is partitioned into specific craft-job units, and the internal wage structure similarly – to illustrate, printers, compositors, and mailers in a newspaper plant. Undoubtedly, printing technology underlies this overall job and wage system, just as technology gives rough form to all internal job and wage structures. However, union-imposed bargaining units impress precise structure and content upon the array of necessary tasks. The system can neither be understood nor explained, therefore, without recourse to its pattern of collective bargaining.

Factory unionism operates somewhat differently, mainly because the problem of job-control is of quite different nature. Normally, the industrial bargaining unit is not tied to a specific skill but embraces a whole complex of jobs. Where it appears, interest in the perpetuation of particular jobs or of crew arrangements stems not from a vested interest in

* Even where union resistance is strong competition will impel technological change, particularly of the "creeping" variety, altering the duties and skills in craft jobs. However, where unions build their jurisdictions around a craft, they can impose an enduring structure for the division of tasks, even if job content is slowly eroded by change. The survival of the railway fireman on diesel locomotives and the traditional job structure in the building industry are strong American cases in point.

skill but from concern over employment security.* Because the perspective of industrial unionism inevitably extends over the whole range of production, and at times even clerical, jobs, wage rate equalities and differentials within the internal wage structures are conventionally decisive focal points for wage bargaining. Because factory labor is usually not "market-oriented," and instead looks up particular promotional ladders, there is relatively low inter-plant labor mobility. Except where major displacement threatens, jobs as such are less sacrosanct, although there will be much specialized bargaining over wage rates for new and changed jobs. Thus the industrial employer ordinarily will enjoy considerable discretion in the design and development of job structure as such. Discretion will be greatest if the initial structure is created before the advent of a union. It will continue relatively large if the firm can evade commitment to negotiated job descriptions, and either avoid major labor displacements or concede cushioning devices to the unions, such as retraining, supplemental unemployment benefits, severance pay allowances, or displacement geared to natural turnover alone.

Viewed as a whole, technology, management discretion, competitive economics, and collective bargaining all enter into the making of internal job structures. There remains a word about the technical characteristics of the latter, made necessary because internal job and wage structures are closely linked to each other, hence cannot be adequately understood in isolation.

Any job structure rests upon a differentiation of tasks In turn, the separation and clustering of tasks involkes both variance and similarities in the main elements of job content – required knowledge, skill, and experience; particular working conditions, such as heat, noise, heavy lifting, or safety; and responsibility for materials, equipment, product, and possibly the work of subordinates. Thus job structure is a method of grading labor, as a condition precedent to its pricing.**

* Overall attrition or stagnation of employment in certain firms and industries thus lies back of recent bitter controversies over work rules. Here the unions are fighting to preserve jobs in order to protect employment and through this, membership size, irrespective of effects on business efficiency.

** To preserve flexibility, gain efficiency, and control labor costs even with rigid wage rates and fixed wage supplements, employers have traditionally favoured full freedom to break down skill content by simple subdivision and specialization. For the same reason, they have sought to limit union challenge in these matters to grievances over the appropriateness of wage rates on new or changed jobs, leaving changes in jobs as such to their own discretion. Along the same line, most managements resist attempts of unions to make job descriptions a negotiable issue, since detailed written descriptions

Most jobs tend to cluster together in small groups, where the weights of the comparative elements suggest a natural vertical hierarchy for each group. In a craft-determined structure, these vertical hierarchies are very restricted, and the notion of a promotional sequence has but very limited meaning. In its larger aspect, this kind of job structure will embrace a lateral system of specialized craft job groups, each insulated from the other, and all of them overlaid by the supervisorial level.

In the factory case, the vertical hierarchy for each job family will normally be much wider in progression, while the number of such job-sequences will be much larger. Further, these promotional sequences will involve a total hierarchy whose progressively higher tiers will reflect the increasing weight of skill and experience. Factory job structure thus emphasizes both vertical and lateral aspects, involves more movement between immediately parallel promotional sequences, and poses far more complex problems of equalities and differentials in basic job rates. These equalities and differentials lie at the very heart of the problem of internal wage structure.

3. The Influence of the Labor Market

a. *Links between the Labor Market and the Internal Wage Structure*

We have already pointed out that, although the internal wage structure is normally not "given" as something imposed from without, external forces do enter into its making. Obviously, the labor market is one of those forces. Its strength and the range of it impacts will depend directly upon the effectiveness of competition, and inversely upon the ability of management and the union to enforce non-competitive rates and practices. Or, to put it a little differently, the market influences internal wage rates through labor supply. It does so in its double role as a source of candidates for jobs and as a channel of escape for employees who are actively interested in looking elsewhere.

The labor market exerts its main force upon internal wage rates through "market-oriented" jobs, that is, jobs that are fairly uniform in duties and vocational requirements as among firms in the local area. Hence both candidates and incumbents can make some comparison of wage rates and other employment conditions. Such jobs will be particularly sensitive

---

tend to freeze the job structure and to establish fixed ideas of wage equity among the employees. Finally, similar purposes are served in some cases by introducing A-B- and C classifications. Obviously, these practices are much more limited in craft industries.

to the market, which manifests itself through the number and quality of new applicants and through the voluntary quit rate. When the market is loose, there will be a rise in number and quality of applicants and a fall in the quit rate. When it is tight, the reverse circumstances will hold.*

In the factory case, there are relatively few market-oriented jobs, for several reasons. As already noted, most factory labor is not actively "in the market" and in fact knows little or nothing about outside alternatives. Also, many factory jobs are often so highly specialized as not to be readily comparable. Beyond this, the dominant importance of promotional sequences means that there is a constantly available internal supply of labor for staffing most of the structure.**

In consequence, market-oriented factory jobs are concentrated at the starting level, in standard maintenance occupations, and in clerical work. Here quality of workers, numbers available, and the quit rate all have importance. Here, also, the market can directly influence job rates, "bending" the internal structure on occasion.

By contrast to the factory case, as Shultz's Boston study suggests, the metropolitan market for clerical labor contains several market-sensitive jobs, making most of the internal salary structure quite vulnerable to outside forces, even without trade unionism. The jobs themselves are usually standard in duties and requirements. Accordingly, the going rate and other conditions have tangible significance to employers and workers alike. Because the market is rather well organized and provides fairly effective communications, each employer is quite sensitive to changes in accessions and retentions enforced by shifts in labor supply and demand. For the same reasons, the internal salary structure and its movements are determined with considerable precision by market forces.

In skilled craft trades, effective unionism of a peculiar type has greatly circumscribed the action of market forces. Unionism and collective bargaining, rather than the market, impose the job and wage structure upon the employer; jobs are not market-oriented but union-oriented. The labor market for each craft is sealed off by the union's system of job control, which regulates entry, turnover, and exits throughout the market.

* Reynold's study of the New Haven factory labor market for manual workers indicates that new applicants come mainly from new workers and the unemployed, and to a much lesser extent from the dissatisfied employee [11].

** Creation of semi-skilled jobs by simple specialization strengthens this advantage, by reducing necessary training time and required knowledge and skill. Thus the number of potential candidates for most factory jobs normally well exceeds the number required. Therefore direct rationing becomes inevitable.

Through its effective monopoly of skill, the union achieves both job standardization and effective enforcement of a non-competitive and generally uniform single rate in the area. Turnover may be quite high, but mainly only where labor engagements are temporary.

However, when the market becomes tight, the effects for the employer are the same as in the industry and clerical markets: available new workers shrink in number and decline in quality, while voluntary quits may become a problem. In time, the employer may have to resort to premium payments to acquire and to hold satisfactory labor, warping his wage structure accordingly.* When the market is loose, the situation is in reverse, although wage rates will stay rigid downwards.

b. *The Labor Market, Wage Contours, and Key Rates*

Dunlop has proposed the concept of a "wage contour" to identify one of the key links between internal and external wage structures.[12] In its strict meaning, the contour suggests a line of strict interfirm equality in the wage rates for comparable jobs. However, Dunlop uses it in two contexts: one to designate a common group of wage-setting agencies, for example, plants, firms, or bargaining units that accept their interdependence; and the other to refer to particular jobs having common significance to a group of interdependent wage setters who are linked together by a common labor or product market or by both together.

For present purposes, market-oriented jobs are one type of occupational contour, while union-oriented jobs are quite another. Both provide some of the main pillars of the internal job and wage structure, the former because their wage rates are so sensitive to external market conditions. Thus they represent one kind of key job, with a key rate in the structure. They do so because the work is comparable, the employers compete for this kind of labor, and mobility is greater among such workers. Accordingly, the rate for a market-oriented key job must be adequate to draw and to hold the quality of labor sought, in the numbers desired. For competitive reasons, therefore, the rates for those key jobs are unusually interdependent as among the employing firms in the local labor market. For the same reason, they will be peculiarly strategic for the internal structure.

However, as will be shown later, there are other kinds of key jobs that are not market-oriented, yet also are strategic for the interior system. Some acquire such status through unionism and collective bargaining,

* Here the market is enforcing a competitive rate. "Red circle" rates for factory labor often have similar origin.

for example, skilled crafts and union-oriented industrial jobs. Others may obtain it because they are cost-sensitive for the product market, and still others because of their technical importance relative to closely related jobs in a given occupational grouping.

Market-oriented jobs vary widely by industry. They are negligible in craft trades, yet quite pervasive in clerical work and in the service industries generally. In factory work they are quite limited in number, yet quite decisive for certain points in the wage structure. Obviously the presence or absence of unionism makes a difference, but even under collective bargaining the labor market may narrow discretion in wage determination for this kind of key job.

c. *Adjusting to The Labor Market: The Wage Rate as a Selective Variable*

Traditional equilibrium analysis has long emphasized changes in the job rate as the main mechanism for internal adjustment to changes in labor supply. Properly understood, however, theory has also recognized other modes of response besides wage adjustments – alterations in non-pecuniary benefits, in average level of worker efficiency, and, to some extent, in total money earnings inclusive of supplements to the base rate. To these should be added variations in recruiting efforts and revisions in job content. For a time at least, manipulation of these other elements can substitute for changes in wage rates for market-oriented jobs and, indeed, for all jobs for which labor supply alters.

For instance, suppose that the local labor market becomes progressively tighter. To avoid raising wage rates, the employer may intensify his recruiting efforts, perhaps improving non-pecuniary conditions as well. In some cases he may be able to simplify certain jobs, breaking them up into multiples requiring a lower grade of labor. If necessary, he may reduce his standards for hiring and for promotion, deliberately accepting candidates of lower efficiency on the premise that the enforced rise in unit labor costs will be temporary, that poorer workers later can be laid off or demoted.[13] For the same underlying reasons, he may tolerate some rise in costs of turnover, and some fall of efficiency among the already employed, the second expressed by increases in absenteeism, tardiness, and bad work, and possibly by slow-down tactics.*

Together, these responses serve as expansion joints for absorbing the shock of a change in market forces, one that enables the employer to put off raising wage rates, mainly by tolerating a decline in labor efficiency

* In market theory, all of these reactions may be depicted as a movement of the labor-supply curve upward and to the left – i.e., as a decrease in supply.

and a rise in indirect employment costs. Although unit labor cost will still rise, to some extent its course will be reversible when the market loosens up. By contrast, a rise in wage rates for practical purposes is irreversible. However, if tightness persists for a long period, eventually the employer will have to raise his wage rates, simply to check the fall of labor efficiency to intolerable levels.*

Turning now once more to rates for market-oriented jobs, we may regard them as efforts of the firm to attain an equilibrium wage, where demand and supply quantities are balanced for conditions then prevailing. The more effective is competition, the narrower will be the discretionary range within which the rate will be set, and the more uniform will be this rate among employers along the same occupational contour. Even with equilibrium, however, there can be interfirm dispersion in such rates, reflecting variance in quality of labor and in non-pecuniary attractions. Long ago both of these were recognized by competitive analysis.[15] However, when market conditions change, the cushioning effect of the expansion joints noted above help to absorb the shock, permitting delay for some time even in the adjustment of market-oriented key rates. In practice, the discretionary range may be quite narrow, but never attaining a point. The theorist's quest for determinacy can never be wholly successful.

4. The Influence of the Product Market

a. *Links Between the Product Market and the Internal Wage Structure*

The product market exerts its main influence upon wages and employment through the rate of sales and through the sensitivity of product price to the actions of close competitors. The relationship between cost and price sets the margin of net profit, and so is the primary determinant of survival or extinction. Here, therefore, economics can powerfully affect wage making.

For a given price and a given sales rate, the margin of net profit will depend upon the level of unit total cost. This, in turn, will depend partly upon the level of unit labor cost. The latter provides the main link from the product market to the internal wage structure. The level of job rates, of course, affects unit labor cost, but so do the rate of output, labor efficiency, the distribution of the work force among jobs, and supplemental employment costs.

* Since other firms competing along the same labor-market contour will be raising rates, any given employer who holds off too long risks loss of his wage-paying reputation as he fall back down the "wage escalator." To stay "in line," he cannot delay a rise indefinitely [14].

From the standpoint of internal wage structure, certain jobs are "cost-oriented." First, they may bulk critically large for unit labor cost because most of the firm's labor force is massed in such classifications, for example, assemblers in an automobile plant, or operators and mechanics in a transit operation, where highly compressed job structures prevail. Second, certain jobs may be cost-oriented not from employee concentration, but because they lie at the center of an occupational planetary system, to which other job rates are closely bound, by custom, contract, or technology. In either case, cost-oriented jobs are major supports for the entire wage structure, because of their strategic importance to unit labor cost, and through the latter, to the margin of profit.

Obviously, the degree of their importance depends in turn directly upon the ratio of unit labor to unit total cost. It also depends upon the state of competition in the product market – the ease or difficulty with which the firm can raise or maintain price without marked collateral effects upon the rate of sales. A favorable cost ratio, or competitive position, or both together, affords a higher ceiling for the internal wage structure, hence more wage space within which to maneuver.* The contrast between an oil refinery and a textile mill, which shows up clearly in wage statistics for these fields, well illustrates favorable and unfavorable configurations here.

The product market can also influence the internal wage structure through the effects of variations in the rate of sales upon the rate of production. Increases in output lead to higher earnings from incentive systems and through increased overtime work. They may also invoke accelerated rates of promotion to higher-rated jobs, again with attendant higher earnings. Yet wage rates need not change at the same time, if at all. Still, relative earnings will alter as among all jobs in the structure. Further, these increases in earnings are reversible in great part. Where sales fall off and production contracts, earnings also drop. Thus here, too, is an expansion joint by which shocks imposed by the product market can be cushioned in their effects upon job rates.

b. *The Product Market, Wage Contours, and Key Rates*

Jobs become cost-oriented particularly where the profit margin is sensitive to changes in unit labor cost. Accordingly, in such cases they

* Some readers will no doubt recognize here the presence of two of Marshall's four factors that conjointly shape the price-elasticity of demand for labor – elasticity of demand for the product and the ratio of labor to total cost. The other two – ease of substitution of capital for labor and elasticity of supply of capital – usually enter over the longer run.

acquire the status of key jobs with key rates for the job and wage structure.* They cannot be easily manipulated as to rate without major effects upon cost, hence they become decisive for wage policy in such circumstances. By contrast, where the job structure is very wide in its vertical range, as in basic steel, few classifications need be cost-oriented, and the strategy of wage-fixing will pivot around other factors. However, this is not to say that considerations of overall unit labor cost need not be decisive, for this will depend upon the amount of wage space available.

Cost-oriented jobs involve a special kind of contour of their own. It takes its origin not from the labor market nor from a particular bargaining system, but from competition in the product market. Competition here aligns certain employers in an interdependent relationship where the ratio of unit labor cost to price is critical, even if the firms operate in different local labor markets. Key jobs of the cost-oriented type thus involve close interdependence of wage rates as among firms. Departures from the norm are not likely undertaken. Put alternatively, the contour imposes a restraint upon the particular wage rate, exerting thereby a stabilizing effect upon the whole internal structure.

Beyond the limited domain of particular cost-oriented jobs, the product market may impose a different and broader kind of contour, made up of a group of firms that compete in the same product market, and whose product prices are thus closely interrelated.** No one producer, acting alone, can raise price to protect his profit-margin when unit total cost is rising, because he then risks a serious loss in sales. In consequence each firm is very sensitive to changes in unit labor cost stemming from higher wage rates and supplements, particularly when labor cost is a significant proportion of total cost. From this it follows that such firms will act "co-respectively" to each other, in raising both average wage levels and product price. Each tries to "stay even with the competition," by holding to the common contour.***

If, further, the overall demand for the products of these firms were to

* They are also likely to be union-oriented jobs under collective bargaining, and on occasion may be market-oriented as well.

** Thus the cross-elasticities of demand among the separate products are very high, because the products are close substitutes for each other.

*** Joint bargaining committees, pattern-following in wage setting, and association bargaining all represent attempts of this kind. In one form or another, these approaches have developed in collective bargaining in the automobile, rubber, basic steel, and construction industries, as well as in many others. The same principle underlay the efforts of steel fabricators to escape from the basic steel contour in the late 'forties, in short, to act from their own product contour.

decline, or to become much more elastic through increased competition from imports or domestic substitutes, each firm on the contour will regard demand as a ceiling that imposes firm limits upon increases in wage rates or supplements at the particular time. This evidently underlay the resistance of both the textile and the boot and shoe industries to union pressure for wage increases during 1947–50. The product-market contour, rather than either the local labor market or union-imposed "orbits of coercive comparison," provided the line against which wages and wage increases were held.

This, it seems to me, was the major economic difficulty underlying the basic-steel strike in 1959. Previously during the postwar years, the industry sustained, indeed, conceded in negotiations, wage increases averaging perhaps 8 per cent a year in cumulative increase of labor cost, raising its prices in parallel during the same period. The producers were following a common product-market contour, experiencing little difficulty in raising prices so long as they did so, because demand conditions were very favorable in the long run.

By 1959, the demand situation had begun to turn adverse, threatening to become much more so. Faced at last with some excess capacity, foreign producers were now competing agressively with American steel exports in third markets. If American prices were to rise much further, steel imports could also become a real threat, because their disadvantage in shipping cost was shrinking rapidly with the continuing rise in domestic steel prices. Along with this, new domestic substitutes – wood, plastic, and concrete – were already cutting into the steel market. In other words, the aggregate demand for American steel had already turned much more price-elastic, promising to become even more so with the threat of increased competition from imports as well. Demand was now starting to cramp further price increases. All the firms along the contour felt it. The situation was therefore clear: further increases in unit wage cost threatened a real squeeze against profit margins. The trend rate of increase in man-hour productivity – about 2.5 per cent annually – was inadequate to offset the eight percent average annual rise in postwar labor costs. To protect the long-run prospective profit rate, therefore, the employers had to reduce their wage concessions below what they had been granting in previous negotations.*

* This is not to say that the desired profit rate was economically appropriate; nor that the companies' sudden precipation of the work-rules controversy was strategically wise; nor that bargaining relations had nothing to do with the intractability of the dispute. All that is affirmed is that the product market posed a major obstacle to easy settlement.

From the economic side, consequently, the product-market contour played a decisive role – in fact, had done so for many years. Given a single great union, whose range of employee organization is virtually product-market wide, a common pattern of wage increases has become institutional. Competition among the steel producers enforces high interdependence of product prices. For the same reason, it imposes interdependence of company wage structures. Operation of the product-market contour thus becomes the key to wage determination in the American steel industry. In many other industries, the same force can be seen at work.

5. The Influence of Collective Bargaining

a. *Bargaining Structures*

We have seen that both the labor and the product markets can give rise to key jobs and key rates in the internal wage structure, as well as affecting it in broader ways. The same is true of unionism, which can impose contours of its own, through collective bargaining.

Considerable diversity is evident here, reflecting the variety of union bargaining structures. In craft trades and industries, the union has a lateral orientation, because it organizes by skill and extends its range over many employers, even in different industries. Its traditional purpose is to achieve job- and wage-rate uniformity for the particular skill that it supplies. The result is to cross-cut the job and wage structure of each employer in the trade with a lateral stratum embracing its own minute job cluster and wage structure. The same phenomenon occurs when the union organizes a segment of factory work, for example, pipefitters or carpenters in an aluminum plant. In other words, the craft union represents a wage contour identified with a key job and a key rate, with interpolated differentials for apprentices and helpers. The employer must then accept multiple bargaining units, each of which involves a quite rigid job and wage structure. Craft unionism thus replaces the work of the unorganized and imperfectly competitive labor market, substituting a peculiar market of its own, governed by the system of rules developed by the union and extended through collective bargaining.*

In a craft industry, the product depends upon a cluster of skills. Thus there may exist close parallelism between the contours imposed by the craft unions involved and that deriving from the product market. Where

* As Kerr has noted, competitive reasoning regards these structuring rules as "frictions." Actually they change the nature of the whole market, allowing a quite different evaluation.

both types of contours match in geographical radius, adjustment to their respective impacts upon wage making becomes a straightforward problem of accommodating union pressures to cost-price resistance. This is the usual situation in the buiding trades, because the product is mainly not exportable. If, however, the union and product-market contours diverge in geographic range, they can clash seriously, posing acute bargaining difficulties. This occurs for specialized firms using carpenters and sheet-metal workers to produce kitchen cabinets and range hoods for regional markets, or for large printing houses selling in a broad market. Local wage-making can then conflict with the product-market contour, indeed, also clashing with local wage-making in other areas embraced by the same product market.

Consider now factory unionism. Here the job structure is vertically oriented within the plant, but the union nonetheless has a horizontal interest, invoked by the other plants and firms with which it deals. This broader organizational interest need not be defined nor limited necessarily by the product market, for the organizational structure of the union may well extend over many different product markets. Thus the particular wage-making contour that an industrial union seeks to enforce upon the employer can pose a conflict with the contour defined by his product markets. Often the union itself must resolve the problem, by segregating its membership and its policies according to industry lines, as the machinists have done in distinguishing railroad, aircraft, shipyard, and job-shop work. Another strong case is the steelworkers' reluctant concession of a separate wage pattern for steel fabricating relative to basic steel production.

Although there is a clear tendency for industrial unionism to develop distinct groups of bargaining units in response to pressures emanating from different product markets, even broader organizational interests may at times supervene – with important consequences for internal wage structures. This occurs in various contexts. To illustrate, inflationary movements such as in 1946–48 enabled unions to impose broad patterns of general increases, with extensive disregard for differences of economic circumstances as among industries.* Other examples would be the spread of automatic wage-increasing mechanisms – escalators and improvement factors – or the rise of health, welfare, and supplemental unemployment benefit plans.

Distinct from these broader organizational interests and objectives of

* Inflation makes this possible by weakening the restraining influence of the product market. Hence the hostility of unions to tight money.

industrial unionism is their approach to the internal wage structure as such. Here the central problem is equalities and differentials as among particular groups of jobs, not general increases for all of them together.

If the industrial union deals with a group of firms having a common product market – local, regional, or national – the forces of technology and of competitive imitation together will impart considerable uniformity of job structure throughout the group. In this way certain classifications readily become key jobs, and as such, important tokens for collective bargaining. Because they are reasonably comparable among the different employing units along the bargaining contour, they afford an easy standard of equity to the union and its members, so becoming union-oriented jobs.* As such they serve as benchmarks for the larger internal structure, hence as critical points in bargaining issues turning upon equalities and differentials in job-rate relationships, within and among the firms involved. For reasons of technology, function, or custom, certain other jobs tend to cluster around these occupations, giving rise in time to strong notions of equitable differentials. By interpolation and extrapolation, these key rates help to give form to the larger internal structure. As compared with the lateral cross-cutting imposed upon the structure by craft bargaining units, however, the interior system in factory organization is much looser, affording the employer far more room in which to maneuver in the pursuit of greater economic efficiency.**

Taken as a whole, unionism has had some broad impacts upon internal structures generally. Where needed, it compels the substitution of explicit job rates for personal rates of pay.*** In factory work, it pushes for fewer classifications, working against the employer's economic interest in diversification to break down skills and to reduce training costs. Often the union functions here as a conserving force, perpetuating traditions in job and wage structure, balking efforts to increase efficiency because of its primary concern for job security and for conventional notions of wage equity.[17]

b. *The Problem of New and Changed Jobs*

Unionism poses special problems regarding the adoption of internal job and wage structures to technological and organizational changes.

* For independent reasons, they may be cost-oriented or market-oriented as well.

** Examples of exceptions are large printing plants and the railroad industry, where the interior job and wage structure is primarily union-determined.

*** A 1951–52 survey by the BLS showed that for production workers on time rates, in only two southern cities out of forty studied throughout the country, did personal rates cover more than a quarter of the employees in the samples. [16]

Change works here in two major ways – as the slow but cumulative accretion of minor modifications in materials, equipment, product, or work flow; and as discontinuous jumps requiring the creation of new jobs and the abolition of old ones. Accommodation of these types of change is one of the major elements in the dynamics of internal wage structures.

As Martin Segal has shown in his study of twelve unionized manufacturing plants, technological change projects two major issues for collective bargaining, both affecting the wage structure.[18] First, it may reduce skill or effort required on the job, justifying a lower rate if customary principles of job analysis are followed. Second, it will probably increase job productivity, justifying a higher rate in the minds of the workers and their union leaders. If the job is on incentive rates, management will favor revision of rates to set tighter standards and so avoid deterioration of the system, while if it is a new job, management will want to fix the rate by careful time and motion study or by conventional methods of job evaluation. On old jobs, the union will normally cling to the existing standards, while on new ones it will press for higher earnings.

Obviously, these situations demand compromise, sometimes only after a long strike or a costly arbitration. In essence, from management's standpoint the compromise requires sacrifice of the integrity of formal job analysis and of a rationally evaluated wage structure in exchange for the continued freedom to make technical innovations and to harvest their fruits in increased labor productivity. To the union, the compromise may mean sacrifice of some occupational groups, by shading the gains in rates and earnings on behalf of the larger interests of the organization.

In the outcome, time and base rates will normally not be cut on changed jobs. In fact, time rates may even be increased, "because" productivity has risen, even though skill and effort may have decreased or at least not increased. The advance in the job rate will then spread quickly to related dependent rates in the cluster. In this way, loose time or incentive rates will gradually accumulate, undermining the consistency of the wage structure, to the despair of the industrial engineer. In time, the drift of the structure away from its original moorings may so impair the firm's cost-profit position that it will have to resort to a major struggle to restore its competitiveness. Meanwhile, it will tolerate the drift reluctantly, avoiding a prematu recrisis and "buying off" the threat of deliberate holdbacks on production. Here a strategy of delay will prove more effective if the product market is expanding. When this is not the case, the firm will be induced to fight hard from the outset.

Management's approach to loose wage structures is thus governed by a calculus of the costs of present and future wage concessions versus the alternative costs of immediate resistance – a difficult strike or slow down tactics, with loss of quick gains from innovation. The union, too, must weigh its course, by considering the political importance of the employees affected, the scale of possible labor displacement, the internal political dangers of excessive concessions extracted from management, and the need to protect the employer's competitive position.

c. *The Union as a Mechanism for the Transmission of General Increases to the Internal Wage Structure*

In addition to influencing relatively narrow relationships within job clusters, unionism can affect the internal wage structure as a whole, through its policy toward general increases. Whatever the way in which it achieves these increases, the union thereby introduces a novel force in the shaping of the structure, one that is often checked or redirected, but not ultimately determined, by the influence either of the labor or the product market. Today in the usual case the "going annual increase" has become both a custom and a political necessity. Union leaders can gain no credit from their constituents by allowing savings from increased productivity to become translated into lower product prices, particularly when the latter event is more honored in the breach than in the observance. Perhaps, too, the widespread prevalence of oligopoly makes it easier for the employer to share the gains of productivity through increased money wages than to court the diverse risks of a major strike, a cut in price, or the threat of a congressional inquiry.[19] At any rate, the problem for collective bargaining centers around the size of the annual increase and the way it is to be distributed.

These questions have particular importance for factory unionism, since the nature of the general increase will determine its effects upon absolute and relative job differentials within the plant. By contrast, because the orientation of the craft union is primarily horizontal rather than vertical, it need worry little about the method of distribution save where time and inattention have caused it to fall seriously behind other crafts in the trade.

Practice reveals three main kinds of general increases: The flat cents-per-hour, the flat percentage, and the differentiated increase. As is now well known and in any case readily evident from an elementary knowledge of arithmetic, flat cents-per-hour increases preserve absolute differentials at the cost of relative compression of the structure – a familiar wartime phenomenon. By contrast, flat percentage increases enlarge absolute differentials but leave relative differentials intact, awarding larger absolute increases to the higher-rated jobs. Because most industrial unions have their memberships concentrated among lower paid workers, they have a natural equalitarian bias in favor of flat cents-per-hour increases. But absent sustained inflation, such unions can neglect internal structural relations only at peril to their ultimate survival.* Institutionally viewed, what then happens is that the higher paid groups in the bargaining unit become restive, posing a problem of internal political unity for the union leadership. Restiveness can lead to a sharp increase in grievances over job-rate inequities, pressures for added adjustments to restore former differentials enjoyed by the upper groups, and even efforts of skilled workers to break away from the bargaining unit (craft severance).

Postwar deterioration of the relative position of the better-paid groups led to renewed union attention to problems of internal wage structure. This shows up clearly in the wage chronologies prepared by the BLS for leading firms and industries. They record a marked shift toward special adjustments to improve differentials for the upper tiers of the job structure, adjustments deliberately sought by the industrial unions. Impressive examples may be found in automobiles, aircraft, and rubber, to cite a few cases.

The predictions yielded by competitive analysis accord with these institutional developments, although the internal wage structures achieved in collective bargaining need not and do not conform closely to the notion of an equilibrium system of internal rates, in which supply and demand quantities are neatly balanced for each job, and equi-marginal returns are achieved from expenditures on each type of labor. However, competitive analysis does work out in a more limited way. It affirms that workers will move until net advantages (wages and working conditions) are equalized as among an array of different jobs in the plant. Since jobs differ in educational and skill requirements, in required special abilities that involve scarce talents, and in disutilities attached to working conditions (heat, noise, danger, etc.), differential job rates will emerge in response to variance in labor supplies.[21] If all jobs in the plant were paid the same rate, some would have surplus supply, while others would be short of the number desired. Accordingly, worker preferences would compel an internal system of job differentials to arise.

Such systems do emerge. When they get out of line structurally, workers respond accordingly. Some jobs become difficult to staff; quit rates

* During the war period, the skill groups got equal or even larger absolute increases, although their percentage advantage declined. The latter phenomenon was acceleration of a long-time trend.[20]

and transfers rise; and efficiency may drop. Thus the competitive analysis has some explanatory value here. It shows that even without unions employers will develop and continuously modify an internal system, that where they do have bargaining relations with a union, pressures for differentials will still operate. However, as a transmitting and mediating agency for competitive forces, collective bargaining has special effects of its own. The wage structures so developed cannot be accounted for from competitive analysis alone. Differentials still have economic significance, but they now possess political and institutional importance as well.

d. *Impacts of Collective Bargaining upon the Internal Wage Structure*

In the first place, the union has wider organizational interests than the firm. This means that both the level and the structure of the interior wage system will undergo change from forces quite divorced from the local labor market, as the union seeks to impose patterns of general increases drawn from afar, or if it succeeds in tying internal wages to mechanisms such as a cost-of-living escalator or an improvement factor.* In these endeavors, the union's influence can reach even from beyond the relevant product market. However, the latter often operates as a restraining influence. Unless an automatic mechanism is at work, the product market will compel deviations from pattern increases of broader origin, to take account of adverse economic circumstances for the firm and perhaps the industry. Even automatic mechanisms need not be permanently exempt. Thus recently employers in some fields have fought hard to eliminate escalator provisions, because these have seriously inflated labor costs.

In the second place, unionism has given added meaning to key jobs, key rates and job and rate clusters. Even without unionism, the key job and its associated cluster are natural units from which the design of the internal wage structure must proceed. Where management is free to act alone, it usually will rank its jobs by efford and skill, tying dependent jobs to key rates. Unionism introduces new elements: comparable rates for comparable key jobs among firms, preservation of customary differentials within clusters, the principle of no-cuts in job rates even if content changes, and linkage of increases in particular job rates to increases in job productivity regardless of cause.

* Changes in the cost of living usually involve a national price index, while the improvement factor rests upon a productivity index for manufacturing industry as a whole. Neither has anything directly to do with local conditions of labor demand and supply.

In the third place, the union contributes to greater uniformity of internal wage structures among employing units located along a given bargaining contour. It does so by compelling management to revise its wage policies, curbing the latter's discretionary power in setting differentials by job analysis or formal evaluation. Here the outcome for the internal wage structure will depend decisively upon whether the bargaining relationship is primarily one of conflict or of cooperation.[22]

In this domain, three main tendencies can be seen at work. In the first, the union takes an active and generally cooperative interest in a rational development or reconstruction of the wage structure, usually to reduce an unmanageable load of grievances over wage inequities. The creation of a new system of time and piece rates in basic steel through the joint program for job evaluation is a good example of a co-operative approach in action.[23] Another strong case is the evaluation program developed during wartime by collective bargaining between the aircraft firms in Southern California and the United Automobile Workers and the International Association of Machinists. Although modified many times since, this wage and job structure still survives.*

The second tendency is for the union to perpetuate tradition, under the threat, not always latent, of open conflict. Here the union is concerned with winning general increases, preserving customary differentials, and protecting job security. It will be indifferent to the employer's interest in economic efficiency, firmly resisting changes in job content and structure. Generally, craft unionism behaves in this fashion.

Finally, where the bargaining relationship is one premised upon thinly veiled or open conflict, the internal wage structure may become increasingly irrational and chaotic with the passage of time. The union insists upon a no-cuts policy whenever job content changes, demanding pro-rata increases in time rates and earnings as productivity increases on the job. As changes in technology and in the organization of work progressively alter relative job content and productivity, the factors of relative skill and effort gradually lose significance for job-rate and earnings differentials. If management follows an appeasement policy, conceding unsound grievance settlements and going along with union pressures in other respects, it will accelerate the deterioration of the structure. If, further, the plant is on incentive rates, cumulative improvements of

* In addition to describing the scheme comprehensively, Kerr and Fisher provide a brilliant analysis of the inherent conflict between the urge for internal rationality and consistency on the one hand, and the disturbances wrought by external forces on the other [24].

productivity will lead to a pattern of relative job earnings that steadily drifts away from that originally intended by the initial design of the base- and piece-rate structure.*

The natural history of deteriorating internal wage structures terminates with a crisis for both sides. Management finally realizes that unit labor cost has soared to levels that are competitively intolerable, deciding that a frontal attack is now unavoidable. The union leaders find themselves beset with internal political problems originating from wage anomalies generated by an increasingly irrational wage system. At this stage it may require a bitter strike to compel a better accommodation between the parties, so that revision of the structure can become possible. In some cases the conflict may go so deep that only the aid of disinterested and informed neutrals can achieve some redesign, for example, resort to contract arbitration of disputed issues, or creation of an advisory committee to study problems and to recommend solution.**

To sum up, the evolution of internal wage structures under collective bargaining depends decisively upon the quality of the relationship between the parties. Because that relationship can vary so much, the development of the structure need not follow a unique path in time.

6. Concluding Remarks

a. *System and Plasticity, Principle and Accommodation in Internal Wage Structures*

Ideally, the purpose of internal wage differentials is two-fold. First, they should provide adequate supplies of labor, of acceptable quality, for jobs that differ in required skills and experience, in associated responsibilities, and in attendant disutilities. Second, they should furnish adequate incentives for high worker efficiency throughout the organization. In purport, job evaluation seeks to achieve these objectives in systematic fashion – if you wish, by substituting technical standards and uniform procedures for the results that otherwise would be provided by an effectively competitive labor market, if one were available.[25]

* Although the jointly evaluated base-rate structure in steel was a remarkable essay in union-management cooperation, conflicting interests between the parties have prevented a parallel approach to incentive rates and earnings. Incentives have large importance in the basic-steel industry. Obsolescence of the system in this respect is now a major cause of acute bargaining difficulties in the industry.

** The leadership of the union can often use these approaches, where it recognizes that the existing structure is obsolete but cannot make concessions alone because of extreme membership pressures stemming from vested interests in the present system.

The very notion of a structure suggests a purposive design, achieved by consistent and precise application of a rational scheme of principles. In the real world, no such precision and consistency are ever realized, ultimately because interests clash over notions of equity, justice, and efficiency. Collective bargaining points up and accentuates the clash, but it exists in any case. There is no such thing as a scientific system of wages, because the human material of the system – management, workers, and the union – makes independent and conflicting valuations about any principles that might be imposed. Wage engineering, perhaps like military intelligence, is a contradiction in terms.

Wherever found, internal wage structures are the product of compromise and accommodation. In their design and modification, they reflect the joint effects of external pressures and internal discretion. There forces may contribute either to coherence and stability, or to disintegration and disruption, depending upon their combined thrusts. Thus any wage structure will exhibit persistence and change, consistency and ambiguity, reflecting as it must efforts at rational action, the inevitable impress of custom, and the untoward results of occasional neglect.

Examined at any given moment, the structure will display elements of order that are the precipitates of decisions taken in past time. For the same reason, it will show some consistency through time. But no system of internal parities and differentials can remain wholly intact for long. The combined effects of changing market forces, changing technology, changing patterns of work organization, and changing union objectives, all dictate that the system must be malleable. No matter how orderly it may be, or how well it may initially serve as an adaptation to a given environment, the system cannot persist unchanged indefinitely. Wage structures are but part of a larger productive organization. No organization can long survive without plasticity in its practices.

b. *Order and Indeterminateness*

Equalities and differentials in job rates represent an ordered set of prices evolved by a common unit of control. Common control imparts some degree of deliberate design to the set. By contrast, the external wage structure, while also an order statistically speaking, in its larger dimensions is not the product of calculated intent. But how free are the designers of the interior wage system?

Behind that system lies the job structure. The job hierarchy is an administrative device for crystalling functions as specific tasks that in turn dictate specialized labor requirements. Thereby it supplies the inner logic for the ordering of job rates. Often there is some room for maneuver at both the job and rate levels. Accordingly, it is tempting to view this logic as flowing from the autonomous thinking of management, operating freely in a virtually unlimited arena for discretion. Yet nothing could be more wrong. Management decisions about job structure and job rates are a vector of several forces, some of them imposed by the larger environment. The system of wage rates emerging will not necessarily be strictly determinate, but the range of indeterminacy is finite – and often narrowly so.

Technology provides the foundation for job structure, but only the foundation. Jobs take their form and substance from the initiatives of management, aided or impeded by unionism and competitive forces. In some cases, the job structure is virtually a given datum for management, as under craft unionism or in the usually well-organized clerical market. In others, the structure admits of more plasticity, although even here firms engaged in common activities will develop considerable uniformity in job patterns, under the impress of a shared technology and possibly mutual bargaining relations with the same union.

Passing now from job to wage structure, internal wage systems fall into four main classes, indicated below.

1. *Primarily union-oriented*: here the wage structure is linked firmly to the union bargaining units, each representing a key job with a few subordinate ones attached to it. To each employer, collective bargaining makes the wage structure almost completely determinate. Craft-union industries compose this category – construction, printing and publishing, the railroads, longshoring and maritime, entertainment, for examples.

2. *Primarily market-oriented*: here the wage structure is derived in great part from a well-organized and competitive labor market, and there is no union. The individual employer has some discretion, but not a great deal, because jobs are easily identified and quite uniform throughout the market. Service industries offer a host of examples – banking, insurance, department stores, and restaurants.

3. *Primarily internally determined*: here the wage structure is not closely linked to the labor market, because the latter is too disorganized to provide adequate grading and pricing, and jobs are too specialized to provide much uniformity. There is no union to impose restraints or imperatives upon management. The product market may exert some restraining influence, but not if labor cost is low relative to total cost. Management then sets wage rates – proceeding from pure job evaluation, or ranking by job analysis, or catch-as-catch-can methods – adjusting the

average level of the structure perhaps with due regard to the latent threat of unionism. Examples would include firms in small towns or predominantly non-union communities, in isolated locations, or in locally unique lines of production. Much of government employment also fits this category.

4. *Primarily union- and product market-oriented*: here the wage structure originates and develops under managerial initiative, but is decisively shaped and restrained by influences beyond management's effective control. Technology contributes some uniformity of job structure for firms engaged in common lines of production. Union relations establish some key jobs and clusters, while others derive their status from their significance to cost-price relations and the product market. Unionism supplies a periodic upward push to the whole structure, imposes certain traditional parities and differentials, and exerts a peculiar impact in the pricing of new and changed jobs. The product market dictates resistance to the upward general push, and compels the employer to undertake initiatives and adaptations in technology and organization, leading to new and changed jobs. If the ratio of labor to total cost and the price-elasticity of demand for the product are favorable, union pressure will be much more effective than where the opposite conditions prevail. Examples of both situations would include many firms in the manufacturing and mining sectors, and in certain branches of the service industries.

The interesting cases are types 3 and 4, because here discretionary wage-setting works much more freely. In practice, the making of internal wage structures in these circumstances centers around key jobs and their associated clusters. Key jobs may acquire such status from the labor market, from the product market, or from unionism with its propensity for inter-plant comparisons and its sensitivity to politically strategic groups of employees. Clusters, in turn, may take their origin from technically related functions – departmental activities, processes, production lines; from skill complexes – job families, team and crew arrangements; or simply from customary association. Managerial discretion is least for key jobs and their minute associated clusters, where custom dictates its own proprieties. Or, speaking figuratively, the cluster is a determinate little planatary system of wage rates. Beyond its immediate gravitational field, there may exist many other jobs that lie in the interstices among narrow clusters, and whose rates will be more susceptible to manipulations because the centripetal force exerted by clusters is too weak to bring them into orbit. Here joint or unilateral job analysis, or job evaluation, serves as a means of extending orderly design over the whole system. If joint, these procedures enlarge the impact of the union beyond the periodic attainment of general increases and the occasional revision of particular rates. If unilateral, they enable management to relate both the level and the structure of the system much more closely to considerations of incentives, efficiency, and control of unit labor cost.

If, now, we take determinateness to mean both precise limits to rate setting and stability in rate relationships over time, to what extent does it rule the internal wage structure? The system of rates may be determinate in three different senses: first, as showing stability in absolute or relative differentials among job rates; second, as reflecting absence of significant employer discretion regarding the absolute level at which a given rate is set; or, third, as revealing absence of significant employer discretion for setting the average level of all job rates within the unit of control.

The first kind of determinateness – stability of equalities and differentials in job rates – occurs most commonly with narrow occupational clusters, where workers' notions of equity and custom are particularly keen. These sentiments can be effective even without a union, for in the interests of efficiency managment will often recognize them. However, the union is the usual agency for the perpetuation of fixed rate relationships. Furthermore, beyond narrow clusters, factory unionism may extend similar stability over the broader reaches of the wage structure, by joining in an overall evaluation procedure, or by negotiating for the maintenance or restoration of traditional relationships. Here, however, stability yields in time to the eroding effects of technological change and, perhaps, of a series of general increases. In such cases, the restoration of the broader rate relationships becomes a task for deliberate negotiation.

The second kind of determinateness involves very narrow limits to the employer's discretion in setting the absolute rate for a particular job. Both market forces and unionism can greatly reduce discretion. If the labor market operates with competitive effectiveness, it will establish firm going rates, for example, for routine white-collar jobs or for starting rates of factory labor in a metropolitan area. The product market may achieve the same effect for key jobs that are cost-oriented, where competition imposes severe restraints upon increases in product price.

Unionism introduces a somewhat different kind of determinateness in job rates, although its actions need not be wholly free of the influence of market forces. First, collective bargaining creates clear-cut contract rates. In the main these must be stable for a considerable period – until they are renegotiated. Second, the union may insist upon a standard rate for those jobs that are comparable among several firms in an area, or firms that share a common bargaining contour. To the single employer, such rates may be imposed by union insistence upon pattern-following, or through binding obligations to an employer bargaining association. Normally such rates bear no close connection to the labor market as a competitive wage-setting mechanism. However, they may still be closely dependent upon the product market, in which case the employer's discretion is narrowed from below by the union, and from above by the difficulty of raising product price.

Last, determinateness, rather than employer discretion, may rule the average level of all the firm's job rates – its actual height and its movement in time. As with particular job rates, this may arise from a competitive labor market in a few cases – for example, white-collar work. More commonly, it may be imposed by the product market, where labor cost is decisive for the profit margin and competition makes it very difficult to raise price. Here the demand ceiling affords little room for raising job rates as a whole, although minor adjustments in rate relationships will still be possible. Indeed, a particularly adverse product market may dictate no increase in job rates at all. Given the difficulty of cutting job rates in these times, the employer in this instance may still get his labor cost down by downgrading the job distribution of his force, by cutting overtime, and by reducing output and incentive earnings.

Unionism, of course, can introduce upward pressure on the wage level of the firm, acting independently even in a soft labor market. However, the union does not eliminate the restraining influence of the product market altogether. Where it is an effective barrier, the employer will resist most strongly. Here various possibilities emerge.

First, the union may make concessions to a single employer whose high costs have placed him in a vulnerable competitive position, tapering the general increase relative to other firms, or allowing him no increase, or taking a general increase in exchange for hidden concessions on other wage costs. Second, where competitors are few, the union may enforce uniformity in general increases by a policy of selective attack, enforcing a common pattern of increases because no firm is willing to stand out alone, and each knows that his rivals will undergo a comparable increase in labor cost, which in turn weakens the price restraint to them all. Third, the union and a group of employers competing in the same product market may seek collective escape from the price restraint, by means of block negotiations involving an employer association or bargaining committee – a method that also affords the employer some defense againt divide-and-conquer tactics.

However, neither pattern-following nor the method of joint negotiation necessarily removes the restraining influence of the product market. Everything depends upon the price-elasticity of demand to the whole industry, and upon the importance of labor to total cost for each producer. Thus, despite a high ratio of labor to total cost, the construction industry has been able to raise wage levels and product prices very rapidly postwar, because easy credit has fostered a building boom involving both highly inelastic and substantially increasing demand. Until 1958, the same general condition prevailed in basic steel. When demand turns much more elastic, however, collective employer resistance will become much more acute. Thus the official policy of restraint of aggregate demand by tight fiscal and monetary methods, by checking the rise of the entire price level, has greatly increased the force of product-market restraints generally. This in fact, it seems to me, is the key to the now widely remarked emergence of much tougher bargaining by employers.

Thus, in the large, the product market enforces selectivity in wage behavior – within a group of competing firms and among separate groups of firms serving distinct product markets. Together with a favorable labor-to-total cost ratio, it may allow much discretion in the upward movement of the employer's average level of job rates. Alternatively, it may narrow that discretion to very close limits. Either way, it shapes the environment for collective bargaining, inducing both the union and management to adjust their wage behavior accordingly.

In all senses, the determinateness of a particular internal wage structure depends upon the strength of competitive forces in the labor market, the restraint exerted by the product market, and upon the nature of the union and the bargaining system. Over time, shifts in the product market and changes in technology are the main forces making for displacement of either the level or the differentials in a given job-rate structure. Here the mediating force of unionism can contribute peculiar effects of its own.

Granted that the notion of a contour, or a cluster, is more a descriptive fiction than it is an operative entity, nonetheless it does describe well certain uniform ways in which men act in erecting and altering an internal wage structure. Parities and differentials, levels and rates of change in levels, do have continuing significance to the actors in a local wage system. They provide the substance that gives shape to the system, and the coherence that causes its persistence through time.

c. *Conclusion*

The disintegration of competitive single-rate theory followed unintendedly from its final affirmation in Hicks' *Theory of Wages*, published in 1932. In the ensuing interregnum, the belief became widely held that internal wage structures and their movements could be explained primarily by appeal to non-market forces. This turn of thought was helped powerfully by certain collateral events – the rapid spread of collective bargaining between 1933 and 1945; revelation in numerous wartime wage surveys that great diversity existed in rates for comparable jobs; and inflationary movements in aggregate demand and in wage-price levels during 1945–48. In consequence, this kind of thinking seemed to affirm that wage rates were no longer determinate in the classical sense, but instead were determined by the discretionary acts of wage-setters themselves. If, as seems to be implied, the politics of unionism are the only external force affecting job rates, then the internal wage structure becomes detached from market forces entirely, to float freely in an administrative void, where it can easily be buffeted by union manipulation, or otherwise by the employer himself if he has no union. If so, the explanation of wage rates is now to be found in politics, and no longer in economics.

This probably overstates postwar thinking, but in any case the latter goes too far in reaction to the determinateness asserted by classical theory. The newer view rightly recognized the weakness of most labor markets as a wage-determining force, hence the existence of a discretionary range for most job rates. Properly, too, it introduced unionism and collective bargaining as a new kind of environmental force, one that also narrows employer discretion – in cluster relations, for particular job rates, and in upward movements of the whole structure. Further, it recognized that the employer has other means of adjusting to changes in labor supply and demand, beyond those involving manipulation of job rates.

However, the notion of a range of indeterminacy can be pushed too far, at the cost of losing all the economics of wage determination. This would be no real loss if economics have little real relevance. But this is not the case, for there remains the restraining influence of the product market. Where that influence is very weak by reason of favorable demand and cost circumstances, discretion can be broad, and opportunity for the union to push successfully can indeed be large. However, this is not the general case. Thus the non-economic approach fails to supply a general theory of wage-making. If, then, we are to account for diversity and selectivity in the behaviour of internal wage structures, we shall have to pay renewed attention to the role of the product market as an environmental force.

References

1. MARSHALL, *Principles*, 8th ed., p. 538.
2. JACK STIEBER, *The Steel Industry Wage Structure: A Study of the Joint Union-Management Job Evaluation Program in the Basic Steel Industry* (Cambridge, Mass.: Harvard University Press, 1959) pp. 311–312, 320–322;
GEORGE P. SHULTZ, "A Non-Union Market for White Collar Labor," unpublished paper delivered at National Bureau of Economic Research, Conference on Labor Economics (Princeton, N. J. April 1960).
3. For evidence about the spread of wage formalization, see OTTO HOLLBERG, "Wage Formalization in Major Labor Markets, 1951–52," *Monthly Labor Review* 76 (January, 1953) pp. 22–26.
4. ROBERT L. RAIMON, "The Indeterminateness of Wages of Semiskilled Workers," *Industrial and Labor Relations Review* 6 (January, 1953) p. 181. Raimon shows how such jobs enable the employer to gain much flexibility in selection and assignment of personnel.
5. For distinction between the two forces affecting specialization and their effects upon the occupational composition of the labor force, see HELEN WOOD, "Trends in the Specialization of Occupational Requirements," ch. vii *in* WILLIAM HABER and others, editors, *Manpower in the United States: Problems and Policies* (New York: Harper, 1954) (Publication of the Industrial Relations Research Association) pp. 103–116.
6. RICHARD A. LESTER, *Hiring Practices and Labor Competition*, Research Report no.88, Industrial Relations Section, Princeton: (Princeton University, 1954), pp. 97–98.
7. CLARK KERR, "Labor Markets: Their Character and Consequences," *American Economic Review*, Papers and Proceedings XL (May, 1950) pp. 278–291; "The Balkanization of Labor Markets," *in* E. WIGHT BAKKE and others, *Labor Mobility and Economic Opportunity* (New York: Technology Press of Massachusetts Institute of Technology and Wiley, 1954) pp. 92–110.
8. On job rationing, see E. ROBERT LIVERNASH, "The Internal Wage Structure," *in* GEORGE W. TAYLOR and FRANK C. PIERSON, editors, *New Concepts in Wage Determination* (New York: McGraw-Hill, 1957) pp. 142–145.
9. SHULTZ, *op. cit.*
10. For the origins, nature, and effects of this pay system, see MORRIS A. HOROWITZ, "The Railroads' Dual System of Payment: A Make-Work Rule?" *Industrial and Labor Relations Review* 8 (January, 1955) pp. 177–194; and MORRIS A. HOROWITZ "Make-Work Effects of Railroad Constructive-Allowance Payments," *Labor Law Journal* 6 (May, 1955) pp. 321–334.
11. LLOYD G. REYNOLDS, *The Structure of Labor Markets* (New York: Harper, 1951) pp. 43–75.
12. JOHN T. DUNLOP, "The Task of Contemporary Wage Theory," in TAYLOR and PIERSON, *op. cit.*, p. 131.
13. MELVIN W. REDER, "The Theory of Occupational Wage Differentials," *American Economic Review* XLV (December, 1955) pp. 833–852; RICHARD A. LESTER, "A Range Theory of Wage Differentials," *Industrial and Labor Relations Review* 5 (July, 1952) pp. 483–500.
14. REYNOLDS describes this mechanism in *The Structure of Labor Markets, op. cit.*, pp. 157–162.

15. See, for example, *Wealth of Nations*, Book II, ch. xiv; MARSHALL, *Principles*, 8th ed., Book VI, ch. ii–iii.
16. OTTO HOLLBERG, *op. cit.*, pp. 22–26.
17. For a classic demonstration of the principle that the trade union is not a natural agency for the promotion of business efficiency, although its officers are frequently compelled to consider it, often at the risk of schizophrenia, see BENJAMIN M. and SYLVIA K. SELEKMAN, "Productivity and Collective Bargaining," *Harvard Business Review*, 28 (March, 1950) pp. 127–144.
18. MARTIN SEGAL, "Factors in Wage Adjustments to Technological Changes," *Industrial and Labor Relations Review*, 8 (January, 1955) pp. 217–230.
19. For development of this argument, see ALFRED KUHN, "Market Structures and Wage-push Inflation," *Industrial and Labor Relations Review*, 12 (January, 1959) pp. 243–259.
20. HARRY OBER, "Occupational Wage Differentials, 1907–1947", *Monthly Labor Review*, 67 (August, 1948) pp. 127–134. In recent years there is some evidence that percentage differentials have been widening again.
    For discussion of how relative compression compels renewed attention to structural problems of wage differentials, see H. M. DOUTY, "Union Impacts on Wage Structures," Industrial Relations Research Association, *Proceedings of Sixth Annual Meeting, Publication No.* 12 (1954) pp. 61–76.
21. MELVIN W. REDER, "Wage Determination in Theory and Practice," in NEIL W. CHAMBERLAIN, FRANK C. PIERSON, and THERESA WOLFSON, eds., *A Decade of Industrial Relations Research*, 1946–1956, a publication of the Industrial Relations Research Association (New York: Harper, 1958) pp. 64–97.
22. See the excellent discussion by E. ROBERT LIVERNASH, "The Internal Wage Structure", *in* TAYLOR and PIERSON, *op. cit.*, pp. 170–171.
23. STIEBER, *The Steel Industry Wage Structure, op. cit.*, pp. 3–118 and 235–332.
24. CLARK KERR and LLOYD H. FISHER, "Effect of Environment and Administration upon Job Evaluation," *Harvard Business Review*, XXVIII (May, 1950) pp. 77–96.
25. See the discussion by WILLIAM H. KNOWLES, "Economics of Industrial Engineering," *Industrial and Labor Relations Review*, 5 (January, 1952); for evaluation principles, see KERR and FISHER, *op. cit.*

Chapter 6

WAGE STRUCTURE AND ADMINISTRATION IN SOVIET INDUSTRY

WALTER GALENSON

University of California, Berkeley (Calif.) USA

The last decade has witnessed the growth of a massive body of Western writing on the Soviet economy. Relatively little attention has been devoted, however, to the important subject of wages. Some efforts have been made to trace the course of real wages, and to compare the living standards of Soviet and American workers. But the literature relating to wage administration, policy, and structure is as yet largely unexplored.[1]

The policy of the Soviet authorities with respect to wage statistics is to a large extent responsible for this situation. The types of detailed data on wage rates and earnings which are generally available in great volume in the West are conspicuous by their absence from Soviet statistical publications. We do not have, for example, aggregate data on wage rates or earnings for any postwar year. Nor do we have regional, industrial, or occupational figures of a systematic character. There is no doubt that a tremendous variety of detailed wage information is available to the Soviet planning agencies, and one can only wonder at the reasons for suppressing its publication.

However, since 1955 there has been some improvement in the situation from the point of view of the Western student. In that year there was established the State Committee of the Council of Ministers of the USSR on Questions of Labor and Wages, charged with the primary mission of subjecting prevailing wage structure and practices to a critical examination. This was not a fortuitous occurrence; the need for some such agency became apparent with the relaxation of direct labor market controls in the early nineteen fifties. With workers once more able to move from job to job, as they had been before 1939, the deficiencies of the wage system as a mechanism for allocating the labor supply were brought into sharp relief. Wage differentials which were at least practicable in a controlled labor market resulted in serious distortions of the available manpower pool under freer conditions. Suppressed wage inequities came to the surface. And what was even more alarming to the Soviet authorities, fierce competition among enterprises for labor resources in short supply threatened the stability of the entire wage level, as well as the wage structure.

The Institute of Labor, the research arm of the State Committee on Questions of Labor and Wages, together with numerous research agencies throughout the country, have conducted exhaustive inquiries into wage practices, and a number of reports have become available as a result of their efforts.* Most of the published information relates to the experience of individual enterprises, though there is occasional reference to data of a more aggregate nature. Many of the recommendations emerging from the studies were put into effect, beginning characteristically with heavy industry. It is anticipated that by the end of 1960, all of Soviet manufacturing will have undergone a thoroughgoing wage reform.

Soviet wage practices take on an added significance because they serve as a model for the other communist countries of Eastern Europe and Asia. The millions of industrial workers in the communist bloc, including the Chinese, are being compensated for their labor on the basis of a fairly uniform set of principles. This wage system is undoubtedly the most widespread of any in use at the present time.

This paper is concerned with only one aspect of Soviet wages: intra-plant structure and administration. Such questions as inter-industrial and regional wage differentials and the relationship of wages and prices will not be dealt with. Limitation of scope to the micro-economic level imposes certain limitations upon the analysis. Too often, however, wage theory begins and ends with macro-analysis, and never really comes to grips with some of the more interesting problems of wage behavior. It is hoped that this paper will contribute to the emerging body of literature on wages at the grass roots level,[2] which is so essential to the achievement of a really satisfactory theory of wages.

* The Institute of Labor published in 1958 a three-year research plan describing some 800 separate labor projects to be carried out by more than 300 research institutes throughout the Soviet Union. One hundred thirty five of the projects were concerned entirely with wage questions, and in many of the others, wages were subsidiary to the main topic. The State Committee and the Institute of Labor publish two monthly journals devoted to labor questions: *Sotsialisticheskii Trud* (referred to hereafter as *Socialist Labor*) and *Byulletyen Nauchnoi Informatsii Trud i Zarabotnaya Plata* (referred to hereafter as *Bulletin on Labor and Wages*).

1. The Basic Wage Scale

The entire Soviet wage system rests upon the basic wage scale (*tarifnaya cyetka*), which provides the basis for classifying all wage earners.* The scale consists of a number of grades expressed as ratios to the first (lowest) labor grade. These grades are peculiar mixtures of job classifications and personal ratings for individual workers. The method of their determination is considered below; suffice it to say here that particular jobs are assigned grades using a kind of job evaluation system, and that while workers are also rated personally according to the same grades, they are generally paid the rate for the job. A recent manual on wages explains the system in the following terms:

> "... the worker's wages are determined not by the grade of the worker but by that of the job. A worker of the fifth grade performing a job of the sixth grade is paid according to the rate of the sixth grade; the same worker performing a fourth grade job is paid according to the grading rate of that job." [4]

However,

> "In those cases when a worker does jobs of a lower category than his own, and the difference is two grades and more, he is entitled, besides his wages according to piece-work rates, to extra pay for each hour of work equal to the difference between the grading-rate corresponding to the worker's grade and the grading rate corresponding to the grade of his job." [5]

This implies only partial protection for the worker employed below his skill, since the compensation is in the form of hourly rates, which are characteristically below piece rate earnings.

The policy in recent years has been to provide a single standard basic scale for each industry, with inter-plant differentials provided for by differences in the money equivalent assigned to the first grade for each plant. The most recent scales promulgated for some major industries are shown in Table 1, arranged in the order of the magnitude of the differential between the lowest and the highest labor grade, from high to low. Several observations may be drawn from this and several subsidiary tables:

* The remuneration of managerial, technical, and clerical personnel is not considered in this paper. These groups are paid according to detailed monthly salary schedules worked out for each industry and plant on the basis of a series of factors established by the central wage authorities [3].

TABLE 1

Basic Wage Scales in Soviet Industry, as of 1960

(Ratios, Grade I equals 1.00)

Industry	Labor grades									
	I	II	III	IV	V	VI	VII	VIII	IX	X
Coal mining [a]	1.00	1.12	1.33	1.66	2.50	3.12	3.33	3.75		
Iron and steel: [b]										
Ore mining	1.00	1.12	1.33	1.58	1.88	2.24	2.67	3.20		
Metal production departments	1.00	1.13	1.28	1.45	1.65	1.87	2.13	2.43	2.78	3.20
Auxiliary depts.	1.00	1.15	1.20	1.52	1.77	2.06	2.40	2.80		
Construction [c]	1.00	1.18	1.40	1.66	1.97	2.34	2.80			
Non-ferrous metals [d]	1.00	1.17	1.37	1.61	1.88	2.21	2.60			
Rubber [e]	1.00	1.14	1.30	1.49	1.71	1.96	2.26	2.60		
Cement [f]	1.00	1.15	1.32	1.52	1.77	2.06	2.40			
Chemicals [g]	1.00	1.14	1.30	1.49	1.71	1.98	2.30			
Synthetic leather [h]	1.00	1.14	1.30	1.49	1.71	1.98	2.30			
Reinforced concrete products [i]	1.00	1.15	1.33	1.54	1.80	2.10				
Machinery and metalworking [j]	1.00	1.13	1.29	1.46	1.72	2.00				
Oil Refining [k]	1.00	1.14	1.31	1.50	1.73	2.00				
Building materials (except cement and reinforced concrete) [l]	1.00	1.13	1.29	1.48	1.72	2.00				
Woodworking [m]	1.00	1.13	1.29	1.48	1.72	2.00				
Textiles [n]	1.00	1.11	1.25	1.40	1.60	1.80				
Baking [o]	1.00	1.11	1.25	1.40	1.60	1.80				
Fish Processing [p]	1.00	1.11	1.25	1.40	1.60	1.80				

Sources for Table 1

a) A. G. AGANBEGYAN and V. F. MAYER, *Zarabotnaya Plata v SSSR* (*Wages in the USSR*) (Moscow, 1959) p. 130. Scale introduced during 1957.

b) *Socialist Labor* (1957) No. 7., p. 78. Scale effective last quarter 1957.

c) *Socialist Labor* (1956) No. 1. Scale effective January 1, 1956.

d) *Socialist Labor* (1958) No. 8, p. 48. Scale introduced during 1958.

e) *Bulletin on Labor and Wages* (1959) No. 6, p. 12. Scale introduced during 1958.

f) *Socialist Labor* (1958) No. 8, p. 54. Scale introduced in 1958.

g) *Socialist Labor* (1958) No. 7, p. 33. Scale introduced in 1958.

h) *Socialist Labor* (1958) No. 11. Scale introduced in 1958.

i) *Socialist Labor* (1958) No. 8, p. 54. Scale introduced in 1958.

j) *Socialist Labor* (1959) No. 5, p. 8. Scale effective October 1, 1959.

k) *Socialist Labor* (1959) No. 7, p. 53. Scale effective fourth quarter 1957.

l) *Socialist Labor* (1960) No. 2, p. 48. Scale introduced during 1960.

m) *Socialist Labor* (1960) No. 2, p. 56. Scale introduced during 1960.

n) *Socialist Labor* (1958) No. 12, p. 46. Scale introduced during last quarter 1959.

o) *Socialist Labor* (1959) No. 12, p. 55. Scale introduced during last quarter 1959.

p) *Socialist Labor* (1960) No. 1, p. 63. Scale introduced during 1960.

a. There is a relatively small number of basic labor grades, the most usual number being six or seven. The customary pattern in American industry appears to be a range of seven to 16 grades.* The general tendency in the Soviet Union has been to reduce the number of basic grades in the interest of a simpler structure. This observation is borne out by the data in Table 2, showing the evolution of basic wage scales since the 1920's. In every case, the number of labor grades in 1960 was less than at the beginning of the planning period, and in the case of only two industries, ore mining and construction, was there a temporary reversal of the trend in the late nineteen-thirties.

TABLE 2

Trends in Soviet Basic Wage Scales, 1931–1960

Industry	Before 1931–1933		Introduced during 1931–1933		Prior to the 1956–1960 changes		In effect, 1960	
	No. of grades	Ratio of high to low grade	No. of grades	Ratio of high to low grade	No. of grades	Ratio of high to low grade	No. of grades	Ratio of high to low grade
Coal	12	1 : 3.5	11	1 : 4.4	8	1 : 3.75	7 [a]	1 : 3.3 [a]
Oil	8	1 : 2.8	8	1 : 3.6	8	1 : 2.6	6	1 : 2.0
Ore mining	10	1 : 3.0	8	1 : 3.6	10	1 : 2.8	7	1 : 2.8
Machinery	8	1 : 2.8	8	1 : 3.6	8	1 : 2.5	6	1 : 2.0
Construction	7	1 : 2.5	6	1 : 2.85	7	1 : 2.8	6 [a]	1 : 2.0 [a]
Leather	8	1 : 3.0	7	1 : 3.0	7	1 : 2.6	6	1 : 2.0
Garments	7	1 : 2.5	—		8	1 : 2.4	6	1 : 1.8

Source: A. G. AGANBEGYAN and V. F. MAYER, *Zarabotnaya Plata v SSSR* (*Wages in the USSR*) (Moscow, 1959) p. 135.

[a] These scales differ from the ones shown in Table 1. They may be slated for introduction, but thus far, no notice of the change has appeared.

The gradual reduction in the number of labor grades is ascribed by Soviet writers to the levelling of skills during the course of industrialization. To quote one source, at the outset of the industrialization process the larger number of labor grades "was dictated by the effort to stimulate the rapid formation of cadres of highly qualified workers, which the country then needed. Now, when there is a highly qualified, highly educated

* The American steel industry, however, has an unusually large number of labor grades, 32, as a result of the Cooperative Wage Study undertaken in the nineteen-forties [6].

working class, the differences in wages must be significantly reduced."[7] Although six labor grades might appear inadequate to achieve sufficient differentiation among workers, the widespread use of piecework systems (discussed below) apparently provides enough flexibility.

b. There is a tendency for basic labor grades to be more numerous in heavy than in light industry. Steel, with 10 grades, may be contrasted with six grade scales in textiles, baking, and fish processing. Two reasons are given for this: the greater complexity of the skill structure in heavy industry, and the goal of providing greater individual incentive for mastering those skills. To quote a Soviet source once more: "of great help in deciding the question of the number of grades in the basic wage scale is analysis of the learning time and the productive experience necessary for fulfilling the complex tasks in each branch of industry. Comparing the number of years of study and working experience required to perform the most highly skilled work in a given branch of industry can determine the differences in the grading established by the wage scale."[8]

The position of the machinery and metalworking industry in the labor grade hierarchy is somewhat surprising. One would have expected it to be closer to the iron and steel pattern than to consumer goods. The industry is extremely heterogeneous, and the uniform scale introduced in 1959 replaced over a thousand different scales with ratios of high to low grades (referred to hereafter as the "extreme ratio") varying from 1 : 1.9 to 1 : 3.5.

In almost every case, the scales introduced after 1956 consolidated a variety of earlier scales. In the fishing industry, for example, the new scale replaced 130 older ones; in the steel industry, "a significant number" of old ones.[9] One of the aims of the State Commission on Labor and Wages is to bring a greater degree of uniformity into Soviet wage structure, and by consolidating the basic wage scales, a long step toward this goal was taken.

The rate of progression from one basic labor grade to the next is determined with incentive factors in mind. It can be seen from Table 1 that in almost every case, the absolute difference between grades rises with each step. This contrasts, for example, with the practice of equal increments between grades in the American steel industry, though American practice in this respect varies a good deal from plant to plant.

The Russian preference for progressively increasing wage grade differences is based upon several factors: (1) it is felt that this scheme provides a greater stimulant toward skill improvement, since the higher the worker goes in the scale, the more money he gains from an additional step upward [10]; (2) total wage cost tends to be less under a progressive scheme, since under this arrangement, even with identical extreme ratios, the absolute level of wages will be less at every step except the first and last, compared with a system of equal increments.[11] In the past, however, equal increments were employed where enterprises were having difficulty in recruiting sufficient numbers of lower paid workers.

c. (1) More extensive comment is in order with regard to the wage differentials implied by Table 1. It is clear, in the first place, that the skill pattern of a particular industry influences the spread in wage rates; the more difficult the acquisition of skills, the greater the premium. However, this is far from being the entire story, for other factors play a significant, and perhaps even a commanding role. To cite one example: a rotary furnace machinist in the cement industry, whose training consists of a one-year vocational course and two or three years of experience, has a basic wage rate 140 per cent over the minimum rate for the cement industry, whereas an assistant foreman in the textile industry, with two to three years vocational schooling and at least one year of experience commands a premium of only 80 per cent above the lowest textile rate.[14]

Inter-industrial differentials are not properly the subject of this paper, so we will content ourselves with the observation that wage structure, as well as wage levels, reflect the priorities of the planners. So-called "leading" industries (coal, iron and steel, non-ferrous metals, cement, oil) are given wage advantages in order to permit them to attract the necessary manpower. Wide skill differentials are merely one means of providing management with the ability to secure and hold skilled people. To quote a recent publication: "The policy of the Communist Party and the Soviet state of establishing higher wages for workers in heavy industry compared with other branches of industry remains the unchanged basis for planning wages and regulating basic wage scales in the national economy of the USSR." [13]

(2) Recent Soviet experience with the width of differentials in the basic pay scale has some extremely interesting aspects. As already noted, the lifting of restrictions on labor mobility and the abandonment of a policy of directing labor made wages the critical factor in allocating manpower. Wage differentials tended to narrow somewhat after the war, due largely to a wage adjustment effected in September, 1946, when, in preparation for the abolition of rationing, minimum wages were increased. Workers earning up to 300 rubles a month received an extra 110 rubles; those earning between 300 and 500 rubles received an extra 100 rubles; those earning between 500 and 700 rubles, an extra 90 rubles; and those

earning between 700 and 900 rubles, an extra 80 rubles. A book published in 1956 said of this policy: "Since the highest supplement to wages (in 1946) was received by the lowest paid workers, the difference between the basic wages of the highest and lowest labor grades was reduced. This circumstance gave the basic wage scale a levelling character and weakened its role in helping raise labor skills." [14]

Under the circumstances, the logical policy was to widen the spread of skill differentials, and there were some voices raised in its favor. At a conference of 1200 administrative personnel in the machinery industry, held in Leningrad in October, 1956, a new basic wage scale with an extreme ratio of 1 : 2.8 came in for considerable criticism. One speaker declared that because of the insufficient wage differences possible under this scale, it became necessary to use inflated piece rates in order to preserve the normal earnings of highly qualified workers. Maximum differentials of 1 : 3.2 or 1 : 3.4 were urged by a number of speakers.[15] Former prime minister Bulganin, speaking at a plenary session of the Communist Party central committee on July 4, 1955, declared that the basic wage scales then in force did not guarantee the necessary differentiation among workers with different skills.[16]

However, an opposite policy was adopted; the government decided to champion the cause of the lower paid workers, and a barrage of statements to this effect emerged from official sources beginning late in 1956. Minimum wages were raised on January 1, 1957. The twenty-first congress of the Communist Party, which was held in January, 1959, made the policy official by calling for "raising the wages of the low and average paid workers and employees and by this means reducing the difference in the pay of the low and average wage groups in comparison with the high paid groups." Those who had favored wider differentials were told that "restoration of the prewar scales signifies in practice nothing else but increasing the wages of the high paid workers by the percentage by which the low paid workers were raised in 1946 and 1957, and this in essence is tantamount to annulling the recently adopted, absolutely correct policy of raising the wages of the low paid workers to a greater extent than the high paid." [17]

But the policy of equalization was not fully consonant with what was desirable from an economic standpoint. Either deliberately or by force of circumstance, the basic wage scales promulgated since 1957 in fact provide for wider differentials, though formally they are narrower. This paradoxical conclusion arises from the circumstance that prior to the inception of the wage reform program, there had been wholesale upgrading of workers, with the result that by 1956 scarcely any workers were left in the lowest labor grades, 1 and 2. The scales introduced after 1956 simply dropped the two lowest, and in some cases the three lowest grades. Therefore the extreme grade ratios in the new scales, though invariably smaller than the old, were actually wider when compared with the *effective* spread under the old system.

The Russians have been reticent on this matter, particularly since the Communist Party line has been strongly for wage equalitarianism since 1957. However, a few examples will serve to buttress the conclusion that the actual tendency may have been in the opposite direction.

(a) The First State Ball Bearing Plant in Moscow reported that prior to 1956, it had been operating with twelve different basic wage scales, the ratios of the extreme grades ranging from 1 : 1.88 to 1 : 2.46.* "The actual differential in the pay of workers with high and low skills was even less, since classification of jobs at grades 1 and 2 was absent. It is obvious that such a wage scale lowered the interest of workers in advancing to jobs demanding greater skills."[19] These scales were replaced in 1956 by one with an extreme wage differential of 1 : 2.8, and in 1959, by the present ratio of 1 : 2. If we take the highest pre-1956 differential of 1 : 2.46, and assume that the rate of progression from grade to grade was the same as in the 1956–1959 scale, the effective extreme ratio before 1956 was about 1 : 1.92. For the narrowest of the pre-1956 scales, the equivalent estimate is 1 : 1.55. Thus, the basic scale introduced in 1959 was between 12 and 45 per cent wider than that of 1956.

(b) Between 1943 and 1945, seven grade scales with extreme ratios of 1 : 3.20 were installed in the food industry. The ratios fell to 1 : 1.85 for day workers and 1 : 2 for piece workers in 1946. It was reported in 1956 that only 0.6 per cent of all work was being paid at labor grade 1.[20] Assuming that the new basic scale for baking is typical for the food industry generally (Table 1), the following comparison emerges:

	Extreme ratio
Old 7 grade scale for day workers, excluding grade 1	1 : 1.62
Old 7 grade scale for piece workers, excluding grade 1	1 : 1.75
New 6 grade scale	1 : 1.80

(c) The Stalinogorsk Chemical Combine reported that in 1956, when it had 7 grade scales with extreme ratios of 1 : 2.27 to 1 : 2.51, no work was

* Before the war, this plant had two basic scales, with extreme ratios of 1 : 2.50 and 1 : 3.50. As a result of the wage increase given to low paid workers in 1946, the differentials declined, giving rise to the new ratios [18].

classified in grade 1. The new scale for the chemical industry, introduced in 1958, retained seven grades, but reduced the differential to 1 : 2.30. If grade 1 is eliminated from the older scales, the effective pre-1958 extreme ratios were 1 : 2 to 1 : 2.18.[21] The same situation seems to have prevailed throughout the chemical industry, to judge from the following classification of workers by labor grade prior to the wage reform: [22]

	Labor grade							
	I	II	III	IV	V	VI	VII	Total
Per cent of workers classified	–	0.8	12.6	21.9	27.8	25.8	11.1	100.0

(d) The machinery industry had operated up to the war with an 8 grade scale containing extreme ratios of 1 : 2.8 to 1 : 3.6. After the war, there were hundreds of different scales in effect, mostly with 8 grades, with the most common extreme ratios being between 1 : 2.4 and 1 : 2.5. "In view of the fact that the scales for machinery enterprises were old, there was in fact no scale work at the first two grades." [23] The six grade, 1 : 2 ratio scale introduced in 1959 was in all probability less compressed than the effective scale in 1956.

(e) The pre-1956 scale for the rubber industry had ten grades, with an extreme ratio of 1 : 2.15. The Red Hero Rubber Plant in Moscow reported that under the old scale, no workers were in the first three grades, and only a small number in the fourth.[24] The eight grade scale introduced in 1958, with its extreme ratio of 1 : 2.6, represented a very considerable widening of basic wage differentials.

Other examples might be adduced in support of the conclusion that basic wage scale differentials were increased, rather than reduced, by the wage reform beginning in 1956. There have undoubtedly been instances in which the opposite occurred, particularly in the heterogeneous machinery industry, but I have been unable to find one in the Soviet literature on the subject. It should be noted, however, that the basic wage scales in effect in 1960 are more compressed than those prevailing prior to the war.

It is important to note that the preceding discussion relates *only to basic wage scales, and not to earnings*. In the absence of adequate statistical data, it is impossible to determine whether the trend of earnings differentials paralleled that of basic wage scale differentials. One crucial factor (to be discussed below) which may have more than offset the formal compression of the basic wage scale was the sharp curtailment of performance premia, which had been received in far greater measure by skilled than unskilled workers. Reduced access to ubiquitous bonus schemes for higher paid people may very well have brought about an equalization of earnings in line with official pronouncements.

2. Classification by Labor Grade

Prior to the wage reform, there was systematic overclassification of workers as a means of evading stickiness in the basic wage rates in the face of price inflation. The result was crowding at the top of the scale, particularly for day rated workers, and haphazard and inadequate skill differentials. In the important Kalibre Machine Tool Plant, for example, assignment of individual workers to labor grades was quite casual, and some low skilled day workers – oilers, warehousemen, elevator operators – were put into the top labor grades in order to maintain their earnings at a level which would keep them from moving.[25] At the Lenin Electrical Equipment Plant in Moscow, "the grades of day workers who were not transferred to piece work were raised. On the average, this increase was one grade higher than stipulated in the wage-qualifications manual." [26] A Moscow watch factory reported that "work assigned by the wage-qualifications manual to grade IV (with a rate of 2.19 rubles per 100 pieces) was actually paid as grade V (with a rate of 2.25 rubles per 100 pieces)." [27] A contemporary writer summarized the situation in the following terms:

> "To the shortcomings of the wage system should be added the fact that in many enterprises, the grades assigned to day workers in fact exceed the grades stipulated in the wage-qualifications manuals . . . It is often the case that grades assigned to piece workers are also higher than provided in the manuals. In the machine tool industry, of the total number of piece workers, only 2.3 percent are in grade II (no one is in grade I), although a classification of grade II is stipulated for a number of machine tending jobs. A great many piece workers perform work one or two grades higher than provided by the manual." [28]

The job classification manuals that were in use in 1956 were quite old, dating from the mid-thirties, and did not reflect the latest technology. Similar jobs often carried different rates because of faulty job descriptions, and confusion was compounded by the practice of having each industrial ministry use its own manual, with the result that within the same labor market there might be quite different rates for identical work, leading to excessive turnover. For example, oxygen machine operators in enterprises of the chemical industry were classified in grades V and VI, while exactly the same work in plants belonging to the oil industry carried the rates of grade VI and VII.[29] In food processing plants, the loading of cans for delivery to warehouses was paid for on the food industry scale, whereas loading them into railroad cars was paid on the basis of higher transportation scales. A worker engaged in capital repair was paid construction rates, but if the same job involved current maintenance, he received the lower food industry rates.* As long as labor mobility was inhibited by law, such differences were not critical. But as soon as workers could move, the differentials became incompatible with labor force stability.

The Institute of Labor, in 1959, embarked upon the preparation of a manual for occupations common to several industries in order to eliminate such anomolies. The descriptions of 281 occupations and 900 labor grade characteristics will, when completed, cover about 60 per cent of all industrial workers, and replace some 2,000 job descriptions.[31] New manuals for jobs which are unique to particular industries are also in preparation.

Soviet job descriptions are divided into three main sections: characteristics of the work involved, skill qualifications required of the worker and examples of the work. Each labor grade within a particular occupation is described separately, as well as the occupation as a whole. With the aid of the wage-qualifications manuals, as they are termed, the classification experts assign labor grades to every job in the plant. Many different systems of job grading are employed, though the Institute of Labor has recently recommended the job evaluation scheme shown in Table 3. It will be noted that one factor, conduct of the work process, is assigned an overwhelming weight, and it is problematical whether this type of job evaluation is of much help in actual classification work, particularly when the small number of basic labor grades is taken into account.

Not only jobs, but individual workers as well, are assigned labor grades, in the latter case by foremen, subject to the approval of the director of the enterprise. Workers are promoted on the basis of examinations conducted by commissions representing management and the local trade

* The following data show the rates that were paid in 1956 for the same occupations in three machinery plants in Penza (rubles per hour) [30]:

Occupation	Bicycle plant	Watch plant	Accounting machine plant
Automatic machine tender	—	6.3	2.8
Machine adjuster	6.9	7.2	—
Stamper	3.6	4.0	3.2
Molder	7.3	6.7	—
Appliance fitter	5.1	5.2	6.9
Stamping fitter	6.8	5.2	5.8
Molding fitter	4.8	6.6	5.0

union organization. A worker carries his personal grade from job to job, and presumably, this helps determine his job assignment. As already noted, however, wages are based on the job grade rather than the personal grade of the worker, with certain safeguards for workers who are assigned to jobs rated more than one grade below their personal grades.

TABLE 3

Job Evaluation System Recommended by the Institute of Labor

Function and factor	Degree of difficulty of function and significance of factor	Weights	
		Minimum	Maximum
1. Computation work	Very simple	0	0
	Simple	4	4
	Medium difficulty	5	7
	Very Complicated	10	13
2. Preparation and organization of work and the workplace	Very simple	5	5
	Simple	6	8
	Medium difficulty	10	13
	Complicated	15	22
3. Conducting the work process	Very simple	75	85
	Simple	95	107
	Medium difficulty	120	135
	Complicated	150	172
4. Servicing and controlling equipment	Very simple	0	0
	Simple	4	4
	Medium difficulty	5	7
	Complicated	10	13
5. Responsibility	Minimal	0	0
	Not significant	5	5
	Significant	7	10
	Very significant	15	20

Source: A. E. GRIGORYEV, *Ekonomika Truda* (Moscow, 1959) p. 295.

There is very little statistical information available on the distribution of workers by labor grade. The data shown in Table 4, for the chemical industry as a whole and for a particular machine tool plant, reveal that the two lower grades and the top grade were lightly populated, even after reform of the wage structure. The impression conveyed by these data is confirmed by an analysis of the vast machinery industry, which indicated that in 1957 only one per cent of all day workers in the industry were in the first two labor grades, and less than 10 per cent in grade 3, the great majority being classified in grades 5 to 7.[32]

TABLE 4
Distribution of Workers, by Labor Grade
(Per cent of total)

Plant or industry	Labor grade							
	I	II	III	IV	V	VI	VII	VIII
Chemical industry (1959):[a]								
Before reform	—	0.8	12.6	21.9	27.8	25.8	11.1	—
After reform	0.6	3.8	12.3	23.1	29.4	21.0	9.4	0.4
Moscow Grinding Equipment Plant (1958):[b]								
Before reform	—	—	17.8	14.0	16.5	20.2	15.7	15.8
After reform	0.3	1.9	21.8	16.6	23.4	22.7	13.6	0.5

[a] P. F. PETROCHENKO, *op. cit.*, p. 80.
[b] M. D. GORSHUNOV, *op. cit.*, p. 91.

Labor grade classification is, of course, an important element in the determination of the average wage level. Without any change in basic scales, average wages can rise or fall with shifts in classification. That this has been a significant factor over the years emerges clearly from the following data on the machine tool industry:[33]

	Per cent of workers classified in stated labor grades		
	1930	1947	1953
Grades 1–3	71.9	29.7	25.7
Grades 4–8	23.7	66.1	73.3
Trainees	4.4	4.2	1.0
	100.0	100.0	100.0

The shift of workers into higher labor grades between 1930 and 1947 is undoubtedly due in large measure to changes in the skill composition of the labor force during the industrialization process. Between 1947 and 1953, however, most of the shift was probably due to artificial upgrading. The great reduction in the proportion of trainees is particularly noticeable. As late as 1960, it was charged that in coal mining, trainees were receiving full pay immediately upon being employed, instead of the trainee scale, which called for 60 per cent of the lowest grade in their occupation for the first two months, and 80 per cent for the remainder of the training period.[34]

The basic wage scales adopted after 1956 in almost every case reduced the number of labor grades. Since under the old scales there were virtually no workers or jobs in the two lowest grades, a certain amount of downgrading was necessary if the lower brackets under the new scales were to be operational. In the copper mines of the Sverdlovsk industrial area, the average labor grade was reduced from 6 to 3.98, with the replacement of 10 by 8 labor grades.[35] In the Stalinogorsk Chemical Combine, the average grade fell from 5.11 to 4.95; in the Voskresensk Chemical Combine, from 5.5 to 5.2;[36] in the First State Ball Bearing Plant, by 0.3 grades; in the First State Watch Plant by 0.4 grades; in the Kolomensk Locomotive Plant, by 0.7 grades;[37] in the Kirov Watch Plant, from 6.9 to 5.8;[38] in the Kishinev Chemical Plant, from 4.8 to 4.6;[39] and at the Omsk Petroleum Refinery, from 5.3 to 5.1.[40]

Generally, though not invariably, downgrading was not accompanied by any loss of earnings. Nevertheless, there is some evidence of worker resistance to the process, for the labor grade carries a status as well as a monetary connotation. The Soviet press is very guarded on the subject, though the following was reported for the Lenin Electrical Equipment Plant in Moscow:

> ". . . of 850 day workers it was necessary to lower the grades of 718 by one, and in some cases, by two steps. Several workers, who had received the higher grades ten to fifteen years ago, reacted very strongly against classifications corresponding to the wage-qualifications manual, although their earnings not only remained at the previous level, but in some cases even rose. Therefore the question of the possibility of reducing grades was submitted to the judgment of the workers themselves. A skilled worker, who had been at the plant over 25 years, came to the labor section with the request that notwithstanding his great seniority and experience, his grade be lowered from 7 to 6." [41]

To judge by the amount of attention devoted to the process of reclassification, not too much reliance has been placed upon the self-discipline exemplified immediately above. Special plant committees, consisting of representatives of management, the engineering staff, the plant department of labor and wages, and the local trade union, were established to carry through the task of reassignment. Appeals commissions were set up to consider individual grievances resulting from reclassification. Only 34 appeals were reported by the Kharkov Tractor Plant, despite the fact that 1754 workers were reduced by one grade and 75 by two grades.[42] Steel industry managers were given the authority, after consultation with the local trade union committee, to classify workers one grade lower than the job is rated by the manual where the worker is not fully qualified to perform complicated work or repair equipment, and also "when necessary to allow for differences in conditions of production and labor.[43]

The main burden of reclassification work fell upon the labor and wage department, which is to be found in all plants of any size. Some firms have been handicapped by the lack of qualified personnel. The department chief in one plant complained that his people were being paid inadequately, with the result that they sought other work at every opportunity. In a large Leningrad plant, 78 per cent of the employees in the labor department were trainees, since it was impossible to keep experienced personnel.[44]

3. The Determination of Base Money Wage Rates

The basic wage scale contains only the ratios of skill grades to the lowest skill grade. There are no money figures attached to the ratios.* The fact that a workers is classified, say, in grade 5, says nothing about his actual earnings. Moreover, grade 5 means quite different things from industry to industry.

The wage structure of each plant is keyed in to the industrial and regional wage structure through the determination of the ruble value of labor grade 1. The factors entering into this determination are not properly the concern of this paper; they involve considerations of inter-industry and regional differentials. We will content ourselves with the hypothetical illustration in Table 5, which shows how the lowest labor grades might be determined for a number of industries with a minimum wage of 400 rubles a month.

There has been some discussion of the question whether the loading for heavy work which is found in some industries should be given as a flat sum to all workers, regardless of skill level, rather than included in the compensation for grade 1, which leads to greater absolute supplements for the higher grades. It is argued that the additional expenditure of energy required for heavy work, reflected in greater food requirements, is the same regardless of skill; and further, that since lower paid workers devote a greater proportion of their income to food than the higher paid, merely giving the two groups the same absolute loading favors the higher paid workers. However, manpower considerations dictate the prevailing practice of including the loading in the basic wage.**

* It should be pointed out that for some industries, absolute money figures rather than ratios are laid down in the wage decrees.

** Undoubtedly the greater degree of risk of injury in heavy work is also a factor behind the extra wage allotted to such work [45].

TABLE 5

Hypothetical Example of the Determination of Grade I Wage Rates for Piece Workers, for Industries With a Minimum Wage of 400 Rubles Per Month

Industry	Monthly base rate	Composition of the monthly total			
		Minimum	Loading for the difficulty of the work	Loading for the national importance of the industry	Other
Coal mining					
Underground	690	400	200	60	+30
Strip	545	400	80	60	+ 5
Ore mining					
Underground	620	400	160	60	—
Open cut	545	400	80	60	+ 5
Iron and steel	580	400	120	60	—
Non-ferrous metals	570	400	120	60	−10
Oil					
Well drilling	570	400	120	60	−10
Oil extraction	480	400	20	60	—
Chemicals and oil refining					
Hazardous and difficult work	515	400	80	40	− 5
Normal conditions	455	400	20	40	− 5
Machinery					
Hot work	540	400	80	40	+20
Cold work	460	400	—	40	+20
Cement	530	400	80	60	−10
Reinforced concrete	460	400	40	20	—
Meat and Milk	400	400	—	—	—

Source: AGANBEGYAN and MAYER, *op. cit.*, p. 127.

In industries subject to considerable variation in labor conditions, different pay may attach to labor grade 1 for diverse groups of workers, although the ratios among the labor grades are generally identical. For example, the following wages for steel workers were stipulated for labor grade 1 in 1957:*

* It might also be noted that workers in heavy and unhealthful work are also entitled to higher fringe benefits, particularly retirement and invalidity pensions [46].

Type of work	Rubles per day, grade 1
Production work:	
Underground ore mining	21.60
Open pit ore mining	19.00
Metallurgical and coke departments	20.00
Non-production work:	
Piece work on hot, heavy and unhealthful work	17.60
Piece work on cold, and day work on hot, heavy and unhealthful work	15.60
Day work on cold work	13.70

As a consequence of this type of differentiation, the spread of differentials within an enterprise may be much greater than those specified by the basic wage scale ratios. In the steel industry, under the above schedule, an underground ore miner classified in grade 8 earned a basic wage of 69.10 rubles a day, about five times that of the grade 1 day worker on cold work. Even within the metallurgical departments, the highest paid production workers were rated at 64 rubles a day, compared with 13.70 rubles for the lowest paid non-production workers, a spread of almost five times.

The following differentials were provided for in the basic scale for the machinery industry introduced in October, 1959:*

Type of work	Hourly wage rate, rubles, grade 1
Day workers on cold work	2.75
Piece workers on cold work, and day workers on hot, heavy, and unhealthful work	3.20
Piece workers on hot, heavy, and unhealthful work, and day workers on very heavy and unhealthful work	3.67
Piece workers on very heavy and unhealthful work	3.90

This type of differentiation is by no means limited to heavy industry, as the following scale for the textile industry, introduced in 1960, indicates:[48]

Type of work	Hourly wage rate, rubles, grade 1
Heavy and unhealthful work:	
Day work	2.92
Piece work	3.20
Normal labor conditions:	
Day work	2.58
Piece work	2.92

* These rates apply to so-called Group I industry – aviation, automobiles, machine tools, radio, shipbuilding, electronics, machinery and equipment for heavy industry, etc. Other branches of the industry have slightly lower scales [47].

Table 6 shows, for a number of industries, the differentials between highest and lowest basic wage rates contained in recently promulgated schedules. For light consumer industries, the labor conditions factor adds only about 20 per cent to the total spread, but in the case of heavy industry, the effect is much greater. The precise addition to the effective spread can be determined by comparing Tables 1 and 6.

TABLE 6

Ratio of Highest to Lowest Basic Labor Rates, Allowing for Differences in Conditions of Labor, Wage Scales Introduced Since 1957

Industry	Per cent highest of lowest rate
Iron and steel (metal departments) [a]	467
Non-ferrous metals (metal departments) [b]	375
Chemicals [c]	346
Synthetic leather [d]	295
Machinery [e]	275
Building materials [f]	257
Wood working [g]	243
Textiles [h]	200
Fish processing [i]	200
Baking [j]	200

Sources:

a) *Socialist Labor* (1957) No. 7, p. 79.
b) *Ibid.* (1958) No. 8, p. 48.
c) *Ibid.* (1958) No. 7, p. 34.
d) *Ibid.* (1958) No. 11, p. 58.
e) *Ibid.* (1959) No. 5, p. 8.
f) *Ibid.* (1960) No. 2, p. 48.
g) *Ibid.* (1960) No. 2, p. 56.
h) *Ibid.* (1959) No. 12, p. 48.
i) *Ibid.* (1960) No. 1, p. 63.
j) *Ibid.* (1959) No. 12, p. 55.

4. Incentive Wages

The Soviet Union, perhaps more than any other major industrial nation, is committed to incentive methods of wage payment. The proportion of workers being paid on the basis of such methods in 1956 is shown in Table 7. Piecework was almost universal among those wage earners classified as direct production workers, and widespread among other groups. The wage reforms may have since led to some reduction in the incidence of incentive work (overall data are not available), but on the basis of fragmentary data, the shift toward day work, if any, would appear to have been minor.

A recent Soviet textbook on labor economics explains the heavy reliance on piece work as follows: "The chief advantage of incentive wages lies in the fact that the worker's earnings are determined by his output of acceptable products. Therefore piece work assures the personal material interest of the worker in the results of his work. At the same time, piecework promotes the growth of skill and the better use of tools and equipment; it cultivates intolerance of loss of working time and idleness, and requires a high level of organization in production, standardization of labor, and accounting for output."[49] It is generally believed – and not only in the Soviet Union – that incentive pay leads to higher productivity than day work, and this is reflected in the almost universal premium paid for piece work. The Russian concern with maximization of physical output, and the rapid growth of their labor force, bringing in large contingents of poorly trained and undisciplined workers, led logically to incentive wages.

TABLE 7

Use of Incentive Wages in the Soviet Union, 1956
(Per cent of total workers paid)

Industry	All workers	Production workers	Non-production workers
All manufacturing and mining	77.5	95.0 [b]	55–62 [a]
Electric energy	27.8	—	—
Coal mining	59.1	89.1 [b]	55.1[b]
Iron and steel	70.9	99.2 [b]	—
Machinery and metal trades	74.2	95.9 [b]	45.7
Chemicals	68.5	—	—
Glass and ceramics	81.2	—	—
Paper	87.4	—	—
Textiles	84.8	99.7 [b]	72.5 [b]
Fur and Leather	84.7	—	—
Shoes	85.6	—	—

Source: Nauchno–Issledovatelski Institut Truda, *Voprosi Truda*, Vol. II (Moscow, 1959) pp. 76–80.

[a] The 55 per cent figure represents the proportion of incentive workers among non-production workers in basic production departments, while 62 per cent is the proportion in non-production departments.

[b] Data are for March, 1956.

However, this increases the difficulty of maintaining an orderly wage structure, particularly when technology is changing rapidly, when the price level is unstable, or when there are severe manpower shortages. Earnings can rise rapidly, and lose touch with basic wage scales, if piece rates become loose. This is precisely what happened in the Soviet Union, and it was one of the major causes of the wage reform movement.

Soviet piece rate determination starts with the basic grade scales discussed above. The wage rate per unit of output is fixed by determining a standard task or norm per unit of time, and then simply applying it to the hourly or daily rate. For example, if a given occupation carries a base rate of 3 rubles an hour, and the norm for the production of a unit of output is set at 2 hours, the piece rate is 6 rubles. If the worker just fulfills the norm, his earnings will equal the specified hourly rate. In order to guarantee the piece worker a differential above the day worker, the new basic scales establish a basic rate differential of from 10 to 15 per cent in favor of piece work. But this is a minimum differential, since the piece worker is expected to exceed the standard task.*

The establishment of output norms becomes the crucial factor in determining earnings. If norms are too low, piece work earnings rise in relation to day work earnings, while if the norms are too tight, the compression of differentials robs the incentive system of its stimulating affect. When the wage reform began in 1956, loose piece rates were everywhere in evidence. The basic scales had remained almost unchanged from 1940 to 1955, but factory earnings had doubled. During the war, low norms had been necessary to accommodate the many women and young people who manned the factories. Many of these were simply carried over into the postwar period as a means of boosting earnings. Day workers were kept from falling too far behind, either by being given periodic premia or by being put on fictitious incentive schemes.

All of this made it extremely difficult for the Soviet authorities to maintain what they considered to be appropriate wage differentials. The basic wage scales could no longer regulate either internal or external differentials, and began to lose their entire meaning. For example, a breakdown of earnings by category of pay for the Kharkov Tractor Plant for April, 1956, showed the following:[51]

	Basic wage rate	Pay for overfulfillment of norms	Wage premia	Other, including vacation pay
Incentive workers	44.9%	36.9%	0.6%	17.6%
Day workers	69.6%		16.4%	14.0%

* Average incentive earnings in the United States steel industry have been running about 20 per cent above the standard day rates [50].

In this plant, less than half of the earnings of incentive workers came from their base pay, and even for day workers, about 30 per cent of earnings were determined by factors other than the basic scales.

Between 1940 and 1955, piece earnings rose more rapidly than day earnings, partly as cause and partly as consequence of the greater divorcement of the former from basic wage scales. A special census of machinery industry wages undertaken in March, 1956, revealed that on the average, piece earnings exceeded day earnings by 33 per cent. However, on a direct grade by grade comparison, the differential was 60 per cent. Day workers had been systematically upgraded in order to keep their earnings in line. Following are the direct labor grade comparisons for 14 machinery plants which were studied intensively (piece earnings as a percentage of day earnings):[52]

	Labor grade					
	III	IV	V	VI	VII	VIII
Cold work	166	160	183	180	173	174
Hot work	165	170	174	176	169	186

The necessity of assigning relatively high grades to day workers tended to undermine the whole system of classification. Day work pay was also maintained by the award of all sorts of bonuses which had little relation to plant performance. Management was constantly obliged to juggle the variables involved in earnings in an effort to keep the workers satisfied.

TABLE 8

Basic Wage Rates as a Proportion of Total Earnings, Before and After the Wage Reform (per cent of total)

Industry	Before reform	After reform
Steel (70 per cent of all enterprises) [a]	56.4	77.4
Fourteen machinery enterprises: [b]		
Day work	67.1	77.2
Piece work	44.4	65.4
Eight chemical enterprises: [c]		
Day work	63	76
Piece work	48	70
Coal mining [d]	66	71
Non-ferrous metals [e]	55–60	70–75

Sources:

[a] *Socialist Labor* (1958) No. 8, p. 39.
[b] Petrochenko, *op. cit.*, p. 11.
[c] *Socialist Labor* (1958) No. 7, p. 36.
[d] *Socialist Labor* (1958) No. 6, p. 37.
[e] *Socialist Labor* (1958) No. 8, p. 47.

One of the major goals of the wage reform was to raise the basic wage scales so that they consitututed a larger proportion of total earnings. The substantial degree of success attained can be seen from the data in Table 8. Only in the case of coal mining, which had the highest basic wage scales of any industry prior to the reform, was the change relatively small.

A second purpose of the wage reform, in the sphere of incentive systems, was to tighten output norms, to prevent piece rate earnings from rising *pari passu* with the increased basic wage rates. There are two basic types of norms, in the Russian lexicon: technical or scientific norms, and statistical or experience norms. The latter are determined by past operations and thus tend, in the Soviet view, to perpetuate performance based upon outmoded technology. Preference is accorded to norms "based on careful and profound investigation of the technological process of each separate operation, and frequently of the elements composing it, upon detailed analysis of the possibilities and power of equipment. The analysis must be supplemented with observation through the use of the stop watch... and must take into account the advanced production experience of innovators." [53]

As a consequence of restudying operations, norms of output rose sharply. In the non-ferrous metals industry, the average increase was 26 per cent.[54] A pilot study in the Fifth of October Cotton Combine in the Vladimir oblast produced a 32 per cent increase in weaving, 43 per cent in finishing, 28 per cent in winding, and 36 per cent in the operation of warping machines.[53] Another index of change in the norms was the fall in performance. In the steel industry, norm fulfillment fell from 150–155 per cent to 113–118 per cent as a result of the wage reform.[56] Norms were raised as much as 80 per cent in a group of machinery plants, with the result that performance declined from 168–224 per cent of standard to 123–145 per cent.[57] Following are similar data for six chemical plants:[58]

	Per cent attainment of norms	
	Before reform	After reform
Bereznikov fertilizer combine	140.2	114.0
Slavyansk soda combine	142.3	112.5
Stalinsk chemical reagent plant	147.5	115.0
Erevansk tire plant	134.1	111.8
Permsk chemical plant	160.0	108.2
Bereznikov soda plant	151.0	113.0

The establishment of new norms was in the final analysis a matter for each individual plant, and the authority of local management to effect the needed changes was broadened in 1957. Plant directors were given the right, in consultation with the local trade union committee, to substitute new norms for existing ones whenever warranted by new technical or organizational conditions.[59] The approval of higher authority was no longer needed in such instances.

A network of some 700 production quota research institutes renders technical assistance to enterprises, apparently much in the manner of American wage consulting services. Among their functions is the preparation of standard norm manuals, which can then be applied, with suitable modification, to individual establishments. By 1959, there were 40 such manuals for coal mining, 22 for oil production, 15 in steel, and 249 for the machinery industry.[60]

Anyone familiar with wage administration is aware of the problems involved in raising performance standards. There is a universally adverse psychological reaction among workers against producing more goods for the same compensation. In the West, the process of raising standards is inevitably beset by grievances and strikes. The Soviet worker cannot express his resentment by striking,* but nonetheless the Soviet authorities have handled norm raising carefully. Management has been cautioned against rapid and arbitrary increases in norms, and urged to plan for gradual revision.[61] Following is a description of how the ground was prepared at the Kharkov Tractor plant:

> "During the course of the preparatory period a great deal of mass educational work was undertaken at the plant. The questions of adjusting norms of output and wages were discussed at meetings of the factory Party committee, as well as the factory trade union committee. There were also meetings of heads of departments and sections, secretaries of the departmental Party organizations, and charirman of the departmental trade union committees. In all departments there were meetings of foremen, trade union activists, and general assemblies of the workers, at which the purpose and content of the reform were explained. For departmental agitators there were printed 600 copies of 'agitator's handbooks" in which appeared material regarding the significance of raising the material interests of the workers in production and increasing the growth of labor productivity... 2,000 copies of the pamphlet 'Concerning Conditions for Adjusting Norms and Wages' were printed . . . The text of the pamphlet, printed in placard form, was posted throughout the plant.

* There were rumors of a sit down strike at the First State Ball Bearing Plant (formerly the Kaganovitch plant) near Moscow when norms were raised, but this has never been confirmed.

Suggestion forms, prepared in the print shop, were distributed to all workers. The plant press and radio systematically explained the progress of the measures undertaken." [62]

The raising of performance standards, and indeed the entire wage reform process, have been made more palatable by preventing earnings from falling,* and by simultaneously reducing, or promising to reduce, working hours. By the end of 1959, some 13 million employees were on a 7 hour day, and the government has pledged that this will be universal by the end of 1960.[64] The goal of the planning authorities was to accomplish the reduction in working hours without any decrease in output, to avoid an increase in unit labor costs. It was claimed that daily output per worker in coal mining rose by 2 per cent in 1959, in iron and steel production by 5 per cent, and in chemicals by 5 per cent despite a cut in working hours in many enterprises of these industries. [65] If these figures are to be credited, what this meant for the steel worker, for example, was that in 1959, as compared with 1958, he worked six hours less each week but produced 20 per cent more for each hour worked. If his weekly earnings remained unchanged, his hourly rate rose by 14 per cent, while his rate per unit of output fell by about 5 per cent.

The inflationary proclivities of incentive pay have also been curbed by the virtual elimination of the so-called "progressive" piece rate system, whereby earnings rose more than in proportion to output above the standard task. For example, the following scale had been used in the machine tool industry: [66]

Percentage production over standard task	Per cent increase in piece rate
From 1 to 10	30
From 10 to 25	50
From 25 to 40	75
From 40 and over	100

Prior to the wage reform, 36 steel mills studied had paid 42.6 per cent of their workers by some form of progressive piece work; this figure dropped to 6.5 per cent after the reform.[67] For 14 machinery plants, the decline was from 13.3 per cent to 6.0 per cent,[68] and for 6 chemical plants, from 23.2 per cent to zero.[69] More generally, it was indicated that about

* This was generally but by no means universally true. In the Zhdanov Printing Plant, for example, hours of work were cut from 8 to 7 in April, 1957. The average wage level in the plant rose by 4.3 per cent from January to June, 1957, but of the 2198 employees, 1092 suffered some reduction in earnings [63].

40 per cent of all industrial workers had been receiving this type of incentive pay in 1956, but that by 1960 it had almost disappeared in heavy industry, and was on its way out elsewhere.[70].

Progressive piece work has been replaced chiefly by "straight" piece work, in which earnings vary in direct proportion to output at all levels of production. There has also been some movement away from piece work altogether, particularly where it had been employed in the face of adverse technological conditions for the principal purpose of avoiding low day rate scales. In many chemical plants, for example, piece rates were being paid to workers tending automatic apparatus, and elimination of this practice brought the proportion of day work in the industry up from 41 to 64 per cent.[71] It was found that piece work in the metal, experimental, and repair departments of machinery plants led to the production of inferior or unwanted products, and its use was sharply curtailed.[72] In non-ferrous metals production, the proportion of day work was raised from 37 to 58 per cent, while in heavy industry as a whole, about two-thirds of all workers remain on piece work.[73] This does not mean that piece work is being abandoned; indeed, in coal mining, its use has become more common recently.[74] By all accounts, piece work will remain the predominant form of Soviet wage payment, although its suitability for particular operations will be scrutinized more carefully.

Mention should be made of another term encountered in the Soviet literature, "indirect" piece work. This refers to the payment of non-production workers not on the basis of their own output, but according to that of the production workers whom they service. This has occasionally led to anomolous situations. In some machinery plants, for example, machine repairmen and adjusters service from five to six machine operators each, and their wages are tied to the output of their group. Consequently, they have little interest in the performance of other operators, and rarely volunteer to help them even when they have spare time. Better results have been obtained by tying the wages of repairmen to the production of the entire department.[75]

5. **Wage Premia**

Systematic wage premia based upon specified standards of performance are quite generally paid to day workers, and to some piece workers as well. Prior to the wage reform, this was an important means by which managers in some critical industries raised earnings without touching the basic pay scales. Bonuses were awarded for many different types of achievement, some of them overlapping. At the Nevski Machinery Plant,

50 different types of premium regulations were in effect, and many of the workers were receiving the maximum allowed by the regulations.[76] Steel workers were often more concerned with the various premia for which they were eligible than with their base pay.[77] For workers engaged in capital repair, there were premia for fulfilling the plan with respect to type of machine, for maintaining tools in good condition, for the absence of defects in their work, for economizing materials, for extending the inter-service period of machinery which they repaired, for reducing idle machine time, etc.[78] In most industries, premia were given for saving materials, fuel, and electricity. Workers in the coal and shale industry engaged in underground work received bonuses for repeated use of metal pit props. In cement plants, bonuses were awarded for increasing the stability of the lining of rotary furnaces. For industry as a whole, premium pay rose from 2.4 per cent of the wage bill in 1940 to 3.3 per cent in 1955. For some industries, however, it was much higher: 7.3 per cent in steel, 7 per cent in chemicals, 6.3 per cent in electric power stations, and 5.9 per cent in machinery production.[79]

It is by no means the intent of the wage authorities to abolish premium pay, for it is regarded as the best means of providing incentives for day workers.[80] To prevent abuses, however, regulations have been promulgated imposing maximum limits on premia. For example, steel workers engaged in the production of metal or the repair of equipment may receive premia up to a maximum of 20 per cent of their base pay, while for all other day workers, the upper limit is 15 per cent. The premium index must be concrete, there must not be more than two types in simultaneous use, and there must be a direct link between the work of the individual and the results of the work for which the premium is awarded.[81] The maximum limit set for most industries varies between 20 and 30 per cent of base pay though in exceptional cases it may rise as high as 40 per cent.[82]

On the basis of a few fragments of evidence, the relative importance of premium pay for wage earners appears to have fallen. In the Moscow Grinding Tool Plant, the proportion of premium pay in the total pay of day workers fell from 31.4 per cent to 18.8 per cent after the wage reform.[83] Bonuses at the Moscow Red Hero Chemical Plant, after the reform, constituted from 9 to 15 per cent of total pay, whereas before they had been as much as 100 per cent of the base pay.[84] For eight unspecified chemical plants, the reduction was from 27 to 14 per cent.[85] Some violations of the new regulations have already been reported, however, [86] and it may be surmised that factory management will manage to evade the maximum limits specified when necessary to preserve or attract manpower.

In the summer of 1959, an interesting discussion began in the specialized labor press regarding incentive wage systems in the steel industry, a discussion that may eventually have widespread repercussions throughout Soviet industry. The desirability and feasibility of individual and group piece work has been called into question, and some form of premium pay system related to total plant performance advocated in its stead. The most obvious index of performance is the output plan, and several steel mills have experimented with systems of this nature, including those at Kuznetsk and Zaporozhe.[87]

Proponents of this so-called "norm-plan," as it is termed, argue that group piece work leads to parochialism among the workers involved, in that they are more concerned with the success of their own particular sections than with the work of the plant as a whole. One shift may fail to make necessary repairs in order to keep its output up, leaving the repair work to the next shift. Types of products with high piece rates may be emphasized at the expense of those with lower rates, although the latter may be more essential to the enterprise. On open hearth furnaces, productivity is generally greater at the beginning than at the end of the life of the furnaces, yet output standards do not change, leading to wage variation which is unrelated to worker effort. There is also the difficult problem of revising established norms under conditions of rapid technological change. In one article, the conclusion was reached that "by comparison with standard norms, the norm-plan results in more fundamental, better considered, multi-faceted objective changes in the process of production." [88]

Those who uphold the more conventional incentive schemes make the following criticism of the norm-plan method:

(a) Aggregate output plans include all productive factors, on many of which the individual worker has no influence. Workers may be discouraged, rather than encouraged, depending on total plant performance.

(b) Wages may fluctuate unduly, and without any relationship to task performance. Table 9 purports to show, by a specific example, how tonnage rates might fall steadily without a corresponding trend in standard norm performance, due to an increase in planned tonnages.

(c) Where the norm plan scheme has been installed, all workers of the same grade receive the same pay, and no one knows how well a particular production team is doing.

One writer sums up as follows:

"The chief cause of the change to the norm-plan was, in our opinion, the fear on the part of some experts in not being able to cope with wage regulation and their efforts to avoid overexpenditure of the wage fund. Of course, when the majority of workers are paid by the day, one does not have to worry about observing the wage fund limits, since overexpenditure is hardly likely . . . The attention of all experts in labor should be concentrated on achieving improved methods of technical norm setting, and not on searching for ways of liquidating output norms, that most important index of labor productivity." [89]

The battle was still raging at the time of the present writing, with no indication of which way the decision would finally go.

TABLE 9

Earnings Under Group Piece Work vs. Aggregate Plan Fulfillment, Based Upon the Experience of the Azov Steel Company

	1958					
	Jan.	Feb.	Mar.	Apr.	May	June
Per cent performance standard norms	111.6	110.6	111.9	114.0	109.1	112.0
Monthly piece earnings of a roller (rubles)	1643	1628	1647	1678	1606	1649
Shift output plan in conventional units (tons)	1553	1532	1566	1571	1684	1756
Per cent fulfillment of shift output plan	102.8	102.1	102.9	100.3	98.4	100.4
Monthly piece earnings of a roller if wages were based on shift output plan	1513	1503	1515	1476	1448	1478
Rate per ton, if shift plan were used (kopeks)	4.12	4.18	4.11	4.07	3.80	3.64

Source: Socialist Labor (1959) No. 7, p. 85.

Several additional forms of premium payment should be mentioned before concluding this section. Long service bonuses are paid to workers in heavy industry and in isolated areas to encourage stability of employment. The minimum term of continuous service required for eligibility for such bonuses is two years for underground workers and three years for other workers. In the chemical industry, for example, the annual bonus is 0.8 per cent for service of three years, and rises to 2 per cent for service over 15 years.[90]

Every plant has a so-called "enterprise fund", built up from above-planned profits, about half of which can be used for wage premia. In addition, many enterprises have special "foremen's funds", into which is paid three per cent of the total wages of the foreman's shop, which each foreman may use to reward individual workers for good production records.

Finally, time and a half is paid for the first two hours of overtime, and double pay for additional hours. The night shift works one hour less than the day shift, but the pay for the two is the same.

6. The Structure of Earnings and Concluding Remarks

Lack of data makes it impossible to do anything more than to present a few illustrations of how the foregoing factors affect the internal wage structure. Table 10 shows the impact of the wage reform upon a group of

TABLE 10

Composition of the Wage Fund of Selected Soviet Industrial Enterprises (per cent of total)

	Piece workers			
	Eight chemical plants		Moscow Grinding Tool Plant	
	Before wage reform	After wage reform	Before wage reform	After wage reform
Basic scale pay	48	70	46.5	62.9
Pay for exceeding norms	34	14.5	42.7	16.4
Progressive piece work	6	0.5	1.3	—
Wage premia	7	10	—	11.2
Other	5	5	9.5	9.5
	100.0	100.0	100.0	100.0
	Day workers			
Basic scale pay	63	76	64.9	75.9
Wage premia	27	14	31.4	18.8
Other	10	10	3.7	5.3
	100	100	100.0	100.0

Sources: Chemical plants: *Socialist Labor* (1958) No. 7, p. 36. Moscow Grinding Tool Plant: Petrochenko, *op. cit.*, p. 81.

chemical plants and a single machine tool enterprise. In both, there were increases in the basic pay component of wages, for piece and day workers alike. Piece earnings declined, as did premia for day workers. Progressive piece rates were practically eliminated. These findings are confirmed by the data in Table 11, which also contains a bit of additional detail on the composition of the pay packet. It is not clear why there should have been a decline in the relative importance of holiday pay, since this is usually calculated as a proportion of average earnings in the preceding year.

TABLE 11

Composition of the Wage Fund of the Lenin Electromechanical Plant, Moscow (per cent of total)

	Piece work			Day work		
	1956	Jan.–Oct. 1957	Jan.–April 1958	1956	Jan.–Oct. 1957	Jan.–April 1958
Basic pay	47.4	60.1	68.3	72.6	77.1	80.5
Piece rate earnings	42.1	28.0	17.8	—	—	—
Premia	1.5	2.7	5.7	20.4	16.6	13.6
Holiday pay	5.9	4.4	3.9	4.7	3.8	3.2
Other pay related to scale	2.0	3.3	3.2	1.4	1.3	1.6
Pay, not related to scale	1.1	1.5	1.1	0.9	1.2	1.1
	100.0	100.0	100.0	100.0	100.0	100.0

Source: GORSHONOV, *op. cit.*, p. 140.

The wage problem facing the Soviet enterprise is conceived of in the following terms:

> "When the enterprise receives its annual labor plan, there is before it the problem of determining the concrete way in which it can assure that labor productivity will rise more rapidly than average earnings. To secure economy in labor, the enterprise has a wide selection of means: the introduction of new techniques and improved technology, automation and complex mechanization of production, better organization of labor, and improved administrative structure." [91]

As long as he stays within the wage fund allotted him by plan, the factory manager has considerable discretion in wage determination. He must abide by the basic scale stipulated for his industry, but there is a good deal of flexibility in the allocation of incentive pay and wage premia. Despite the increased relative importance of the basic pay scales, other forms of pay continue to be an important part of earnings.

Low output norms remain one of the principal difficulties in wage administration. Failure to tighten norms when basic wages were raised resulted in very sharp wage increases in some branches of industry.[92]

At the beginning of 1960, a writer in *Socialist Labor* found it necessary to admonish some enterprises which were in the process of restudying norms, in the following vein: .

> "Some industrial experts object to restudying output norms as workers, through better habits, acquire greater mastery of their jobs. It is objected that downward correction reduces individual incentives in raising output and hinders the growth of labor productivity. One cannot agree with this point of view. The determination of time and its elements always reflects the summation of existing levels of skills and practice . . . In the course of time the skills of all workers increase, and the norms must be raised. This stimulates the better workers to higher output. The conclusion is that the correction of old norms must be based upon present reality." [93]

The ambitious program of wage reform undertaken by the Soviet Government in 1956 is due to be completed by the end of 1961. It is hoped by that time to have raised basic wage scales throughout industry to a realistic level; to have reset standard norms of output at levels consistent with current technology; and to have eliminated methods of wage payment which jeopardized the stability of wage levels and rendered difficult the maintenance of appropriate differentials among and within occupations.

Perhaps at that time the Soviet authorities will release some of the abundant data on wages and earnings which they have gathered. When this is done, it will be possible to compare Soviet wage structure, both internal and external, with that of other industrial nations. But until this is done, it is extremely hazardous to draw any general conclusions not only about comparative wage structure, but even with regard to wage developments internal to the Soviet Union. Such findings as we have been able to make on the basis of incomplete data must remain provisional. We can only hope that the policy of greater frankness on matters of economic statistics which has prevailed in Russia since 1956 will be extended to the labor field.

References

1. ABRAM BERGSON's book, *The Structure of Soviet Wages* (Cambridge, 1944) relates largely to the period prior to 1937, almost a quarter of a century ago. Two articles by MURRAY YANOWITCH, "Changes in the Soviet Money Wage Level Since 1940", *The American Slavic and East European Review* (April 1955) p. 209, and "Trends in Soviet Occupational Wage Differentials", *Industrial and Labor Relations Review* (January 1960) p. 166, deal in part with more recent data.

2. Among the most important of the recent publications are the following: Jack Stieber, *The Steel Industry Wage Structure* (Cambridge, Mass., 1959); K. G. J. C. Knowles and T. P. Hill, "The Structure of Engineering Earnings", *Bulletin of the Oxford University Institute of Statistics* (September–October 1954); T. P. Hill and K. G. J. C. Knowles, "The Variability of Engineering Earnings", *ibid.*, (May 1956); S. W. Ostry, H. J. D. Cole and K. G. J. C. Knowles, "Wage Differentials in a Large Steel Firm", *ibid.* (August 1958).
3. For a brief account of this system, see Leonid Kostin, *Wages in the USSR*, (Moscow 1960) pp. 57–69.
4. L. Kostin, *op. cit.*, p. 36.
5. *ibid.*
6. Charles W. Brennan, *Wage Administration* (Homewood, Ill., 1959) p. 174.
7. A. G. Abanbegyan and V. F. Mayer, *Zarabotnaya Plata v SSSR* (*Wages in the USSR*), (Moscow 1959) p. 134.
8. Aganbegyan and Mayer, *op. cit.*, p. 131.
9. *ibid.*, p. 173.
10. A. E. Grigoryev, *Ekonomika Truda* (*The Economics of Labor*) (Moscow 1959) p. 300.
11. G. A. Petukhov, *Tarifnaya Sistyema Zarabotnoi Plati Rabochikh* (*The Tariff System of Wages*)(Moscow 1958) p. 20.
12. Aganbegyan and Mayer, *op. cit.*, p. 133.
13. G. A. Pethukhov, *op. cit.*, p. 50.
14. A. S. Kuznetzova, *Organizatsiya Zarabotnoi Plati Rabochikh na Promishlennikh Predpriyatiyakh SSSR* (*The Organization of Wages in Soviet Industrial Enterprises*) (Moscow 1956) p. 20.
15. *Socialist Labor* (1956) No. 11, p. 11.
16. *Pravda* (July 17, 1955) p. 1.
17. G. A. Petukhov, *op. cit.*, p. 31.
18. *Socialist Labor* (1956) No. 8, p. 8.
19. P. F. Petrochenko (editor), *Ulucheniye Organizatsii Zarabotnoi Plati i Normirovaniye Truda* (*Improvement in the Organization of Wages and Norm Setting*) (Moscow 1958) p. 83.
20. *Socialist Labor* (1956) No. 11, p. 63.
21. *Socialist Labor* (1958) No. 2, p. 120 and Table 1.
22. M. D. Gorshunov (editor), *Iz Opita Perekhoda Predpriyatii na Sokrashchenii Rabochi Dyen* (*Experience in the Change-over of the Enterprise to a Reduced Working Day*) (Moscow 1959) p. 91.
23. Aganbegyan and Mayer, *op. cit.*, p. 169.
24. *Socialist Labor* (1958) No. 7. p. 99.
25. *Socialist Labor* (1958) No. 6, p. 112.
26. P. F. Petrochenko, *op. cit.*, p. 95
27. *ibid.*, p. 109.
28. *Socialist Labor* (1956) No. 2, p. 77.
29. *Socialist Labor* (1956) No. 2, p. 81.
30. *Socialist Labor* (1956) No. 6, p. 100 and *Socialist Labor* (1958) No. 10, p. 28.
31. *Socialist Labor* (1959) No. 5, p. 64.
32. *Socialist Labor* (1958) No. 10, p. 71.
33. *Socialist Labor* (1957) No. 12, p. 30.

34. *Socialist Labor* (1960) No. 1, p. 49.
35. *Socialist Labor* (1958) No. 9, p. 98.
36. M. D. Gorshunov, *op. cit.*, p. 22.
37. P. F. Petrochenko, *op. cit.*, p. 13.
38. *ibid.*, p. 113.
39. *Socialist Labor* (1958) No. 6, p. 108.
40. *Socialist Labor* (1958) No. 4, p. 129.
41. P. F. Petrochenko, op. *cit.*, p. 101.
42. P. F. Petrochenko, *op. cit.*, p. 123.
43. Gorshunov, *op. cit.*, p. 58.
44. *Socialist Labor* (1956) No. 4, p. 103.
45. Aganbegyan and Mayer, *op. cit.*, p. 128.
46. *Socialist Labor* (1957) No. 7, p. 79.
47. *Socialist Labor* (1959) No. 5, p. 8.
48. *Socialist Labor* (1959) No. 12, p. 48.
49. A. E. Grigoryev, *Ekonomika Truda* (*Economics of Labor*) (Moscow 1959) pp. 307–308.
50. Jack Stieber, *op. cit.*, p. 220.
51. *Socialist Labor* (1958) No. 10, p. 72.
52. *Socialist Labor* (1958) No. 10, p. 71.
53. Aganbegyan and Mayer, *op. cit.*, p. 92.
54. *Socialist Labor* (1958) No. 8, p. 47.
55. *Socialist Labor* (1959) No. 12, p. 99.
56. Gorshunov, *op. cit.*, p. 58.
57. Petrochenko, *op. cit.*, p. 9.
58. *Socialist Labor* (1959) No. 10, p. 65.
59. Decree of the Council of Ministers of the USSR (August 15 1956).
60. *Socialist Labor* (1959) No. 2, p. 77.
61. See, e.g., *Socialist Labor* (1957) No. 12, p. 11.
62. Petrochenko, *op. cit.*, p. 117.
63. *Bulletin on Labor and Wages* (1958) No. 4, p. 10
64. Kommunist (1960) No. 3, p. 24.
65. *ibid.*
66. Kusnetzova, *op. cit.*, p. 34.
67. Gorshonov, *op. cit.*, p. 60.
68. Petrochenko, *op. cit.*, p. 15.
69. *Socialist Labor* (1959) No. 10, p. 66.
70. *Kommunist* (1960) No. 3, p. 35.
71. *ibid.*, and *Voprosi Truda*, Vol. II, p. 24.
72. *Voprosi Truda*, Vol. II, pp. 123, 129, and Petrochenko, *op. cit.*, p. 64.
73. *Kommunist* (1960) No. 3, p. 35.
74. *Voprosi Truda*, Vol. II, p. 101.
75. *Socialist Labor* (1959) No. 5, p. 72.
76. *Socialist Labor* (1956) No. 8, p. 18.
77. *Socialist Labor* (1956) No. 7, p. 45.
78. *Socialist Labor* (1958) No. 10, p. 78.
79. *Socialist Labor* (1959) No. 9, p. 31.
80. See, e.g., Grigoryev, *op. cit.*, p. 315.

81. *Socialist Labor* (1957) No. 10, p. 140.
82. *Socialist Labor* (1959) No. 10, p. 17.
83. Petrochenko, *op. cit.*, p. 81.
84. *Socialist Labor* (1958) No. 7, pp. 101–103.
85. *ibid.*, p. 36.
86. Gorshunov, *op. cit.*, p. 90.
87. *Socialist Labor* (1959) No. 6, p. 83; *ibid.* (1959) No. 7, p. 85.
88. *Socialist Labor* (1959) No. 9, p. 87. See also *ibid.* (1959) No. 5, p. 81; *ibid.* (1959) No. 10, p. 95.
89. *Socialist Labor* (1960) No. 1, p. 77.
90. L. Kostin, *op. cit.*, p. 48.
91. *Socialist Labor* (1960) No. 1, p. 70.
92. *Socialist Labor* (1960) No. 2, p. 65.
93. *Socialist Labor* (1960) No. 1, p. 70.

SUBJECT INDEX

NAME INDEX